Relationships

FOR

DUMMIES®

Relationships FOR DUMMIES®

by Dr. Kate M. Wachs

Wiley Publishing, Inc.

Relationships For Dummies®

Published by
Wiley Publishing, Inc.
909 Third Avenue
New York, NY 10022
www.wiley.com

Copyright © 2002 by Wiley Publishing, Inc., Indianapolis, Indiana

Published by Wiley Publishing, Inc., Indianapolis, Indiana

Published simultaneously in Canada

For general information on our other products and services or to obtain technical support, please contact our Customer Care Department within the U.S. at 800-762-2974, outside the U.S. at 317-572-3993, or fax 317-572-4002.

Wiley also publishes its books in a variety of electronic formats. Some content that appears in print may not be available in electronic books.

Library of Congress Cataloging-in-Publication Data:

Library of Congress Control Number: 2001092913

ISBN: 0-7645-5384-4

Manufactured in the United States of America

10 9 8 7 6 5 4 3

About the Author

Dr. Kate M. Wachs is a clinical psychologist, relationship expert, and sex therapist. She is Founder and Director of The Relationship Center™ in Chicago and The Relationship Center Online™ the only full-service introduction and counseling center of its kind. Dr. Kate is the only matchmaker-psychologist in the USA, and has been working in the business for about 20 years. For the past seven years, she has worked with America Online in several different capacities, including Psychologist and Relationship Expert for Love@AOL, one of the most popular areas of America Online, where she has received well over a half million letters to date. Dr. Kate's AOL site (*AOL Keyword: DrKate*) and Web site (www.drkate.com) have amassed several million hits/visits over the years. The sites include a free newsletter, a form you can use to e-mail a question to Dr. Kate, an enormous amount of archived advice (browsable and searchable by topic), interactive questionnaires, popular polls, and much more.

A member of the American Psychological Association, Dr. Kate has twice been awarded the honor of "Fellow" for outstanding and unusual contributions to the science and profession of psychology, particularly in the areas of media psychology and independent practice. She has hosted her own *Dr. Kate Radio Show* — heard across the country on top-rated WGN, and written national columns with circulations over 1,500,000. She is a nationally recognized expert on relationships, dating, online dating, singles, marriage, and sex, and has contributed her expert opinion to *Oprah, Donahue, The New York Times, the Chicago Tribune,* the *Chicago Sun-Times, L.A. Times, Washington Post, USA Today, Time, Newsweek,* most of the top U.S. publications and quality TV shows, hundreds of radio programs, and many other national and international media.

Dr. Kate is also the author of *Dr. Kate's Love Secrets* (Paper Chase Press, 2000, go to www.drkate.com), which has been translated into Spanish (*Los Secretos del Amor*, 2001, Amat Editorial, see drkate.com) and distributed to Spanish-speaking countries and Spanish-speaking areas of the U.S. She has also created a tape series on her books. Dr. Kate is a popular speaker and workshop presenter — helping people everywhere to create healthy, joyful relationships and live happy, fulfilling lives.

Dedication

This book is dedicated to my family, my extended family, and my very dear friends: *Thanks for giving me a solid home base from which I can venture out to help others. I couldn't do it without you.*

Author's Acknowledgments

Many people have nurtured this book to fruition in a variety of ways. First, thanks to my clients and patients at The Relationship Center™ and The Relationship Center Online™, to the readers of my **AOL Keyword: DrKate** and www.drkate.com Web sites, and to my patients at Bay Medical Center, who have allowed me to learn through them and pass that knowledge on to you. I've enjoyed you all and hope I've given you something useful in return.

To my loyal and talented staff at The Relationship Center™, especially Claude, Joy, Walt, Mary, Pat, Patti, Lisa, Kristen, Jeff, and Ed — thanks for being patient and working hard so I could make time to write; your efforts and support are very much appreciated. I couldn't have done it without you.

Thanks to my AOL coworkers, who have been an absolute joy to work with for the past seven years, especially my *Big Bosses*: Heather Perram, AOL Executive Director of Creative Programming, known to all as a very kind lady; and Bill Schreiner, currently VP of Product Management/AOL Box Office and former CEO of Love, a loyal friend and family man who puts the "C" in charisma. Thanks to both of you for making it personal — like a team and family, rather than a slice of big business. *Special* thanks to Andrew Howley, Makis McDonald, Matthew Meyers, Maria Monteverde-Jackson, Clarisse Perrette, and Heather Dove for making the **AOL Keyword: DrKate** site wonderful, and for encouraging me in the creation of this book. Thanks to Ron Casalotti, Sally Taylor, and Diane Caesar, for helping with the technical aspects of my site and the advice letters, and to Diane for cataloging the older letters. Thanks to LynnRenee Miller and Kelly Milne for skillfully handling numerous paperwork challenges. And special thanks to Miguel Monteverde — for having faith in me and trying so hard to find me a special niche at AOL, and for hooking me up with AOL Greenhouse and Love@AOL. I've enjoyed being part of these teams, and a finer group of coworkers could never be found. Special thanks to Steve Case and the upper management of AOL for allowing the advice and questionnaires I wrote for Love@AOL to be included in this book, and to singer/songwriter Marty Axelrod and the multi-talented Bill Schreiner for allowing me to include their "In Real Life" song lyrics.

Thanks to the Hungry Minds and John Wiley & Sons staff, especially VP/Executive Publisher Kathy Nebenhaus, for taking such a personal interest in this book and giving it even more than your usual 200% effort. We will do that *case* of wine in NYC very soon. Special thanks to Karen Young, Acquisitions Editor, for finding my first book on Michigan Avenue, loving it, and campaigning to get me involved with the *For Dummies* lifestyle group. Thanks to Tracy Boggier, Managing Editor, and Stacey Collins, Jennifer Ehrlich, Alissa Schwipps, Corey Dalton, and Mary Fales for your manuscript suggestions. Special thanks also to Walter Perschke in Chicago for reading the text and making suggestions. And thanks to Werner Reifling for finding me on AOL and publishing my first book, *Dr. Kate's Love Secrets* (Paper Chase Press, 2000), and to Alexandre Amat, for publishing it in Spanish (*Los Secretos del Amor,* Amat Editorial, 2001) after finding me in that same bookstore on Michigan Avenue! Thanks for seeking me out and immersing me in the fascinating, challenging world of book publishing.

Many thanks to my solid home base of friends/colleagues, including the professors who encouraged me and went out of their way to make me feel special: Dr. Carl Sipprelle, Dr. Joe Rook, Dr. Bill Cammin, Dr. Rulon Gibson, Dr. John Stumpf, Dr. Ted Balsam, Dr. Frank Leavitt, Dr. Rosalind Cartright, Dr. Maristella Goebel, and all who raised me academically. I thank all my supportive colleagues/friends at the American Psychological Association, especially Dr. Fred Koenig, Dr. Lawrence Balter, Dr. Stuart Fischoff, Dr. Michael Broder, Dr. Michael Mantell, Dr. Frank Farley, Dr. Alan Entin, Dr. Val Farmer, Dr. Susan Kastl, and everyone in APA Division 46 — Media Psychology who taught me how to give psychology away through all forms of the media, including books — and enriched my life so much in the process.

Many thanks to the hard-working staff of the APA Public Affairs Department, especially Pam Willenz, Dave Partenheimer, Mara Greengrass, Doug Fizel, Rhea Farberman, and Lisa Bacote. Thanks for encouraging me, for all your press efforts over the years, and for our special camaraderie. Thanks also to astute thinkers Margaret Durante and Lisa Wyatt for your enthusiasm, encouragement, and valuable media advice and support, and to Margaret for your wonderful circle of friends! Thanks to all my friends in the print, radio, online, and TV media — for helping me see psychology through a different set of eyes and providing me with opportunities to give psychology away.

Before any psychologist can help others, she needs to feel grounded and balanced herself. I'd like to particularly thank my parents, Charles and RoseAnn Wachs, for showing me how to love, and for always working hard so I could have the best in life. Thanks for teaching me integrity and how to work my butt off for a good cause. Thanks to my terrific brother and sister, my wonderful nieces and nephews, and to all my extended family for being such a staunchly loyal, incredibly supportive, solid base, and — *they made me add this!* — for doing without me for holidays, birthdays, parties, picnics, reunions, and . . . , and . . . , so I could finish this book. *Merci bien!*

And finally, I'd like to thank my very old and dear friends, who know me so well, yet love me in spite of it: Dr. John Roraback, Donald Donner, Walter Perschke, Dr. Robert Beiter, Sigalit Zetouni, The Honorable Judge Sandra Otaka, Dr. Mythili Sundaresan, Rick Karr, Dr. Tiffany Field, Dr. Dick Booth, Jim Giambalvo, Pat and Jay Inendino, U.S. Representative Jim Barcia, and Dr. Tom Burk. I have been exceptionally blessed to have you in my life; thanks for always being there for me over the years. ***This book is yours, too.***

Kate M. Wachs, PhD
Chicago, December, 2001

Publisher's Acknowledgments

We're proud of this book; please send us your comments through our online registration form located at www.dummies.com/register.

Some of the people who helped bring this book to market include the following:

Acquisitions, Editorial, and Media Development

Acquisitions Editors: Tracy Boggier, Karen Young

Editorial Manager: Jennifer Ehrlich

Cover Photo: © Corbis

Production

Project Coordinator: Dale White

Layout and Graphics: LeAndra Johnson, Erin Zeltner

Proofreaders: David Faust, Andy Hollandbeck, Marianne Santy, TECHBOOKS Production Services

Indexer: TECHBOOKS Production Services

Publishing and Editorial for Consumer Dummies

Diane Graves Steele, Vice President and Publisher, Consumer Dummies
Joyce Pepple, Acquisitions Director, Consumer Dummies
Kristin A. Cocks, Product Development Director, Consumer Dummies
Michael Spring, Vice President and Publisher, Travel
Brice Gosnell, Publishing Director, Travel
Suzanne Jannetta, Editorial Director, Travel

Publishing for Technology Dummies

Andy Cummings, Acquisitions Director

Composition Services

Gerry Fahey, Executive Director of Production Services
Debbie Stailey, Director of Composition Services

Contents at a Glance

Cartoons at a Glance

By Rich Tennant

"When we met we seemed to be on the same track, so we hitched up. Then, just when I thought the relationship was gaining a head of steam, something derailed it. I don't know—maybe I was sending the wrong signals."

page 295

"I knew they were writing their own vows, but I expected quotes from Robert Frost poems, not The Geneva Convention."

page 225

"It's an agreement Michael and I made—he agrees to stay home from the gym 2 nights a week, and I guarantee that he'll still burn over 300 calories each night."

page 135

"My wife and I were drifting apart. We decided to go back to doing what we used to do when we were first married. So we called her parents and asked to borrow money."

page 325

"I KNOW WHAT A ROMANTIC GETAWAY IS. IT'S WHEN MY PARENTS TELL ME TO GET AWAY FROM THE HOUSE FOR A FEW HOURS."

page 187

"I don't know, Susie - sometimes I get the feeling you're afraid to get close."

page 81

"I'm looking for someone who will love me for who I think I am."

page 9

Cartoon Information:
Fax: 978-546-7747

E-Mail: richtennant@the5thwave.com
World Wide Web: www.the5thwave.com

Table of Contents

Introduction

Relationships make life fun. They don't solve your problems, and they don't even make you happy — only you can do that. But having a lifetime partner can certainly help you weather life's storms and enjoy the best that life has to offer.

"No man is an island," wrote John Donne, a very wise poet. You can deny your relationship needs for extended periods of time, but when it comes right down to it, it's normal and healthy to want a supportive companion, a lifemate, a great sex partner, and someone to play with — all in the same person.

Yet finding and making a good relationship is not easy. Even when you know the basics about how to find a partner and how to make your relationship grow, doing the work takes energy, an upbeat attitude, and perseverance.

Relationships For Dummies is written to help you understand the basics, and to encourage you as you do the work to find and make a healthy and fulfilling relationship. It celebrates the humanness in all of us. Everyone can use a little help in understanding how to find and grow a relationship. And it's for people like you that I wrote this book.

Why You Need This Book

This book will help you organize your thoughts about relationships. It will help you sort through the myriad of relationship myths permeating our society today, to discover exciting realities that you can use to make your love life more satisfying. It will reveal how to differentiate a healthy, compatible relationship from an unhealthy one. It will show you how to strengthen and nurture that healthy relationship once you find it, working through the inevitable problems you encounter along the way. It will encourage you to think in a healthy fashion and assist you in finding the *positive* and *fun* in any relationship stage you encounter — so that no matter what happens, you'll stay fundamentally happy today and in all the days to come.

Assumptions About You

In this book, I make several assumptions about you, the reader.

✔ You have an open mind and are eager to discover new and interesting ways to improve your love life.

✔ You're ready to act, move, and make things happen.

✔ You're not a dummy, but rather an intelligent, competent person who probably knows a lot of what's in this book. *For Dummies* is the name of a brand of lifestyle books that many readers love. To help readers identify the series, certain styles are used in all *For Dummies* books, including the affectionate use of the word, "dummies." Rest assured that no one, especially this author, thinks you or anyone else reading this book is really a "dummy." After all, you bought this book, didn't you?

✔ You're reading this book to discover a new, organized perspective on your relationships, and to gain especially useful tips that you can apply in a systematic way to your life.

✔ You don't want to be overwhelmed by a lot of theory or research data about relationships. Instead, you want me to tell you what I think about relationships, based on my education, training, and practical experience of working with singles and couples over the past 20 years. You want me to draw on my unique experience as a matchmaker-psychologist, therapist, and online/offline advice columnist and radio host, to give you the benefit of what I've learned from the hundreds of thousands of people who have confided in me. And you want me to organize all that information into practical tips that you can immediately use to improve your love life.

✔ I assume you're a heterosexual, and this book refers to heterosexual relationships. However, if you're gay, lesbian, or bisexual, you can adapt and apply much of this same relationship information to your life as needed. Although some considerations are different in these groups, intimate relationships have much in common in all of them.

✔ You are probably female, or a very enlightened male. Most relationship-oriented books are read by those two groups. For that reason, and to avoid cumbersome sentence structure, I have tended to use more pronouns referring to you as "she" and your mate as "he." If you are one of those very enlightened males, I'm extremely happy to have you aboard! Congratulations on reading this book, and for exercising your power over your life and relationships.

How to Use This Book

Everyone has difficulty with different parts of the relationship process, and everyone has different kinds of relationship problems. But fortunately, many people tend to have the same pattern in relationships: Either they consistently pick the "wrong" people, or they consistently make the same kinds of mistakes that keep the relationship from developing.

As you read this book, think about your pattern: What do you do that helps or hurts your relationships? Look for sections that specifically address your difficulties. When you find one, highlight it, underline it, circle it, bend the page corner down, stick a flag on the page, attach a flare — or do anything it takes to help you find that section again later. Then review those sections often when you're having a relationship, and use that information to make your current relationship better than the last one.

Throughout the text, I include advice letters from my *AOL Keyword: DrKate* site and www.drkate.com. In my work as Psychologist/Relationship Expert for AOL over the past seven years, I have received well over a half million online letters asking for relationship advice, and visits/hits from many more times that number. I include some of my favorite advice letters in this book to illustrate valuable points and expand on others. Reading these letters can help you remember important, practical tips. Although the situations described in the letters are probably not exactly like yours, you can often adapt the general ideas from my advice to your particular circumstance.

I also include two interactive quizzes from my AOL site. Take *The Dr. Kate Compatibility Quiz* and *The Dr. Kate Communication Quiz* (in Appendix A and Appendix B respectively), to add to your knowledge about yourself and your relationships. Also, be sure to use the Table of Contents at the front of the book and the Index at the back of the book to help you locate chapters that specifically address your relationship needs.

Please note that in order to make this book fun and easy to read, I use collo-quialisms throughout, including a few words like, "good," "bad," "best," "better," "worst," "right," "wrong," "should," and "shouldn't." In keeping with *For Dummies* style, I also start many sentences with the word, "You." While such terms make the book more casual and easier to read, I just want to remind you to avoid using those words when discussing problems with your mate, and also avoid using them in your thoughts if you tend to suffer from black-white thinking. See Chapters 11 through13 for more on why, as well as how to use more accurate, appropriate words to turn tense discussions into amicable agreements. Also, see Chapters 10 and 20 for how to use more precise words to change irrational thoughts to more rational ones — and feel happier in the process.

How This Book Is Organized

Like all *For Dummies* books, *Relationships For Dummies* is organized to make an enormous amount of practical information easily accessible. This book includes seven main parts and two appendixes. Here's how I divvied them up:

Part I: Relationships 101

In Part I, I review the important elements of a healthy relationship. I challenge common relationship and compatibility myths that cause people enormous grief, and explain how reality is actually much more enjoyable than the nonsense. I outline the different stages of relationships, and show you how to use that information to your advantage — to either make a relationship thrive, or survive a stage you don't like with the least amount of grief, so you can move on to a stage you prefer. I also discuss the "must haves" (the qualities you need to have in a good relationship), the "good to haves," and the "don't need to haves" — and how to find a compatible sweetie in the way that best suits you at this time.

I recommend that everyone read or skim Part I, so you can be grounded in your relationship efforts. To find and make a healthy relationship, you need an understanding of what that is and isn't. It's also critical that we be on the same page when discussing the rest of the material in the book.

Part II: Getting Closer

This part suggests ways to grow your relationship and make it more intimate. I examine some of the common myths about intimacy, and how you can use more rational ideas and expectations to make your love life more satisfying. I discuss how intimacy develops, and how to use that information to pace your relationship in a realistic, yet enjoyable way. I outline the pros and cons of having sex early in the relationship, and give you some guidelines for making the choice that seems best for you. I also suggest factors to consider when deciding if you want to be exclusive with your partner. I outline when living together can be helpful, and when it's not, and top-o'-the-list topics to discuss *before* moving in.

Part III: Staying IN Love — Psychological and Emotional Intimacy

Now that you've found a good partner, how do you stay in love? In this part, I explore myths people hold about what makes them happy, and how those fictions lead to fractious relationships. I reveal the five secrets of happiness, and how you can use them to find joy and happiness in your relationship, your life, and your world. I explain why healthy communication and realistic, positive thinking are so important for staying in love and feeling psychologically and emotionally connected to your partner. I outline practical steps you can take to immediately improve your communication and thoughts, deepen the intimacy, and strengthen the ties that bind you and your honey.

Part IV: Feeding the Flame — Physical and Sexual Intimacy

In Part IV, I challenge some common myths about sex, and how you can use the realities to make your sex life more satisfying. I discuss the difference between great sex, good sex, and maintenance sex, and how to get the most out of all three. I discuss sexual differences that can be compromised, and those that aren't healthy to concede. I explain why sexual intimacy is so important to staying in love and feeling connected to your partner physically and emotionally. I point out useful, relatively easy ways to keep your romance and spark alive, and specific steps you can take to rekindle the fire if your passion has already grown cold.

Part V: Moving Forward Together

Relationships never stay static. They either move forward or backward; they either grow or decay. In this part, I discuss when it's best to move forward toward marriage — how to know when you're ready and when you're not. I discuss strange ideas people hold about marriage, and how you can use more rational ideas and expectations to make marriage work for you. I explain the timing of relationships, the shelf life of the average relationship, and special considerations. I describe *marriage phobia,* an irrational fear of marriage, and suggest ways to increase your partner's motivation if he or she runs for cover each time "mmmmmmarriage" is mentioned.

I also show you how to keep your relationship healthy and enjoyable. And, because no relationship is ever perfect, I detail which problems can be solved, which ones can't, and how to tell the difference. That way, you won't have to waste your time trying to get the earth to move with a partnership that's as stable as quicksand.

Part VI: Moving Forward Separately

Few relationships make it past the beginning stages. Interacting with someone long-term is challenging for everyone, but when it works, woooo - ey! The rewards are tremendous. When it doesn't, there are better and worse ways of making the best of it and recovering from the pain.

In Part VI, I describe how to break up with someone in a kind, empathic way that shows respect for your partner's feelings. I also outline how to handle it when someone breaks up with you, and reveal specific steps you can take to get closure, cope with the pain, and live through it with the least amount of suffering. I describe the stages of healing, and how to know when you're ready to move on. I tell you how to glean the "right" lesson from your experience, and how to apply that knowledge to make your future relationships more productive and enjoyable. And finally, when you're ready, I suggest ways to rejoin respectable society again — how to look at the surf (get out of the house with your support group), stick your toe in the water (meet strangers), wade in (meet singles casually), and slowly, but surely start swimming (date more efficiently). I also tell you how to avoid the *DRR* — The Dreaded Rebound Relationship — and find a more compatible honey this time around.

Part VII: The Part of Tens

This part contains important things to remember to help make your relationship happy: ten (+1) ways to pace your new relationship to get it off the ground, and ten great ways to light your relationship fire and stay a desirable, fun partner forever. I've organized these ideas into lists to help you recall them more easily when you need them!

Appendixes

In the appendixes at the back of the book, I include a compatibility quiz to help you explore who may or may not be compatible with you, and a communication quiz to help you understand how you and your partner communicate. If you're currently attached, take these quizzes, score yourself, and use that information to make your relationship better! If you're presently in between "attachments," take the quiz for your past partners, compare the results, and look for patterns. If you find one or several, how can you change your modus operandi to help your next relationship last longer and better? Then continue to take the quizzes for each potential sweetie you meet, and use the info you gain. Remember, if you only make each mistake once, you'll be *way* ahead of everyone else — and you'll greatly improve your odds of eventually finding and keeping a great relationship. You'll also enjoy your life a whole lot more along the way!

Icons Used in This Book

I've used icons in the margins to help organize the material and point you toward the information you want.

As Psychologist/Relationship Expert for Love@AOL (*AOL Keyword: DrKate* or www.drkate.com), an online site, I have received well over a half million letters asking for relationship advice. You betcha, that's a *lot* of letters! To illustrate valuable points and expand on others, I've included several of the letters — identities kept secret, of course! This icon appears beside those advice letters. I strongly encourage you to read the letters — to help you remember important points and practical tips, to let you know that you're not alone in your problems, and to demonstrate how clear, organized thinking can often lead to successful resolution of The Love Duds, aka your love blues.

These are the most important ideas to remember forever and always. When you see this icon, think, *"Dr. Kate wants me to wake up and pay special attention to this!"* These sections feature pearls of wisdom I've gleaned as a result of my unique matchmaker-psychologist and advice maven roles.

This icon marks items that are specifically geared toward women. However, a smart man will be sure to read these parts, too.

Similarly, this icon marks items specifically geared toward men. But a bright woman will make a beeline to devour these sections as well!

This icon highlights practical, helpful information that you should file in your brain.

Paragraphs marked with this icon offer short and simple time-, energy-, or frustration-saving ideas. Sometimes this icon will clue you to other sections in the book that contain more information on the current topic.

In various chapters, I discuss myths about relationships, compatibility, intimacy, happiness, communication, sex, and marriage, and how believing in those myths causes enormous grief in relationships. The Myth Buster icon appears when I present the saving reality — the important info that pulverizes the myth and presents exciting news that you can use to make your love life more satisfying.

Now, Remember . . .

This book represents my opinion about relationships; it's not set in stone. There can always be exceptions to what I've written. If something doesn't apply to you or doesn't seem healthy for you, then don't use it.

Keep in mind that you're reading this book to understand relationships better — so you can either find a good partnership or improve the one you have. You're not striving to be perfect, to find a perfect partner or relationship, or to have a perfect life. I'm not perfect, you're not perfect, and no partner, relationship, or life is ever perfect. Nevertheless, life is a truly wonderful experience, and to me, people are the best things in it. I hope you find this book stimulating and chockfull of helpful ideas you can use to aid you on your journey through life. I care about you, and I wish you love, joy, *fun!*, and happiness always.

Part I

Relationships 101

The 5th Wave — By Rich Tennant

"I'm looking for someone who will love me for who I think I am."

In this part . . .

You're probably reading this book because you want to find, make, and keep a good relationship. But before you can do that, it's essential to organize your thoughts about relationships. You need to understand what a good relationship is and isn't — and when someone is and isn't compatible.

So, in this part, I discuss the most important points to remember about romantic relationships. I separate the myths from the realities, showing you why the realities are healthier and more enjoyable than the myths. I explain that relationships actually have stages, and describe how you can use that information to your advantage. I point out qualities you absolutely need to have in a compatible mate, those you can do without, and just how picky you should be. Finally, I review how to find people who fit those qualities — which methods to use, when, and why.

Chapter 1

Is It a Good Relationship . . . Or Not?

In This Chapter

▶ Celebrating a good relationship

▶ Identifying a bad relationship

▶ Recognizing the difference

▶ Sidestepping the "unhealthy hook pattern"

Are you happy with your relationship? Or do you get involved with people time and again, only to figure out later that you've once again made a lousy choice? Maybe you don't even have a relationship right now because of those bad choices — or because it just seems too hard to keep trying. Well, if you've had trouble telling the royalty from the toads, you aren't alone. Separating the substance from the flash can be difficult. And when you can't do it, the ensuing mess can be very discouraging.

But don't sweat it. Help is here! In this chapter, I describe how to tell a good relationship from a bad one. I explain why people are often attracted to mates who aren't good for them, and how to recognize when you're in that trap — before you spend years making the same mistakes over and over again. If you use this info when choosing a partner, you can maximize your chance of relationship success. And best of all, you'll never have to tango with a toad again.

When It's Good . . .

Nothing's better than a good relationship (although some people might make an argument for chocolate). When you're in a good relationship, the birds sing and the sun shines — even in the dead of winter. You have love in your heart and a certain bounce in your step. Everything seems more alive and interesting, and you feel hopeful and full of life. Aaah, this is what life is all about.

So what exactly is a good relationship? By my definition, a *good relationship* has two major components — it's healthy for you, and it's fun. The fun part is usually easy to figure out. But what about the healthy? How do you recognize a healthy relationship when you see one? Read on.

Respect and emotional support

In a good relationship, both partners respect, esteem, and approve of one another. They feel like their mate is special — and they act like it. They don't demand that their partner change to be more like them. Rather, they appreciate one another as individuals and respect each other for their differences. They show their support by acting in an emotionally supportive way.

What does that mean? Well, when you're emotionally supportive, you say things like, *"I hope the meeting goes well for you, Honey,"* or, *"I'm so happy for you that you got that new job!"* or, *"Don't pick on your love handles, Sweetie. I like a man who's bigger than me — you sexy man of substance, you!"*

When you show your emotional support for your partner, he feels encouraged, reassured, and appreciated — and you'll also feel similarly when he acts emotionally supportive toward you. You each validate the other's feelings, and that feels grreaaaatt! For more on how to word sentences to express your support, see Chapters 12 and 13.

You can support your partner and his or her right to feel a certain way, even if you wouldn't feel that way in the same situation. Just like respect, when you're emotionally supportive to your partner, you allow him or her to be separate and distinct, yet very valued and special.

Honesty, loyalty, intimacy, trust, and friendship

Question: "How can you have a relationship if you don't have these?" Answer: "You can't."

Intimacy — being really close to someone — develops when you and your partner share thoughts, feelings, and experiences *only* with each other — not with every Tom, Dick, and Harry (or every Tina, Jane, or Mary!). The more you share only with each other, the closer, more bonded, and more intimate the two of you will become.

Of course, none of it is worth a rat's nest if you don't share those thoughts and feelings honestly. Honesty is implicit in any good relationship. If you're telling tales, then your alter ego or fairy tale self is having the relationship, not the real you. In contrast, if you share your real thoughts and feelings, you'll just naturally become closer and more bonded with your partner.

As the two of you feel closer, you also feel like protecting each other. And when you go out of your way to look out for one another's best interest, that loyalty brings you even closer together. Of course, in order to feel free to reveal your innermost thoughts and feelings — "your *soul*" — and to share such personal experiences, you've got to trust each other. In a good relationship, both partners trust each other implicitly and look out for one another without being asked to do so. They are basically "best friends." Friends respect, admire, trust, support, and care about each other, and they act in ways that show it. Makes sense, doesn't it?

Giving and taking

Whether you're Superman and Wonder Woman, or Mr. and Ms. Normal Earthling, you and your partner need to be approximately equal in power in your relationship for your union to be healthy. It's OK if he's Superman-in-the-Boardroom and you're Normal-Earthling-in-the-Workplace, or vice versa — provided you each respect one another as equals in your relationship — and act that way.

When you value each other as equals, all the great qualities I've mentioned in this chapter — respect, emotional support, honesty, loyalty, intimacy, trust, and friendship — flow back and forth between you in a fairly even way. You both share things with one another that you wouldn't share with other people, and you both interact with each other in a very positive way. You're both attracted physically, mentally, and emotionally in some way that seems about even, and you both recognize the relationship as equally important and valuable.

That *reciprocity* — that give and take of feelings, behaviors, and goals — is important to keep your relationship happy, healthy, and balanced. And let's not forget one of the main ways your relationship needs to be reciprocal: In a healthy relationship, you both share a similar goal for the relationship. If you'd like to marry your mate someday, he or she needs to feel similarly — now or in the near future — to make the relationship prosper.

Improvement in the overall quality of life

To figure out if someone's healthy for you, ask yourself the following questions:

- ✔ Has my life changed for the better since this person entered it?
- ✔ Have I grown and become a better person?

✔ Has this person allowed me to be myself and feel good about my uniqueness?

✔ Have I accomplished more, expanded my horizons more, or in some way bettered my life or that of others since I've known this person?

✔ Have the good times pretty much outnumbered the not-so-good times?

✔ Have I experienced more *joie de vivre* — more joy in living — as a result of this person being in my life?

If you answer "yes" to these questions, the relationship is probably healthy for you. In a healthy relationship, the overall quality of your life improves. You grow as a person because your partner gives you the support you need to take more risks and face more challenges.

Remember the monkeys. What? A classic psychology experiment was conducted ages ago by Dr. Harry Harlow, a very astute scientist. He separated monkeys from their natural mothers at birth, and compared their behaviors. When he gave them a warm, soft, stuffed-animal-of-sorts surrogate mother, the monkeys took time from clinging to her to explore various items placed in the cage. When they didn't have that mother surrogate, they anxiously rocked back and forth in the corner instead.

While I feel sad thinking about those monkeys, the "Love In Infant Monkeys" study was vitally important because it said a lot: When we feel loved and supported, we're able to venture out into the world and take risks, always returning to that love and support for more. As we repeat this pattern, we gain confidence, wisdom, and maturity. And we enjoy *living* so much more.

A healthy relationship helps you feel good about yourself, other people, and your life. It allows you the freedom to relax, to be yourself, and to reach out to others in friendship. It emphasizes the positive and *joie de vivre,* bringing sunshine into your world and radiating it to those around you. No relationship is ever perfect. But in a healthy relationship, you and your partner weather life stresses together as a team, and the fun times outnumber the bad overall.

. . . And When It's Not Good

Just as the birds sing and the sun shines in a good relationship, an unhealthy relationship feels like a trip to Hell. I'm talking lakes of fire, an ugly-looking dude with horns, and trolls perpetually pushing rocks up hills. A bad relationship saps the energy and life from your step. It wears you down and eats at you day after day, month after month. The present and the future seem dark and gray, as though life has no use, no hope. Tension and negativity hang in the air, and heaviness sits on your heart.

Studies have shown that it isn't enough to have a relationship. The quality of that relationship is extremely important — not only to your happiness and mental and emotional health — but to your physical health as well. Happily married people are happier and healthier than happy singles, but happy singles are much happier and healthier than unhappy marrieds. So being alone and happily single is better than being involved in an unhealthy relationship. Unhealthy relationships cause stress, and stress is basically cumulative.

Say that you stay up late, fighting with your partner. He announces that the conversation is over, slams the door, and goes to bed. An hour later, he's sawing logs, but you're still pacing, muttering, and doing your best Lady Macbeth imitation. The sight of your "beloved" sleeping peacefully adds to your frustration. When you're finally exhausted enough to drift off to sleep — an hour before you have to get up — you have a whopping nightmare. The alarm goes off, and you dutifully drag yourself to work. You look like Godzilla in a daze, ready to cry or yell at any provocation. You obsess and obsess and find it difficult to eat. You're not only emotionally stressed; you're physically stressed as well. A couple of days like this later, you grab the doorknob right after a sick, sneezing coworker does — and whammo! You come down with the same cold, flu, or other similar scourge.

This happens because your immune system is weakened by stress — physical or psychological — including emotional upset, worrying, fatigue, lack of sleep and healthy food, overworking, and not enough joy. All that stress adds up, and when it reaches a certain point, your weakened immune system can't protect you against a virus or bacteria. So you become physically ill. And, of course, that physical illness makes it even more difficult for you to communicate with your mate and resolve the emotional problems. Now you not only feel the same psychological and emotional stress, but you're also in physical pain — sneezing, coughing, nose running, and very grumpy and impatient. You're not functioning well because you're not feeling well. So the psychological influences the physical and vice versa in an endless circle.

So rather than going through this cycle of Doom and Gloom, pay attention to your relationship life. Instead of letting your heart hurt figuratively — and literally — avoid Relationships from Hell. How? By recognizing the signs of trouble before you get too involved. And how do you do that? I'm glad you asked!

Disrespect, emotional coldness, and lack of support

Have you ever listened to a couple screaming at one another, and wondered why they stay together? I have, too. It's amazing how many couples treat each other with less respect than they treat total strangers. Just as a good relationship includes respect, a relationship in which the partners don't respect each other is very unhealthy. Respect is different from agreeing with someone. You can disagree with someone on many issues, but still hold that person in high esteem and treat him or her with respect.

When someone tries to control or manipulate you instead of appreciating your differences, that person doesn't respect you. The special attention may initially seem like caring and respect, but it's just the opposite. When someone doesn't allow you to be yourself — to think your own thoughts, feel your own feelings, and choose your own behavior — the relationship is extremely unhealthy. You're not a cavewoman getting hauled off by the hair by your caveman, and you shouldn't be treated that way either.

Similarly, if you or your partner is cold and unfeeling toward the other, your relationship is definitely *not* healthy. Perhaps one of you is just a cold person in general. If so, the more supportive partner is not going to be happy in that relationship and needs to find someone more supportive.

Caring, affection, and interpersonal warmth are learned at a very early age. An adult who doesn't care about others is not suddenly going to stop in midstream and — presto chango! — develop that quality. Empathy can be increased, but it takes psychotherapy and a very motivated patient. If your partner really doesn't care and doesn't care that he or she doesn't care, then no relationship with that person is ever going to be healthy. Regardless of whether the coldness was inbred or learned in an unloving home, this is *not* a relationship for you.

Best enemies

Say your mate lies, cheats, or puts his own needs ahead of yours. How can you ever trust him again? When you or your partner lie, cheat, say disloyal things, or betray one another through action, word, or deed, the relationship suffers greatly.

Just as people become close when they share experiences together that they wouldn't share with others, that intimacy is gravely injured when one partner breaks the trust. Instead of a happy, healthy, "we" looking out for each other, the relationship becomes each person for himself or herself, "you" against "me," and vice versa. And of course, that's *not* what a healthy relationship is about. In fact, when you and your partner treat each other that way, you'll generally become best enemies. After you've shared your most intimate secrets with one another, you and your mate can use that information to either help or hurt each other. Just as best friends know one another's innermost secrets and look out for each other's welfare, best enemies do their best to sucker-punch their partners where they know it hurts most.

Being at odds

What if you think the world of your partner, but he or she doesn't return the favor? Ah, unrequited love! It happens to all of us. Unfortunately, I have no miracles up my sleeve that can make it all better. I wish I did.

In fact, relationships are very fragile, especially in the beginning. If you respect, value, or desire your partner more than your partner respects, values, or desires you, then he or she has more power and will tend to take you for granted. If you stay in the relationship despite the imbalance, don't expect your mate to appreciate your good will and sing your praises from the mountaintops. Rather, he'll usually lose more and more respect as time goes on, until the relationship deteriorates into your subbasement.

And if your partner values the relationship more than you do, the opposite will happen — you'll continue to take him more and more for granted and lose more and more interest and respect. Whoever cares *less* has *more* power in the relationship. And whenever the feelings are very discordant, the relationship is bound to fail.

A variation on this theme occurs when your partner demands that the two of you live by a different set of rules. If your mate holds you to a more stringent standard of behavior, the power is uneven, there is lack of give-and-take, and the relationship is not healthy. For example, if your boyfriend wants to hit the bars with his friends whenever he likes, but demands that you stay home because "good girls don't do that," you can do a whole lot better with another partner — and you should.

All relationships require approximately even amounts of give and take and fairly even amounts of control and power. Whenever a relationship has uneven control and power, and one person takes more than he or she gives, the relationship suffers.

Try this: Change places with your partner in your mind. Imagine that you are your partner and he is you. He is now held to the standards that he holds for you, while you live by the rules that he sets for himself. Picture the scene. If you laugh, chances are the situation is highly discordant. There's a double standard in your relationship that simply isn't kosher.

If you want to marry your partner, but he doesn't feel that way about you, then he has more power in the relationship, and the lack of give-and-take is likely to end your union. He may already be married, he may not want to get married to anyone, or he may simply not want to marry you. Or vice versa. Or perhaps he doesn't share your sexual orientation, or he's married to his work, and/or he's married to God and has taken vows to remain celibate. Whatever the reason, it simply isn't wise to fall in love with anyone who doesn't share your relationship goal, who can't reciprocate your love, or with whom you cannot continue a permanent relationship for any reason — no matter how wonderful he or she may be. If you try to sustain a crush or romantic relationship with that person, you're just fooling yourself and setting yourself up for a lot of pain.

Also, a healthy relationship does not exist in a vacuum. If you can't introduce your partner to other people because she's already taken or because he's never around . . . hello! Wake up! *What* are you doing in that relationship?

You can't make someone love you or want to marry you, no matter how much you want to. If you stay with someone who doesn't share your relationship goal, you'll eventually feel sad and/or angry that the two of you haven't married, and the relationship will falter. The more you want marriage, and the more your partner stalls, the faster your dissatisfaction and frustration will escalate. Instead, when you feel yourself falling for someone who is a "no-no" for you, take steps to avoid that person as much as possible — completely, if you can. Then stay away until you at least have a satisfying romantic relationship with someone else who does share your relationship goal — and you can become just a platonic pal to your old crush.

Heading in a negative direction

No relationship is ever perfect. In an unhealthy relationship, however, the bad times outnumber the good times overall. Just as a healthy relationship helps you grow and blossom as a person, an unhealthy relationship hurts the overall quality of your life.

Close your eyes, take a deep breath, and pause a moment. Think about how you've changed since you first met your partner. Think about how you felt and behaved when you met, and how you feel and behave now. If the changes have been in a negative direction, then the relationship is not healthy for you. You may feel nervous around your partner, constantly on edge, or down on yourself. You or your mate may be chronically irritable or quick to cry about the littlest things; perhaps one of you yells, while the other cries. You don't feel good about yourself, other people, or your life. You may be unable to relax, be yourself, or reach out to others in friendship. Your relationship is full of tension, negativity, and criticism.

There's a war going on, you and your partner are on opposite sides, and you're both under siege. When you and your mate fire cannonballs at one another, your health and your relationship health both suffer greatly. As I explain earlier in this chapter, a relationship that is intensely negative and critical is emotionally and physically stressful for both partners. Over time, that cumulative emotional and physical stress wreaks havoc on your bodies and leads to serious physical problems and accidents.

On the other hand, if you and your partner once loved each other, your relationship may actually be salvageable — if you go to therapy. The passion occurs because you care. You're upset, angry, and fighting dirty with each other because you're so invested in one another. If you go to therapy together, the two of you may be able to use that energy to turn your relationship around and become best friends and allies again. However, you'd best head to therapy as soon as possible — stat, as in right now — before you burn out, and before too many cannonballs make one of you abandon the fort.

And When You Just Can't Help Yourself

So maybe you already know all this stuff about what's healthy and what's not, but no one would ever guess it by looking at your relationship or lack thereof. Are you one of those people who can't resist someone who's bad for you, even though you *know* that being with him or her is contrary to your best interests? Do you break up with an unhealthy mate only to find yourself involved with one of his clones?

If you've been your best enemy in this way, ask yourself: Who does this person remind you of? Does she look or act like your mother in some way? Does he remind you of your father? Your first love? Your first crush? The first person who seduced you?

People often get involved with partners who are *unhealthy hooks from the past* — people they know aren't good for them, but they feel comfortable in a sick sort of way, like an old, dilapidated shoe. For example, if your parents were always negative and critical toward you, you may be drawn to negative and critical romantic partners. People often gravitate to what they've known before in their lives — the familiar.

If you're one of those people, you can change your unhealthy hook pattern, but don't expect it to be easy. If it were easy, you wouldn't have this problem to begin with. To change, you'll need concerted effort, a conscious plan, and the patience and endurance to continue working on your problem, even when unhealthy choices seem more attractive to you at the moment. You must first recognize the problem and understand that you probably won't be attracted to someone who's good for you right away. A healthy partner will need to be an acquired taste — like scotch or caviar.

In contrast to liquor and salty roe, however, the effort to acquire a healthier taste in partners is usually well worth it. If you ask an introduction service or friends to match you, hire a counselor to coach you along the way, and make a concerted effort to find partners who are distinctly different from your unhealthy hook, you can eventually become attracted to someone who is both healthy and fun. Now, wouldn't that be nice?

❤ ❤ ❤ ❤ ❤ ❤

If This Is Sex, It Must Be Friday!

Dear Dr. Kate,

My age: 28   **My gender:** Female

I've been in a relationship with a man for four years. I love him, but he hardly spends any time with me. The only time I see him is on Fridays, late at night, and you know the only thing that can be done then! We don't go out. I sit by the phone and wait for him to call. I have a 3-year-old son who adores him, but there's no interaction there. I feel really stupid waiting all the time. My heart says, "Hold on," but my head says, "Get out." What do you think?

Dear Calendar Girl,

Listen to your head. The man is obviously using you for sex. He gets sex for free, without even taking you out for dinner. And while you may love him, it really isn't good for you to wait on him. It's also not good for your son — or even your boyfriend.

Get an answering machine and hire a babysitter. Then get a social life. Go out with your friends, meet new men (try joining an introduction service or running a personal ad). Date other men casually — *no sex*. Don't let any of them meet your son until you're fairly sure that you're going to marry. Otherwise, your son may attach to each person, then be disappointed when you break up, and eventually be unable to feel anything for the guy you end up marrying.

The first time you aren't available when your friend calls, he'll probably appreciate you more. That's fine. If he makes dates in advance, go ahead and see him if you like. But if he calls at the last minute, say that you're *"busy — how about some other time?"* And be sure that he asks you out somewhere, rather than just dropping by.

There's nothing wrong with staying home once in awhile. However, you should be *dating* someone, not living with him one day a week.

All the best, and please let me know how it works out.

Dr. Kate

Chapter 2

Taking a Ride on the Cycle of Love

In This Chapter

▶ Deflating seven problem-causing relationship myths

▶ Understanding the realities that can save your relationship

▶ Grasping the biggest reality of all: *The Love Cycle*

▶ Exploring the stages of relationships

A lot of funny ideas are floating around out there about relationships. In fact, knowing what to think about *The Big R* is really kind of tricky. For example, forming an opinion about relationships based on your own experiences and those of your friends is natural. Buuuttt — depending on how healthy those friends and their relationships have been, you can also end up in real trouble by following their lead. After all, you can't expect to end up happily married if you model your relationship behavior after Uncle Bobby, who's been married and divorced six times!

In this chapter, I review seven common relationship myths that can really mess up your life. But don't worry; I reveal the seven relationship-saving realities, too. I also describe what I've named *"The Love Cycle"* — the series of relationship stages you go in and out of during your lifetime — and how to use that information to make your love life what you want it to be. Finally, I explain how even relationships themselves have stages — and how you can use that information to your best advantage, too.

Discovering the Seven Relationship Myths

Now's the time to examine those funny little thoughts you hold in your mind about relationships — the myths you accept as truth and don't even question until someone like me encourages you to do so. Now, I'm not talking about the Zeus and Hera variety myths. I mean, it's easy to know that they're mythical figures — because they obviously reside in Greece, and you don't! No, the myths

I'm talking about are the fairy-tale variety that just kind of slip into your consciousness as if they might be real. You know, the Prince Charming/Cinderella stuff that the average kid in the United States gets read to him or her — and goes on to read — growing up. Kids have less experience with life than adults do, and much more experience with magic. After all, they spend hours watching cartoons where the hero gets flattened by a steamroller, quickly gets up, returns to normal, and then goes on to save the day. Kids even confuse their dreams with real-life events. All that creativity, joy, spontaneity, and imagination is great, but from those stories, our ideas about romance and relationships begin to form. Because you were a kid at the time, you probably never even thought about how much those fairy tales influenced your ideas about relationships. But little by little, they did.

Then as adults, you get exposed to the *romance movie* (also called the "chick flick"). *Sleepless in Seattle, It Happened One Night, Starman* — the list can fill a whole book, and believe me, I've probably loved them all. They're all wonderful movies that take our minds off our troubles and entertain us. But just like reading the Greeks, it's important to go home at night and remember how reality *really* is — so you don't expect your own life to be magical and get disappointed when it's not.

As I review some common relationship myths, consider which ones cause you grief. Think about the fairy tales and movies you've grown up with, and how they may have influenced you to believe those myths. Then read the reality following each myth, and consider how much more realistic and "better" it is. You really don't have to believe in fairy tales; real life is pretty amazing, too.

Myth #1: We fell in love at first sight

The myth of "love at first sight" assumes that love is magic — that you can instantly "fall in love" with someone without any previous experience with him or her. *"I loved Johnny from the moment I saw him." "When my eyes met Jill's, I knew."*

If you believe in the love-at-first-sight myth, you tend to overlook people you're not instantly attracted to. You may give someone 5 to 15 minutes to make an impression, and refuse to see anyone who doesn't rock your socks on the first date.

Believing in this myth also means that you can fall out of love just as suddenly and magically. As time goes on, you'll probably learn more about ways in which you and your mate aren't compatible. Then if you believe in this myth, you may not work hard enough at making the relationship thrive. After all, if falling *in* love was beyond your control, then falling *out* of love must be, too, right? If forces outside you control your life, then giving up is easy. The intense feeling fades away, and you move on to the next person and the next "love at first sight."

Love at first sight is really infatuation or lust. You like what you see right away, and you want to be in love, so you assume that what you don't know about this person will also be wonderful. You're overwhelmed with an intense feeling of desire. If you're correct, and those puzzle pieces come together in a positive way, you may keep that intense feeling for your partner. But initially, you just don't know if that will be the case.

If you challenge the myth of love at first sight and understand that, in reality, love grows over time, several good things can occur:

✔ You open up your pool of possibilities immensely, and are less likely to overlook a good partner.

✔ You give people more than a few dates to make an impression. You realize that you don't have to be powerfully attracted to a person right away. Instead, you can date someone with average looks, grow to love her over time, and come to see her as very attractive.

✔ You take responsibility for locating a partner and making the relationship thrive. If you want to find a mate, you put yourself in situations where you're most likely to meet people. If you and your mate are having trouble, you try to fix those problems together.

✔ If the intense feeling ends, you don't waste time crying into your beer because the magic in your life has dried up. Instead, you recognize infatuation and lust for what they are, recover from the loss, and move on to find a more compatible and enduring relationship.

Myth #2: I've found my soulmate — "The One"

The soulmate myth claims that there is just one person who is *destined* to be with you — your soulmate. All you have to do is find that person; then everything else automatically falls into place, and you live happily ever after. But think about that — what does this magical thinking really mean? How can you make sure that the person you're with right now is "The One" you were meant to be with? What if someone better comes along? Or what if your soulmate lives in Nairobi, Antarctica, or some place you'll never visit? Are you doomed to be alone forever?

By definition, a *soulmate* is a perfect partner for you. So when you meet someone you like, you tend to gloss over his incompatible qualities for as long as possible, to allow yourself to believe that he's your soulmate. You're less likely to work on your relationship. After all, if this person is really your soulmate, the relationship should just magically *flow*, right?

You may also stay in an unhealthy relationship for a very long time. After all, if you were destined to be together, how can you fight fate? And if that person just happens to be a *hook from your past* — someone you're powerfully attracted to because he or she reminds you of someone you knew in an unhealthy way in the past — staying longer can be *very* unhealthy.

And when you finally realize that your partner and relationship aren't perfect, you're likely to dump them to pursue someone else who once again seems like your soulmate. Instead of accepting reality and working out the problems in your current relationship, you might even desert your spouse and family, and high-tail it miles away to live with that next "soulmate" who's just swept you off your feet.

The good news is that there's no such thing as a soulmate, that *one* person who's perfect for you. Instead, there are actually many, *many* people who can be a good mate for you! The story will just be a little different with each.

So you don't have to look for a needle in a haystack, or worry that you'll never find a good partner because he or she lives in another country. You don't have to move 5,000 miles away to start over with Mr. Dreamboat, who seems perfect. You know that he isn't really perfect — because no one is. You don't have to deny incompatibilities in your mate or the relationship, trying to believe that they're perfect. Instead, you can recognize both the positive and negative qualities in your relationship and work on the problems that you and your partner can realistically change. Isn't that great?

In addition, when someone is an unhealthy hook from your past, you'll recognize it sooner. Instead of getting frantic or avoiding the issue, you'll realize that he or she isn't your "soulmate" (because no one is), and it's OK to move on when the problems are too unhealthy. You'll be more confident and calm, and you'll know that if this current partner isn't healthy or compatible, there's someone else out there for you who *is*.

Myth #3: Being "in" love is better than loving someone

Many people believe that the heady excitement that comes in the first stages of seeing someone (being *in* love) is essentially better than that subdued, comfortable feeling that occurs after you've gotten to know someone a little better (loving someone). This view implies that if you don't have that heady feeling, something must be wrong with the relationship. It also implies that if/when you lose that intensely excited feeling for your mate, it's OK to break up and pursue the "rush" with someone else. After all, you love your partner, but you're not *in* love with him, so why not go for the pot of gold at the end of the next rainbow? Don't you deserve to feel that incredible high?

Sure you do. However, the heady excitement that occurs when you first meet someone, the feeling that people commonly call "being *in* love," is actually being in infatuation or lust. Certainly, there's a "chemical" process occurring. Your heart is pounding, and your brain is firing *endorphins* (opiate-like substances) and producing adrenaline, so you feel very excited and "up."

Part of this excitement comes from the fact that you don't know if you can count on your partner to be there tomorrow. You don't know how things will develop, so risk is involved. The longer you stay in the relationship, and the more you want it to continue, the more it will hurt if it ends. The relationship is also new, and new experiences are often more interesting and exciting.

In a good relationship, however, that feeling eventually becomes more subdued and comfortable. As you get to know someone better, you begin to trust that he'll be there for you tomorrow. As you become more comfortable, the crazy excitement wanes a bit, and a more cozy, snuggly feeling replaces it. You trade off a little of the excitement for a lot more stability.

For more on the stages of a healthy relationship, see the last section of this chapter. Then if/when you're tempted to pursue a rush with someone else, ask yourself: Wasn't your current relationship also exciting in the beginning? Of course. So instead of starting all over with a new person — someone who may not stick around long enough to build a history together — why not work on the relationship you have and make it thrive?

Challenging the "*in* love" myth means that you can appreciate a relationship that doesn't start with infatuation. In other words, you can be happy being with someone you love, even when the beginning was much calmer. You can stay with one relationship and make it better, and you can have a stable love life. You can experience the plusses of growing with your partner over a long period of time. You can eventually get married, stay married, and raise children. Now, that doesn't mean that you can't keep your relationship interesting, pleasurable, and fun. *Au contraire!* Working on the relationship can keep the spark and romance flowing. See Chapters 16 and 24 for more.

Myth #4: I've got to have a partner

Another relationship myth states that you are nothing without a mate who loves you. People who buy into this myth believe that when they're with someone they love who loves them back, life is simply wonderful. When they're not, life — and everything in it, including themselves — is worthless. If you believe this myth, you measure your self-worth by whether you're involved in a relationship. But if your value as a person changes depending on the behavior of others, how can you ever feel secure and confident?

You don't *have* to have a partner to be worthwhile. Your worth as a human being is not contingent on you being coupled, married, or anything else. You can live a happy, productive life without a partner. You have worth just because you exist.

Believing that you can't be happy without a partner is a self-fulfilling prophecy. If you devalue yourself because you're not in a loving relationship, you're likely to feel depressed and worthless, and you'll act accordingly. Then others are more likely to avoid you, and you'll feel worse about yourself. So in essence, your belief comes full circle and causes you to feel miserable.

In contrast, if you love yourself, single or coupled, you're more likely to feel happy and cheerful. You'll then act happy and healthy, and attract other happy, healthy people to you. And that will greatly increase your chances of finding a happy, healthy partnership!

Myth #5: I don't need anyone

You may have been tempted to just chuck it all and say, "Well, love hasn't worked for me, so I don't need anyone anymore!" Most people who've dated for any length of time have felt that way at one time or another. But when you say that you don't need anyone, you're usually saying a whole lot more. Perhaps you've just broken up with someone. You want your partner back so badly, but at the same time, you're disappointed, hurt, and angry. Or maybe you've just been looking for so long, it's getting to you; you're disgusted with the entire process of looking for love. Because you feel like you'll never be successful at love, you reassure yourself that you "don't need anyone." Saying those words to yourself temporarily makes you feel less dependent, hurt, and angry. You feel stronger — even if just for a little while.

But just like the "I've-got-to-have-a-partner" myth, telling yourself that you "don't need anyone" is also too extreme to be true. Being independent is good, and you do need to be happy single, but pretending you're invincible won't make you happy either.

If you tend to be too needy, and if telling yourself that you don't need anyone helps you stay independent to a healthy degree, then go ahead and tell yourself this myth. However, don't say those words to a potential partner, because he or she may actually believe you and leave you for someone who wants a real relationship. And don't use this myth to completely avoid meeting people for extended periods of time. After all, you're human, and studies have shown that when you share your problems with a supportive person, you can minimize stress and live longer. Having a good friend or mate to talk to can be a very good thing.

Myth #6: If I find my perfect partner, my life will be perfect

Here's a riddle: You're human, but what isn't? Perfection. Perfection and humans just don't go together; one excludes the other. Yet another myth (often held in conjunction with the soulmate myth) assumes that people can be perfect, relationships can be perfect, compatibility between two people can be perfect, and life can be perfect. This myth holds a standard — perfection — as attainable, and encourages you to seek a level of compatibility that is basically unattainable.

It also implies that someone else can come along and save you from your life. Prince Charming comes along on his big white horse, kisses you, and saves you. "Someday my prince will come."

Just like the soulmate myth, this myth encourages you to gloss over incompatibilities and flaws in your mate in a desire to find him "perfect." Of course, when you finally realize he isn't perfect and isn't going to make your life perfect, you become angry and blame him for not coming through with the rest of the perfect dream. Instead of taking responsibility for your own life and happiness and trying to fix the problems, you either wallow in unhappiness, believing it's your partner's fault — or you toss your imperfect relationship to pursue someone else who currently seems perfect for you.

The reality is: Where people and life are concerned, perfection does not exist. You're not perfect, your mate is not perfect, no relationship will ever be perfectly compatible, no one's life is ever perfect, and the only person who can save you from your life is you. After you understand this statement, several wonderful things happen:

- ✔ **You become happy with less than perfection.** Rather than focusing on the negative and summarizing your mate, your relationship, and your life as *"no good"* because they aren't *"perfect,"* you give yourself permission to be happy and content with mostly positive and realistic experiences.

- ✔ **You start looking at your mate more realistically.** Instead of glossing over her incompatibilities trying to find her "perfect," you can relax and accept reality. Instead of blaming him for not being perfect, you can praise his efforts and small steps to improve — even if the result is less than perfect.

- ✔ **You stop blaming your mate for your mistakes.** Because you're also not perfect, you accept responsibility for your less-than-perfect actions and work on improving them.

- ✔ **You stop expecting your mate to save you from your life.** Once you remove the possibility of someone else saving you, it's much easier to accept responsibility for your own life and become proactive in changing it. You understand that you're the only person who can make yourself happy — the only person who can do the work and make your life more of what you want it to be.

✔ **You realize that since no relationship is perfectly compatible, disagreements are inevitable.** Instead of getting upset when problems arise, you cheerfully and realistically work out compromises with your partner.

✔ **You stay faithful to your mate.** Even though someone else may initially look perfect and cheating might cross your mind, you quickly recover. You know it'd only be a matter of time before you'd discover that person's imperfections and incompatibilities between the two of you. And since you've already got a wonderful partner who's proved pretty compatible and put so much into your current relationship, why switch?

Myth #7: We'll be together forever

Nothing lasts forever. Except maybe fruitcake or bills or taxes — but definitely not love! Yet many people believe the myth that says when you find true love, it lasts indefinitely — just like the fairy tales and modern movies, where boy meets girl, they fall in love, and they all "live happily ever after" in a cute little house with a white picket fence and 2.2 children.

Although watching your favorite (albeit unrealistic) romance movies may be fun, don't let those images control your expectations of reality. If you truly expect to stay with your partner forever, you'll be devastated when your relationship ends. Since roughly 50 percent of all marriages end in divorce, and one mate usually outlives the other even in happy marriages, believing that the two of you will be together forever virtually assures that you'll eventually be devastated when reality occurs.

But don't get your knickers in a knot! Losing a partner does *not* have to devastate you. Yes, you'll feel pain. However, if you have realistic expectations going into the relationship — if you understand that it can end at any time, you'll enjoy the present for all it's worth, and act and speak in ways that show your appreciation to your partner. So if your relationship does end, you'll be better prepared to handle it. You'll be sad, but not shocked, which will allow you to greatly shorten the time you spend grieving.

Reviewing the Myths and Realities

Table 2-1 reviews the seven myths and realities I've mentioned in this chapter. So whenever you feel one of those dastardly myths creeping into your brain and usurping your consciousness — Wait! Stop! Review this table and rescue yourself with a saving reality.

Table 2-1	Seven Relationship Myths and Realities
Grief-Causing Myth	*Saving Reality*
M1: We fell in love at first sight.	R1: It might be infatuation or lust at first sight, but it just ain't love, Babe!
M2: I've found my soulmate — "The One."	R2: There are many compatible people out there for you.
M3: Being *in* love is better than loving someone.	R3: Loving someone is just as good as being *in* love.
M4: I *must* have a partner.	R4: You can live a happy and productive life without a partner.
M5: I don't need anyone.	R5: People live longer with someone to talk to.
M6: If I find my perfect partner, my life will be perfect, and I will be saved.	R6: No partner will ever be perfect, and the only person who can save you is *you*.
M7: We'll be together forever.	R7: Relationships end through breakups and death, but you can live happily and love again.

Accepting the Greatest Reality of All

No, this isn't about Whitney Houston's hit "The Greatest *Love* of All." I'm talking "greatest *reality* of all" here, as in *relationships*. And what is that greatest reality?

The greatest reality of all is that most people go in and out of various relationship stages over their lifetimes, a pattern I've named *"The Love Cycle."* Simply put: *Life is one big Love Cycle consisting of relationship stages that tend to repeat over and over and over again.*

And what are the relationship stages that make up *The Love Cycle*? Thanks for asking:

1. **Finding Love:** Before you can make a relationship, you have to flirt, date, and find a reasonably compatible partner. Some relationships end right there, never progressing past a first date or casual dating. If yours does progress, however, you then assess his or her compatibility. Are the two of you compatible enough for a good relationship? If you continue to see one another, you gradually grow closer. You may or may not have sex

together. But when you feel like a couple, with some expectation and assumption that you'll see one another again, you're traversing Stage 1 and entering Stage 2 of *The Love Cycle*.

See Chapter 5 for help with dating, Chapters 3 and 4 and *The Dr. Kate Compatibility Quiz* in Appendix A to assess your compatibility with someone, and Chapter 7 to make rational decisions about sex.

2. **Making the Relationship Work:** Now you're past casual dating; you're *having* a relationship. You both see yourselves as a couple, and expect to see one another rather frequently for a while. This stage includes becoming more and more intimate by sharing ideas, thoughts, feelings, and experiences with one another that you don't share with anyone else. Sex is usually one of those experiences, so this stage usually includes making a commitment to be monogamous with each other. It also includes working out problems through good communication and mutually satisfactory compromises. You may choose to move the relationship forward by living together or getting married. Or, if you're not doing very well at making the relationship work, you may traverse into Stage 3 of *The Love Cycle* instead.

See Chapter 6 on intimacy, Chapter 8 on exclusivity, Chapter 9 on cohabiting, Chapter 10 on staying happy in your relationship, and Chapters 11 through 13 and *The Dr. Kate Communication Quiz* in Appendix B for more on communication. See Chapters 14 through 16 and Chapter 24 for sex and romance info, and see Chapters 17 through 19 for marriage tips.

3. **Letting Go:** This stage occurs when you realize that somewhere along the way, your relationship has deteriorated to the point where it's in serious trouble. You may seek couples counseling to try to fix it, but if things don't improve, you may have to let go and break up. This stage also occurs when you lose a partner to death. It includes weathering the breakup, dealing with the pain of losing a partner and a relationship you wanted, and grieving. It also includes getting closure and forgiving — yourself, your partner, and especially in the case of death, even God. It may also include seeing a psychologist to help you heal faster.

See Chapter 20 for more on when your relationship is and isn't fixable, and Chapter 21 on breaking up with less pain.

4. **Starting Over:** After you've grieved your loss and healed enough, you begin to rebuild your love life. Stage 4 includes the steps you take to get back in touch with people and outside activities. It involves getting out of the house and starting to socialize, then eventually dating again. If you have children, it also includes helping them through the transition.

See Chapter 22 for tips on starting over, and when you're ready to date, review Chapter 5. Then starting over with Stage 1, review each chapter mentioned when you get to that *Love Cycle* stage with your new mate.

DR. KATE SAYS

Always look at the big picture. Understanding love as a series of relationship stages is vitally important for two reasons:

✔ If you like the stage you're in, remembering that it's temporary helps you appreciate your partner and show it. It helps you do the work to stay in that stage as long as possible.

✔ If you don't like where you are, understanding it's time-limited helps you work through that stage with the least amount of grief, so you can move on to a stage your prefer.

Recognizing That Relationships Have Stages, Too

Besides moving through various relationship stages of *The Love Cycle*, relationships themselves tend to have stages, which I explain in this section.

The Infatuation/"In" Love Stage

Early in this chapter, I talk about the heady excitement that comes in the beginning of the relationship. Your adrenaline rushes, your blood pressure and heart rate increase, you feel your heart pounding, and you are intensely interested in your partner. In fact, that first stage of relationships includes a variety of biochemical changes (ergo the term "romantic chemistry"). It's also called the *endorphin stage,* because your brain emits neurochemicals called "endorphins." Like heroin and morphine, these neurochemicals make you feel high, on top of the world, invincible. You have an intense desire to spend more and more time with your partner, and find it difficult to concentrate on anything else.

The relationship is interesting and exciting because it's new, unknown, and a bit risky. At any moment, you could lose whatever you've invested in the relationship. You don't know your partner well, so you don't know if you can trust him or her to be there tomorrow. You don't know if the feeling will continue either; the infatuation/lust may or may not grow into real love.

At this stage, your mate is a giant puzzle, and although you may like what you see so far, pieces of information are still missing. Gradually, over time, you begin to see your mate around different people, in various situations, and under different kinds of stress. The puzzle pieces fill in. As time goes by, if you continue to like those pieces and the positive feeling lasts and grows, you pass into the next stage of the relationship, the Nesting/Loving Stage.

The Nesting/Loving Stage

As you begin to trust that your partner will be there for you today, tomorrow, the next day, and the next, you begin to relax. As you gradually learn more about each other and like what you find, you relax even more. Your adrenaline decreases, your heart stops pounding, and that crazy excited feeling starts to subside. You still feel great around your partner, but it becomes a more comfortable, snuggly feeling. A neurochemical called *oxytocin* fires in the brain, adding to the nesting feeling. You and your partner love one another, but you're also comfortable at the same time. Part of the excitement goes away, but it's replaced with a calm, secure, happy feeling.

Many relationships start with the Infatuation/*In* Love Stage, and progress to the Nesting/Loving Stage when the partners have seen each other often enough to really get to know each other. Getting to the Nesting/Loving Stage usually takes about three to four months of seeing someone three to four times weekly. If you haven't been dating one another that much or that often, then the strong feeling you have may be infatuation, and it may die out before you reach the love stage. The only way to tell if an early strong feeling will develop into real love is to wait and see. You have to get the rest of the puzzle pieces to know, and that takes time.

It's normal and healthy to go from the Infatuation/*In* Love Stage to the Nesting/Loving Stage. If you stay in the Infatuation/*In* Love Stage, your relationship may be unhealthy or too difficult. For example, if you're not able to see one another very often because you live miles apart, getting to know one another will take a longer period of time. If your partner is cheating or has serious psychological problems and you're in a constant stage of relationship schism, never knowing if your relationship will be there tomorrow, you may also stay in the infatuation stage. But most healthy relationships move on to the Nesting/Loving Stage. And that sure is a great place to be!

Chapter 3

Is It a Match?

In This Chapter

▶ Deflating six problem-causing compatibility myths
▶ Understanding six compatibility realities that can save your relationship

*I*n the movie *White Palace*, three friends are sitting on a couch observing the other party guests. Two of them are encouraging the third friend, Max, to date the hostess because she's beautiful, talented, and a great cook. Max looks at the couples in the room and asks, "How do you know who's right for each other? The Goodmans, or the Clarks, or Andy and Jasper — we all said that they were perfect for each other, and they didn't even last a year. Larry and Sherry? I've never heard Larry say a decent word about his wife."

There's no question about it: Figuring out compatibility — who is and isn't compatible for you — is a tough nut. Compatibility is one of the most important questions in life, but it isn't even taught in school! Yet to succeed at a relationship, you've got to find a compatible partner and identify that person as having potential. So your beliefs about compatibility will make or break any relationship you have. They'll have a direct impact on the people you choose to date and keep dating, as well as your choice of a long-term partner or spouse.

If you hold irrational ideas about compatibility, you're more likely to choose unhealthy people, stay in an unsatisfactory or harmful relationship, and experience considerable distress and upheaval in your life. Just as there are myths that can wreak havoc on your relationship (see Chapter 2), there are also many strange ideas about compatibility floating around out there. In this chapter, I discuss the six most common grief-causing compatibility myths and the six realities that can save your relationship.

I suggest taking **The Dr. Kate Compatibility Quiz,** located in Appendix A, for the person you're dating right now or the most recent relationship you've had. Score yourself and read the results. Be sure to note the compatibility elements addressed by each question, and keep them in mind as you read this chapter.

Debunking Six Compatibility Myths

As I discuss the following compatibility myths, ask yourself: Do I hold any of these beliefs? If so, think about how that belief influences your life. Then reflect on the reality and how your life could be improved by letting the reality guide you.

Myth #1: I've got to find a partner "the natural way"

Many people believe the myth that they must find a partner "the natural way." Right from the start, this myth causes trouble by assuming that there are "natural" and "unnatural" ways of meeting suitable partners! The person holding this belief generally thinks that meeting through friends and family is fine, meeting through work is fine, and meeting through activities is fine. Bumping into someone on the street is even fine. Using more direct methods, however, like online and offline personal ads and dating services, is not fine.

If you believe this myth, you're likely to waste a lot of time chasing your tail while trying to find a suitable partner. This is the new millennium, so why keep yourself in a Relationship Dark Ages? People are often suspicious of the unfamiliar, but there's no such thing as an "unnatural" way to find someone. In fact, modern dating methods like introduction services and personal ads can help you be more efficient and successful in your search, saving you time, energy, and money. See Chapter 5 for more on how and when to use online and offline personal ads and dating services.

Here's the bottom line: There's no one right way to date. How you find a suitable partner depends on what relationship stage you're in, and how ready you are to make a permanent relationship. If you're not done healing from a divorce or breakup, for example, or if you're too young to get married and want to date casually, you may find social activities a fine way to meet new friends. On the other hand, if you're old enough, mature enough, and ready for a serious relationship leading to marriage, introduction services and personal ads may be the best, most efficient option for you. For more on choosing a dating method that's best for you, see Chapter 5.

Myth #2: I deserve the best; I shouldn't settle

This myth assumes that people come with quality tags attached to them: for example, "good person," "bad person," "best person," and so on. The person who buys into this myth often makes statements like, "I deserve the best, and I won't settle for less!" She's quickly judgmental of others and assumes that whenever someone differs from her, that person must be less of a catch. After all, since she's such hot stuff, being like her must be the best, right? That makes other people not good enough for her.

This myth encourages people to look at differences between people as a sign of being "better" or "worse" than someone else. A woman using these judgmental terms to differentiate potential from "non-potential" mates has usually discussed the subject with girlfriends and decided that she's a great catch. So, of course, she "deserves" the best, and she shouldn't compromise her high moral grounds to date anyone of lesser quality.

People who believe in this myth look down on others for being different, and overlook many compatible matches to pursue some kind of *idealized mate* — a fantasy person "just like them," and therefore perfect in every way. While these judgmental mythbelievers hold very highly inflated opinions of themselves, they rigidly reject others on the basis of insufficient data. They come across to others as arrogant, rude, cold, egotistical, and egocentric.

The surprising thing about it, though, is that the person who has to believe in this myth is generally insecure and frightened deep down. She lacks real confidence and self-esteem. After all, if she really believed in her self-worth, why would she have to put others down to feel good about herself?

You can be different from someone, and those differences may mean that the two of you are not compatible for a romantic relationship. However, just because another person is different from you does not make him better or worse — it just makes him different.

People come in so many combinations and permutations — no wonder the world is such an interesting place! No two people are ever totally alike, and frankly, a normal person would be bored silly dating his or her clone. But it's a real mistake to use *moral* words (for example, "good," "better," "best," "bad," "worse," or "worst") to describe human beings. Only a higher moral power (God, for example) has the right to judge anyone's worth as a human being. Since presumably, no reader can claim that distinction, rest assured that every person alive is a valuable yet unique individual — and banish moral words from your compatibility descriptions and decisions. Besides, as I discuss in Chapter 2, there's no such thing as a perfect person anyway. Everyone has plusses and minuses; it's all just part of being human.

Beware people who try to judge you. They usually have so many longstanding personal problems, it's just not worth trying to pursue a relationship with them. They need psychotherapy, not a romantic partner.

Myth #3: I want it all in one person

Just as the previous myth assumes that people can come in the "perfect" variety, some people foolishly believe that relationships can also be perfectly compatible. They're convinced that if they look hard enough, they can locate someone who fits them perfectly, and all their needs will be magically fulfilled in that relationship. In making statements like, "I want it all in one person," they're either extremely naive and prone to believing in fairy tales — or arrogant and prone to judgments like those described in the previous myth. Because they believe that compatibility can be perfect, they also overemphasize what they have in common with their partners and overlook any evidence to the contrary: "We're exactly alike in every way. We're just perfect together!"

When the mate ends up being a mere mortal, the partner often becomes irrationally upset at him or her. Unfortunately, if that person continues to believe in the myth, he often breaks up and dates someone new whom he has designated as "perfect" this time, and the pattern just repeats and repeats. That person is never satisfied or happy — and tends to bestow that unhappiness on his or her partners as well.

Just as no person is ever perfect, no relationship is ever perfectly compatible. Because you'll never find anyone who is perfectly compatible, it's important to analyze which elements of compatibility are most important. (See Chapter 4 for more on compatible characteristics.) Then try to find someone who is compatible with you in those ways. Once you find that person, be sure to appreciate him or her and show it — verbally and through your actions — so your relationship stays alive and kicking.

For example, if you want to get married and/or raise a family, finding a partner who shares that relationship goal is extremely important. Otherwise, no matter what other qualities that person might possess, the relationship will not be compatible enough to satisfy you over time. See Chapter 2 for more on how the "perfect" delusion adversely affects relationships.

Myth #4: I can tell in five minutes if we're compatible

Many people believe they have some kind of inherent ability to size someone up and grasp that person's essence in a matter of moments. Other people may need time to get to know someone, but these folks are *Superpeople!* — or so they believe. They have the power to see through walls, brains, and personalities — to foretell the future and whether they have a snowball's chance in hell of relationship success with someone.

Of course, people who believe in this myth tend to overestimate their people sense. All they're doing is a quick assessment of whether or not they're immediately attracted to the other person. Their rationale: "I only end up getting involved with people I find attractive right away." This reasoning is unfortunate because:

- ✔ It's a self-fulfilling prophecy. If you only date people you find gorgeous at first sight, then of course, anyone you form a relationship with will be someone from that small subsection of the population. To then turn that around and say, "See, I was immediately attracted to everyone I eventually fell in love with," is to use twisted logic.

- ✔ If you only date people you're instantly attracted to, you're overlooking many people who could be compatible with you emotionally, intellectually, and in many other ways.

In reality, initial impressions of people are frequently very distorted. Allowing that impression to determine whether or not you'll get to know someone is to seriously compromise your love life. What really matters is not how you initially perceive someone, but how you see him or her over time. Yes, you have to eventually be attracted to someone physically or sexually for a romantic relationship to work. After all, you do want to have sex with your mate. However, most people are capable of growing to find someone more or less attractive over time.

For example, someone very close to me once described an initial encounter with her mate: "He had red, bushy, windblown hair, a sunburned complexion — and the biggest freckle I'd ever seen on the end of his nose. He was wearing a turquoise shirt and burgundy shorts that didn't match, and he smelled of beer." She had never dated a redheaded guy before, and she was struck by his strangeness/uniqueness. Her thoughts continued: "Wow, look at all those freckles! He's got that kind of skin that gets skin cancer. Boy, I hope he doesn't get it. He seems like a nice guy. But he's so wild looking . . . is he crazy?" Of course, while all this was going on in her head, she was trying to answer the man's questions! How did the story end? Well, this wise woman overlooked her fears and fell in love with the gent — then realized he was quite handsome, especially to her.

If you get to know someone who doesn't initially strike you as attractive and then fall in love, one day, you'll wake up and say, "Wow, she's really gorgeous. How come I never noticed it before?" And the opposite is also true. If you initially find someone very attractive, but become less than pleased with his personality over time, you'll eventually be able to say, "He is physically attractive, but I'm not attracted to him." And that relationship will not survive as a romance.

Society would not exist if people couldn't grow to find other people attractive. After all, most people aren't model-gorgeous; yet they still manage to find partners because they fall in love with the *complete* person, not just the visuals. Still skeptical? Look around you. If only model-perfect people married and had children with other model-perfect people, barring a few genetic anomalies, humanity would be full of model-perfect people!

Myth #5: Opposites attract

The myth that "opposites attract" isn't terrible; it just causes some difficulty over time. It assumes that people go best with those who are their total opposites. Of course, if you take this myth to its logical conclusion, you would date someone unlike you in most ways. If you were a short, 75-year-old, staunchly rigid Republican and quiet homebody, you'd choose a 21-year-old, tall, very liberal Democrat who loved to party every night.

And what if you want to marry and your mate never does, or if you want a child and your partner is adamantly opposed? What if your partner loves sex and you can't stand it? Or if one of you believes in making a difference in the world, and the other is more than content sitting around and watching TV?

You may initially become very attracted to someone who seems very opposite, but eventually, those same qualities that you once prized may come to repel you. It all depends on what the quality is and how much you differ from your partner in that way.

For example, very talkative people often enjoy people who listen more. If their partner talked as much as they did, how would they ever find time to say all they wanted to say? Quiet people frequently tell me they open up more around gregarious, chatty people. Similarly, if you tend to be a little timid, you might appreciate a mate who encourages you to be more adventurous. His energy and spirit might energize and stimulate you.

If you're a very left-brained female who excels at verbal and analytical skills but can't cook, and always manages to just miss the wastebasket with a paper ball, you might appreciate a husband who's better at right-brain activities, like fixing things around the house, working with his hands, and cooking dinner for you after a long work day. To be happy together long-term, however, you'll still have to talk to one another about feelings and thoughts and feel understood. But if your mate looks at your near-miss paper balls as cute, rather than hopelessly messy, then you may have found your little piece of relationship heaven!

And on some issues, especially your relationship goal, it's extremely important to be similar to one another. Otherwise, the relationship won't survive long-term. In areas like values, ethics, life goals, and how you see yourself and the way you fit into your world, it's usually better if you and your partner are more similar than different.

The bottom line is: It's the big picture and how the two of you interact over time that counts. If you share the same relationship goal and can appreciate and enjoy each other's quirks as "cute" and "unique," you're far more likely to stay happy and together.

Myth #6: Distance makes the heart grow fonder

I'm sure that you've heard the myth "distance makes the heart grow fonder," which assumes that what is scarce or rare is more appreciated or valued. In many situations, this maxim holds true. For example, imagine that your boyfriend has been taking you for granted, blaming and yelling at you rather than losing his job by yelling at his boss. If you went out of town for a few weeks, your boyfriend might realize how much he loves and misses you, and start acting that way when you return.

On the other hand, what if you're a guy whose girlfriend has to stay out of town for weeks or months at a time? What happens when you feel lonely or sad and want to talk with a trusted friend? Maybe your partner is available, and maybe she isn't. And how do you feel when you call late at night and she isn't in the hotel room? How does she react when you're not home watching TV as usual on Thursday night? Do the wheels start turning?

And what happens if you meet a really great person on the Internet, and over time, you end up chatting more and more, and looking forward to getting to know one another better, but you just happen to live 5,000 miles apart?

The reality is: Relationships need frequent, quality, in-person time to flourish. People become intimate by sharing experiences with one another that they don't share with anyone else. If you and your partner are separated for long periods of time, you're not suddenly going to turn into a machine, without any feelings or needs. You may be able to get by on telephone calls and e-mails for awhile, but eventually, you're going to crave the in-person contact. Cybersex notwithstanding, virtual reality has only so much benefit!

If you enjoy a thriving offline relationship for a lengthy period of time, and one of you then has to be away for a while, it'll be difficult enough to keep the relationship going. If you've just met and you live far apart, your relationship will probably never develop or last long-term. And if you meet over the Internet and have *never* shared any in-person relationship together, the prognosis is even bleaker. If that person also lives halfway around the globe, consider the task impossible.

Unless you're independently wealthy, there usually isn't enough emotional investment to warrant the expense of frequent phone calls and trips to someone who lives in a different state or country. Every time you leave one another, parting becomes more painful. Sooner or later, one person generally decides that he's better off pursuing someone closer to home — a partner who can be there when he wants to be emotionally and physically intimate.

If you have to be temporarily separated from a long-term partner, make a concerted effort to keep in touch as much as possible through phone calls, e-mails, instant messages, and *snailmails* — the good old envelope and stamp kind of mail. If you can, plan frequent visits of long enough duration so you and your mate can really relax and enjoy one another. Don't just run in and out of town, becoming more and more tense and frustrated. And if you meet someone new (online or offline) who doesn't live within one or two hours of you, cut your losses and find a Honey closer to home.

Reviewing the Myths and Realities

Believing in myths can cause you lots of grief, so always keep the realities in mind. Table 3-1 can help; use it wisely!

Table 3-1	Six Compatibility Myths and Realities
Grief-Causing Myth	*Saving Reality*
M1: I've got to find a partner "the natural way."	R1: Modern dating methods are more efficient and successful.
M2: I deserve the best; I shouldn't settle for less.	R2: "Different" may mean "incompatible," but it doesn't mean "better" or "worse."
M3: I want it all in one person.	R3: You'll never find a perfect partner or perfectly compatible relationship.
M4: I can tell in five minutes if we're compatible.	R4: Relying on first impressions can seriously compromise your love life.
M5: Opposites attract.	R5: Some opposite qualities can initially attract, but eventually repel.
M6: Distance makes the heart grow fonder.	R6: Relationships need frequent, in-person, quality time to thrive.

Chapter 4

What Makes Someone Compatible?

In This Chapter

▶ Differentiating the "must haves," "good to haves," and "don't need to haves"

▶ Examining compatibility in unique situations

▶ Taking a hint from the experts — people who've been married long-term

Ahhh, compatibility — the 64,000 dollar question! As I note in Chapter 3, compatibility is a very complicated, yet critically important subject. It's at the heart of whether a relationship will be healthy and long-term — or unhealthy and fleeting.

So, if you've not yet taken **The Dr. Kate Compatibility Quiz** located in Appendix A, don't be lazy — do it *now!* Take it with your current partner or most recent love in mind. Score yourself, then read the interpretation of your score. Pay attention to the qualities listed for each question, and keep those in mind when reading the rest of this chapter. Also, review Table 4-1 (later in this chapter) frequently to help you remember which qualities are most important to compatibility — and which aren't important at all. Understanding those distinctions can mean the difference between enjoying a healthy, fun relationship long-term — and wasting years with a partner who'll never give you that joyful companionship.

In the following sections, I discuss the "must have" qualities that you need to have in a compatible relationship, the qualities that are "good to have," and those that you really don't need at all.

The Must Haves

In Chapter 1, I mention the qualities commonly found in healthy relationships. Another way to look at these qualities is to say that they're extremely important to compatibility. In fact, to be compatible with your partner, you both must have the qualities discussed in the following sections.

Honesty

To form a bond with someone and become emotionally intimate, you need to share experiences and secrets with your partner that you don't share with anyone else. That kind of intense, intimate, highly private interchange requires both parties to be honest with one another. Honesty involves giving accurate information about events that are known or have already occurred.

But what if your honey asks you about someone else's secrets? Or his latest clothing purchase? Should you really tell him that his new Hawaiian shirt would make a better bedspread? Should you tell your girlfriend that the woman coming down the street is "really hot?" See the sidebar "How much honesty?" (in this chapter) for how to be truthful while keeping your body parts intact.

Trust

It's impossible for you and your partner to know what the other is doing every moment of every day when you're not around one another. So instead of checking constantly, it's important that you both *trust* each other — you believe that your mate will always act in ways that protect your best interests, without being asked to do so. Good will is a prerequisite to intimate sharing and communication, so giving each other the benefit of the doubt and assuming the best is important.

Loyalty

Very closely related to trust, loyalty involves keeping your commitments and being there for one another. You can both count on each other to be stable and reliable and come through in a pinch. You protect your partner's best interests without being asked to do so — and your partner protects yours.

Loyalty and integrity are much-underrated qualities in the modern world. To maintain a good relationship with anyone, it's critical to keep your word and stand by that person when he or she is in need. In an intimate relationship, those behaviors are even more essential.

Monogamy

Monogamy is really a type of sexual loyalty. When you're monogamous with someone, you have sex only with that person. Sex involves getting up close and personal with someone. Your bodies get as close as anyone can get, short of donating an organ. So it makes sense that being sexually exclusive helps the relationship grow emotionally.

Maturity

To have a healthy, happy relationship with someone, both partners have to function at a fairly high level of *maturity* or emotional development. They have to be willing to consider the "big picture" — how they fit into their world, considering not only their own point of view, but their partner's as well. Both need to see things from their partner's point of view, and treat one another with respect, in an adult fashion.

When both partners are mature, they want to treat one another well — just because they believe it's the best thing to do. They understand they won't get everything they want the minute they want it, to the degree they want it, in any relationship. Living with a mate includes compromise, but mature people enjoy the satisfaction that goes along with being able to give, as well as receive. In contrast, immature people focus on their own needs. They look out for themselves first, and try to control or manipulate to get the upper hand.

Psychological health

Similar to maturity, psychological health is a "must have" in any successful relationship. A psychologically healthy person is emotionally stable, responsible, independent in living skills, and reasonably competent in social skills. He's in touch with reality, free of serious addictions and self-defeating behaviors, and has thoughts, feelings, and actions that are within normal limits. If either partner is unhealthy, the relationship will be skewed. If the psychological problems are severe enough, the relationship will either suffer greatly or end. The partners must each deal with their own personal problems before they can resolve any disagreements between them.

Shared relationship goal

For any relationship to thrive, both partners have to feel good about where it's going. If one wants a long-term committed relationship eventually leading to marriage, and the other just wants to have fun with that person, as well as others, the relationship is *not* going to work. You can compromise on when to marry, how to marry, and how to act after you're married, but marriage is an all-or-none condition; you can't be half married.

Timing

Ever meet someone who seemed *sooo* compatible with you, but the timing was just off? In addition to a shared relationship goal, timing is extremely important. People who are in the process of divorce, or just recently divorced or widowed, should give themselves time to heal before marrying again. If you meet someone in that stage and you want to get married soon, the two of you aren't compatible in the here-and-now. Even if your new partner cares for you, it's just too soon to remarry. He can't magically skip his recovery time any more than you can magically change to be in his relationship stage.

Many relationships end because the partners can't agree on their future together. You and your partner need to be in sync with regard to your relationship goal, and fairly close in your timing with regard to reaching that goal. Otherwise, you may be better off cutting your losses and looking for someone who's more compatible with you in those ways.

How much honesty?

Honesty is telling the truth as you know it about factual events that have already occurred. Honest partners do not knowingly give misinformation. However, *being honest* doesn't mean being rude, unkind, or aggressive. It doesn't mean sharing things to hurt your partner or "spilling your guts." *Discretion* — using good judgment about what to reveal and what not to reveal — is also important in any relationship.

So it's usually best not to attack your boyfriend's new clothing or make remarks about another woman's "hotness." It isn't necessary to share these feelings, and doing so may hurt your partner. If you're going to leave your girlfriend for that "hot" female, you will need to tell your mate that you want to break up. However, you still don't have to tell her that she "isn't hot enough." There are far kinder ways to break up. (See Chapter 21 for more on this.)

In addition, you don't have to reveal *everything* you think and feel to anyone, including your partner. You can always opt to keep something confidential because you've promised someone that you would, because you don't feel comfortable sharing the information, or just because you want to keep it to yourself. You also have the right to be vague if you don't want to respond to someone's detailed questions. But don't lie about an issue. Just tell your partner, *"I don't feel comfortable sharing that information,"* or,

"I don't feel comfortable sharing that information at this time." If it relates to a secret someone else has told you, you can say, *"That information was given to me in confidence, so I can't share it with you."* It's much better to hold back information than to give inaccurate information.

It's also OK to talk about your goals and intentions in good faith, then not be able to follow through all the time. That's not lying. However, if you're unable to keep your word for any reason, discuss that with your partner as soon as you realize it, and try to find an acceptable solution that also protects your partner's best interests. Isn't that what you'd want your partner to do for you? Don't just go out and do something that you promised not to do, or fail to do something that you said you would do. If you decide that you don't want to date your boyfriend exclusively any more, for example, tell him before you start dating other people.

People generally trust that someone is being honest with them until/unless they find out differently. After someone violates the code, however, there's no way to know when that person will cross the line again. That's why cheating is so destructive to a relationship, and why trust is so difficult (and sometimes impossible) to repair. For partners to remain strong, they must remain bonded to one another in honesty and good will.

The Good to Haves

So now that I've listed the "must haves," the time has come to consider the qualities that are good to have in a relationship. The more of these qualities that you and your mate have in common, the more compatible the two of you usually are. You can be incompatible in one or a few of these areas if you're strongly compatible in some or all the others. However, the more you're different in any particular area, the more you'll need to respect one another's differences and find respectful, satisfying compromises. In a nutshell, the more you're different in the following areas, the more you'll need to have compatibility in the first area on the list — good communication.

Good communication

Superglue #1! Where would the world be without ways to hold things together? Your books would fall apart, your house would fall down, and you'd be standing there naked in a pile of your clothes! Similarly, without communication to hold your relationship together, it too would fall apart. (Although your mate might not care if you're standing there naked with book pages, two-by-fours, and clothes on top of you!)

Communication is the glue that holds the relationship together. You can disagree on many issues and still enjoy a thriving relationship — provided you discuss your differences assertively (not aggressively), and make mutually satisfactory compromises. Good communication is *extremely* important to the lifespan and quality of a relationship. I put it under the "good to haves" rather than the "must haves," however, because you or your partner can start with mediocre communication and still enjoy your relationship long-term — *if* one of you is communication savvy and leads the other through the maze. Also, everyone can improve his or her communication with training and effort, so it's more easily changed than any of the "must have" qualities. (See Chapters 11 through 13 for more on the benefits of good communication.)

Overall fun and chemistry

Everyone needs some fun in life! To spend considerable time with someone and stay with that person, you need to enjoy his or her company most of the time. That's why you can't will yourself to love someone who seems like he or she should be perfect with you. For love to develop and continue, you have to genuinely enjoy each other.

Buuuuttt — life can be stressful, and stress can cause you to temporarily lose your sense of humor and fun — until you're boring yourself and your sweetie. It's quite possible to resuscitate your joie de vivre, however, with some effort, rest, and attitude readjustment. (Some mouth-to-mouth doesn't hurt either.) For some tips on how to play it smart and keep the fun and chemistry thriving in your relationship, see Chapters 16 and 24.

Compatible intelligence

To become emotionally close and stay close with someone, you both need to understand each other. To do that, you need to be reasonably close in intelligence. However, keep in mind that there are different kinds of intelligence. Your mate may be very proficient at right-brain activities, like working with his hands, manipulating objects in space, and doing creative, artistic activities, while you're more left-brained and excel at verbal, analytical, and logical tasks. The two of you can still get along very well — *if* you respect and appreciate your differences and communicate that understanding.

Physical attraction

Think about it — how often do you look at your own face and body, compared to how often you look at your mate's? Because most "normals" look at their mate far more often, partners have to be attracted enough physically to enjoy being with each other and having sex. Often, physical attraction is the first quality that draws you to another person, and the first quality that draws someone to you. This is particularly true of men, who are usually more visually motivated than women. While women are often drawn to a man's prestige and social standing (his power) and find the total package important, guys tend to focus on how someone looks. Everyone tends to perceive someone as more attractive after they fall in love with him or her, however, so a smart person allows himself that opportunity. See Chapter 3 for more on this topic.

Sexual attraction and orientation

Superglue #2! Just as good communication is the superglue that keeps you and your partner emotionally bonded and intimate, sex is the superglue that keeps you and your partner physically bonded and intimate. And in doing so, sex also helps you stay emotionally bonded and intimate. What a bonus! Because your mate is presumably the person you want to be most emotionally and physically intimate with, and also the person you want to have sex with if you're having sex with anyone at all, it's very important to have compatible sexual orientations and be sufficiently attracted to participate in sex together. Although physical attraction influences sexual attraction, other factors (like how much you love someone, how much fun you have together, and your partner's skill in the bedroom) can add or detract from the mix.

Similar interests

If you and your partner enjoy the same activities, spending quality time together will be easier. And the more you spend quality time together, the closer you'll feel toward one another.

Howeevvverrrrr — you and your mate don't have to have all your interests in common. If you're willing to share most activities, but loathe a few of each other's, you can each do those activities with other people. For example, if your man wants to go hunting but you strongly object to killing Bambi, you can spend that hunting weekend seeing relatives or friends he doesn't enjoy — or those who don't enjoy him. If your woman loves to shop and shop and shop until you both drop, drop, drop, you can encourage her to go with friends, while you go golfing, work on your car, or hang out with your buddies (especially those she can live without). Just limit the number of "loathsome activities" to three, tops. Otherwise, you and your mate will spend a lot more time with other people than with each other, and over time, that can kill any relationship.

Similar investment/power in the relationship

For a relationship to get off the ground, both partners have to want it to happen about equally as much. If one wants the relationship a whole lot more than the other, that person will have less power in the relationship. The other partner will sense that he or she has the upper hand and will often take the first person for granted, seeking out someone who is more "hard to get."

For example, consider how people act at an auction. If you want to buy a piano and are planning to bid on the brown one, but everyone else bids on the black one, you'll question your decision. Perhaps you've underestimated the black one's worth. Conversely, if you bid on the brown piano and no one else does, you'll wonder if your choice has some flaw that you've overlooked. It's just human nature; we all tend to devalue anything that comes too easily and prize something that is rare and more difficult to obtain.

A relationship is very fragile in the beginning, so power differences are more difficult to overcome at that time. But it's always good to keep the power — and the financial, emotional, sexual, and other investments you have in your union — about equal. Otherwise, one of you may lose interest.

Shared life goals and plans

Although not as crucial as sharing the same relationship goal, it's helpful if you and your partner are in sync with how you see your *raison d'être* — your reason to be. How you view your life's purpose has a lot to do with how you spend your time. So the more you share life goals and plans, and the more similar your approach to setting goals and making plans, the better.

Similar financial attitudes and practices

Money, money, money — you can't live without it! So it's no surprise that money — how to make it and how to spend it — is one of the most common topics of disagreement between partners. If your relationship is to thrive long-term, you and your mate will need reasonably compatible financial attitudes and practices.

Shared history

If you and your partner are together for two months, you may enjoy one another to the max while it lasts, but your lives won't blend much during that time. And it's way easier to spend two months with someone than to spend years together. In fact, the longer a couple stays together and the more life they live together, the greater the likelihood that they'll continue to stay together. The longer you stay with your partner, the more common history and positive traditions you'll amass together. Those customs and routines are uniquely yours as a couple, so they feel comfortable and safe, and they bond you together. Although every healthy relationship includes some change, spontaneity, and growth, it's also important to maintain a number of customs and routines. The key to success is to balance the "old" and "new" in a way that most pleases you and your partner.

Support of family and friends

No relationship exists in a vacuum. Eventually, you'll meet each other's friends and family. The more your family and friends support your relationship, the easier it will be to continue seeing one another. Conversely, the more your family and friends disapprove of the relationship and make that disapproval known to you, the more stress you'll have to endure to continue seeing one another.

Similar culture/religion/ethnicity

The more similar you and your partner are with regard to culture, religion, and ethnicity, the more comfortable you may feel with one another. You'll tend to share customs and traditions, and that shared history can make you feel closer to one another. It can also comfort your family and friends.

At the same time, people are often attracted to people who are slightly different from them — the difference adds to the "mystique." If both partners continue to respect their differences, they can make a fine match. However, families often pressure young adults to marry within their race, culture, or religion, and friends can also cause problems. So if you and your mate are from different races, you'll need to be strong enough to withstand ugly remarks and strangers staring at you from time to time. If you decide to become seriously involved, discuss your differences in a straightforward way and, together, make a plan for how to deal with outside pressures that arise as a result of those differences. Then if/when that stress occurs, you'll be better prepared and much more able to handle it together.

Perseverance

Because no two people are ever perfectly compatible, every couple has to work at keeping their relationship flourishing. They need to discuss their differences amicably and work out compromises they both find satisfactory. They also need to make time for each other, carving out time for dates and sex.

So the more you and your partner believe in working hard on your relationship, giving it attention and care and doing your best every day to make it thrive (in short, the more perseverance you have), the more likely your relationship will survive.

The Don't Need to Haves

The "don't need to haves" are things that you and your partner don't need to have in common to enjoy a satisfying, long-term relationship. You might be able to find these features, as well as the "must haves" and "good to haves," when you have a big pool of potential dates. But keep in mind that the smaller your available pool, the more important it becomes to distinguish essential from nonessential qualities. See the letter on age odds at the end of Chapter 5 for more on this. To begin distinguishing the "don't need to haves," consider how much each element affects your relationship, and how difficult it would be to change. For example, all the qualities listed under "must haves" are both extremely important to the relationship and very difficult to change. If your mate isn't honest by the time you meet him, he's not likely to become so during your lifetime. In contrast, the qualities in this section are both unimportant to your relationship and/or fairly easy to change.

Same taste in dress

In the grand scheme of things, clothing isn't nearly as important as the character of the person wearing it. So separate the person from the clothes when evaluating your relationship.

Don't stop dating someone just because you're turned off by his or her clothing or style of dress. Instead, wait until you have a solid relationship, then start buying your partner clothing when special holidays arise. Eventually, suggest helping him or her shop. Most partners, particularly those who are fashion-challenged, are usually happy to have their mate's help.

Same neighborhood

You and your mate don't have to live in the same neighborhood to develop a compatible relationship. Contrary to some popular biases, city people often enjoy going to the country, and people often live in the 'burbs not because they're ignorant or culturally illiterate, but because they enjoy the less expensive, relaxed environment and don't mind commuting to the city for cultural entertainment. As long as the distance isn't more than 90 minutes or so, dating someone from a different neighborhood can give you a chance to explore fun activities in that area.

Same education

As I mention earlier in this chapter, it's important for both partners to be roughly similar in intelligence. However, it's *not* important to have the same amount of formal education. As long as you understand one another, share similar interests (including intellectual interests), have fun together, and mix well with your respective work groups, family, and friends, the two of you can be quite compatible.

Same politics

Several high-ranking members of opposing political parties have managed to enjoy stable, loving relationships over the years. If you and your partner truly respect one another and your right to hold different political views, and as long as you don't feel compromised in your career or livelihood by those differences, there's no reason why you can't disagree on politics and still enjoy compatible coupledom.

Exactly the same marital and family status

It *is* vitally important that you and your partner be emotionally available, so neither of you should be married to other people. However, as long as you each have some kind of single status (single/never-married, divorced, or widowed), with or without children, then dating one another is often fine, even if you vary in your specific marriage and family experiences. The more you differ from the experiences of your age group, the more important it is to be flexible in this regard.

For example, if you're 28, never-married, with no children, it should be fairly easy to marry someone who shares these qualities because there are many never-married, childless, 28-year-olds out there. However, when you hit 45, a large percentage of people in a compatible age range will be divorced with children. So if you're still never-married then, it's best to maximize your chances by being open to them, even though they differ from you in that way.

There are also plusses and minuses to both sharing and differing in these qualities. If you're a divorced parent, you may feel comfortable with another divorced parent because you share that history and understand your stresses. At the same time, however, dating another divorced parent often means more logistical complications, like dating around your visitation schedules. So don't stereotype on this issue. Just take each person as an individual, and see how the relationship plays out for the two of you.

Special Compatibility Considerations

There's no question about it — compatibility is complicated, and there's no let-up in sight! Although I review many of the most important compatibility elements in previous sections, it's important to understand how to prioritize and assess compatibility in your unique situation. First, take a look at Table 4-1 to organize your thoughts about compatibility. Then read how to assess compatibility in a few example situations.

Table 4-1	Elements of Compatibility by Importance	
Must Haves (Extremely Important and Very Difficult to Change)	Good to Haves (Moderately Important and Difficult to Change)	Don't Need to Haves (Unimportant or Easy to Change)
Honesty	Good communication	Same taste in dress
Trust	Fun and chemistry	Same neighborhood
Loyalty	Compatible intelligence	Same education
Monogamy	Physical attraction	Same politics
Maturity	Sexual compatibility	Same marital/family status
Psychological health	Similar interests	
Shared relationship goal	Similar investment/power in the relationship	
Timing	Similar life goals/plans	
	Similar financial views and practices	
	Shared history	
	Support of family/friends	
	Similar culture, race, and religion	
	Perseverance	

Avoiding "impossible" partners

Keeping in mind the basic groupings in Table 4-1, if you're heterosexual, monogamous, and desire marriage and children in the near future, how would you assess your compatibility with someone from the following groups: married partners; gay partners; people who practice open relationships; or people who engage in swinging and group sex?

In each of these cases, your relationship goal (listed under "must haves") would differ from your partner's. Because *shared relationship goal* is a "must have" — extremely important and difficult to change, and *sexual compatibility* is a "good to have," a relationship with someone belonging to any of these groups would be doomed from the start. Although a married person could eventually divorce, *timing* (another "must have") is definitely incompatible right now. And although it's possible for someone who has practiced open relationships and swinging to stop those activities, it's best not to bet on it. Someone who isn't heterosexual isn't going to be compatible with you at all, so it's self-defeating to establish a romantic relationship with a gay person. Instead of dating that person and becoming attached to him or her, it would be better to find someone more compatible in these areas.

"Oh, that's obvious," you say. Nevertheless, many women become attracted to married men, men who engage in sexual practices they don't find comfortable, and gay men. See the letters at the end of this chapter and at *AOL Keyword: DrKate* and `www.drkate.com` for more on this topic. Just because someone has different sexual practices and orientations doesn't mean that you can't connect with him or her on many other variables. So if/when you do, you'll just need to exert extra control over yourself to avoid becoming romantically involved. Otherwise, you're just setting yourself — and the other person — up for emotional pain.

Considering socioeconomic status

What if a man and woman are both 28, but he's a high school educated janitor who makes 25K a year, while she's an MBA-educated investment professional, making 200K annually? They could certainly have honesty, trust, loyalty, monogamy, maturity, psychological health, a shared relationship goal, and compatible timing — all the elements in the "must have" column. They might also have great physical attraction, sexual compatibility, fun, and chemistry. However, they might have *less than compatible interests* outside the bedroom. She might prefer theater, opera, and ballet, while he enjoys sporting events, camping, and bowling. In addition, since they have different lifestyles, "collars," and *socioeconomic differences* (less shared history and dissimilar financial practices), they may receive *less support from her family and friends*, particularly if they view her education as an important step in family progress.

On the other hand, if she's the only one in her family with an MBA and everyone else has a high-school education and blue-collar job, her family might actually be more accepting and emotionally supportive of her boyfriend than someone who shares her education and "collar." And just because her boyfriend has a different collar doesn't necessarily mean that they won't enjoy the same activities. By assessing all the compatibility factors in her particular situation, she can estimate how likely it is that the two of them will be able to sustain their relationship. If she intends to continue despite the differences, she can brainstorm steps to take (deciding with her boyfriend how to handle unsupportive family and friends, for example).

Dealing with the disapproval of family and friends

If a man and woman in their late 20s marry, and the man opts to stay home with the kids while the woman works, or if they come from different racial backgrounds, any *family disapproval* could increase. Although there's really nothing wrong with reversing traditional male-female roles, family and friends can cause stress if they don't share those progressive views. In addition, because both partners are younger, they're more likely to be sensitive to such criticism. If the couple stays together, they need to discuss how they'll handle rude remarks, while always presenting a united front. In contrast, if both partners are 55, their family and friends might not care about socio-economic power, lifestyle, financial, or even racial differences. And if they did, the couple might find it easier to ignore the criticism.

Meeting online

What if a couple meets online and lives 1,000 miles away from each other? Another curve ball, but if you consider Table 4-1, it's easier to estimate potential compatibility. For example, they can certainly be compatible with regard to honesty, trust, loyalty, monogamy, maturity, psychological health, relationship goal, and timing. But they might have trouble telling whether they're compatible in these ways — because they don't see one another in an everyday environment. It'll take longer to develop the relationship, and longer to tell if the other acts in *emotionally healthy* ways or ways that suggest a *shared relationship goal* (both "must haves"). For all they know, the other person could be married or dating a lot of people while promising fidelity at the same time. The man might be trying out a different identity to see how he likes it. The woman might be telling him what she honestly believes to be true about herself, but he might not agree with her if/when they meet in person.

Similarly, although she might notice if he's extremely irresponsible and laissez-faire with money, she can't really tell if he has *similar life goals* or *similar financial views and practices* ("good to haves"); she's not there watching him spend money, pay bills, or run up credit cards.

They can't meet each other's friends and family online, so they can't observe how they each interact with them. Since they're communicating online, through written messages, they can't assess their *verbal communication*. They can exchange pictures, but since physical attraction and sexual compatibility are based on much more than physical attributes, they really can't tell if they'll have *physical attraction, sexual compatibility, fun,* and *chemistry* (all "good to haves") offline.

If they keep the relationship online, there's no problem. But if they are ever to become a real couple, they'll need to assess all these variables offline. Until then, determining whether the relationship could ever get off the ground is difficult. They would certainly need a lot of *perseverance* (another "good to have") to do it. They'd also need a lot of money, energy, and time.

Relating long-distance

Engaging in a long-distance relationship is never easy, especially when the participants have widely different incomes. A woman making 200K might have no difficulty paying for phone calls and plane fares, but a man making 25K probably would. The financial demands of the long-distance situation might bring any *socioeconomic differences* (differences in *history* and *financial practices* — "good to haves") to the forefront very quickly. If the difference in their incomes bothered the woman, it could upset the *power in the relationship* (another "good to have"). Or the fact that the woman is putting so much into the relationship might cause the man to value her less. Or lead to *less family and friend support*. In addition to the money and logistical problems, the couple wouldn't be able to spend much time together, which would hinder their *communication* (a "good to have"). Someone would eventually have to move to live with the other to allow the relationship to progress. Whoever did that would immediately have less power, because he or she would be investing more into the relationship. When one person leaves family, friends, job, and an entire life to live with someone far away, that person takes an enormous risk. The resulting difference in *interpersonal power* could add yet another stress to the mix. In this case, if the woman moved to be with the man, it might ruin the relationship because she's already contributing more money. On the other hand, if the man moved, it might strengthen the relationship because his sacrifice could balance her financial contributions, making the partners more similar with regard to power in the relationship.

In contrast, if the couple met online but lived locally, they could move the relationship offline as soon as possible and assess their compatibility just as they would with any other relationship. If they met offline and then moved some distance away from each other, they'd also have a better idea about their "must haves" and "good to haves." But they'd still need a lot of *perseverance* to make the long-distance relationship last over time.

Determining Compatibility

Whenever you want to figure out your compatibility with someone, take *The Dr. Kate Compatibility Quiz* in Appendix A. Then review Table 4-1 and consider the ways you and your partner are or are not compatible, as I've done in the previous examples. Brainstorm the compatible qualities you seem to have, as well as what kinds of problems you might expect to encounter. Then, considering the number and seriousness of the problematic areas and how difficult those items are to change, and factoring in how any "must have" or "good to have" qualities might help, estimate your chance of relationship success, and make a decision as to whether or not to pursue the relationship.

"Wow," you might say, "That's really pessimistic — hypothesizing possible problems before they occur." Au contraire. For one thing, you're estimating both your possible compatibility strengths, as well as your possible weaknesses. In addition, if you follow this advice, your thoughtful preparation can actually help the relationship stay on a more realistic, yet satisfying and slowly progressing path. If you decide to get involved, you'll go into it with realistic expectations. You'll be able to recognize and address various problems more quickly and efficiently because you've thought them through and brainstormed possible solutions in advance. That clarity, speed, and forethought can increase your chance of relationship success. If the relationship works out, great. But if it fails, you're less likely to be shocked or emotionally creamed. You went into this partnership with your eyes wide open, and you chose it knowing the risks. So you'll reach closure more quickly and be able to heal and move on more quickly, too.

So, How Picky Should You Be?

You should be picky enough to rule out people who:

- ✔ **Abuse you or your children physically or sexually.**

- ✔ **Are psychologically unhealthy to a degree** that being with them would compromise your psychological health.

- ✔ **Don't share your relationship goal.**

- ✔ Are *emotionally unavailable* — unable to give you what you want emotionally, either because they're already taken or for any other reason.

In addition, be very careful about dating the following types of people:

- ✔ **People who abuse you verbally.** If you date, attend couples counseling together, too. Your partner needs to learn to speak assertively, not aggressively, and work with you to reach compromises you both find acceptable.

- ✔ **Anyone suffering from self-defeating behaviors or serious psychological, personal, or interpersonal problems.** You can't make anyone get well; you can't even make that person seek treatment or stay on his medication. So it's far better to date people who are psychologically and emotionally healthy and stable.

- ✔ **A partner with a less serious psychological/emotional/behavioral problem, if it will adversely affect your life and your relationship, and he or she refuses to get help.** If you're thinking about marrying or linking yourself financially, legally, or emotionally to someone who isn't stable or doesn't take care of himself, it's best to reconsider. Over time, that chronic stress — which is totally outside of your control — can really take a toll on your physical and mental well-being. Eventually, you may have to leave the relationship to protect your own mental health.

- ✔ **An alcoholic, drug abuser, compulsive gambler, or sex addict.** These addiction problems must be treated before your relationship can progress.

- ✔ **An emotionally immature person, or someone who isn't competent in daily living skills.** If your partner refuses to work and loses job after job, or if he quits whenever he feels like it, despite the bills, it's probably best to cut your losses and move on. Remember, love *can't* conquer all — you also need money, emotional maturity, and psychological health.

See Chapter 20 for more on differentiating problems that can be fixed from those that can't.

Take a Hint from Long-Term Marriages

Another way to consider which elements are important in compatibility is to ask the lay experts — couples who have been married long-term. How *do* they stay together year after year despite today's high divorce rate? Studies suggest that the following qualities are extremely helpful:

- ✔ Being best friends.

- ✔ Believing that marriage is forever, that it's a sacred bond.

- ✔ Knowing that there will be good and bad times, but if you persevere, the good times will come again. (So you don't have to have fun every moment of every day in the relationship. Always look at the big picture.)

- ✔ Flexibility, a good sense of humor, and being able to laugh at yourself and roll with the punches.

Long-term marrieds, as a group, have much insight. If you want your union to last, emulate these qualities — and choose a partner who'll do the same!

❤ ❤ ❤ ❤ ❤ ❤

Date Bisexual/Homosexual/Priest/Married Man? Why Set Yourself Up for Pain?

Dear Dr. Kate,

My age: 26   **My gender:** Female

I'm heterosexual, but I'm crazy about a bisexual co-worker.

My age: 20   **My gender:** Female

I'm in love with a gay man. What should I do?

My age: 27   **My gender:** Female

Three years ago, I met this man through work, and fell in love with him. The problem is, he's a priest. I've tried so many times to forget him, but I can't; he feels the same way.

My age: 45   **My gender:** Female

I've fallen in love with a married man. The moment I met him, I felt like I'd known him all my life, and every logical thought went right out of my head.

Dear Confused Women,

Do you ever want to have a satisfying romantic and sexual relationship? If so, then forget about these men. Gays, bisexuals, priests, and married men may seem very attractive, but you're fundamentally incompatible. So don't start a relationship, or you'll be setting yourself up for a lot of pain. If you already have a relationship, the sooner you break it off, the better. You can certainly become platonic friends in time, but if the feelings are strong, you'll probably need to stop all contact for awhile before you'll be able to stop loving him.

Try joining an introduction service and running a personal ad to find appropriate dates. Limit yourself to people who are single and emotionally available, who share your sexual orientation and your relationship goal, and also live within 90 minutes of you.

Be thankful you've only invested as much time as you have. The longer you stay involved, the more you'll fall in love, and the worse the pain will be when you eventually break up. And of course, you will eventually need to break up — because there isn't anywhere to go with these relationships.

Use thought-stopping and *The Dr. Kate Quick & Dirty Grieving Technique* (see Chapter 10) as needed to get through your pain. Focus on how fortunate you are to be moving on, not how much you miss your friend. Then get busy and start dating more appropriate men.

All the best. Please let me know what you decide to do and how it works out.

Dr. Kate

How to ID an Abusive Man Before Falling for Him

Dear Dr. Kate,

My age: 47   **My gender:** Female

You recently advised an abused woman to learn to recognize signs that a man is abusive and controlling before becoming involved with him. How can I do that? My first husband was emotionally and physically abusive. The second seemed anything but — until we were married!

Dear Drawn To Fire,

Good question. Start by asking yourself these questions about the man you're interested in:

- **Does he remind you of someone in your past?** Your father? Somebody important who was abusive to you early on? A critical, blaming alcoholic who was never pleased with you? People often become drawn to hooks from their past who are comfortable in a sick kind of way.

- **Did his father abuse him or his mother?** If so, he's much more likely to abuse you. Abused kids don't all go on to abuse others, but most abusers were abused or witnessed abuse growing up.

- **How does he react when he does something inappropriate?** Does he apologize, or blame you instead? Abusers are quick to criticize or blame you; it's always *your* fault.

- **How does he handle stress?** Is he chronically angry, resentful, and unpredictable? Do you feel like you can't be yourself around him? Like you're walking on eggshells? Abusers are very unpredictable, quickly going from affection to rage over very small issues. You never know exactly what will set it off — just that something will before long.

- **Does he have double standards for your behavior and his?** Wants to know your every move, but not keep in touch with you? Does he become jealous when you so much as talk to another man, but think nothing of kissing or fondling a woman right in front of you? When you're not satisfied with something, does he make an honest effort to change it? Abusers assume a "right of entitlement" — that is, they deserve everything just because, and you don't deserve anything because you're not them. Change places with the man in your mind: Imagine that you're treating him the way he's treating you and vice versa. If you suddenly laugh, the relationship is very discordant — beware!

- **Does he overstep his boundaries and try to manipulate you?** For example, does he call in sick for you when you weren't going to — pretending to do you a favor? Abusers begin by overstepping boundaries in little ways that you might write off as romantic. Then they quickly become extremely controlling and manipulative.

- **Do any of his old girlfriends become platonic friends, or do they always cut ties?** Beware of a man with no respectable long-term friends, someone who always burns bridges. Perhaps he treated his exs the way he's going to treat you in the future.

Usually, the important data is right in front of you. Ask yourself these important questions and listen to your gut — don't try to explain away his behavior, even if he tells you to!

Best wishes! And please keep me posted on your progress.

Dr. Kate

They Share Custody of the Dog!

Dear Dr. Kate,

My age: 25 **My gender:** Female

I've been with my boyfriend for six months now. We have a wonderful relationship. He treats me great, and we talk about a future together. But he has a dog and shares "custody" of Fido with his ex-girlfriend. That isn't all. Fido lives with the ex, so during the day, my boyfriend's mother picks Fido up and keeps him at her house, and my boyfriend takes him back at night. Or the ex will come and pick him up. This is the only thing my boyfriend and I ever argue about — I just don't understand why they keep doing this. Fido is only 2 years old, so he'll certainly be around awhile. Am I overreacting?

Dear Suffering from Canine Envy,

Yes, I think you're overreacting. Your boyfriend is with you, not his ex. When people don't have kids, they often feel like their pets are their children. Animals are much smarter than we give them credit for being. Once you cross the line and see them as "a different kind of human," it's easy to become extremely attached.

Your boyfriend basically feels like he shares child custody with his ex. So if you end up marrying him, he'll probably be very responsible to you and any children you have together. I think that's great — not something to worry about. If he and his ex wanted to be together, they would be. He's choosing to be with you instead. He just wants to stay in touch with his child/dog, too.

Be thankful for what you have. Don't sweat the small stuff.

All the best, and please let me know how you're doing from time to time.

Dr. Kate

Chapter 5

Finding That Special Someone

• •

In This Chapter

▶ Considering your readiness state

▶ Exploring the many ways to meet your significant other

▶ Choosing the method(s) that will work best for you

• •

Four score and many hundreds of years ago, everyone lived in a small town where it was really easy to meet everybody. They didn't have to work too hard to find a partner because there weren't many to choose from, so they couldn't be too picky. When the town got bigger, they relied on their friends and relatives to introduce them to compatible mates. But as time went on, more and more couples had babies, and those babies grew up and had babies, and their babies eventually had babies. It now became much harder to find compatible mates. There were just too many people, and no one could know everyone. So many choices, so little time. Then one day, someone finally admitted the job was too hard and too important to do alone, and he paid a professional to help. Before long, other people caught on and went to see the matchmaker, too. Instead of spending all their free time looking for spouses, they just registered with the matchmaker, and she did the work for them. And then they all found significant others, and lived happily ever after — even the matchmaker. The End.

In the new millennium, there are millions of potential mates to choose from. Luckily, there are many ways to meet compatible singles, and they all come with plusses and minuses. In this chapter, I describe those methods, their pros and cons, and their efficiency and intensity levels. I explain which singles benefit most from each method, based on sex, age, and readiness for a long-term relationship. I also suggest ways to locate each method. And I describe how to use a professional matchmaker for faster, more convenient success. Enjoy!

Determining Your Relationship Readiness

You can choose from many different ways to meet other singles. The method you choose should depend on your relationship goal, how soon you want to reach it, and your relationship readiness state. Your choice may also be governed by what's available in your area of the country. To determine how ready you are for a short- or long-term relationship, consider your age, maturity level, relationship goal, life goals, and life stage. For example, if you're a single, never married, 27+, mature-for-your-age person who eventually wants to get married and raise a family, it's time for you to use a more efficient method to find a compatible spouse. If you're 18 and itching to settle down, but you're just finishing high school or beginning college, with no profession at this time, you're not going to be mature enough for a healthy marriage for about seven to ten years yet, so you don't need a particularly efficient method for finding people. You'd be better off dating around and making friends while you finish your education, get career training, and build a stable career.

If you've been coupled or married to the same person since age 16 and are just divorced at age 42, you're as emotionally mature as you're probably going to get, but you've been coupled all your adult life. You need time to live as a single person, to date around and figure out what kind of person is compatible with you and vice versa, before you get seriously involved again. If you're so recently divorced that you're still hurting, you may just need to make friends and hang loose before even starting to date. (See Chapter 22 for more on starting over.) If you're 38, female, divorced, and have dated for three or more years post-divorce, you need an especially efficient method to find a suitable spouse, particularly if you want to have kids.

So, depending on your specific situation, you may or may not be ready to meet someone for a long-term, serious relationship. Begin by reviewing Table 5-1, where I compare and contrast the various methods. Figure out which readiness level applies to you, and pay special attention to the methods described in that section, so you can choose one that's best for you.

Table 5-1	Ways to Meet People for Romantic Relationships		
Efficiency Level	**Method**	**Best for People Who Are**	**Not for People Who Are**
Mild/casual	Community and church activities, events, classes, clubs, and gyms open to the general public; Volunteering; Anywhere you are.	Not ready to marry soon; looking for friends or just casual fun. Includes: Young people; college students; newly relocated; recently divorced or widowed.	Psychologically ready and mature enough to marry; want long-term relationship or marriage in the next few years.
More efficient	Introductions from friends; Activities, dances, events specifically for singles; Computer chat rooms; Speed dating.	Ready and able to marry in the next 5 years. Includes: Single, never-married, aged 23–26, who've dated enough and want to marry in about 5 years; and divorced/widowed awhile, ready to start dating.	Ready and able to marry in the next 2 years and need a more efficient method; or need more casual fun.
Most efficient	Online/offline personal ads and online dating services; Offline dating services, including: Library services, and Personal match-making services (usually the best).	Ready now and want to marry in the next 2 years. Includes: Never-married, 26+, want to marry and raise family; recovered from divorce or relationship loss and dating comfortably.	Not ready or able to settle down right now; need to date more before getting serious. Includes: Young and inexperienced; married or still coupled; just recently divorced, widowed, or broken up.

Bumping into People: The Casual Methods

If you're looking for something to do, but aren't looking to get married in the near future, these casual methods are for you. While it's always possible that you'll meet a special person while participating in these activities, it's not very probable. But if you're just looking for friends, just dating around, or won't be ready for an intense relationship for quite awhile yet, this is your section.

Sampling activities, events, and special interests

There are lots of activities and events open to the general public in most communities. Ready? Deep breath . . . fairs, festivals, ethnic celebrations, harvest fests, Octoberfests, garden walks, open houses, dances, concerts, sing-alongs, sports, nature hikes, hay rides, rummage sales, flea markets, stamp shows, coin shows, auto shows, auctions, art shows, arts and crafts fairs, bird shows, dog shows, cat shows, even Civil War reenactments. There are also museums, historical museums (like Greenfield Village, MI, or Williamsburg, VA), nature parks (Busch Gardens), and zoos. Indulge your special interests by visiting with others who share those interests. The list is endless.

Plusses: These events allow you to see the world while making new friends who may also share a special interest. If you're not ready for anything more intense (for example, if you're just divorced, widowed, or broken up), here's your chance to get out of the house and get your mind off your pain.

Minuses: The crowd is usually mixed in age and marital status, so it's often difficult to differentiate the attached from the unattached. If the crowd is large, people often bring dates or friends. That, plus the sheer volume of people and noise level, often make meeting someone new more difficult.

But hey! You can always bring a platonic friend and just enjoy the event! Or go by yourself, bring a camera, act like a tourist (smile and look around a lot), and chances are, you'll run into other friendly people who are there doing the same thing. In fact, you'll usually meet more people if you go by yourself.

To locate: Contact your local chamber of commerce or mayor's office, and auto groups, like AAA. See local newspapers, especially the weekend editions, local magazines, special interest publications, and *Chase's Calendar of Events* (a reference book carried at local libraries and bookstores). Check train stations, parks, highway rest areas, and online sites for special event schedules. Ask your friends for their favorites.

Keep a file of events and activities taking place in and around your town. Include your city, your 'burbs, and those that can be reached for weekend trips. Become an expert on your area. Save your computer searches by "favorite placing" them (click on the heart at the top of the screen on AOL, or mark it as a "favorite" in other browsers), or print them and keep a copy in your paper file. If you're ready to meet potential dates, pick events that encourage interaction and tend to attract opposite-sex people close to your age.

Chatting it up at church events

Most churches hold activities open to the public, including potluck dinners, bingo, fairs, carnivals, and baked-good sales. Some even have events and dances open to singles of all religions.

Plusses: Attendees are usually very positive, warm-hearted, and emotionally supportive, so you might find it easy to make friends there. If you're just divorced, hurting, and need to get out of the house, but you aren't ready for anything one-on-one, church events can help you mix with people again.

Minuses: You have to decipher the coupled from the non-coupled. You might end up liking someone who doesn't share your religion. But if you don't care or if you're only going to be friends, it might not matter.

To locate: Check with your own church about their activities and events. Then, using online or offline Yellow Pages directories (look under "church"), call nearby churches. If church membership isn't required, ask to be placed on their social events mailing list.

Enrolling in adult just-for-fun classes

Want to learn to cross-country ski? Mambo? Two-step? Invest money? Speak French? Tell good wine from poor wine? From sports to dancing to languages, finances, arts and crafts, nature, antiquing, food, cooking — so many different kinds of classes — you could never experience them all. But you can certainly have a good time trying!

Plusses: You can expand your mind, get in shape, and become interested as well as more interesting. If you're post-breakup, you can keep your mind occupied with more pleasant thoughts — while you also meet friendly people.

Minuses: As with community activities, special interests open to the public, and church events, you'll need to distinguish the single from the coupled.

To locate: Just-for-fun classes are offered by many universities and colleges, community centers, park districts, Ys, museums, churches, various clubs, and some adult education firms. Call your local chamber of commerce, the mayor's office, and park districts to request a list of classes. Check city and community newspapers, magazines, special mailed ads, online sites, and the phone book. Ask your friends.

Choose a class that allows you to relax, laugh, interact, and get physical with people your age who might eventually become dates. For example, men might attend ballet class to meet young, sensitive women, and women might choose an improv class.

Clubbing with sport and special-interest clubs

Looking for a more regular way to indulge your interest in a particular activity — tennis, running, golf, skiing, French, the great outdoors, public speaking, whatever? Join a club that caters to that interest. Generally open to the public, these kinds of clubs arrange events and trips that allow you to participate in the activity with other friendly people.

Plusses: You'll have an opportunity to make friends who might grow into dates who share your special interest. It's often easier to start conversations — you can always talk about the special interest at hand. You may also feel safer and more relaxed in a group of regular members.

Minuses: If you break up with a fellow club member, searching for another date at club events is tacky. You may have to change groups to avoid your ex.

To locate: Check local newspapers, magazines, your mayor's office, Web sites, and online or hardcopy Yellow Pages directories (look under "clubs"); ask your friends.

Joining a gym

Consider your choice of a gym not only for its equipment and activities, but also its clientele. Although the gym isn't an efficient way to meet singles, it's always possible that you'll run into a prize while you're stationary biking.

Plusses: You have to work out anyway. Many gyms have rest areas and juice bars, where you can meet and mingle. Many also offer classes, dances, and other special events.

Minuses: Sweating in front of a potential date may not be your cup of tea. You'll also need to distinguish the coupled from the single and emotionally available. They all tend to look alike in sweats!

To locate: Check online or offline phone directories; keep your eyes peeled as you drive down the road; ask your friends. Take advantage of guest passes and visitors' rates to see if you really like the place (and its clientele) and will keep going — before plunking down serious money. And if funds are tight, don't forget the local Y!

Volunteering your time

Volunteering allows you to do something worthwhile, while meeting warm-hearted people.

Plusses: People will benefit from your efforts, and you'll benefit even more from the warm, fuzzy, satisfied feelings you get. If you're post-breakup, helping people in greater need can pleasantly distract you and keep you connected to your world.

Minuses: No minuses here!

To locate: Ask around at community centers, churches, and hospitals. Check online and offline Yellow Pages directories; do an online search; check out *AOL Keyword: Volunteer* or www.helping.org; ask friends.

Ask the director about the sex and age of most of the volunteers, then pick a group and activity likely to attract potential dates. For example, men could hold cocaine babies at a local hospital (think about all those nurses!), while women could mingle with Habitat for Humanity guys who are good with their hands! See Chapter 22 for more on volunteering.

Encountering singles in everyday places

If you're an outgoing person with good people sense, you can occasionally make friends on the street whenever and wherever you feel safe. See an interesting person on the train to work, or in your grocery store or elevator? Flash a smile and introduce yourself!

Plusses: You have to shop and go to work anyway, so why not do two things at once? Keep your eyes and ears open (and a pen and paper handy for phone numbers!), and make that dry cleaning trip an opportunity to make a new friend.

Minuses: It's a little awkward to hand a stranger your phone number. Also, do *not* use this method if you lack people sense or frequently get involved with people who take advantage of you. The life you save could be your own. See the section on meeting through the personal ads later in this chapter, and follow those safeguards when meeting strangers.

Dating Around: The More Efficient Methods

It takes time to cultivate a relationship using the following methods, but less time than the casual methods described in the previous section. See Table 5-1 to review the "More Efficient" methods and when they're best used.

Meeting through friends

Live dangerously — let your friends fix you up every now and again. If your friends have good judgment, can keep your confidences, and understand your likes and dislikes, it's not a bad way to meet people. Thank your friend for his or her fix-up efforts, no matter what the outcome, to keep whatever supply there is flowing.

Plusses: This method is usually safer than many because there's a paper trail. Your friend knows the other person, and that person knows that your friend knows him, so the odds of your date being a mad rapist are extremely low.

Minuses: Everyone has only so many friends, and they may only know incompatible people. If you don't get along with your fix-up, your matchmaker friend may take it personally. If running into your ex-date at parties thrown by your mutual friend would make you uncomfortable, skip friendly matchups.

Exploring singles-specific events

Most communities arrange activities and events just for singles: dances, parties, dinners, *progressive dinners* (where you change seats for every course to allow you to meet more people), volleyball games, softball tournaments, and other outdoor activities. Singles attending vary in age and background, depending on a number of factors like how and where the event is advertised.

In Chicago, for example, my corporation, Advanced Degrees Introductions, Inc., throws book signings, cocktail parties, and other singles events from time to time. The Council on Foreign Relations usually throws two cocktail parties per year. The World's Largest Christmas Party attracts the after-work singles crowd. There are Christmas Eve dances for Jewish singles, and Valentine dances for people of all faiths.

Plusses: You can participate in an activity you enjoy, while mingling with other singles who are also looking for dates and possibly more. If the activity is thrown for people with a certain characteristic (Jewish, Catholic, parents, or softball lovers, for example), people you meet will either share that quality or be open to it.

Minuses: The groups don't check backgrounds, so once in awhile, the person you're chatting with may actually be married. The smaller, more personal the event and sponsoring group, the more likely it is that the attendees are single. Also, whom you meet and how many people you meet at these events is governed more by outside forces (like seating arrangements or who's blocking the bathroom door when you're in need) than actual compatibility considerations. If you date and then break up with someone from that group, you may want to skip the activity in the future to avoid seeing your ex.

Only participate in activities you *really* enjoy. Don't play softball just to meet a guy, or you may end up meeting a sweetie who craves softball while you despise it. Similarly, only go to dances if you love to dance. While you'll probably be successful in dancing with people, it's very unlikely that you'll meet your next husband or wife. If you're going mainly for that reason, you'll get bummed out when it doesn't happen. If you're feeling vulnerable, you might even take someone home with you and later regret it (ever been in a singles bar at its 2 a.m. closing?). And Ladies, if you *do* enjoy dancing, try dancing with everyone who asks you, provided you feel comfortable with them. Other men are more likely to ask you to dance if they believe you'll accept the invitation.

Logging on

Up late, and feeling lonely at 1 a.m., when all your friends are asleep? Go online and chat with a fellow insomniac or someone many time zones away, where it's only 7 p.m.!

Plusses: There's always someone up and eager to talk in real time, a.m. or p.m.

Minuses: You can't always trust what people say about themselves online. So if you intend to meet in person, *only use this method if you have good judgment about people.*

If you're chatting on AOL, check out that person's posted profile. If you hope to continue the relationship offline, chat only with people who are single, emotionally available, and living within one to two hours from you. See the section and sidebar on personal ads for more.

Experimenting with speed dating

For roughly $25 a pop, you chat one-on-one with people of the opposite sex, one right after the other, to find suitable dates. Conversations are timed (about seven minutes long) to allow you to talk briefly with every possible candidate in the room in about 90 minutes. The number of men and women are kept even. You mark which people you'd like to see again on your card, and turn it in at the end of the night. If they've also selected you, names and numbers are exchanged, and you call one another to connect for your date.

Plusses: You meet about 10 to 12 potential dates — more than you'd meet at most other singles activities. It's also acceptable to ask direct questions upfront — saving you gobs of money and time that you might otherwise drop on someone who doesn't share your relationship goal. And it's new, so you can't be burned out on it yet!

Minuses: While you're meeting lots of potential partners on the same evening (which sounds efficient), you have no control over which people are invited to the event. Usually, sponsors just limit each group to a certain number of opposite-sex people in a certain age range. They don't consider many other factors that will either make or break compatibility (see Chapter 4 for a list of "must have" and "good to have" qualities), so you may not be compatible with anyone attending the event. In addition, there's no real screening of the people involved, and their answers to your questions might be false or quite subjective. Because speed dating is brand new, such events aren't available in many to most cities. And of course, finding something to say in seven minutes when the pressure is on can be quite difficult. These events favor those who are terrifically charming under pressure, and that isn't the most important compatibility criteria for any relationship. You might be overlooked or overlook someone else who could be a terrific partner in a more natural, relaxed setting.

To locate: Keep your eyes and ears open for print and radio ads. Do an online search, and ask your friends.

Dating for Keeps: The Most Efficient Methods

Looking to cut to the chase and find a partner to settle down with? You're in luck! Many methods are available to help you find a *long-term relationship* (LTR), or a LTR leading to marriage. The methods in this section are *most efficient* because they allow you to access a group of people who are more likely to be single, to openly state your relationship goal (for example, marriage, marriage and kids, living together, just dating), and to ask for the same relationship goal in anyone you meet.

In all the methods mentioned previously in this chapter (other than the speed-dating method), asking someone about their relationship goal is really not appropriate. You can't really walk up to someone at a dance and ask, "So, how do you feel about getting married?" A healthy person would be gone in a flash, whether he or she wanted the same goal or not. It's just not appropriate to ask a new acquaintance that question, and it won't be for several months. So the woman usually waits until her boyfriend makes an offhand comment about someone else's marriage, then tries to figure out how he feels from his remarks! It can take months for marriage to come up in the conversation, and sometimes it never does. So you can be very attached to someone before learning that the two of you really aren't compatible!

In contrast, the following methods allow you to restrict the people you meet to a certain relationship goal, and/or to exchange relationship goal information with your date before meeting. So you can skip over anyone who's totally incompatible with you — before you get involved.

Placing a personal ad

I recommend running an ad rather than answering them, to get a much better response for your time and energy. Read the ads published in offline publications and online sites, and choose one with people you'd like to meet, a fast turnaround time, and low cost. To place a personal ad:

Step 1: Set up a suitable e-mail box, phone number, or P.O. Box to receive responses. Online: Use a new screen name or one you won't mind dumping if necessary. Do *not* use your master account or any other box that can't be easily changed, and don't use a screen name that identifies you. **Offline:** Invest in a second, unpublished phone number, pager, or cell phone, and an answering machine that allows for two-way recording. Each venue publishes their procedures; read them and use them properly. If you want respondents to leave voice mail (recommended): Record the voice messages on your answering machine as you retrieve them; review them later and take notes. If you also allow respondents to write you: Give the publication a post-office box, not a home or work address. *Never* put your address/phone number in an ad, online or off.

Step 2: Read some ads to learn what goes into them and get creative ideas.

Step 3: Outline (rough draft) the information you want to include in your ad. Describe your personality (like "playful," "fun," "intelligent") and the kind of person you seek ("responsible," "monogamous," "loving" — whatever qualities you consider most important). Mention some favorite activities and your relationship goal.

Don't give out your income, and don't talk about sex. If you're placing an ad online, go to *AOL Keyword: Love* or www.love.com, and their form will take you step-by-step through the ad-writing process.

Step 4: Try to make your ad stand out; make it special. If you're funny, use humor. If you're not, try to say something in a more poignant or romantic way. Be friendly and upbeat.

Step 5: Have a single, platonic pal of the sex you're looking for review the ad and make suggestions.

Step 6: Send in your ad. Follow the directions noted in the online or offline publication running your ad. **Online:** Unless you feel that a picture might identify you too much and damage your confidentiality, I recommend using a photo. Choose one that shows you smiling and at your recent best. **Offline:** Carefully consider your potential liability before posting a photo offline. Online ads are usually only viewed by other singles searching the database, while many people skim offline newspaper and magazine ads just for fun. Depending on your occupation, how conservative your community is, and other factors, it might be best to skip offline photos.

Step 7: Enjoy! If you don't receive any responses you like, check the publication again to see if they have people of the appropriate age and sexual orientation, and if your ad appeared, correctly printed, in the proper category! If necessary, fix your ad and try again.

Tips on meeting through the personals

If you're interested in meeting someone who has responded to your personal ad:

1. **For awhile, chat via phone or online.** Women should talk to a potential date on the phone for at least an hour before meeting in person. If you've already been chatting online, phone time doesn't have to be that long, but do get to know someone better before agreeing to meet.

2. **Never give out your identifying data (last name, address, or where you work) right away.** Remember, after someone has the information, you can't take it back. Women, get the man's number first. If your city has a "name and address" service, call that number to find out what name and address are listed to the man's phone number. Similar services are available online (do an online search for "reverse caller" services). Before dialing the man's phone number, press "*67" first, so your number won't show on his caller ID.

3. **If you decide to get together and need to give him a phone number, use your pager, cell phone, or unlisted number you got just for this purpose,** so your date can't find your address the same way you found his. Always use a number you can dump if necessary. Men don't need to be as cautious, but take some care, lest a smitten suitor show up unexpectedly at your office!

4. **If you decide to meet, do so during the day-time, in a public place with many people around, where you can leave easily if you like** (like Sunday brunch at a busy restaurant). Keep the first meeting short (a few hours). You can also take a friend along or meet in a group setting. Drive yourself to and from the date, and take plenty of money. Women, tell a friend where you'll be, and give her your date's name, address, phone, and any other important information. Arrange to call in once from your date and when you're finished, and tell your friend when you expect that to be. If you meet your date in another city, be sure to do all this, plus call in several times.

5. **Limit yourself to people who live within one to two hours from you,** so you won't have to deal with long-distance relationship challenges (see Chapter 4). If you do decide to meet someone in a different city, book and pay for your own hotel and flight arrangements. Do *not* stay with your new date. Be sure to follow the recommendations in #4 (above) as well. Don't have sex or invite your date to your home or hotel room the first time you meet. (See Chapters 6 and 7 for more information.)

6. **Stay safe.** When you're out, listen to your gut. If you don't feel comfortable, excuse yourself and leave early. And if you don't have at least fairly good people sense and common sense/judgment, if people tend to use you or you tend to have bad luck with them, *don't use personals of any kind, online or off!*

7. **Follow the suggestions in Chapter 6 about moving slowly and gradually from being a "stranger" to becoming more intimate.** Keep in mind that you can meet honest and dishonest people online and off. *You are meeting a stranger*, and you need to trust gradually and slowly, as you determine that he or she is worthy of your trust.

8. **Don't be too invested in pleasing your date, and keep your expectations in check.** Remember, if it doesn't work, it just means the two of you aren't compatible. And don't see so many people that you burn out on dating. It takes time to meet this way, so pace yourself!

Finally, a few cautions from Love@AOL:

"Don't believe everything you read. . . . Remember that the person at the other end may not be who they say they are. *Don't* respond to any correspondence that's lewd or crude or in any way makes you feel uncomfortable. AOL offers you the option of Mail Controls, which allow you to block unwanted mail and attached files, among other options." They also add that you should forward any obscene e-mails and *IMs* (Instant Messages) by using *AOL Keyword: Notify AOL,* and they will take appropriate action.

Using personal ads, online or off

Personal ads have been around for at least 20 years, and are now more readily accepted and easier to use. You can opt to have people write you, e-mail you, or call you. Each method has its perks. Snailmail allows you to see the paper and handwriting of the person answering your ad, but it's much slower. Voice mail allows you to hear the responder's voice and, if you listen closely, to learn more about his or her personality.

Plusses: Personal ads are usually inexpensive, and they work well for people with more time than money. While placing an ad in an offline city magazine can still cost several hundred dollars, you can place an ad at *AOL Keyword: Love* or www.love.com, and pay a small fee or nothing at all. It's not only appropriate, but also customary to clearly state your relationship goal in a straightforward, matter-of-fact manner, and to ask that people only respond if they share your relationship goal.

Minuses: If you're placing the ad, you have to do all the sorting and screening of responders yourself. That's a time-consuming job, and since everyone has only so much energy to do any activity, you can easily burn out before you get through a stack of 100 e-mails or phone calls! And while most people don't deliberately lie in their self-descriptions, some do. Also, the information is very subjective — at the very least, everyone is telling you their own opinion of themselves, and you may disagree with some of those descriptions when you meet. If you're answering an ad, you may not receive an acknowledgment from the person you contacted. That can get frustrating over time, especially since your response has to be original and personal to make the grade in the first place, and constructing that response takes time. Since the ads are confidential and no one else is screening anyone, there's very little paper trail if something goes wrong. So don't use online or offline personal ads of any kind if you don't have good people judgment (a "good gut"). For more, see the sidebar on placing a personal ad, located in this chapter.

Using online dating services

"Online dating services" are really evolved personal ads with a twist. First you answer some profile questions, giving objective demographics about yourself and stating various preferences for your match. Then the service's computer program selects certain people who match you in certain ways (for example, on age, race, religion, sexual orientation, and other preferred demographics) and sends those profiles to your e-mail.

Plusses: Most online dating services charge little, but prices vary depending on the program you choose and its length. If the fee is low enough, you may want to try their computer selections to see how well they turn out, and whether or not they allow you to use the personals for a longer period of time before burning out. Programs that take into consideration both parties' profile preferences and rule-outs should theoretically be more successful than a program considering only one person's data.

Minuses: While the service uses your personal data to select matches for you, the computer program can't really screen for personality. Your matches are only as good as the accuracy of the data, which depends on the honesty and objectivity of the person completing the form. No one interviews the applicant or verifies the accuracy of the responses. Since most people are quite subjective in their self-opinions, you may disagree with the match's description after interacting with him or her. Don't confuse this kind of "dating service" with offline dating services, where someone interviews the person in real life, and there is more of a paper trail.

To locate: Go to *AOL Keyword: Love* or www.love.com and follow the links. Or find others through online searches.

Trying a library introduction service

Offline introduction services, which are usually much more involved and thorough than the online kind, come in many different forms. But there are really two major divisions: the "library" dating service, and the more exclusive personal matchmaking service (discussed in the next section).

In a library introduction service, you purchase a membership, which buys you the right to peruse the profiles, photos, or videos in the library for a period of time, and to put your profile, photo, and/or video in that library for others to view and choose. In most places, you fill out the profile yourself. You choose the people you want to meet, and an effort is made to contact that person, who then has a period of time to accept or decline meeting you. That person may or may not take the opportunity to visit the service's office and review your profile, photo, and/or video before deciding. If there is no response or a negative response, nothing takes place. If the person you choose replies in the affirmative, you are each given the other's name and number, so you can contact one another and arrange a date.

Plusses: You get to control whom you choose, and see the entire population you're choosing from. You can state your relationship goal on your profile, and search profiles for members who have stated a similar goal. You can see the person if the service offers photos or video clips, and you can observe the person's handwriting and use of the language if the person completes a profile himself. Some offer activities for members.

Minuses: Since the member completes his or her own profile, the information volunteered is still largely subjective. So it may be incorrect or very slanted, and you may not agree with that description when you meet your date in person. Also, many, if not most, people find it difficult to make a videotape that captures their essence in three minutes or less. Yet people viewing the tape tend to give that small sample of behavior much more importance than it deserves. Also, because many people skip the written profiles and just look at the pictures and videos on file, the very attractive tend to have long waiting lists, while others who photograph or videotape less well go unnoticed. The most popular people may give their potential dates very little attention or fail to respond, while others may receive no dates at all during a lengthy membership costing thousands.

Library services sell you the right to use their library during a certain period of time; they don't promise you matches. Because they don't have to do your matches and they're not promising that you'll find a compatible person or even get matched, most take people of any age and condition, as long as they pay the fee. Once you join, you may find very few people who match the demographic or personality preferences you requested on your form. In fact, if the service doesn't make an effort to keep the age and sex of members approximately even (which is often the case), they generally end up with a lot of men below age 30 and a lot of women over 50. (See the ***AOL Keyword: DrKate*** letter at the end of this chapter for more on this.) Unfortunately, those two groups don't usually want to date each another! If you're trying to date people who are statistically more rare in the population, you'll experience the same problem finding such a person inside the service.

Doing your own matching is basically like doing intense research on an ongoing basis. You'll need to regularly spend hours of your free time researching possible matches, stopping in regularly to review the profiles of any new members who have joined since your last search, and checking out anyone who chooses you. If someone rejects you, feedback is very limited.

It sounds like I'm very much against library services, doesn't it? Well, I'm not. In my recommendations, they're actually second in line after the more personalized matchmaking services. And everybody doesn't always have the luxury of being able to choose a classy boutique service of quality. So if your town only has a franchised library service, it may still be much more efficient than other ways of meeting people, particularly if you:

> ✔ ***Don't* tell them your income on the phone or in the interview.** Library services, particularly the nationally franchised ones, often quote different prices for the same membership, depending on how much money you make and how eager you are to sign up. They often start around $4,000 or more!

✔ **Don't accept their initial price.** Continue to resist, and don't buy on the first day. Chances are, the price will tumble, and you can get the program for a fraction of what they initially charge (around $900 at the present time). That's even more true if you belong to a statistically rare group. The reason? Their service costs are minimal because you're doing your own matching. They've just spent all the time they're going to spend with you (interviewing and signing you up), and you may have to pay extra for the photos or videotape anyway. So there's no reason not to give you the service at a lower cost. Most of the money taken in goes for the rent, advertising, or direct mail, so they can afford to cut costs here and there. Their whole sales approach is geared toward bargaining, so be sure you do, or you'll pay too much for the same service other people get for less.

✔ **Do ask the important questions and compare several services before choosing any.** This is even more true if you're in a group where it's more difficult to find available partners (men under 30, women over 50, and so on). For more on how to choose a service, see the sidebar "Questions to ask when choosing an introduction service," in this chapter. Also, keep in mind what you're buying — the right to use the library. Don't expect miracles just because you're paying a fee.

Signing up for a personal matchmaking service

These services vary enormously, depending on their population; the credentials, training, skill, professionalism, and ethics of the matchmaker; whether the company is a nationwide franchise or a more personalized boutique service; whether the matchmaker meets you or not; and whether the service is a real business or a hobby the owner is doing to meet a special someone. There's also a difference between businesses run predominantly to make money, and those run by someone who actually cares about the service sold.

Most personal matchmaking services will interview you extensively, asking questions about your relationship goal and match preferences. The service screens and researches matches for you, then notifies you via mail or phone that your match is ready. If both parties accept the match, names and numbers are exchanged, and you and your match get in touch to arrange a date. So the service does the work while you have all the fun. Not bad, eh?

Prices vary from almost nothing ($150) to $4,000 or more, depending on your city and the type of program involved. Good services cost at least $1,000 because of all the work involved and the cost to the company. Services go by time (one or two years), or by the number of matches you're given. Prices for personalized matchmaking services tend to be firm — *and should stay firm.* In contrast to library services, where you basically do all the work and can consequently bid down the price, personalized matchmaking services do as much of the work for you as possible. So your membership fee has to cover the more in-depth interviewing and screening, the matchmaker's time, and the salary of the people informing you by phone or letter about your match. And just like library services, personal services also have to pay for rent, office expenses, advertising, and direct mail. So, these services have much less profit than library services and, hence, less room to cut costs. The plus of all that, however, is that you'll feel less like you're buying a used car!

Plusses: There are many advantages to using a credible matchmaking service. If you're a busy person with many responsibilities, you'll appreciate the convenience and time saved. Because the service does everything that you don't have to do (interviewing, screening, and researching your matches), and you spend your time doing what only you can do (dating the people and figuring out who's more compatible for you), this is the easiest, most time-efficient way to meet people. Since everyone burns out when they do too much of something for too long, allowing a service to do what you don't have to do allows you to date longer before burning out. Since dating burnout is often a problem with other methods, this is a big advantage over library services, personal ads, and any other dating method where you do more of the work.

The personalized, confidential attention is often more comfortable than flipping through photos of prospective mates in a large room filled with strangers — or putting your personal information on a library shelf or in an ad for others to review. In addition, because the matchmaker has to match you, she has to keep the numbers relatively even with regard to sex, age, and other variables. This is a *huge* advantage over the library services — *huge*. (See the **AOL Keyword: DrKate** letter at the end of this chapter for more information.)

Minuses: Nothing in life is perfect. So like all methods of finding a special sweetie, personal matchmaking services have their drawbacks, too — the amount depending on the specifics of that service. For example, some services have you fill out forms and interview with someone other than the matchmaker. Others claim to send your data out of town to a person or computer program that supposedly matches you. Do not use these kinds of services. If a matchmaker hasn't met you, that person knows very little about your personality, so your matches are less likely to be compatible. Also, be wary of any service that says it's testing you. Valid, standardized psychological tests must be administered, scored, interpreted, and kept under lock and key by a psychologist. Chances are, the tests you take are just quizzes, and results may not even be taken into consideration. Quizzes aren't necessarily bad, but don't let a service convince you that it's best simply because it uses non-standardized, unreliable quizzes.

See the "Questions to ask when choosing an introduction service" sidebar, in this chapter, and follow those suggestions to help you locate a credible service that fits you best.

Questions to ask when choosing an introduction service

Before you choose an introduction service of any kind (the personal matchmaking variety or a library service), do some homework. Find services in your area by checking online and hardcopy Yellow Pages directories, singles publications, and city magazines, and by doing an online search. Ask the services you call where they advertise, then check those publications for more services. Narrow down the field to four services that seem reputable. Visit those services, ask the following questions, take notes, and review them at home. Wait at least a day before deciding which service to join. Then, of the services that answer your questions best, join the one that feels most comfortable. If none do, start over again and do more research.

1. **How long has this service been in business?** Beware of new companies. They have fewer members and, hence, less compatible matches, and they often go under in less than five years.

2. **What kinds of programs do you have? How much do they cost?** Avoid services that will not give you a description and price or price range over the phone before you state your income or visit their office for an in-person interview.

3. **How many members do you have? What age, profession, religion (add other variables here that are important to you) are your members? What's the range? The percentage of males to females in my age range? How many members do you have who (have a certain characteristic) and would also be willing to meet me?** Try to join a service with 750 to 2,000 members, with approximately equal males to females at all age levels. More than 2,000 members is not personal; fewer than 500 is too small for much compatibility. (It's OK to join a smaller service, but the price should also be smaller.) The service should

be willing to tell you the parameters of their membership (age range, professions, degrees, religions, races, relationship goals, what members are looking for, and why they use the service). Avoid services loaded with young men and older women, those that give older men more matches or lower prices, those that seem unaware that there are differences in the pool of women and men available at certain ages, and those that give you canned, rather than thoughtful responses, to these questions.

4. **What are the relationship goals of the membership — are most people looking for marriage or casual dating?** Make sure that the majority share your relationship goal! For example, if you want a long-term relationship or marriage, skip a service that considers a second date a success, and instead, join a service that emphasizes your long-term relationship/marriage goal and/or only accepts people with similar goals.

5. **Who does the matching? How long has the interviewer been working for the service? What are his/her credentials? What makes that person competent to match me?** The person interviewing you should be matching you. This industry suffers from high turnover rates, so if you later find that your interviewer has moved on, ask for another interview.

6. **On what variables will I be matched?** Beware services promising to match you within "X amount of points" from some test score, or according to some very specific type of system. None really exists, and their claims are most likely unjustified. Conversely, avoid services that interview superficially, or remind you of used car sales; show little ability to describe personality or intelligence; seem more interested in your

money than you; and/or imply there's something wrong with you because you want to sleep on it before signing up.

7. **How will I be informed of my matches?** Look for a service that phones you to describe your match and obtain consent before exchanging your data with another client. Avoid those that mail other members your identifying data — and run like crazy from any that send other clients your videotape!

8. **What steps are taken to ensure the confidentiality of my information?** All data should stay under lock and key. Staff must be trained in confidentiality procedures, including how to protect your personal information and how to answer people pretending to know you.

9. **Why do you think the program you're offering me fits me? Whom do you turn down?** The interviewer should describe exactly what kinds of people the service does/doesn't accept, and in what ways you fit the accepted group. Don't join a service that accepts everyone as long as they can pay. All services interview people who are incompatible with their group, and accepting them is equivalent to ripping them off.

10. **Do members give feedback about the service? Will the service share it with me?** They must get feedback from their members, and it's best if they're willing to pass it on to you.

11. **When people are unhappy with this program, why are they dissatisfied? What do I do if I'm dissatisfied?** Beware those who tell you that everyone is satisfied; there's no such thing. The interviewer should describe procedures available to help clients resolve problems.

12. **What makes this service better than its competitors?** *Think* and make sure that the answer makes sense!

Note: Avoid services where the staff dates the members, or where staff members aren't professional. The service should have an office and caring staff who treat you with respect. Be extremely wary of services that come to your home or meet you in a hotel lobby. Avoid services that seem like a "mill." They won't remember anything you tell them the minute you're out the door. Avoid companies with canned responses, hard sells, or "I'm not sure that you're right for this program" (take away) sales maneuvers. Read the contract carefully before you sign it, and ask questions until you completely understand it and are comfortable with it. Take a copy home with you. Make sure that you understand how the service works. Staff should give you a handout detailing the policies and procedures. If not, take lots of notes. Trust your gut, and join a service only if you feel comfortable there.

I'm Prime Age for a Female? Age Odds!

Dear Dr. Kate,

My age: 26   **My gender:** Female

People say I'm at the prime age for a female, but I don't feel it. I feel middle-aged. I'm fun-loving, caring, sensitive, trustworthy, honest, sensitive, respectful, and in shape, with a good sense of humor. But I can't seem to find someone to love and marry. The more I get to know the guy, the more disappointed I become. I'm beginning to give up hope. Help!

Dear Feeling Hopeless,

My goodness, Girl, you're not middle-aged! Even if you're pessimistic and think you won't live past 65, you're not even halfway. In fact, I'd say you're just beginning your adult romantic life.

However, you are correct that you're going into your prime age for finding a husband. There are more men born than women, but they die at a faster rate, beginning in infancy and childhood. Men have more muscular strength, but women are more resilient overall. At 26, the odds are greatly in your favor, since you're still outnumbered by men. However, when you're about 37 and dating men 40+, that group will shrink as more of them die from heart attacks. Then strokes will thin the group of men 50+, slowly and gradually diminishing the number of available marriage candidates as you grow older. Gay men are thought to outnumber lesbian women, so that also skews the numbers. And if there's a war, more men are killed than women, which also shrinks the pool.

More women are expected to die from Alzheimer's in their 80's, leading some to predict that if we live past 100, we'll once again be outnumbered by men! However, the years from 37 to 100 can be a little challenging. Women in that age range need to be smart and diversify their efforts when looking for partners. They also need to make sure that they're focused on the qualities that are most important, while overlooking those that aren't.

So, while your girlfriends may already be marrying and settling down, you've got about eight years before you need to be concerned. And since the odds are in your favor now, you can meet wonderful men in many different ways. Try running a personal ad or joining an offline introduction service. You're a *great* age for an introduction service. Since men your age outnumber women your age, most services have too many young men and need young women to balance the population. Most professional services attract men who are goal-oriented, sincere, and gainfully employed, and who want to find a good partner as much as you do. Pick a service that caters only to marriage-minded people. If you choose well, you should find that their members are much better matches than men you meet at bars, and the whole process is far more efficient than other methods. If you use personal ads, limit your contacts to marriage-minded, emotionally-available men who live close enough to develop a healthy offline relationship.

Stay positive. If you follow this advice, you should be well on your way to reaching your relationship goal by age 30. Best wishes and happy hunting!

Dr. Kate

Part II
Getting Closer

The 5th Wave   By Rich Tennant

"I don't know, Susie – sometimes I get the feeling you're afraid to get close."

In this part . . .

*O*nce you've found a compatible partner, the real work
begins. As difficult as finding a compatible partner
may seem, growing that relationship is much more
challenging. It involves constructive effort, energy, and
determination. Relationships are extremely fragile in the
beginning, and whether or not you move closer to one
another depends on many factors that all interact with
one another.

In this part, I discuss why and how people become
intimate. I examine common myths about intimacy,
how believing in those myths can cause problems for
your relationship, and how challenging them and understanding the realities can actually make your relationship
thrive.

In addition to your ideas about intimacy and commitment,
how you handle sex the first time in your relationship can
affect its future. Exclusivity and cohabitation are also
important considerations. So I discuss all these steps on
the path to togetherness, and show you how to pick and
choose among your opportunities and possible behaviors,
to continue moving your relationship forward — in a
positive, enjoyable direction.

Chapter 6

Growing More Intimate

....

....

*E*ver met the "right" person at the "wrong" time? Well, it happens to all of us. Unfortunately, when it happens, there's usually nothing much that you can do about it. As I discuss in Chapter 4 on compatibility, *timing* — sharing the same relationship goal on similar timetables — is important if you and your partner are to succeed long-term as a couple.

How you pace the relationship will have a lot to do with whether or not it survives the early, more fragile stages. *Intimacy,* that very close, personal, special bond you feel with someone you love and know well, can't be forced or speeded up. It has to occur naturally, as you get emotionally and physically closer with your partner.

In this chapter, I discuss two common intimacy myths that cause people to push their relationships to the breaking point, and how believing in the realities instead can help you relax and pace yourself. I also explore the role that timing plays, and how realistic expectations and pacing can help the relationship survive and grow.

Squashing Two Intimacy Myths

Ask yourself: Do you hold either of the following intimacy myths? If so, think about how that belief influences your life. Then reflect on the reality and how letting it guide you could be an improvement. Use Table 6-1 later in this chapter to remind you of each myth and reality.

Myth #1: If some is good, more must be heaven

Many people believe that when it comes to relationships, if some is good, then more must be even better. For example, if someone likes some of your company and you get along superbly during that time, then naturally, that person would enjoy more of your company. This myth presupposes that you and your new partner will continue to get along well, no matter how much time you spend together. It encourages people to give in to their powerful urges to see one another as frequently as possible. As they continue to enjoy one another, people usually increase their time together. So why not see each other several times a week? Why not go on vacation together? Your lease is up for renewal, and you're spending your free time together anyway, so why waste all that money on two apartments? Why not move in together instead?

The reality is, however, that less can be more — especially in the beginning of a relationship. Remember, you can't ever be perfect at anything, so you probably won't hit the exact "optimum length of stay" factor right on the head.

It's better to leave someone wanting more of you and fantasizing about "the next time," than to overstay your welcome and bore him or her silly. Relationships are enormously fragile in the beginning stages, and excitement is an important part of The Infatuation Stage in any relationship (see Chapter 2 for more on this). If you vow to stay until the time you spend together is no longer pleasant, you're shortening the overall length of time that your relationship will stay exciting and fresh.

Also, no two people ever feel exactly the same at any one particular time in the relationship. So just because you think your partner is wonderful and you can't get enough of him, it doesn't mean that he feels as strongly as you do. Overstaying your welcome further assures that your partner, who desires you and your company less, will come to desire you and your company even less.

Myth #2: Online love = Offline love

Have you met anyone online and developed feelings for him or her? People who haven't done this usually think it's a little nuts, but I can reassure you that perfectly sane people of both sexes have experienced the incredible excitement of what seems like "online love." It's amazingly powerful. You find yourself wanting to talk to your new friend more and more, and looking forward to the e-mails and instant messages. You have an intense desire to get to know the other person as much as possible — as quickly as possible.

Many of the people who experience this phenomenon end up believing that online love is just as powerful and valid as anything you could experience offline. Unfortunately, believing in this myth encourages you to trust and totally give in to the intense positive feelings you experience when interacting with someone online. You assure yourself that chatting online for hours and hours day after day to someone 5,000 miles away is a match made in heaven! Why not exchange phone numbers and schedule an in-person visit? Surely the distance won't matter. You can go visit one weekend, and finally find the love you've been waiting for all your life! After all, your experience online has been nothing short of fantastic, so how can anything go wrong?

Now I'll slowly count backwards from "3" to "1." And when I reach "1," I'll snap my fingers, and you'll open your eyes, *wwwwake up!*, and return to reality as we know it. Ready? 3 . . . , 2 . . . .

Unfortunately, falling in love with someone you've never met *in person* is impossible. You can develop very powerful feelings while interacting online, but true love develops in person over time. See "In Real Life," a song by Marty Axelrod and Bill Schreiner, at the end of this chapter, to help you remember that "It Ain't Real Love 'Til It's In Real Life."

If your relationship is going to stay online — no problem. But most people meet online because they want to eventually make an offline relationship. And offline relationships involve a ton of variables that you can't assess online, including verbal communication, physical/sexual attraction, and how you each smell, feel, taste, sound, smile, laugh, tease, make love, and conduct yourselves in everyday life. Online photos and e-mail just aren't enough.

Many people express themselves differently online than off. They may take on a different persona — a different personality style, and verbalize fantasies that they wouldn't have the courage to carry out offline. So if you believe in those fantasies and assume that nothing stands in the way of fulfilling them, you could be very disappointed when your partner does not come along as expected on your dream voyage.

On the other hand, online relationships *can* develop into successful, enjoyable offline relationships. It takes time, however, and it takes interacting with that person *in person* over time. It also takes good judgment in people, and realistic expectations. You can e-mail someone several times a day, chat in real time through instant messages, and speed up communication that would normally take months to occur in an offline relationship. But don't be fooled into thinking that speeding things up this way also means you can fall in love that fast. In the end, online experiences can augment, but never take the place of offline interactions. See Chapter 5 for tips on how to safely and successfully use online personal ads and other online resources.

Reviewing the Myths and Realities

Use Table 6-1 to remind you of the intimacy myths and realities.

Table 6-1	Two Intimacy Myths and Realities
Grief-Causing Myth	*Saving Reality*
M1: If some is good, more must be better.	R1: Less is often more, especially at the beginning of a relationship.
M2: Online love is the same as offline love.	R2: "It ain't real love 'til it's in real life." And even then, it takes awhile.

You Can't Hurry Love!

Most people like the idea that magic exists — the notion is creative, awe-inspiring, and fun. They want to believe that love is magic — that it can take on magical forms and happen in magical, instantaneous ways. However, as I point out in Chapter 2, people often confuse infatuation with love in the early stages of a relationship. Making a relationship is like putting a huge puzzle together. You've found some of the pieces and connected them, and you like the way the picture is coming together so far, but lots of pieces are still missing. You want to believe — and you hope — that the rest of the pieces will come together the way you want them to.

But that doesn't always happen. In fact, those puzzle pieces frequently don't line up the way you'd like. At any point, you may discover something about your date that causes you to lose respect. In fact, since many pieces have to be in sync for compatibility to occur, it's surprising that any relationships work out for any period of time! As challenging as it can be to work with someone eight hours a day or befriend him or her for a platonic relationship, developing an intense, intimate relationship is often much more complicated!

Real love takes time — because getting to know someone takes time. You have to see him or her under different conditions — happy, sad, tired, hungry, cold, inconvenienced, stressed out, and so on. You need to see your sweetie around family, friends, coworkers, supervisors, supervisees, and strangers. By interacting with your mate in different situations and under varying conditions, you learn about his values, hopes, and dreams, as well as his behavior, character, and attitude toward life and other people. Sure, your partner can tell you what she believes herself to be like, and she may be telling you as honestly as she can. But it's always a *subjective* description — she's telling you her own opinion of herself, as she sees herself through her values. When you get to know your mate better, you may find that you don't agree with that description at all!

There's no set time exactly, but in general, if you've seen someone in person at least three to four times a week for at least three to four months, and the strong positive feeling continues, you're probably developing real love. In contrast, if you've only or mostly experienced him or her online, there's no way to tell if that intense feeling is really love or just infatuation.

Keep this in mind: Easy come, easy go. When someone comes on to you very intensely, he probably wants to be in love so much right now, he's shoving you into that box in his mind. If you weren't present, someone else would do. And because you're not really that special to him, he can easily replace you, too. So when an attraction happens very quickly, online or off, go ahead and enjoy it. In the back of your mind, however, take it with a grain of salt. It could end at any moment, and if it does, just take it in stride. Don't get discouraged or give up on love altogether. And if the feeling lasts and grows into love — be pleasantly surprised and enjoy it to the max while it lasts!

Nurturing Intimacy

Have you ever known anyone for a long time, but felt as though you didn't know that person at all? Perhaps you've spoken with him for extended periods of time, but he's still an enigma to you. Yet with another person, you've had briefer, more rushed conversations, and still felt closer. The difference has to do with how intimate the conversation is — how much that person reveals himself to you emotionally and psychologically. Some people talk a lot and say very little. Others talk very little, but say a lot. And most people are somewhere in between. It's not the amount of words that grows intimacy between two people, but rather, how much personal and emotionally revealing information is passed back and forth.

What causes emotional intimacy to grow?

Emotional intimacy grows when you and your partner share very personal and private *thoughts, feelings,* and *emotional experiences* with one another that you don't share with anyone else. You begin to feel bonded, and your union becomes more unique and special *because* you've shared those intimacies.

If you're visiting a foreign country and you suddenly bump into someone from your own country, there's an immediate feeling of camaraderie, even though you've never met that person before. The reason? You share a unique experience: You're both citizens of your country wandering around a foreign land, and you're the *only,* or two of the only, compatriots you know there. Everyone else belongs to another group. Similarly, you might initially feel more intimate with someone who comes from the same "old neighborhood," the same religion, the same ethnic background, or the same school.

But that's not enough to make intimacy thrive. Besides sharing activities and experiences, you need to freely share your thoughts and feelings about those activities and experiences, as well as other parts of life. Thoughts and feelings are internal and personal; the other person doesn't know about them unless you share. So sharing thoughts and feelings is extremely intimate. When you and your friend discuss how you each feel and think about your world, then listen supportively to each other's thoughts, feelings, anxieties, joys, and sorrows, you feel closer — more emotionally intimate with one another.

What stifles emotional intimacy?

Emotional intimacy is stifled when:

- ✔ **You try to rush or force it.** Intimacy develops over time, in relaxed, reciprocal, one-on-one interactions.

- ✔ **You or your partner only talk about events, and never share your feelings and thoughts about those events with each other.**

- ✔ **You or your mate *expect* or *demand* that the other share his or her feelings with you.** You can't make anyone care for you or want to share secrets with you. Trying to do so will lead to disrespect and resentment — not respect, desire, and affection.

- ✔ **You share too much with too many people.** If you tell everyone your secrets, they're no longer secrets. You and your partner become intimate when you share your private thoughts and feelings in a special, unique way. If you share with everyone, it's not unique or special. You can't be emotionally close to everyone. When you try, you become close to no one — and usually end up feeling alone and very depressed.

What causes physical/sexual intimacy to grow?

I mentioned earlier that emotional intimacy grows when you and your partner share very personal and private thoughts, feelings, and emotional experiences with one another that you don't usually share with anyone else. Similarly, *physical and sexual intimacy* grows when you and your partner share very personal and private *physical and sexual experiences* with one another that you don't usually share with anyone else — at least not at this time. The relationship becomes more unique and special because you're enjoying those intimate acts together. And when you share intimate sexual acts with one another that you don't share with anyone else, you also feel closer emotionally — provided your relationship is ready for the intensely private sharing. (See the following section for what happens if it isn't.)

What stifles physical/sexual intimacy?

Physical and sexual intimacy is stifled when:

- ✔ **You have sex in a routine, impersonal way, without ever sharing intimate feelings and thoughts.** Just as emotional intimacy is stifled when you and your partner don't share your innermost feelings and thoughts, sexual intimacy is, too.

- ✔ **You try to push someone into sexual intimacy.** Similar to emotional intimacy, you can't make anyone want you sexually. If you force someone to have sex too soon, it constitutes rape, and the other person usually feels a lot of resentment and hostility.

- ✔ **You have sex with a consenting partner, but one or both of you don't feel that emotionally intense about the other.** If you and your partner share sexually intimate activities before enough emotional intimacy is present in your relationship, you'll both tend to notice — and feel uncomfortable about — the incongruity and discordance.

- ✔ **You have sex with too many people.** Just as sharing thoughts and feelings with everyone makes the experience less special, sharing sex with everyone makes that experience less unique and special, too.

Pacing Your Intimacy

One way to understand how healthy intimacy develops into a healthy relationship is to picture six concentric circles, one inside the next. You can use these intimacy circles to remind you to gradually share with someone over time, as you get to know and trust him or her more.

When you first meet someone, you start at the outermost circle. As you get to know that person better, you advance, circle by circle, toward the innermost circle — self-intimacy.

- ✔ **Circle 6 — Strangers:** When you first meet someone, you're strangers. You don't know one another, so you have no idea if you'll end up liking or disliking each other. You begin to share information on a very superficial level, revealing no personal or private information. If you're attracted to each other, perhaps you flirt a bit. If you both respond in a positive fashion, you may then advance to the next circle.

- ✓ **Circle 5 — Casual Dating:** In the next circle, the two of you begin to date. You still don't know one another very well, so you don't share anything personal just yet. Privacy is important, and you don't even know if you'll see each other again! So you engage only in "press release talk" — info you wouldn't mind seeing in 4-inch high letters on the cover of your local newspaper the next morning. You share feelings and thoughts, but only positive feelings and thoughts about positive, non-controversial topics. You're there to have fun with one another, and you keep it light. As you date more and become more interested in each other, you grow closer. If you both appreciate the other's interest and reciprocate it, you may progress to the next circle.

- ✓ **Circle 4 — Romantic Friends:** As you move into this circle, you begin to trust one another more; you're having a relationship now, and growing more emotionally intimate. You know one another well enough and feel secure enough to be able to tease and be more spontaneous. You also reveal more of your thoughts and feelings about more serious, sensitive topics. It's OK to discuss negative topics, as long as you always spend more time talking about positive ideas, and always leave the date on an upbeat, emotionally supportive note. In this stage, you feel more affectionate toward one another, so you hold hands, put your arms around each other, and kiss. You look forward to spending more time together and getting to know one another better.

- ✓ **Circle 3 — Romantic Lovers:** At this point, you're having sex. You've crossed a boundary and are now sharing an extremely personal physical experience with one another that you don't share with anyone else. You've become physically and sexually intimate. That unique interaction bonds you together even more tightly, and increases your emotional intimacy in the process. You enjoy giving and receiving love and emotional support, along with physical and sexual pleasure.

- ✓ **Circle 2 — Deep Intimacy:** This stage takes much longer to reach; by this time, you and your partner know one another extremely well. You've heard each other's stories and have experienced one another so closely for so long that you trust each other deeply. You're best friends and exclusive, intimate partners. You both know you can trust the other to look out for your welfare through thick and thin, without being asked to do so. Your relationship has been tested and has survived with flying colors, so you trust the emotional support between you to continue indefinitely. You and your partner have seen each other at your worst, and have continued to love each other. This is as close as you can get with another human being, and it's enormously rewarding and comforting to most people.

✔ **Circle 1— Self-Intimacy:** This innermost circle consists of you and only you. It's healthy to keep some thoughts, ideas, and feelings totally to yourself, no matter how much you and your partner love one another. (See the sidebar in Chapter 4 on how much honesty is too much.) In fact, if you don't maintain this circle, you're acting as though you have no self, no ego — and that's very unhealthy. On the other hand, staying too much in this circle is also unhealthy, because then you're closing yourself off and not letting anyone know and get close to you.

A healthy relationship slowly and gradually moves from the outermost circle, Circle 6, to the innermost circle that another person can occupy, Circle 2. To start the process, take a small risk and reveal something small about yourself. If your partner seems supportive and reciprocates with some personal information, you'll probably feel a little closer and trust a little more. Little by little, reveal more about yourself and take more risks, slowly and gradually over time, as you grow to know and trust one another more. As you do, you'll move from Circle 6 to Circle 5 to Circle 4 to Circle 3 to . . . .

It's *not* healthy to try to jump from *Circle 5 — Casual Dating* into *Circle 3 — Romantic Lovers* on a first date. You're skipping too many boundaries all at the same time, without getting to know each other first. Your young relationship isn't ready for such advanced intimacy; you don't even know if you're going to like one another enough to continue dating, much less cavort naked in the sack together! When you push a relationship too fast, the relationship takes a hit. Since relationships are extremely fragile in the beginning, they often don't survive that damage. (For more about this, see Chapter 7 on sex early in the relationship.)

To pace the relationship and keep it thriving, try to keep the emotional intimacy and physical/sexual intimacy in sync with your partner and with the time you've actually spent in the relationship. For tips to successfully pace a new relationship, see Chapter 23.

❤ ❤ ❤ ❤ ❤ ❤

Beware 180-Degree Man! Here Today, Gone Today!

Dear Dr. Kate,

My age: 48   **My gender:** Female

I've been dating a recently divorced man, and I thought we had a wonderful relationship. He took me to his club's party, introduced me to his friends, had me host the Holiday party for his employees, and bought me a beautiful gold chain. We had eight dates in a month, talked on the phone every night, and planned dream vacations. Then out of nowhere, he told me he needed time to think. And now he's dating others. I'm crushed. Advice?

Dear Crushed,

I get many letters like yours. Here's the bottom line: Easy come, easy go. Beware of anyone who comes on so strong so fast. He may leave just as fast.

Now, there are exceptions. I know a man who told a woman on their second date that he was going to marry her. He turned out to be a great guy — not a psychopath or abuser overstepping his boundaries — and they've now been happily married for over 30 years. But they are an incredible exception. For every one of those relationships, there are millions more that work out like yours or fall apart in some other way.

Your friend has problems. He's on the rebound after his divorce. Be especially careful with newly divorced men. They don't know what they're doing much of the time. They may be acting out of loneliness, sadness, regret, hurt, anger, or low self-esteem. They're too upset with what's happening in their own lives to be considerate about how they're treating you. They're not thinking, "Gee, I'm coming on kind of strong. Maybe I should back off a little before I give her the impression that I'm definitely going to be part of her life!" Men usually don't think that far in advance about personal issues — especially not when they're stressed. They just *react*.

In addition, males, as a group, tend to "talk out loud" — they don't really mean a lot of the dreams they spin. So don't take them too literally. In the future, pace your relationships. Give the man some competition so he'll stay interested in you. If you decide to go faster, just take it with a grain of salt, and remember that 180-degree turns are common. So enjoy it while it lasts, but don't believe everything he tells you. He may think he means it, but he may not know what he feels, and he may not feel any need to be consistent either.

Get busy meeting other men. If your friend calls for a date, turn him down for the first night, and ask him for a different night. *"I'd love to see you, but I can't make Saturday night. How about Sunday brunch instead?"* Don't be too available. Let him wonder what you're doing on Friday and Saturday.

All the best, and please keep me posted on your progress.

Dr. Kate

Those Three Little Words — "I Love You!"

Dear Dr. Kate,

My age: 21   **My gender:** Female

I've been dating a guy for almost seven months now. We connect on so many levels, and I really love him. But he hasn't said those three little words I've been longing to hear — "I love you." I've mentioned that I'm insecure about his feelings toward me, and he's told me that his actions speak loud and clear. He says that he really cares for me and has no desire to see anyone else. Help!

Dear Confused and Lost,

You've only known him seven months, and if he's around your age, he's still quite young. It takes men a bit longer to get in touch with their feelings, and some really never do. As women, we talk to our friends about our intimate feelings from the time we're little, but men don't. So they usually lag behind women in being able to identify their feelings and express them to others.

He's already told you that he really cares for you and has no desire to see anyone else. That's fine for seven months, especially at your age. On the other hand, if he continues to say that and only that when you're 28, *then* you can move on to men who are able to express love and make an emotional commitment. You're only 21 and nowhere near ready to get married now, so there's no harm in giving your boyfriend time to get comfortable with his feelings.

Dear Dr. Kate,

My age: 38   **My gender:** Female

I've been dating a man, 40, for almost two years now, but he won't tell me he loves me. He avoids any discussion about commitment. He's with me 95 percent of the time, so why can't he just say those three little words??? I think he loves me, but unless he tells me, I can't be sure. Should I continue or try someone else? I'm not getting any younger!

Dear "No Spring Chicken,"

At two years, your boyfriend should be able to tell you he loves you, and he shouldn't be dodging questions about commitment. He's plenty old enough to make that decision. Perhaps he's afraid to say anything because he knows you'd like to get married and he doesn't want to. You're 38, so you need to date only marriage-minded people who can see you as appropriate marriage material in the near future. It doesn't sound like your boyfriend fits that bill, so try dating other people casually. If your boyfriend then perks up, invite him to couples counseling with you.

All the best,

Dr. Kate

In Real Life

Words and Music by Marty Axelrod and
Bill Schreiner, CEO of Love

She was raised outside of Baltimore,
The youngest and the wildest child of four.
Her favorite color: bright lime green,
Her guilty pleasure: People Magazine.

I fell in love when I saw her face,
The prettiest girl in cyberspace.
Before I ask her to be my wife,
I really ought to meet her in real life.

> In real life, face to face,
> Pounding hearts, first embrace.
> Romance sure is sweet online,
> But it ain't real love 'til you're in real life.
> It ain't real love 'til you're in real life.

I've told her most of my fantasies,
I'd feel the heat right through the keys.
We burned a hole in private chat,
Now we're both ready for more than that.

She'll be wondering if I like her dress.
I'll be thinking my hair's a mess.
For all those jitters we might feel,
There comes a time when you've got to deal...

> In real life, face to face,
> Pounding hearts, first embrace.
> Romance sure is sweet online,
> But it ain't real love 'til you're in real life.
> It ain't real love 'til you're in real life.

No turning back now,
We're on our way
To a rendez-vous at the ol' cafe.
I think we're gonna be OK

> Right here in real life, face to face,
> Pounding hearts, first embrace.
> Romance sure is sweet online,
> But it ain't real love 'til you're in real life.
> It ain't real love 'til you're in real life.

©1999 Marty Axelrod and Bill Schreiner

Chapter 7

Sex Early in the Relationship

. . . .

In This Chapter

▶ Exploring how and why men and women differ in their sexual thoughts, feelings, and behaviors

▶ Assessing risk/rewards when deciding to have sex for the first time or with a new partner

▶ Choosing what's best for you and then acting responsibly

. . . .

*T*hink about it: How many people have you shared a bus with? How many dinners or movies have you shared with other people? How many people have you told secrets to from time to time? Now — *how many sex partners have you had in your life?*

The reality is: The number of people with whom you share sex is very small in the grand scheme of things. So when you do have sex with someone, the event is special, unique, and important — even if you don't immediately realize it — and even if you *never* consciously realize it.

In Chapter 6, I explain how people become emotionally and sexually intimate by sharing special experiences only with each other, and why it's best to keep your emotional intimacy and physical/sexual intimacy in sync with each other — and with the time you've actually spent in the relationship. In this chapter, I explore what happens when you don't do that. I discuss emotional and physical risks of *sex early in the relationship* (SEIR), and how to estimate the risk you have with a particular partner. I also discuss how differently men and women view sex — and why — in the next section.

All Sexual Reasons Aren't Alike!

Men and women aren't identical creatures, and they never will be. Their differences have been documented through brain studies, psychological testing, and behavioral and historical data. Their brains tend to be wired differently, and males and females are raised differently as well. So from the perspectives of *nature* (genetics and brain function) and *nurture* (learning and conditioning — being raised to think and behave a certain way), men and women have many differences. How they consider the act of sex is just one of those differences. Table 7-1 shows those differences.

Table 7-1	How Men and Women View Sex
Men, as a Group, Tend to . . .	**Women, as a Group, Tend to . . .**
Peak at ages 18–21.	Peak in their late 30s to early 40s.
Focus on biological/physical aspects of sex.	Emphasize the emotional and psychological context of sex.
Find it easier to have sex with someone they dislike.	Find having sex with someone they dislike quite difficult.
Be more practical. If they don't want to see a woman again, may have sex to get something from the date.	Be more idealistic and romantic. View sexual interest as a sign that he really wants to know her better.
Be more visually inclined, and more stimulated or bothered by physical appearance. Care less about her intelligence, personality, success.	Be stimulated by the "whole picture" — power, success, personality, intelligence — and care less about physical attractiveness.
Think competitively about sex. Sex is a sign of prowess, an arena to compete in, even notches on a belt.	View sex as a sign of being loved, and prize belongingness and affection above competition.
Exaggerate and boast to their buddies, especially in their teens, about their sexual conquests. The less experience, the more they boast.	Share emotional and romantic details, not sexual fine points, with close friends. The relationship is more important than the sex itself.
Focus on their own sexual impulses, not realizing that the woman interprets sexual interest as a desire to get to know her better.	Assume that men feel as they do about sex — that men also have sex to develop the emotional and romantic parts of the relationship.
Press for sex, especially when they're peaking sexually.	Misunderstand a man's sexual peak because they haven't yet had one.
Look down on women who give in.	Respect the man, even when he's pushing for sex.
Impulsively say, "I love you," in the heat of passion — when they mean, "I really, really, *really* want to have sex with you right now."	Say, "I love you," when they think they mean it. Believe a man when he says, "I love you." Take men's statements too literally.
Become confused, blame the woman, and avoid her after having unexpected sex.	Want to continue relationship and help the emotional intimacy catch up to the sexual intimacy. Feel hurt and confused when the man blames them and exits quickly.

Women, as a group, tend to emphasize the emotional, psychological, and romantic aspects of a relationship. Men, as a group, tend to emphasize the sexual, physical, and practical aspects of a relationship. When I say, "as a group," that's exactly what I mean. This statement is not true of *every* woman, but of women in general. The same holds true of my statement about men. It may not be true of a particular man you know, but it's true about men in general. When considered as a group, men and women tend to think and feel differently about sex.

So women may choose SEIR to be accepted or loved, whereas men usually choose it for the sexual stimulation involved. Having sex may not even be a compliment to the woman, but rather, a sign that the man *hasn't* had a good time on the date and wants to salvage something for his money.

If everyone discussed his or her reasons for having sex in advance, there wouldn't be any problem. If they understood why their partner wanted to have sex with them and didn't like it, they could just opt out of the activity. However, while having sex is private, discussing sex seems to be even more private. An amazing number of people are willing to have sex, but not discuss it before it takes place. As a result, people usually guess at the reason their partner wants sex, then act on their assumptions. If those ideas are incorrect, they find out after the act is over and the repercussions hit the fan.

So how do men and women acquire these divergent sexual attitudes and behaviors? Glad you asked! Let's look at the anthropological, neurological, genetic, and social learning data.

Anthropological data

Women have always had the babies, and it's pretty difficult to carry a baby while hunting or moving quickly on your feet. So in ancient times, the woman stayed home and tended to the baby and the field, while the man went off hunting. The woman depended on her man to bring supplemental food for her and the babies, so she tended to stay with one stable, reliable guy for this reason.

In contrast, men competed for the available women, because snaring a good one meant that their lineage would continue in a "survival of the fittest" fashion. Men also tended to have sex with more than one woman, because that further strengthened the likelihood that their lineage would survive. Today, men are still more competitive in their sexual conquests, and still more likely to have sex with different partners, even when they're committed to others. While WWII, the sexual revolution of the 1960's, and the need for two incomes to support a family have encouraged women to work outside the home in bigger numbers than ever, women are still more likely to be the one staying home with the kids in single-income homes. That makes the man more sexually available — and the woman less available — to others outside the relationship.

Brain differences

Men, as a group, tend to be more *right-brained* (spatially-skilled) than women. They tend to excel more at performance and mechanical skills than verbal skills, making it more difficult for them to communicate verbally. They also use fewer areas of their brains when solving problems than women do. That tends to make them more focused and less intuitive than women.

What do these differences mean in the sexual arena? Well, men tend to be more focused on the purely physical aspects of sex, while women tend to notice the context more. To a woman, the lighting, the music, the person involved, the relationship, the romance, and all the sights, sounds, smells, and tastes of the environment in which sex occurs tend to be important. Because it's easier for the man to compartmentalize and focus solely on his sexual pleasure, it's easy for him to have sex with someone he doesn't really like much, or to round out a bad date. Women, on the other hand, have a more difficult time blocking out all the social cues. Later in the relationship, women are more bothered about having sex when they're not getting along with their partners. They're more likely to bring up and try to resolve issues because they find it difficult to just carry on with sex like nothing is amiss.

Genetic differences

Men, as a group, are usually more aggressive than women, even in childhood. Little boys tend to be much more rough-and-tumble than little girls; the aggressiveness is conditioned into them through learning (discussed in the next section), but it's also programmed in their genes.

Fast forward: Those little boys grow into men who tend to be more sexually aggressive than women. They've had the lead role for many thousands of years, and they're not in any danger of losing it. Unless they're shy and realize they lag behind their peers in aggressiveness, men seem content to do the chasing — and often look down on women who appear to be too pushy, too aggressive, or "less feminine."

But women usually can't tell which men have these biases until it's too late. As a result, they often try to find a way for their man to lead, even while chafing at the bit. Partners always need to balance their roles and keep the relationship power fairly even, but that's especially true when the relationship is new and more fragile. This balance is also extremely important in the bedroom. If the woman comes on too aggressively during sex, the man often disrespects her and blames her for their sexual involvement. He may then redirect his energy to someone else who plays the feminine role more skillfully — someone who doesn't threaten him emotionally or sexually.

Compounding this male-female difference is the fact that women and men reach their sexual peak (when their hormones are surging and they're experiencing intense sexual urges) at different ages. Men peak between ages 18 and 21, while women don't peak sexually until their late 30s to early 40s. (Go ahead and wonder about the wisdom of this. I have!) This variance makes it more difficult for one sex to understand the other's sex drive. It means that adolescent and young adult males think about sex an enormous number of times per day, while adolescent and young adult females don't. Instead, young females spend hours daydreaming about love and romance.

Not until they're 38 through 40+ and experiencing their own sexual peak do women begin to understand what young men go through 20 years before them. It's one thing to intellectually know that sexual peaks exist, but quite another to experience one! Once a woman peaks, she understands the young man's sexual aggressiveness and how to handle that pushiness without feeling guilty. Too bad she's not programmed to feel that difference 20 years earlier! But maybe — just maybe — men and women are genetically programmed *not* to peak at the same time to avoid millions of babies being born to sex-crazed adolescents!

The role of learning

Learning also plays a big role in how men and women acquire different sexual attitudes and behaviors.

A little girl grows up playing with dolls and playing "house," which focuses her attention on relationships. She roleplays taking care of babies, instructing those babies how to interact with other kids/dolls in the house, cooking, cleaning, and juggling all the roles her mother plays. She learns to model her behavior after her mother's, being responsible for the emotional connections in the family, as well as most of the practical chores of the household. She also learns to demur to boys — to let the more aggressive males lead.

Fast forward: The little girl grows into a woman who emphasizes the role of relationships in sex. She grows up sharing close intimate relationship details with her girlfriends. As a teen, she spends hour after hour on the phone, dissecting her relationship possibilities and interactions. She doesn't usually brag about sexual conquests; she views sex as a sign of being loved, accepted, and belonging to a family. As an adult woman, she goes on to analyze her emotions and her dates in the context of her overall relationship goal. She gets a lot of experience in identifying emotions, sorting through emotional problems, and devising effective follow-up action. And she uses these same skills after having SEIR with a man. Instead of getting completely flustered by unexpected sex, she's able to face it, cope with it, and try to work it out.

Because she discusses love and relationships so much during childhood and adolescence, the woman is comfortable thinking about and encouraging emotional intimacy. She wants the man to be the sexual aggressor, and she's more likely to be the spouse staying home to raise the children in one-income families. Her early roleplaying often encourages her to place more emphasis on the mothering and housekeeping roles of "mother" than the sexual duties of "wife." Think about it — little girls play "house," not "dating" or "sex." As a result, her husband may later complain, as many husbands do, that she loses interest in sex after marriage.

In contrast, the little boy plays with trucks and cars — which emphasize the role of *function* in life. Or he might play "war" or "cowboys and Indians" — games that emphasize aggression and competition. He gets involved in competitive sports early on — baseball, basketball, football, you name it. All of these emphasize achievement, winning, defeating a competitor, and performing well in an outside environment. In contrast, girls tend not to join or even have access to those kinds of teams.

The boy is raised to believe that he must be tough, independent, and self-sufficient. He's not supposed to play with dolls, or dwell on or care that much about relationships. That's for sissies. Instead, he *competes* with his friends in sports and games; he doesn't talk to them about his thoughts and feelings.

Fast forward to the future: The little boy grows into an adolescent who boasts to his buddies about nonexistent sexual conquests. As a man, he emphasizes how well his career is going, and whom he beat in the boardroom or on the racquetball court. He becomes a man who shares sports and games with other men, but wouldn't dare ask "the guys" about his love and relationship problems. He wouldn't want to expose himself in that way.

As a result, the man has much less practice identifying emotions and coping with unexpected events like SEIR. When a complicated emotional situation arises, he frequently doesn't know what to do. He's confused, and his emotional problem-solving skills are much less developed than the woman's. He's had much less experience, so he isn't confident that he can discuss the issue and resolve it successfully. He may not be able to identify what he's feeling or know how to describe it to the woman. Because he's also learned not to appear vulnerable or incompetent by asking for help, he often finds it easier to blame the female and avoid her — which then ends the need to solve the problem!

So the man tends to emphasize function, doing, accomplishing, achieving, and winning. The woman tends to emphasize relating, sharing, loving, and communicating. They each bring those roles into sex, where the man is more likely to focus on orgasm as the goal, and the woman is more likely to focus on sex as a way to express love. She's more likely to emphasize their relationship, how much the man loves her, and how he shows it through verbal and romantic expressions of endearment.

As more and more progressive parents try to raise their kids in a more even-handed, "genderblind" manner, these stereotypes are slowly changing. During your lifetime, however, you can expect the differences outlined in this section to continue. If you're a heterosexual, understanding how the opposite sex thinks and feels about sex is extremely helpful. You're going to be interacting with mates who tend to think differently, feel differently, and then behave differently — in a manner consistent with those thoughts and feelings.

If you don't understand the basis for those actions, you'll end up with a lot of hurt feelings. You might assume that your partner is putting you down, for example, instead of realizing that it's not personal. You'll also need accurate assumptions in order to decide what to do in certain contexts. If you can see the man's point of view, as well as the woman's, you can wisely choose behavior more likely to be respected and valued by your partner in that context.

You'll also be able to keep your emotional and sexual intimacy more balanced and make better decisions about SEIR. And if you and your partner do become an emotionally and sexually intimate couple, you'll be able to use your knowledge about your differences to improve your communication and enhance your long-term sex life as well.

Think about how you select presents for people. When you choose a gift, you don't buy what you'd like to have. Rather, you consider your partner, and what he or she would like. The same wisdom holds true when giving the gift of sex, and when addressing the most common sex questions — the *when*, *where*, *how*, *how much*, and *with whom* questions of sex. When you keep in mind the differences in Table 7-1 (earlier in this chapter), answering these questions gets easier.

WHEN to Have Sex

I will never tell you exactly when or when not to have sex for the first time ever, or when or when not to have sex with a particular partner. You have to make that decision for yourself. However, I have heard many stories from people who've made unfortunate choices and suffered as a result, so I sometimes make strong recommendations. Please don't take my suggestions as commandments that you must follow. When and with whom you choose to have sex always has to be your choice.

However, the one commandment that I will give you is that *if* you have sex, you *must* be responsible and mature about it. Inform yourself about how the male and female body works, and how you can help protect yourself — and your partner — from *sexually transmitted diseases* (STDs) and unwanted pregnancies. Then be responsible and take those precautions every time you have sex. Be considerate and loving toward yourself, your partner, and any babies you may bring into the world by using the protections that I mention later in this chapter, and by letting your partner know — and possibly abstaining from sex — if you have a STD. If you don't feel like being that responsible and mature, then avoid sex — to protect yourself, your partner, and his or her future partners.

It's also important to examine your motives for having sex — and be honest with yourself about the emotional risks you take each time. While the emotional risks aren't usually life-threatening, they are important. Using Table 7-1, consider your possible motivation and your partner's possible motivation for having sex, and estimate your emotional risks. Then taking all of that into consideration, make your decision.

Whatever behavior you choose — to have sex or not to have sex — do it with your eyes wide open. Be honest with yourself. If things don't work out as you want, don't beat yourself up emotionally. Just learn from the experience, and use that knowledge the next time — when you make your next sexual decision.

There are two parts to the "when to have sex" question: when to have sex for the first time ever, and when to have sex for the first time with a particular partner.

Having sex for the first time ever

The first time you ever have sex should be an experience you'll always want to remember, because, in fact, you *will* always remember it — good or bad. Ask any of your friends, and they'll all remember the first time. It's special by virtue of being first, and no other sexual episode will ever be first again in your lifetime. So you'll definitely remember your first intercourse. And you may also remember the first time you have oral sex and the first time you orgasm, especially if they don't all happen on the same night.

So if you decide to have sex for the first time ever with someone, just be sure that you're comfortable with that choice. Don't do it because your partner is pressuring you or because it's a special occasion (like Valentine's Day, or your 6-, 12- or even 24-month anniversary). Don't decide to do it because you've put it off for so long and feel so out of touch with your peer group that you just want to find someone and get it over with. Don't do it under rushed, awkward conditions if at all possible. Above all, make sure that the person with whom you're having sex is someone you want to remember for the rest of your life — because, plain and simple, you will.

Exploring sex with a new partner

Not as important as your first time ever, but still extremely important, is the first time you choose to have sex in a particular relationship. No matter how many times you've had sex before, the first time you indulge with a new partner becomes significant by virtue of being the first sexual experience in that relationship. Because sex is so physically intimate — regardless of the emotions of the partners involved or how they feel about one another, I highly recommend that you consider your choice carefully before jumping in. As I discuss in Chapter 6, a relationship is very fragile in the beginning stages, so it's always best to keep the physical/sexual experiences in sync with the emotional intimacy and the time you've spent in the relationship. It's also important that you and your partner care for one another about the same amount at about the same time. When one of these aspects gets out of sync, discomfort usually results, and one or both parties may attempt to resolve the awkwardness by terminating the relationship.

Before you can make an informed decision about *when* to have sex or *with whom* to have it, it's important to realize how men and women differ in their attitudes toward sex and why. Reviewing Table 7-1 at such times can help you organize your thoughts and make a decision.

There are many pros and cons of having SEIR with a new partner. While it may temporarily please a partner who is pushing for sex and likewise allow you to satisfy your own sexual needs at the moment, SEIR also has many cons, as shown in Table 7-1. In addition, when you have SEIR, your partner may be less invested in giving you pleasure, less likely to tell you about a STD, and less likely to take proper STD or pregnancy precautions. In contrast, if you delay sex, many of the people who are only interested in you for sex will tend to drop out. You'll have fewer sexual partners and, hence, fewer possibilities for unwanted STDs and pregnancies. In addition, by keeping your physical actions in sync with your emotions, thoughts, and timing in the relationship, you'll also feel more centered, upbeat, and psychologically healthy.

WITH WHOM to Have Sex

When deciding with whom to have sex, it's also good to factor the information from Table 7-1 into your decision.

For example, if you're a woman and want a more complete, long-term relationship with a man, you may decide not to risk having sex with him. Perhaps he's the kind of guy who'd pressure you to have sex, then disappear in confusion the next day. You understand that giving in won't help him love you more; in fact, having sex might help him devalue you instead. You'll be able to see "the big picture" and factor in his aggression. If the man is 21, you'll also understand that he's peaking sexually and likely to be acting on impulse. And because you understand all of this, you'll find it easier to turn down his advances and wait until the emotional aspects of your relationship catch up to your sexual urges. You won't feel guilty or bad about yourself for turning him down.

It's interesting to note that women who have brothers are generally more aware of male motivation and behavior. A woman who loves her hot-blooded brother finds it easier to say, "This man tells women he loves them to get them into bed, but he's usually a nice guy." In contrast, a woman who doesn't have that experience often assumes that no guy, and especially not a nice one, would actually stoop that low during passion. When she learns that a man has done just that, she's more likely to internalize it, and feel hurt and belittled. She considers the man's behavior to be a statement about her unworthiness rather than a symptom of his sexual peaking.

Because women usually don't have sex just for the sake of physical gratification, the woman should carefully consider her real motivation for having SEIR, and whether sex with this particular person at this particular time is likely to accomplish that goal. If she wants the relationship to continue and doesn't know how sex will affect their union, and if she doesn't feel comfortable discussing the issue with her partner — or if she doesn't know him well enough to know if he'd be honest with her — she's often better off avoiding the risks by choosing not to have sex at this time.

If you've had a tendency to rush the sexual aspect of your relationships, consider changing your "MO" — *modus operandi* — your way of accomplishing something. You've already discovered that what you've been doing hasn't worked very well. So why not try something new? Try building the psychological and emotional aspects of your relationship before engaging in sex; keep your thoughts, feelings, and behaviors in sync with one another. Your relationships may improve as a result, and you'll probably feel a *lot* more balanced. Then other people are more likely to sense the changes in you, and look at you with more respect and esteem. And that could very well lead to a healthy, fun relationship with one of those people!

Of course, if you choose to have sex with someone purely for sexual gratification or to go with the flow at the moment, that's your choice. I'm not telling you that you shouldn't. Just be honest with yourself, consider the risks, and differentiate between the real and imagined rewards beforehand. If you don't care about the relationship continuing, and as long as you and your partner are in sync as to why you're having sex — or you both understand why the other is having it and you accept those terms — then there's no reason why you can't choose to have sex just for the sake of having sex.

WHERE To Have Sex

Because you'll definitely remember the first time you ever have sex, it's very important that the first episode occur in a pleasant, relaxed, private environment. Because you're also likely to remember the first time you have sex with a particular person, the "where" it takes place is also important.

Having sex hurriedly in the back seat of a car is not most women's idea of sexual bliss. (It's also a good way to develop a premature ejaculation problem, because you're constantly getting rewarded for climaxing as soon as possible.) Because women place a lot more emphasis on the context of sex, pay attention to where it takes place. A woman needs more time to feel the sexual sensations, and if she's feeling anxious, that anxiety will get in the way. She'll also need more foreplay, and that's impossible if you're out in the woods, steps away from a boys club camp!

A woman is also more likely to interpret your choice of settings as an indication of how much you value her. If you constantly have sex in places where she can't relax or feel valued, she may avoid the entire experience to avoid what she perceives as the "sleaziness" of it. It's sometimes difficult for teens and young adults to find respectful places to enjoy lovemaking. However, keep in mind the importance of the setting, and do your best to make it pleasant. Your partner will be more inclined to relax, make noise, and get into the act if she's not trying to have sex with you in your dorm closet while your roommate is sleeping!

Some women enjoy the possibility of being discovered by strangers in an outdoor or other environment, but it's not the norm. Women are far more likely to appreciate a relaxed, pleasant setting — and a man who makes sure that she's comfortable, pays attention to little details (like the lighting, scents, music), and provides anything she needs, including a lot of kissing and foreplay.

When the location isn't the best, Ladies, don't immediately assume that the gent doesn't value or respect you. Be positive, and don't internalize and exaggerate. Depending on his family and home situation, it's very difficult for a young boyfriend to have access to good places for having sex. Of course, you can always encourage his mother and father to join a weekly bowling league or golf tournament!!!

And when you're older and have more locations available, don't insist on always having sex in the same place. Try to compromise with your partner on location, perhaps by using more variety. (Time to christen that other room?) For more on how to vary the "where" of sex in a long-term, established relationship, see Chapter 15.

To grasp just how much women notice details that men don't, try this experiment: Take a piece of paper and write down everything you can remember about your first date with your partner. Have your mate do the same — without conferring. Then when you're both finished, compare notes.

A woman tends to remember what she and her date wore, including the color and style of every piece of clothing — except anything that she didn't see! She'll remember a lot more of the conversation, and she may even recall some exact sentences that were exchanged. She's more likely to remember what kind of music was playing in the car, how much lighting was in the restaurant, if the waiter was polite or rude, and if anything was unusual in any way. If you ask the woman to tell you about the date, she'll give far more details. The man will usually give a very brief summary, and when asked specifically about the above elements, won't be able to recall what he was wearing that night, much less what she was wearing! However, if he noticed something sexual about the woman (like her big breasts), *that's* the information he's likely to remember!

For more on making your sexual experiences more rewarding, see Chapters 14 and 15 on sex, Chapter 16 on lighting the fire and keeping it lit, and Chapter 24 for ways to rekindle your flame.

HOW to Have Sex

Because sex is an extremely intimate activity, it's best when both people are equally involved in giving and receiving pleasure. That makes the experience more reciprocal and keeps the power in the relationship more evenly balanced. ***Note:*** The goal of sex is *not* orgasm; it's giving and receiving pleasure and having fun with your partner. And the bottom line of how to have sex is that it should be *fun* for both partners.

If you don't like the man or woman enough to focus on him or give her pleasure, or to reciprocate his or her pleasuring of you, then you shouldn't be having sex with that person. If you have to fantasize about someone else to submit to sex with your mate, then you and your partner need to either fix the relationship or end it. Or perhaps it's way too early for the two of you to be involved in such an intimate activity, and you just need to wait for your emotions and your relationship to catch up to your sexual desires.

Orgasms just naturally occur when you're relaxed and comfortable and the sexual sensations increase past a certain point. But women usually need a lot more time than men to let the sensations cross into their awareness. A woman of any age is usually more able to feel sexual pleasure when she receives more foreplay, including manual and oral stimulation.

However, if the woman is worried about what the man thinks of her, anxious about whether or not she should even be having sex, or is having sex to be loved, the anxiety will interfere with the sexual sensations. So she often finds sex better in a more permanent relationship. And of course, the man who has an investment in the relationship is more likely to take the time to give her the foreplay she needs. In contrast, a man who is only out for his own pleasure is far more likely to do a "Wham-Bam-Thank-You-Ma'am!"

Avoiding STDs and Unwanted Pregnancies

Over the past century, modern medicine has battled fatal STDs and emerged victorious — only to have other STDs take their place. For example, after many years, the once fatal syphilis was finally cured with the discovery of penicillin. Then for a few years, most common STDs were eliminated and the physical threat of casual sex seemed eradicated. Unfortunately, however, other STDs soon emerged to do havoc. At the present time, AIDS is both fatal and incurable, while herpes and genital warts are incurable, but not life-threatening. In time, those diseases may be wiped out, and others may emerge. But all things considered, it's extremely important to have safe sex whenever you decide to have sex.

Soooooo . . . that brings us to this section, where we have to discuss some important realities. I've included this information not to scare the living daylights out of you or to make you *phobic* (irrationally fearful) of sex — but to help you take normal, rational precautions during sex so you can keep it healthy and fun.

You're the only person who can decide whether or not you should have sex — for the first time or with a particular partner. However, if you're going to have sex, always have it responsibly. It takes only one mistake to mess up a lot of lives. The amount of time, energy, and cost it takes to protect yourself is so little in comparison to the amount of heartache and stress caused when you don't! Even if you don't get pregnant or acquire a STD, you may spend weeks worrying about it if you don't use proper protection.

So here are the absolutes that must be followed to have responsible adult sex: No method of birth control is 100 percent effective (except abstinence, of course) — *not ever.* Every method, even the most effective, has a chance of failing. Although the percentage of failures may be small considering the entire group of people having sex while using that method, if you're in the small percentage that ends up pregnant or gets someone else pregnant, you're still going to be a very unhappy camper.

As for STDs, the latex condom is the best method presently available to help prevent their transmission during sex. But the latex condom is not foolproof; you can still acquire many STDs while using it. For example, most STDs can be passed orally, and many can be passed through touch. Also, people frequently aren't aware that they have a STD until *after* they've passed it on to someone else. And some people can even be "carriers," passing herpes on, for example, without ever getting the symptoms of herpes themselves. The symptoms of STDs can mimic other diseases, and some don't have any obvious symptoms. And remember, anyone from any social class can be a carrier. So to be safe*r*, *always* use a new latex condom for every act of sex and try to limit your sexual contacts.

To protect against both STDs and pregnancy, it's best to use *two* forms of birth control — a fresh latex condom, along *with* another highly effective form of birth control (like the pill, contraceptive implants, contraceptive shots, the IUD, the sponge, or the diaphragm) for every episode of sex. But keep in mind that even these precautions won't completely protect you from all STDs and unwanted pregnancies. So take that into consideration when deciding whether or not to indulge at this time with this particular person.

The bottom line is: Any time you have sex with someone, some risk is involved. That's another reason to carefully consider whether or not you want to have sex with someone *before* you have it. If he or she isn't special, do you really want to take the risk?

Consult a gynecologist or a doctor at Planned Parenthood. Based on your history and medical exam, the doctor can recommend a birth control method that's best for you. Use this, along with a latex condom, to help protect yourself and your partner from pregnancy and STDs.

If you're going to have sex with a woman who isn't on any of these methods, use an appropriate form of spermicide along with the latex condom. In addition to the condom and spermicide, you may also wish to withdraw your penis prior to ejaculation to provide even more protection. Also, while you can see if you're using a condom, you can't really see the woman's protection. Many a woman has deliberately tricked a man into getting her pregnant. So men, don't be naïve. Use your head, and if you're not sure that a partner is using a second form of birth control, supply a second yourself.

Keep in mind that someone can tell you he doesn't have any STDs, while carrying one at the same time! If you don't feel comfortable asking your partner to wear a condom or use contraceptive pills or devices, then you should reconsider whether you feel comfortable enough to have sex with that person. Similarly, if you don't feel comfortable talking about sex — asking your partner if he or she has or has had any STDs, then you're not comfortable enough to be having sex with that person.

See the sidebar in Chapter 15 for more information on STDs and pregnancies. You can also find a wealth of material on the subject at *AOL Keyword: Health* and www.plannedparenthood.com.

Being Honest with Yourself

It's extremely important that you always be honest with yourself — and face your life and its challenges in a calm, direct, mature, down-to-earth, realistic way. Being honest with yourself includes admitting that you're not perfect (because no one is), and that as an imperfect human, you find doing some things extremely difficult. Acknowledge these things and, if they're important, either find a way to do them more easily or change the situation to eliminate the pressure. But don't just deny the problem until you really mess up your life.

For example, if you want to have sex right now no matter what, don't try to hide that desire from yourself. Don't try to convince yourself that you'll never have sex before love or marriage, then get drunk at a party and have sex on the spur of the moment without using any protection. Delaying sex until marriage is difficult, but perhaps your religion and family and friends think you should. Fine. But factor in your ability to live up to that standard. If you feel yourself weakening, don't just put it out of your mind and go to the party. Trust me — many people end up pregnant that way. If you want to have sex right now no matter what, admit it — then get those two forms of protection and use them. If you're not currently on birth control, carry spermicide and latex condoms with you. You can still try to avoid having sex. But if you feel yourself giving in, at least you'll be protected, and your decision won't bring another unwanted baby into the world.

And if you only want sex when you're drinking and you really and sincerely do want to wait, take some other precautions. Try masturbating to orgasm before you attend a party to reduce your sex drive. But just to be safe, tuck some latex condoms and spermicide into your purse, wallet, or glove compartment, and try to forget about them. Then if you do find your resolve weakening that night or another, you can remember that you have them.

You can also avoid drinking or taking drugs before and at the party so you'll have more self-control at your fingertips. You can also arrange never to be alone with someone you find sexually tempting. Or you can skip the party altogether and get busy doing some kind of *competing behavior* — something you can't possibly do and have sex at the same time! Try a movie with mom, donating your time to the homeless, taking your kid sister to the park, whatever.

With regard to any situation: If you're not feeling like yourself or if you're not sure if you should be doing something (for example, having sex with a partner), you're usually better off waiting until you *are* sure — or at least until you feel better and can make a calm, mature decision.

The point is, there are many ways to handle any situation, including sex. The only really rotten way is to lie to yourself, and end up pregnant or carrying a STD, harming another person in the process. So always be honest with yourself about *you*, your strengths, your weaknesses, and how you *really* think and feel — not how you're supposed to think and feel, or how someone else wants you to think and feel. Then if you do decide to participate, go into the situation with your eyes wide open. That will reduce your emotional risk. If you're aware of the risk you're taking and accept it, you'll be better prepared to deal with any repercussions.

Before you decide to have sex with someone, ask yourself the following questions — and make sure you're being honest with yourself:

1. How long have I known this person? Is this person really special to me? Do I want to remember this person as being one of my sex partners?

2. Am I really special to him or her? What behavioral evidence do I have to know that I am special, other than him saying, "I love you," or giving other forms of flattery to encourage me?

3. What's likely to be my partner's motivation for having sex with me? What factors are motivating me? What do I hope to accomplish by having sex with this person at this time?

4. Do I want to remember this time and place as being the first time we had sex?

5. What risks am I taking with regard to STDs, pregnancy, and the relationship if I decide to indulge? How am I going to handle those risks? Do I have the protection necessary to protect myself from unnecessary STDs or pregnancy? How might having sex with this person change our future relationship together? How will I handle any risks to the relationship?

6. Can I handle it if the SEIR doesn't work out the way I want it to? Will I be able to chalk it up to "experience" and be happy with my decision, no matter what the outcome?

7. Am I thinking clearly? Am I under the influence of alcohol or drugs, feeling bad about myself, or stressed or fatigued? Is any other factor influencing my decision?

Sex is one of the most important activities you can ever share with someone. Sex is also a natural, healthy drive, like eating, drinking, sleeping, and curiosity. And sex with the "right" person at the "right" time is a lot of fun. So use your head, as well as your heart, when deciding to participate. Once you've decided to have sex, have fun and enjoy it. See Chapters 14 through 16 and Chapter 24 for more on making sex an enjoyable part of your love life.

❤ ❤ ❤ ❤ ❤ ❤

Another One Bites the Dust — Sex Too Soon!

Dear Dr. Kate,

My age: 21   **My gender:** Female

I started seeing this guy two weeks ago, and things seemed great. He was exactly what I'd been looking for to recover from the breakup of my six-year relationship. We got pretty close, and ended up having sex. Since then, he hasn't called. Should I call him, or just let him be? My friends say not to call; if he likes you, let him chase you. What do you think?

Dear Recovering,

You're trying to recover too fast. Your friends are correct about not calling him and instead, letting him be the aggressor, but did they also remind you not to have sex with anyone so quickly?

First of all, there's no way you could know that "he was exactly what you had been looking for" in two weeks time. He may have seemed that way, but at two weeks, you don't know much at all about him.

Many men lose interest in women who have sex with them early on. It doesn't matter if they pushed for it; they just lose interest and stop calling. Some men are happy with the conquest and move on to conquests elsewhere. Others just feel uncomfortable, because they weren't expecting sex so soon. Instead of continuing to date the woman and letting the relationship catch up with the sex, they avoid the woman to avoid feeling uncomfortable.

And yes, there are guys out there who don't have either of these two reactions. The problem is they all look alike on the front end, and by the time you know which guy is which, it's already too late to do anything about it. If you have sex, you can't undo it. On the other hand, if you wait awhile before sex, many of the men who are only interested in carnal pursuits will drop out. And you'll get a better chance to see the man's character and behavior over time.

You also need to be concerned about getting too emotionally involved too quickly. You were in a very long relationship, especially for a woman your age. It's time to hang loose and be single for awhile. Date men casually — no sex. If you get intensely involved too soon, you may end up in a rebound relationship. Then you'll just have to break up and deal with the pain all over again.

Don't call him. If he calls you, don't have sex with him again for a long time (try to wait about three months if you can). Let the relationship and your emotions catch up first.

All the best. Please let me know what you decide to do and how it works out by writing me an update letter.

Dr. Kate

Chapter 8

When (And Why) to Talk Exclusivity

. . . .

In This Chapter

▶ Being realistic about your maturity level, your relationship goal, and your life stage

▶ Examining your feelings and the timing in a relationship

▶ Knowing when to commit, when to date casually, and when to move on

. . . .

*O*K, what if you've found a partner, grown more emotionally and physically intimate, shared more and more special moments, confided more and more secrets, and enjoyed sex together? Now what? What do you do next?

Well, maybe you decide to have an *exclusive* relationship with your partner — you decide to be emotionally committed and sexually monogamous with one another. In this chapter, I discuss when exclusivity is a good idea, and when it's not. I review issues to consider — like your feelings for one another, and your relationship goal, maturity levels, dating histories, life stages, and timing. I explain why casual dating makes more sense than serial monogamy. And finally, I encourage you to explore your relationship expectations to decide if they're timely and wise.

The WHY of Exclusivity

When the time seems "right," you may want to become exclusive with your partner. There are times when exclusivity is healthy for you and helpful to a developing relationship. When are those times? Read on!

Limiting your physical and emotional risks

As I discuss in Chapter 7, becoming sexually involved with someone includes risking sexually transmitted diseases (STDs). If you or your partner have sex with other people, your STD risk increases exponentially. You multiply your risk by how many partners you and your partner have, how many partners those people have, and so on. So being sexually exclusive greatly limits your risk of contracting an STD.

In addition, the longer you continue to have sex with someone, the greater the emotional risk you're taking. If that person left you today, it would hurt more than if he'd left you months ago — before you became so attached. Being sexually exclusive with one another makes it more likely that the emotional attachment will grow between the two of you, not between you and others.

So it's easy to see why people usually desire exclusivity as their relationship progresses. The closer you get to someone, the less you want to share those special experiences with anyone else, and the less you want your partner to share himself or herself with others. After all, one reason those experiences are so special is because you're sharing them only with each other.

Increasing your sexual and emotional comfort and closeness

Being sexually exclusive also strengthens the emotional intimacy and the psychological bond between you. You're sharing an incredibly intimate act only with one another because you're more emotionally intimate with one another than with anyone else. In effect, you're now *making love,* not just having sex, and that distinction can help the relationship grow. Making a commitment to be exclusive with one another allows both parties to relax a little. You're choosing to concentrate on one another over the myriad of other possibilities. You're acknowledging that this relationship is special — that it will be there in the future. You call one another "girlfriend" and "boyfriend" — and let the world know that you're a couple. And when you gradually relax, that comfort also enhances your enjoyment of sex. So the emotional intimacy reinforces the sexual intimacy, and the sexual intimacy reinforces the emotional intimacy in one big, continuous circle.

The WHEN of Exclusivity

Just as anything "*good*" or healthy can become "*bad*" or unhealthy if used at an inappropriate time, exclusivity is healthy only when certain conditions are present. I describe those conditions in the following sections.

Really loving, not just lusting

It makes sense that you want to commit only to someone you love. Otherwise, why settle down together? But keep in mind that infatuation and lust can mimic love. (For an explanation of the differences between love, infatuation, and lust, see Chapter 2.) If you haven't seen your partner in person three to four times per week for three to four months, the powerfully intense feeling you're experiencing may be lust or infatuation, not love.

Before you make a commitment to your partner, make sure you're really feeling love for him or her. Make sure you've known one another long enough and seen one another often enough that the feeling is reliable and stable — that you can count on it to be there today and for the foreseeable future.

Sharing the same relationship goal

Does your partner ever want to get married or get married and have children? About when might that be? If you don't know the answer, it's too soon to commit to each other. You may be committing yourself to someone who's basically incompatible. And if you already know that you and your partner *don't* share a relationship goal (if you want marriage and children, but your partner doesn't, for example), it's a mistake to commit to that person.

Unfortunately, many marriage-minded women make that mistake. Often, the woman unconsciously hopes that her partner will change his mind and realize his true path toward marriage and kids. She may even waste years wishing and hoping. But of course, wishing and hoping don't make it so. In the meantime, she passes up valuable opportunities to find someone more compatible, and squanders many of her childbearing years.

If you disagree with someone's relationship goal, it's OK to date one another casually. Just don't put all your eggs in one basket, particularly when you already know that your partner is not compatible with you in this crucial area. If you can date your friend while also dating others, fine. But if dating that person distracts you from finding someone more compatible, it's usually best to terminate the relationship and search for a more compatible partner.

Having enough casual dating experience

If you're 18 and haven't dated much, it's a mistake to settle in with one person. You need to date a variety of people before you're ready to settle down with anyone in particular. The same is true if you've just gotten divorced at age 38 after being married to the same person since age 18, or because you've just left the priesthood or convent after 40 years! Or maybe you came from a country where young people didn't date, or attended all-girl schools and concentrated on your studies, or you were shy and awkward. Whatever the case, you need to *casually date* a variety of people — to date around without having sex — to figure out what you need in a relationship and who's more compatible with you. If you settle down before doing that, you may later wake up and want to explore dating again.

Sharing similar relationship stages

In Chapter 2, I discuss **The Love Cycle** and how we all go in and out of various relationship stages throughout our lifetime. To make a committed, exclusive relationship with someone, you need to be in a compatible relationship stage. For example, if you've just recently divorced, widowed, or broken up, you're not ready for another commitment right now. You're in the *Loss and Letting Go Stage*, so you're not compatible with someone who's been in the *Finding Love Stage* for years and is more than ready for a committed, exclusive relationship.

You still need to grieve your loss, get closure, and heal. Then you have to start over by being single for awhile and gradually increasing your contact with other people. It's normal to feel quite needy, sad, and insecure at these stressful times. If you grieve effectively, you'll eventually heal and be able to start over. But you can't skip over the grieving part just because you want to.

If you jump right into another relationship during one of these traumatic times, you're probably choosing a partner for reasons that are important to you now (to avoid being alone at night), not reasons that will become important to you in the future (because you're highly compatible with that person). Once you get better, you'll notice your incompatibilities, and end your "rebound relationship." To save both of you the stress of breaking up, don't commit to be exclusive with anyone when you're not in a compatible relationship stage. Instead, acknowledge that you're not ready yet, and continue to date casually until you're ready for more.

Sharing similar life stages and timing

Just as you and your partner need to be in compatible relationship stages before committing to one another, you also need to be in compatible life stages at the same time. Timing is important in any normal relationship. If you and your partner are in different life stages, you may be incompatible at the current time — even if you'd be compatible at a different time.

For example, if you're a 29-year-old, never-married male graduate student, with no children, who wants to get a doctorate and secure a tenured position at a university, you're in a very different place from a 35-year-old divorced woman with two kids who wants to get remarried and have another child in the near future. You still have more grad school, an internship, and a few more moves before you secure a teaching position at a suitable university. You want to get settled careerwise before you marry and start a family. However, your 35-year-old girlfriend may not want to uproot her two kids to move across the country with you as you pursue your dreams from state to state. If she shares custody of those children with the father, she may not be able to take them out-of-state. If she marries you now, she'd lose the alimony her husband is paying her, and you can't support her and the kids on the peanuts you're making as a research fellow. You'll eventually make a fine salary, but not for several years yet. And your girlfriend doesn't have that much time. She wants to have another child while she still can.

Although you both share the same long-term relationship goal (getting married and raising a family), you're in different life stages, and the timing is off. So it would be a mistake for the two of you to commit to each other. It's just delaying the inevitable breakup and preventing your girlfriend from meeting other men who may be ready for marriage and kids now — or at least way before you are.

There are all kinds of scenarios like these. Life is complicated. And as I mention in Chapter 4, it's fairly common to meet the "right" person at the "wrong" time. You may share the same long-term relationship goal with someone, but because of where you are in **The Love Cycle** or in accomplishing your life goals, you may not share the same short-term relationship goal or timing. So committing to one another would be a mistake. It could tie you up in an unfulfilling relationship for years, and keep you from meeting someone who's more compatible with you at this time.

Being emotionally mature

Maturity is a little difficult to define. When you're *sexually mature,* your reproductive organs have developed to the point that they're fully grown and able to reproduce. Similarly, *emotional maturity* refers to how emotionally developed you are, and how fast you're growing and changing emotionally. Until you reach emotional maturity, you grow and change a great deal emotionally and psychologically as you meet various people and encounter different life experiences. So to become emotionally mature, you first need to experience life. Then you need to gather knowledge from your experiences and apply that knowledge in the present and future to live wisely and avoid mistakes. While people can mature faster by encountering more experiences at a faster rate (by relocating from country to country as a military brat, for example, or by raising younger siblings when both parents die), most people living a normal life take awhile to acquire enough experience. Acquiring that knowledge base and being able to see "the big picture" of life takes time, and some people never get there.

In my observation, women tend to mature around age 27 to 28, and men around age 30. Before the age of emotional maturity, both sexes change a great deal, which is normal. As you add more experiences and learn from them, you change how you relate to the world. So committing to someone before you reach maturity is a big risk — betting that you'll feel the same way toward your partner through all the changes you'll make. Since your partner is usually in the same age range and can also be expected to change a great deal, there's no way to guarantee that both of you will change in the same direction. And just like relationship and life stages, maturity can't be rushed. If you or your partner isn't mature enough to settle down, it's a mistake to force the issue by marrying one another at this time.

On the other hand, if you're not ready for marriage, but you have dated enough, being exclusive with another person can move the relationship forward and give you valuable experience. Just as it's important to date casually before selecting a lifelong mate, it's helpful to have some long-term relationships before finally settling down in marriage. You'll learn a lot from them — knowledge you can later use to choose a better partner and be a better spouse.

Being mutually committed

Some people deliberately have sex with more than one person to decrease the likelihood that they'll become emotionally involved with anybody. For commitment to advance your relationship, it has to be mutual. If you and your partner are supposed to be having an exclusive relationship, but you're being faithful and he or she isn't (or vice versa), then there's no real commitment or exclusivity taking place.

Relationships should always be fairly reciprocal. When one person wants to be special and the other doesn't, the person who cares more generally has less power in the relationship. The other partner quickly takes that person for granted and cares less.

So, if you suspect that your partner is having sex with others, you may want to reconsider having sex with him. If you aren't special enough that he would share sex exclusively with you, why would you want to share such a special experience with him? If you resist having sex with your partner when other people are having sex with him, acting differently at least distinguishes you as special in one way, if not exactly the way you'd like.

Avoiding the Serial Monogamy Trap

I sometimes get letters from people who practice *serial monogamy* — that is, they date one person at a time until the relationship ends, and then they start over with another person. If they date more than one person at a time, they feel like they're cheating. If you start with that idea, though, how can you ever figure out who to be with? *Dating* is the process by which you compare the way you think and feel around one person to how you think and feel around someone else. Only by comparing and noticing the differences can you figure out who is more compatible with you.

When you only date one person at a time and try to take that relationship as far as it can go, it's easy to doubt the relationship in the future. How do you know if he or she is the *most* compatible person for you — or even one of the most? You may seem compatible, especially during the first three months of infatuation. However, once you begin to find out your partner's liabilities — and believe me, everyone has some — you may begin to wonder whether you should continue your exclusive relationship. If you think you've made a mistake and want to stop being exclusive and start dating around, your mate will probably feel rejected and hurt about his or her change in status. In fact, the two of you will probably break up shortly afterward.

Expecting someone to become exclusive with you without first dating you for a considerable period of time is also illogical. When someone *is* willing to do that, look for the possible reasons. Is he on the rebound? Is there some financial reward? Is she trying to escape something that she doesn't want to deal with? If you haven't had time to become special to your partner, why does he or she need to see you as special? How long has it been since she's had a good relationship? Is that neediness getting in the way of his judgment?

Instead of going too fast and then trying to back step, try to move the relationship along in a slower, steadier, more forward-moving direction. Even if you think someone will turn out to be very compatible, it's usually best to keep dating others until you've dated your partner long enough and often enough to know that the two of you really are compatible and in love. Table 8-1 summarizes when and when not to consider commitment and exclusivity in your relationship.

Table 8-1	When to Consider Commitment and Exclusivity
When to Consider . . .	*When NOT to Consider . . .*
When you've seen your partner in person at least 3 to 4 times a week for at least 3 to 4 months, and you both continue to experience intense pleasurable feelings for each other.	When you've just met your partner and don't know if your strong feelings are really love, or just lust or infatuation.
When you and your partner are emotionally mature.	When you or your partner are quite emotionally immature.
When you've dated enough to know that this person is pretty compatible with you.	When you don't have enough dating experience to know.

(continued)

Table 8-1 *(continued)*	
When to Consider . . .	*When NOT to Consider . . .*
After you've casually dated a number of people and are ready to commit to a longer-term relationship.	When you need to explore casual relationships with a variety of people.
When you and your partner are in life and relationship stages where commitment is a good idea.	When you or your partner need to heal before settling down with anyone (for example, at least 2 years after divorce or death of a spouse, and a considerable period of time following a serious breakup).
When you and your partner share a similar relationship goal, and committing to one another is a step toward that goal.	When you and your partner disagree about your relationship goal, and committing to one another is a step away from achieving your goal.
When you want to have sex only with each other.	When you want to have sex with other people as well.

Being Realistic

Use the information presented in this chapter to help you decide if commitment is right for you and your partner at this time. If you're not sure, list the pros and cons on a piece of paper. Remember to face the situation realistically — consider what the situation really is, not what you want it to be. To learn more about whether the two of you are compatible, see Chapter 4 and use *The Dr. Kate Compatibility Quiz* and *The Dr. Kate Communication Quiz* in the appendixes. To learn more about marriage and its timing, see Chapter 17.

If your partner is pressing you for commitment and you don't feel ready, pinpoint what leads you to feel the way you do, and discuss your feelings with your mate. Similarly, if you want commitment and your mate doesn't, use all this information to understand your differences and decide what to do about them. By facing all these factors realistically, you can make a choice that's best for you.

Chapter 9

Is It Time to Cohabit?

In This Chapter

▶ Realistically examining your reasons for cohabiting

▶ Knowing when living together is a good idea and when it's not

▶ Maximizing your cohabiting potential, if you make that choice

*T*hink back to your childhood. Did you have any trouble getting along with your mom, dad, sisters, or brothers? How about when you were in your teens? How about now — do you have any family members that you dearly love, but if you spend too much time with them, you find yourself going absolutely *nnnnuuuutttttttsss*? How about at work — are there any people who just get on your nerves? Most workplaces report that their greatest problem is staff relationships — helping employees get along together. And that's when they're only spending eight hours, five days a week together. If human interactions are so problematic during the eight hours people generally spend together at work, imagine how much energy and effort it takes to get along with someone 24/7!

Living with someone day and night — through ups, downs, fatigue, sickness, hunger, and stress — can be a real challenge, even when you love that person dearly.

In Chapter 8, I discuss when and when not to become committed and exclusive with your partner. In this chapter, I consider when and when not to *cohabit* — live together — when you're *not* married to one another. Cohabiting is a special kind of commitment — one that puts a lot more strain on the relationship than just promising to be sexually and emotionally faithful to one another.

In this chapter, I explore when cohabiting is a good idea — and when it's not — so you can make the decision for yourself. And in case you do decide to live together, I give you tips for making the experience more satisfying and productive.

When Living Together Is a Good Idea

As one of my clients once said, "Living together is a *lot* different from dating!" I'll say. When you live with someone, you experience each other at your best and your worst. Although you can keep up appearances while dating, managing to look your best for a block of time, you can't keep that going around the clock. And when you see each other 24/7, you also see the sick, tired, hungry, grouchy, smelly, bedhead, no makeup, stinky breath, 5+-o'clock-shadow version of each other. And you get to *hear* one another at your worst, too — making all those rather odd sounds that humans sometimes make.

So given all this, *when* is cohabiting a good idea? Thanks for asking! Read on.

When you've dated enough, but are not yet ready to get married

If you're 24 and have been dating since you were 15, but don't feel ready for marriage yet, then living with someone may be just the ticket. Cohabiting will give you the chance to discover how another person perceives your behavior and how you need to grow. You'll also practice empathy and patience. When the inevitable problems occur, you can discuss them assertively and forge satisfactory compromises. Then when you eventually marry someone, all that practice and experience should come in handy to help you be a better spouse.

Recently divorced, no kids, not ready to remarry

What if you're emotionally mature enough to marry, but not ready because you're currently healing from a previous relationship or marriage? If you've dated your current partner long enough, you might decide to live together for awhile.

Of course, if you were formerly married a long time, it'd be better to get some recent dating experience under your belt before you start living with a new partner. However, if you just feel the need to connect more firmly with one person, moving in with that person is far better than jumping right into marriage. That way, if you find that you and your new partner are incompatible after you've healed from your past relationship, splitting up will be much easier than if you had married on the rebound.

Of course, this only works if neither of you has children. If either of you does, it's not wise to put them through the stress of revolving live-in mates.

When enduring a temporary, but long-term, stressful situation together

If you and your partner are attending graduate school, living together may be a great idea. Graduate students have very little time to date, and living with an emotionally supportive partner can be helpful in getting you through the intense academic stress. Money is usually scarce in graduate school (affording dates is tough anyway), and two people can often live more cheaply than one. If the environment is also stressful — for example, if your school is located in Alaska or one of the Dakotas and it's 10 degrees below zero outside — having a warm bod in bed with you has even more benefits!

If graduation finds the two of you very attached, you can move together to a place you both find acceptable. But such moves have also broken up relationships, so it's probably better to experience the change as single, cohabiting partners first — before finalizing a marriage. There are other situations where similar reasoning applies — for example, enlisting in the armed services, joining the Peace Corps, or going to a third-world country as a temporary, but long-term missionary or relief worker. In general, whenever you have to endure some kind of stressful environment for several years, but you're eventually going to return to a more relaxed, normal environment, it's usually better to cohabit rather than marry.

When moving from place to place to further your career

What if you need to relocate frequently to advance in your profession? In academia, for example, there are only so many vacancies at different levels at any one time at any institution. If you want to move up the ranks from professor to university president, you'll probably have to change institutions and cities. In companies with a national or global presence, people commonly move around to build their resumes and advance their careers. In the arts, actors and musicians frequently travel and live on location as part of the job. In news, the anchors, reporters, sportscasters, and weathermen move from town to town until they reach a market where they want to stay.

Needless to say, jumping around from city to city or country to country does not a great relationship make. It has also made mincemeat out of many marriages. So it may be better to live with your partner until you think you're done moving for the foreseeable future — or you believe that the two of you will be able to work it out if another transfer occurs.

To stay financially independent

If you have a lot of money or, conversely, if you have next to none, you might also choose not to marry. If you're very wealthy, you might prefer to remain single rather than risk splitting up assets in the event of a divorce. Sure, you can get a prenuptial agreement, but asking for one can provoke a lot of bad feelings, and you can still end up in an extended property battle.

Conversely, if you're living on social security or some other kind of aid and marrying someone means getting fewer benefits, you might choose to cohabit rather than marry. Similarly, it might be more practical to remain single if you're receiving alimony after a divorce. After all, what would happen if you marry a new partner and then divorce? You might find yourself much worse off than if you'd just lived with your new partner instead of marrying him.

To preserve certain benefits

Sometimes people end up in complicated relationships where it seems better not to rock the boat and cause extreme changes in living situations. These situations are largely practical, involving money or restrictions imposed by the outside world. For example, if a couple wants to divorce, but one partner is suffering from a serious illness and needs the other's insurance coverage or other benefits to survive, it may be better if they avoid divorce for the time being. That's particularly true when that person would be unable to obtain insurance or similar benefits on her own. At the same time, the couple is not emotionally married. Both may even be seeing other people. Yet divorce and remarriage is out of the question, at least for the time being, due to the practical problems that would arise if they got divorced. So they stay married and live with other people instead.

Today's world is complicated, and some practical considerations may warrant cohabiting rather than marrying, at least temporarily. Please note, however, that this is *not* the answer to the usual extramarital affair. In the overwhelming number of cases, married partners should either choose to stay married and be faithful — or divorce and seek other partners.

When the end goal is cohabitation

Partners who have previously been married to other people often don't want to get married again. If two of you find one another and decide that cohabitation is the end goal for you, living together is fine. The relationship can be happy — provided you both continue to feel the same way about your relationship goal.

Some people prefer cohabiting to marriage; they just feel it works better for them. Perhaps they have an independent streak that feels trapped in marriage. Cohabiting helps them relax and enjoy their partner; it helps them be a better partner as well.

Older couples

Older partners often feel less compelled to marry again. If they've both raised families and their spouses are now dead or divorced, they're probably not going to start another family. If no one in their families, neighborhood, or circle of friends cares whether they're formally married, they might opt to live together instead.

When NOT to Live Together

Many people are happy when their relationship has progressed to the point where their partner wants to live with them. To them, this move signifies that their mate is willing to become more committed. Not only is the person dating them on a regular basis; he or she is now willing to commit to spending most free time together as well. Both parties answer the phone, and people know they're a couple. They buy things together and share responsibilities and activities like cleaning, cooking, paying bills, socializing, and sleeping. They're faithful, and they act like a more permanent couple. So given all this good stuff, why isn't cohabiting always a good idea? Read on!

To determine marriage compatibility

Many people think of living together as a step toward marriage, which, unfortunately, it isn't. The myth suggests that cohabiting before marriage is like a trial marriage. By living with one another in advance, you can figure out if you're compatible enough to marry. This myth seems very reasonable and logical. But if it were true, then couples who lived together successfully would be expected to marry each other and stay married longer.

Studies show, however, that people who live together before marriage tend to go on to marry other people, not one another. In addition, cohabiting successfully before marriage does not guarantee a happy, long-term, or successful marriage. Rather, couples who live together before marriage get divorced at about the same rate as couples who don't.

In general, living together lacks many of the plusses of marriage, but it does include many of the negatives. For example, marriage carries extra status because it's a rite of passage. Relatives and others usually treat the couple like adults able to make their own decisions. A title change even accompanies the promotion — the "Ms." becomes "Mrs." People act like you're a couple, so you feel more coupled. You get married in front of your friends and family. This isn't a trial run — it's the real enchilada. It's time to pull out all the stops and be the best partners ever, because marriage is the end of the line.

In contrast, people tend to have mixed reactions to cohabiting couples. They may harbor sexist attitudes and assume that the man must be holding out: "If he really loved her, he'd marry her, so something must be wrong." Or they may think: "He's still on the market. After all, if he isn't married, he's still fair game, right?"

When you're not married, buying things together can also be more difficult. You're more of a credit risk because you can split up a lot easier, leaving the lease, house, car, or whatever dangling. And whom should people invite to weddings, birthdays, holiday celebrations, and other shindigs? How do they address more formal invitations? Do they list both of you, or say "So-and-so and Guest?"

At the same time, living with someone comes complete with all the negative aspects of marriage. Your partner gets to see you when you're definitely *not* at your best — and vice versa. Is that the suave, sophisticated, desirable person you once dated?

Many partners behave worse when cohabiting. They take one another for granted. They put off having sex because they can now have it almost any time. They drift apart emotionally and sexually/physically. And if one partner actually wants to be married rather than just cohabiting, that person usually becomes frustrated and resentful over time — until the relationship begins to fall apart.

When your relationship goal differs

If you want to get married and start a family, but your partner doesn't, then living together only delays the inevitable breakup. Your mate probably won't change his mind in the near future. Meanwhile, you're passing up other potential partners who do share your relationship goal.

A woman has very few good childbearing years. Although she's physically able to have children at puberty, she's not emotionally mature and ready until she's about 26 to 28. Yet the odds of her having a baby with birth defects increase beginning at about age 35. So that leaves a total of seven to nine years when the woman is in her childbearing prime, both physically and psychologically.

When a woman is involved in a self-defeating relationship but loves her partner, she does what people often do when faced with a difficult issue — she ignores it. Yet as painful as it may be to break up with a man who doesn't share your relationship goal, it's nothing in comparison to how painful it will be when you wake up and realize that you've squandered your ability to have children.

In my opinion, no woman over the age of 26 should waste her time dating or living with a man who doesn't share her relationship goal — particularly if she wants children.

When one of you is afraid of marriage

A variation on the previous theme occurs when one or the other partner is actually afraid of marriage. Perhaps your mate was married before and feels like he was "taken to the cleaners" emotionally and financially. Or perhaps he believed that marriage and being a good husband meant making his wife happy. If his wife then divorced him, he may have learned the "wrong" lesson. Instead of realizing that no one can ever *make* someone else happy (after all, *you* have to make *yourself* happy), the man now believes that marriage is not for him, that he's a failure at it, and that any future attempts he makes will only result in more failure and pain.

Marriage to you doesn't bother him; marriage to *anyone* bothers him. Because he has irrational fears about marriage, he allows himself to avoid it and, in doing so, he never learns that there really wasn't anything to be afraid of.

If you end up living with a marriage-phobic partner, that person will never marry you. You are essentially giving your mate what he or she wants — without asking him or her to take a risk and marry you. For more on this topic, see Chapter 19.

If You're Going to Live Together

It's extremely important to discuss practical issues and potential problems *before* you move in together. If you and your partner disagree about something, it's far better to work it out in advance — while your motivation is high and you still have other options. That way, if you can't compromise successfully, you can always opt to continue living alone — while you still have an apartment! After you move in together, there's less incentive to please, more opportunity to take your partner for granted, and more trouble relocating.

Most couples fight over the same kind of things: money, sex, kids, family, friends, how to spend spare time, who'll do what around the house, and where the relationship is going. So discuss these problems before moving in. To get a head start, see the following sections.

Managing your moolah

Discuss how you'll handle the bills. Who will pay for what? Will you each pay certain bills from your own checking account, or will you get a joint account instead? Will you combine all your money, none of it, or just some of it? There isn't one right answer; many plans can work. Just discuss your ideas with one another in advance, and make a plan together.

Making time for sex

Don't expect your sex life to improve when you live together; it usually doesn't. In fact, it frequently gets worse. People often appreciate what is difficult to achieve and devalue things that come more easily. When they live together, many partners begin putting other activities ahead of sex, or postponing love-making because they're tired, or hungry, or it's late, or . . . , or . . . , or . . . .

Nip this problem in the bud — before it jeopardizes your emotional closeness. For more on sparking your love life, see Chapters 14 through 16 and Chapter 24 of this book. Check out www.drkate.com and **AOL Keyword: DrKate** for lots more advice I've written on this topic. You can also see *Rekindling Romance For Dummies* and *Sex For Dummies,* both written by Dr. Ruth Westheimer and published by John Wiley & Sons, Inc.

Disciplining the kids

Do either of you have children? If so, how will you handle the discipline? Do you both agree to use time-outs, and know how to use them effectively? How will you handle discipline of older children? Have you discussed reasonable expectations, as well as reasonable rewards and take-aways? Do you want your partner to direct the kids, too? If not, how will you avoid the children looking down on him or her? If you both have kids, how will you handle their interactions? What if some are older and some are younger? How will you explain that the older ones get more freedom because they're older — without alienating the younger kids?

Children have a way of quickly figuring out what they can get away with, and they will just naturally press their limits. It's extremely important to discuss how you'll manage them in advance. Decide on a plan, then carry it out consistently. If it needs changing, change it together, make the changes known to the kids, then follow those changes consistently. If you disagree with how your partner is handling a child — but the situation is not dangerous or physically abusive — don't interrupt your mate, embarrass him, challenge his authority, or reprimand him in front of the child. Instead, talk to him in private as soon as possible.

If you expect your mate to accept your children, and your children to accept your mate, it's important to act like he's part of the family, too. If you don't want your partner to direct or discipline the kids in any way, then your relationship probably won't work out long-term.

Even when you try to bring up every possible problem you can think of, other situations will arise that you've forgotten. So spend considerable time discussing as many potential problems in advance as possible. That way, you can create a consistent, stable, loving environment for your kids, while keeping your sanity and handling the unexpected in between.

Be careful when deciding to live together with children. It can be very confusing for the kids. Depending on the details of your situation, you may be better off living single until you decide to marry, then blending your family at that time. If you decide to live together with the kids, expect there to be problems, discuss them as much as possible in advance, and make a plan. Keep a united front with your partner, and make the house rules clear and consistent. And be sure to seek family counseling — with all family members present — as soon as possible when problems arise. Counseling can keep problems from getting out of hand and help your new family blend.

Fitting in family and friends

How will you handle seeing relatives and friends? Will all of them know that you're living together? Will you and your partner visit them together, as a couple? How much time will you spend seeing them alone? How will your family and friends take your decision to live together? If someone may be a problem, how are you going to handle that person? Discuss all these issues and more before you move in.

Spending your spare time

How will you spend the time you're not working or sleeping? How much of it do you want to spend together versus how much with other people? It's fine to occasionally do things with other people rather than each other, but you need to discuss how much time that will be and when (for example, what day of the week and what hours). If your friends and family get all your quality time and your sweetie gets you only at your worst, don't expect the relationship to thrive. Also, be sure to discuss how much time you'd like to spend hanging out together at home versus how much time you'd like to spend out and about — doing the town or just smelling the roses.

Distributing the domestic goddess duties

Who's the lucky person who gets garbage detail? Who scrubs the toilets? Mows the lawn? Takes the dog to the vet? Cooks? Does laundry? There's no right or wrong per se; many plans can work. But be sure to discuss your ideas in advance to avoid misassumptions that then lead to misunderstandings and hard feelings.

And what if the situation changes? What if your man gets laid off and you get a promotion, complete with more responsibilities and hours? Will your Romeo automatically take over more responsibility for the home? Or will he expect you to handle the housework and your day job, too? The more you know in advance about your honey's perspective on the pots and pans detail and other Happy Homemaker chores, the better.

If one of you is Mr./Ms. Clean and the other's the Slob of the Known World, take *extra* care to discuss how you'll handle those discrepancies. Will you hire a maid to help out? Will you designate a certain room as that partner's Hard Hat Area, agreeing to keep the overflow stashed there, with door tightly closed to protect the innocent? Trust me: This one needs to be discussed well in advance to avoid nuclear fallout.

And how much time do you want to spend vegging out versus taking care of household obligations and chores? Some people spend most of their waking time *moving* — always fixing, cleaning, or doing something. Others are enormously proficient couch potatoes as they recuperate from the stress of their day job. Again, there's no one right way. But the more you're upfront about each other's habits, the better.

Confidentially speaking

How do you and your partner feel about your priorities as a couple? In order for any couple to survive, there has to be a willingness to put your union first, as a top priority. That means that neither partner goes gossiping to their family about the other's flaws. Even if you're "mad as hell and you're not going to take it any more" (like the newscaster dude in the movie *Network*) — stuff it. Resist the urge to tell all to Mom, who never liked "that guy" in the first place. Remember, when everything calms down again and you've made up with *that guy*, Mom will still remember everything you told her — and she'll give you lots o' grief about taking him back. And she'll probably give him lots o' grief as well!

So make your partner your trusted ally and friend. Be loyal and keep confidences and secrets. Remember, you got close in the first place because you shared experiences with one another that you didn't share with other people. So keep the intimacy sacred, and don't let it all hang out with everyone else.

If you know you're likely to receive disapproval from family or friends, discuss it with your sweetie, and come to some kind of agreement about how you'll handle it. If a family member or friend tries to pry you apart, will you both talk to the offender together (preferred option)? Or will the partner related to or emotionally closest to that person have a little chat with him or her? Whatever you decide, make sure it's a joint decision between you and your mate, and remember to stand together as a united front.

Comparing relationship goals

Ahhh, here's the big issue: What is this arrangement all about? Is cohabiting a permanent goal for both of you? How long do you expect to live with one another? What do you expect to happen after that? Before you move in together, have the big pow-wow and get this out in the open.

It's enormously important to be on the same page with regard to your goal for this relationship, or you could easily end up hurt later. If you're going to rent an apartment or buy a house together — or if any of your possessions or finances are going to get intertwined — that relationship goal is going to make a big difference.

How committed is your mate to working out problems? How will you handle it if one of you wants to bail? What if your partner decides he doesn't like the suburban house and moves back to a city apartment by himself? How will you handle the mortgage? Whose name is on the house? The furniture loan? What does that mean in terms of your responsibility and payments? If your partner views this move as experimental, with little risk on his or her part, you may want to reconsider. Do you really want to take such a risk for someone who has so little invested in you and your relationship?

I strongly urge you to write down any agreements, compromises, and plans you make together. Then read the list aloud, give your partner a copy, keep a copy, post a copy in your joint home, and reread it periodically. If you do all these things, you'll both tend to notice four great outcomes:

- ✔ **You'll find it easier to notice any overlooked topics or details.**

- ✔ **You'll remember the information better.** Memory is very fragile, and people often forget details. The more senses you use to process information, the more likely you are to remember it. So when you write a list, you're using your sense of touch. When you read it, you see it. When you read it aloud, you also hear it. When you review it periodically, you're seeing it again, and the repetition also aids learning and retention. So you're much more likely to remember the details when you do all of these! And before you can act in a certain way, you certainly need to remember what you agreed to do, don't you?

✔ **You'll notice and clear up any disagreements sooner.** Sometimes partners reach an ambivalent, awkwardly worded compromise. As you draft the note together and read it aloud, the disagreement will be more obvious. It's better to raise the issue and find a better compromise now, rather than letting it slide and later having an argument about who is — and *isn't* — remembering correctly.

✔ **You'll be more likely to respect and honor your agreements.** You can't see ideas, thoughts, and verbal statements — they're intangible. But if you do all these things — if you write them down, read them aloud, share copies, post copies, and review them — it makes your agreements, compromises, and plans more legitimate, real, and tangible. Then if either of you decide you don't like something you've previously agreed to, you'll be more inclined to admit your change of heart and deal with it by renegotiating — instead of pretending you didn't make that agreement in the first place.

If your partner questions why you're doing all these things, explain that you want to make sure you understand one another. That way, you can both get your needs met and be happy living together.

Paperwork and details are not romantic in the traditional sense, but they're often necessary for the day-to-day life of the relationship. By doing a little work ahead of time, you can spend less of your time arguing — and a lot more of it enjoying each other to the max!

Sex Has Changed Since We've Moved In Together

Dear Dr. Kate,

My age: 38   **My gender:** Female

I've dated my boyfriend for six years on and off, and we've lived together for 11 months. Sex while dating was great, but now that we're living together, it's terrible. He's started working two jobs, getting up at 5:00 a.m. and working until 7:30 p.m., so he's always tired. But when we have sex, he lays on his back and expects special treatment. I perform oral sex and am very receptive to his needs, but I get nothing in return. I've nicely said, "Remember when you did this or that? It felt so good, please do it again." But he gets mad. I'm starting to feel resentful. What do I do?

Dear Resentful,

People frequently have sex more often when they're dating than when they're living together. When cohabiting, they know they can have sex whenever they want it, so it becomes less of a drive. It fades in priority because it can always be put off until tomorrow. If you both thought that today was your last chance to make love, you'd suddenly find a lot more energy for it. You'd remember to appreciate it — right now, today — and you'd act like it.

In addition, it's usually better not to live with anyone. If you cohabit, you get all the problems of living with someone — including the reduction in romance — but none of the plusses of marriage. For most couples, marriage is a very important rite of passage; it cements and legitimizes the relationship and motivates them to try harder. Living with someone is OK if you're not old enough to get married. But you and your man have had enough dating experience, you're plenty old enough — and you should be mature enough for marriage. In any long-term relationship, the couple has to work on keeping the spark alive and kicking. But people are usually more invested in doing that when they're actually married.

I'm sure that working long hours has also hampered your boyfriend. Why is he working two jobs? Why are you living together instead of marrying? If you feel strongly for one another, perhaps he should reduce his work hours, and the two of you should get married.

Instead of having sex and feeling resentful, wait until the weekend or whenever he's more rested. But if he's never rested, just wait until he wonders why you don't want sex any more. When he brings up the topic, ask him how he feels your sex life is going. Let him talk. Be understanding and supportive. Agree with whatever he says that you *can* agree with, so he feels understood. Then gently tell him how you feel. Remember to tell him what a great lover he can be, and how much you'd like to do that again. Offer to help him get more rest, so you can have better sex. Try to find a workable compromise.

Normally, I'd tell you to initiate the conversation. However, it seems that you have been trying to talk to him, and he hasn't been receptive. If you stop having sex with him, he should eventually be receptive to talking it through. But let him lead the conversation, so he feels that you're also willing to listen — that you're not just nagging. Avoid power struggles and stay calm, so he'll be more able to hear you and negotiate compromises. And be sure to see Chapters 11 to 13 for more on how to amicably discuss and resolve important topics.

Best wishes! I hope it works out for you.

Dr. Kate

Part III
Staying IN Love — Psychological and Emotional Intimacy

The 5th Wave   By Rich Tennant

"It's an agreement Michael and I made - he agrees to stay home from the gym 2 nights a week, and I guarantee that he'll still burn over 300 calories each night."

In this part . . .

So, after you've found a compatible partner, fallen in love, and developed intimacy — what's next?

Well, *next* is the most challenging part: Staying in love. How do you keep the closeness between you growing and thriving? Intimacy is deepened in two big ways: A) Psychologically and emotionally, by sharing thoughts and feelings with one another through verbal communication; and B) Physically and sexually, by staying close through sexual communication.

In this part, I discuss the "A" — how to grow psychologically and emotionally closer to your partner. First, I describe how to *think* about happiness, yourself, your partner, and your relationship to fully appreciate what you have and get the most out of it. Then I discuss how to use verbal communication to increase your emotional intimacy and keep it growing. I also give you practical tips that you can use to effectively share your thoughts and feelings with your partner. By using these techniques on a daily basis, you're more likely to stay in love — and make the love last as long as possible.

Chapter 10

Come On, Get Happy!

*W*hen God made man, he forgot the owner's manual. And man's been trying to write one ever since! Luckily, one of our biggest advances has been in figuring out what causes happiness — and what doesn't. For example, everyone wants to be happy. But have you ever noticed how some people have few material possessions, yet seem very happy, while others have an abundance of material wealth, yet seem very unhappy? How can some people remain strong through many crises, while others fall apart over nothing? If money and possessions don't determine happiness, what does? And if the amount of stress you feel *isn't* determined by the intensity of an event, then what does control it?

In this chapter, I consider four happiness myths and how believing such fantasies can cause you to become very unhappy indeed. Then for each myth, I present the reality, and how it's actually more pleasant. Finally, I show you how to use the five secrets of happiness to make your life as enjoyable as possible for as long as possible. So what are you waiting for? *Come on, get happy!* Don't you owe it to yourself?

The Four Happiness Myths

As I discuss the following myths, consider which ones cause you grief. Then read the reality following each myth, and consider how believing in it could actually change your life and make you much happier.

Myth #1: Optimism isn't realistic

Negative, pessimistic people think that optimists are delusional; they pity them for their inability to see life as it *really* is. In contrast, they see themselves as understanding the "truth" about the world, and not being afraid to face it. They tend to be critical and cynical, even putting a negative spin on their humor. They look around them and find proof for their pessimistic ideas, interpreting ambiguous situations as negative.

Their negative observations *seem* correct, but it's really a vicious self-fulfilling cycle. Doom-and-gloomers *think* negatively, so they *feel* critical and pessimistic, which then makes it easy for them to *act* in negative, distrustful, critical ways. Then other people either shy away or react negatively to them — which then confirms their belief that the world really is a pretty lousy place. And so the cycle continues downward. In essence, pessimists trap themselves in a self-perpetuating cycle of gloom and doom.

In reality, escaping this cycle is easy. If you think that the glass is half empty, it is. On the other hand, if you think the glass is half full, it is. In fact, the glass is both. But how you *think* about the situation determines how you *feel*, and how you feel makes *acting* in an optimistic, uplifting way more or less difficult. And how you act greatly influences how others respond to you.

If you *think* about life in a positive way, you'll *feel* more satisfied with what you find around you, and you'll *act* in more optimistic, supportive ways. And, guess what! People love being around others who are optimistic and emotionally supportive. Ask yourself: Would you rather spend the day with someone who's constantly complaining — or with someone who finds joy and fun in everyday things? The optimist generally gets treated better than the pessimist, and that, in turn, confirms his or her view of the world as a pretty wonderful place.

Myth #2: Other people are happier than me

If you believe in this myth, you probably notice other people a lot — too much. And you idealize the relationships of others. You believe that other people have better lives and perfect relationships. You see a loving couple cuddling on the street and assume that those people have no real problems. Then you look at your own life and your own relationship, and feel very unhappy because you're not as happy as others seem to be. And nothing will make you more miserable than thinking that everyone else is having more fun than you are.

No one has a perfect life or a perfect relationship. People who enjoy great blessings often find themselves dealing with great tragedies as well. For example, if you have money, you have to take precautions so others don't steal it. If you don't have money, you don't have to worry about anyone loving you for your money; you just need a way to pay the bills. Money never makes anyone happy, and not having it doesn't have to keep you from being happy either. Likewise, no other material possession ever equals happiness either.

Never assume that someone else is happy because they were given more than you. It simply isn't true.

Myth #3: Other people and things make me happy

The person who believes this myth uses expressions like, "You *made* me mad!" and, "You *make* me so happy!" Although these figures of speech are very colorful, they also imply that the responsibility for your happiness lies outside you. If someone *makes* you feel happy/sad/mad/whatever, then that person can also *make* you feel unhappy/less sad/not mad/whatever. And if your mental state is controlled by what another person does, then you can never be truly stable. After all, you can't control what anyone does, so how can you ever be truly happy for extended periods of time?

Well, the good news is: No one and no thing can cause you to be happy. In fact, people and things don't cause happiness at all. It's what you *think* about those other people and things that determines whether you *feel* happy or sad. Your thoughts — not outside events, the presence or absence of material objects, or other people — cause your feelings.

Just as money can't make you happy, other people can't make you happy either. *No one can make anyone think or feel or do anything.* The only person who has that distinction is the person who owns the thoughts, feelings, and behavior. When you accept this truth, then and only then can you be truly happy. If you stop waiting for circumstances to change in your life, you can make yourself happy — every day — no matter what life brings.

When you take responsibility for your feelings, including your happiness, you exercise one of the highest powers you have — the ability to control your thoughts and emotions to make them what you want them to be.

Myth #4: I can't be happy single and alone

Many people believe that they can only be happy when they're with a partner. If you believe this myth, you may also believe that your partner makes you happy (see the preceding section for more on this). Not only does such a belief place responsibility for your happiness outside you, it puts that responsibility smack dab on your partner. Wowwweeee! That really leaves you dangling in a precarious position, doesn't it? Even if you have a partner for awhile, eventually that person will leave or die. So believing in this myth guarantees that you'll be unhappy for a substantial period of time.

Also, when you believe that your mate makes you happy, you tend to blame him or her when you don't feel happy. Doing that will virtually ensure that your relationship will either become very unhappy or nonexistent before long. And, of course, if you believe in this myth, losing that mate will cause you to feel even more unhappy.

In reality, making you happy is not your mate's responsibility — it's yours. Accepting that responsibility is one of the most freeing experiences in life.

Because happiness is a state of mind, not a reaction to a particular person, thing, or event, you can be happy no matter what happens to you. You can be happy married, widowed, divorced, or single — or in whatever marital state you find yourself. You can be happy at any age. As long as you're alive, you can make yourself happy, no matter what. Accepting that truth and acting accordingly makes you an extremely powerful person.

Reviewing the Myths and Realities

Review Table 10-1 often to remember the four happiness myths and remind yourself to use the four powerful realities to make yourself happy.

Table 10-1	Four Happiness Myths and Realities
Grief-Causing Myth	*Saving Reality*
M1: Optimism isn't reality.	R1: "Reality" is largely how you view it.
M2: Other people are happier than me.	R2: Everyone has problems. You can be as happy as anyone — if you make yourself happy.

Grief-Causing Myth	Saving Reality
M3: Other people and things *make* me happy.	R3: Only *you* can *make* yourself happy, sad, or any other emotion.
M4: I can't be happy single and alone.	R4: You can be happy in any marital state.

DR. KATE SAYS

Thought-stopping

Thought-stopping is a simple technique that you can use in many different situations — whenever you need to replace bothersome, nonproductive thoughts (like worries, obsessions, and internal monologues that blame yourself or others) with healthy, productive thoughts. To identify whether a particular thought is productive, keep this in mind: If you review a past event one or two times to learn what you can from it and use that knowledge in the future, that's productive. However, if you continually run the same scene through your mind over and over again, that's nonproductive. You won't learn anything else; you're just making yourself sick. The same holds true for events in the future. You can rehearse a future scene once or twice in your mind to practice what you're going to do or say, but any further thought will just wear you out. To do the thought-stopping technique, follow these steps:

1. **Identify the type of thought you need to change.** If you're obsessed with your ex, stop all "ex thoughts." If you worry too much or feel blue, stop your anxious, self-doubt thoughts.

2. **When you get one of these thoughts, say, *"Stop it!"* to yourself.** (Not aloud, unless you want to get arrested!) That stops the irrational thought; you can't think two thoughts at exactly the same time.

3. **Say the opposite of whatever is bothering you, using the most positive, yet realistic terms.** If you've just been dumped and you think, "I miss him so much, I'll never be happy again," say: *"Stop it! I loved him, **but I can be happy** without him. And when I'm ready, I'll find a new partner."* Be sure to say your positive thought after the *"Stop it!"* In other words, don't just stop the negative thought; *replace it* with a positive thought (and make sure it's upbeat). Otherwise, you're just yelling, "Stop it!" at yourself, and thinking negatively.

4. **Turn your attention to what you're doing or have a positive fantasy.** If you're working on a task that requires attention, focus on the task at hand. If not, imagine a trip to Europe, floating down a river on a raft, or just plan your day. You can have any kind of fantasy — if it's positive or neutral, and doesn't remind you of what you're trying to forget.

5. **Calmly repeat this process every time you get an unhealthy thought.**

This technique *always* works. Every time you use it to replace a negative thought with a more positive, realistic thought, it's working. In the beginning, you'll find yourself thinking the unhealthy thought for awhile before you catch yourself. You'll also find that after you stop the thought, it

(continued)

(continued)

quickly returns. You'll be floating down your fantasy river, and suddenly, your ex appears on the shore! The more you practice this technique, however, the quicker you'll catch yourself and the longer you'll be able to keep the thought away — until one day, you'll suddenly remember that you've forgotten your bothersome thoughts altogether! That's the nature of this technique. To realize that it's worked, you have to remember that you once had this problem!

One caution: Every psychological technique can be used in an inappropriate way or at an inappropriate time — making it unhealthy, rather than healthy. For example, if you use this technique to forget about paying your bills, it's not healthy. If you use it to avoid feeling guilty about having an affair or deserting your mate, that's not good either. Basically, use the technique to end thoughts that are *really* hurting you — not uncomfortable thoughts that you need to remember. If action is warranted (if you need to pay a certain bill, for example), do it. If you can't because it's 2 a.m., write yourself a note to do the task in the morning. Then use thought-stopping to fall asleep so you can wake up fresh and handle the problem at that time.

The Five Secrets of Happiness: Make It Happen!

Now that you understand what's real and what's fantasy, use the following five-step program to make yourself happy: ,

1. **Change negative statements to positive ones.** Changing the way you think is difficult because thoughts are intangible; you can't see them. So it's easier to start reprogramming yourself for happiness by changing the way you speak. After all, if you're saying it, then you know you're thinking it, too, right? So start listening to the way you talk. When you hear yourself making a negative statement, change it to a more positive statement: "It was the worst . . . *no, that's not true. It wasn't the worst time I've ever had; I just didn't enjoy it as much as I'd hoped I would. But overall, it was OK."*

2. **Change negative thoughts to positive ones.** Once you've mastered your verbal remarks (see the preceding bullet), try changing the thoughts you don't say aloud. Start noticing how you think. If you catch yourself thinking negatively, stop yourself. Say: *"Stop it!"* Then say the exact opposite of what you were thinking. (See the "Thought-stopping" sidebar in this chapter to become a whiz at this incredibly simple, yet profoundly useful technique.)

3. **Grieve when necessary, then go back to being positive.** No one can deny that bad things happen to good people. When something bad happens, admit that you don't like it and you'd have preferred something else. But don't rant and rave or leap into a chasm of suffering. Instead, face the pain head-on and grieve. Allow yourself to vent; get it off your chest. Then get up the next day and pull yourself back together again. (To grieve efficiently, see *"The Dr. Kate Quick & Dirty Grieving Technique"* sidebar in this chapter.)

4. **Sell yourself on life.** See the positives and beauty all around you. You can find millions of reasons to be happy to be alive. When they don't instantly come to mind, go outside and let them come to you.

People tend to get neurotic when cooped up, and these days, almost everyone gets cooped up inside more than they should. When you're surrounded by pressure and demand after demand, escape to the country and let everything settle out. Get the cobwebs out of your brain by getting close to nature. Take a drive, sit on a riverbank, and let your feet dangle in the water. Watch the squirrels and birds play. Walk and get some fresh air. The oxygen will help you think better, and the exercise-fired endorphins will help you feel better, too. Then write down what's good about your life. Add to this list daily, and when you're not feeling so great, reread the list. The bottom line: Everyone, including you, has much to be thankful for. You just need to remind yourself about what that "much" is.

5. **Make every day count; take charge of your destiny.** When people are dying, they don't dwell on the car, house, or education they should have acquired, or the places they should have visited. Instead, they think about the people in their lives — the ones they should have been nicer to, the ones they should have married, and so on. It's all about *people*, not material objects. Dying people are in a unique position to review life. By emphasizing their people experiences, they demonstrate what's really important.

Don't walk around in a fog; live every day like it could be your last Notice every experience — *feel* it, savor it, appreciate it — and make it an occasion for joy and wonderment. Do the same with your mate. You'll never know how much time you have together, so appreciate every day. Don't dwell on the negative; emphasize the positive. Look at your relationship as special and enjoy it as much as you can. Then if it lasts, you'll enjoy it all the more. And if it ends — well, at least you enjoyed it while it lasted!

The Dr. Kate Quick & Dirty Grieving Technique

When you experience a major loss, use thought-stopping (see the sidebar in this chapter) to replace your irrational thoughts with more rational ones. Talk to a psychologist to vent your thoughts, feelings, and fears. Review your relationship in a productive fashion and get closure; learn what you can from the experience so you can apply that wisdom in future relationships.

But what if you're doing all that, and one day, the irrational thoughts seem to be winning? The lump in your throat is so big, it's difficult to swallow. Listening to the news on the way to work makes you teary-eyed, and by the time you get there, you're so irritable, you snap at your coworkers. What's a person to do? Use *The Dr. Kate Quick & Dirty Grieving Technique* as soon as possible to get your irrational thoughts and emotions out. One warning: Don't use this technique if you've had problems with *psychosis* (losing touch with reality) or suicidal thoughts or attempts. However, if you have no such history, try these helpful steps:

1. **Arrange your living situation so no one will hear you or interrupt you.** If you have kids, wait until they're asleep, then put some music on and shut the bedroom door. Or ask a friend to take your kids for the evening.

2. **Think about every irrational thought you've been trying to stop; exaggerate each as much as possible, and cry for as long as you can.** You might think, "I was so happy with my ex; I'll never be that happy again!" Or, "She was the best thing that ever happened to me! I'll never find anyone that terrific again!" Think about all those nagging fears in the back of your head — and sob for as long and as hard as you can. Spread his pictures across the bed and take a long look. Remember how much you loved your mate, how happy you were, and how much you wanted your relationship to work. Pull out all

the stops and sob for at least a half-hour, or two or three hours — and this includes you guys, too. Don't be afraid; as long as you're a relatively healthy person in touch with reality, with no history of psychosis or suicidal thoughts or attempts, you'll be fine. You're still in control; you're just allowing yourself to vent for an evening to get the pain out.

3. **Go through a whole box of tissue.** Just keep sobbing and sobbing until you find yourself saying, "No one will ever love me again" (or one of your most irrational thoughts), and a little voice finally answers, "I don't give a damn!"

4. **Take some headache medicine and go to bed.** By this time, your eyes and lips will be all puffed up. You'll look a little like Godzilla, and you'll probably have a whopping headache.

5. **When you get up the next morning, resume thought-stopping and replace all your irrational ideas with more positive, realistic thoughts.** If you're not sure which thoughts are irrational or why, ask your psychologist to point out the self-denigrating, blaming, or otherwise catastrophic thoughts bothering you and why they aren't realistic.

Use this technique as needed to work through your grief and speed your recovery. Use it to rid yourself of stressful thoughts and emotions so you can relax and go back to being rational the next day. When you use this method, you exercise some control over how and when you grieve. *Remember:* This technique is not a substitute for therapy. Rather, it's an adjunct that can help you face your fears, deal with them, reduce the time you suffer, heal faster and more completely — and survive the days in between with as much dignity, grace, and comfort as possible.

Chapter 11

Superglue #1: Good Communication — The Nuts

- -

In This Chapter

▶ Understanding the role communication plays in any relationship

▶ Debunking three common communication myths

▶ Reviewing the most common topics people fight about

▶ Adopting the proper communication mindset — expectations and attitudes

- -

*N*o two people ever think or feel alike, and no two people ever agree on everything all the time. If they do, they're probably not being honest, or they're trying too hard to agree. Sooner or later, every couple disagrees about something. If disagreeing broke up relationships, no relationships would exist; so obviously, disagreeing doesn't end relationships. In fact, studies show that people can disagree often and still get along very well — provided they discuss disagreements amicably and resolve them through satisfactory compromises. So instead of avoiding disagreements, hone your communication skills and make them work for you.

Communication builds emotional intimacy. You become close to your partner by sharing thoughts and feelings with one another that you don't share with anyone else, and you do that sharing through verbal and nonverbal communication. Then to stay close, you must continue to share through healthy verbal and nonverbal communication. So communication is Superglue #1 — bonding you together and keeping you closely bonded, day after day, month after month, year after year.

In this chapter, I discuss the important role communication plays in growing and sustaining relationships. I debunk three common communication myths, and review the most common topics partners tend to fight about. Finally, I describe the attitudes and expectations you need to communicate well.

Before reading this chapter, take *The Dr. Kate Compatibility Quiz* located in Appendix A to discover how you communicate. Score your quiz and read the results. For each question, pay close attention to the attitude or behavior assessed (listed in the scoring table); keep those in mind when reading the rest of this chapter. Then try the suggestions in your results summary to improve your communication with your partner.

Exposing Three Communication Myths

In the same way that people hold myths about relationships, compatibility, intimacy, and happiness, they also harbor funny ideas about communication. Since communication is the superglue holding your partnership together, it's vitally important to maintain realistic ideas about the communication process.

Myth #1: My partner should know how I feel

Many people believe that their partner should "just know" what they're thinking and feeling — as if they had some highly select, focused form of ESP. This myth says that partners can do just that, and it also implies that the more the partners know and care for each other, the more they can read each other's mind. So if you believe this myth, you probably also believe that if your partner can't or doesn't want to read your mind, then he or she doesn't care — or hasn't paid enough attention to you — to know your thoughts and feelings without being told.

In Chapter 7, I discuss how men often feel more comfortable *doing*, rather than *speaking*, and how genetics, learning, and early development trigger this. In fact, many men emphasize action over words, and this can cause a great deal of communication problems. The man might believe that his mate should be able to interpret his thoughts and feelings from his actions alone — no words needed. He shouldn't have to tell his mate, "I love you," because he informed her of that fact 10 years ago, and besides, it's obvious how he feels, isn't it? He helps her around the house and takes her car to the shop. Why else would he do that? Meanwhile, his female partner, being the opposite sex in many more ways than one — longs to hear those three little words. Like most females, she tends to be verbally inclined, so the actions just aren't enough. She wants to hear words of endearment — lots of them.

In fact, neither partner should expect the other to "divine" thoughts and feelings, or conversely, attempt to read their partner's mind. Rather, it's each partner's responsibility to share his or her feelings with the other partner, and vice versa. Expecting your mate to read your thoughts and feelings through your actions — or any other method other than hearing them out of the horse's mouth — is not only unfair, it's also very unwise.

So don't expect your girlfriend to tell how you're feeling by observing your behavior. Don't expect your boyfriend to read your mind, and for heaven's sake, don't take it as an insult when he can't. In fact, be happy that he doesn't want to try, because it's much better if your partner does not presume to know how you think or feel. When a partner incorrectly presumes your feelings and then responds to you based on that incorrect assumption, he or she is not responding appropriately to the situation at hand, and more and more problems can result. Solving a disagreement then becomes peeling off layer after layer of the onion to solve the next misunderstanding that it's based on, and the next, and the next, and so on. By the time the two of you unravel what you're really thinking and feeling — if you ever do — you may find a lot of hurt feelings and much wasted energy.

In contrast, if you accept that it's your responsibility to share your feelings with your mate in an appropriate way, you'll be more inclined to do so. That sharing will then draw the two of you closer.

Myth #2: Talking is talking — everyone does it the same way

Another myth states that talking comes in one variety — talking. Sure, there are different languages, but beyond that, talking is talking, and everyone does it the same way. If you take this myth seriously, you overlook the subtle nuances of communication and how these subtleties can either make you successful at life and love, or regularly land you in hot water.

In reality, communication involves not only language, but many other verbal and behavioral cues as well. Your choice of words (and how you put them together) is one important part of communication. The context in which that verbal comment occurs is also significant. You can change the meaning of a sentence by emphasizing a different word, or by using a different tone, volume, or speed. How your message is received will also depend on the accompanying behavioral cues (like eye contact, facial expressions, gestures, body positions) and other behaviors (like whether you cut someone off and give unsolicited advice, or act patient and emotionally supportive).

Myth #3: If I'm angry, I have to be aggressive

This myth states that the way you express your emotions is dictated by the type of emotion. For example, if you feel angry, you have to be aggressive when expressing that feeling. This myth assumes that you have no control over your feelings and behavior — that once you feel angry, your words will inevitably come out in an aggressive manner. This myth also suggests that aggression must be natural and normal because everyone gets angry sometimes, right?

Wrrronggo! The *feeling* (anger) is different from the *behavior* (communicating aggressively). You can be angry and communicate passively, aggressively, or assertively — the same holds true for any emotion. *Feeling angry* does not make you a sick person; anger is a normal emotion, and everyone experiences it from time to time. However, you can express that anger in a sick, inappropriate way — or in an appropriate way — and you are responsible for whichever way you choose.

When you feel angry, that's the *emotion*. How you express that anger is the *behavior*. You might choose to say nothing, which would be *passive* (also known as nonassertive) — not standing up for your rights. Or you might choose to act *aggressively* — standing up for your rights, but going too far and taking advantage of the other person's rights in the process. Or you might choose to be *assertive,* standing up for your rights in a way that shows respect for the other person's rights. Speaking aggressively is never appropriate in a romantic relationship, no matter what you're feeling or with whom you're speaking. In fact, aggressive statements are almost always inappropriate — the one exception being when speaking aggressively prevents someone from taking aggressive action against you. For example, some bullies will back down when someone speaks aggressively to them in a show of strength. However, even then, speaking aggressively is a risk — the bully might decide to aggress against you rather than back off.

It's important to note that some people (and even some dictionaries) use the words *assertive* and *aggressive* interchangeably, as though they are synonyms. That's inaccurate and unfortunate, because it overlooks real and important distinctions between the two behaviors — distinctions that can make or break any relationship. Assertive communication can bring you closer to your partner because it's direct, intimate, and respectful, whereas aggressive communication is vague, disrespectful, and always inappropriate — and one of the main reasons that relationships fall apart. To find out more about these passive-aggressive-assertive distinctions and how to use assertive communication to enhance your relationship, see Chapters 12 and 13.

Reviewing the Myths and Realities

Review Table 11-1 frequently to help you think rationally about communication.

Table 11-1	Three Communication Myths and Realities
Grief-Causing Myth	*Saving Reality*
M1: My partner should know how I feel.	R1: It's each partner's responsibility to share his or her feelings with the other.
M2: Talking is talking; everyone does it the same way.	R2: You can communicate passively, aggressively, or assertively, and how you communicate makes a big difference in how your message is received.
M3: If I'm angry, I have to be aggressive.	R3: The *feeling* (anger) is different from the *behavior* (communicating aggressively). As with all emotions, you can be angry and still communicate passively, aggressively, or assertively.

Communication Qualities: The Nuts

In Chapter 1, I describe the qualities characteristic of a good relationship — the qualities that must be present to make the relationship thrive. Those attitudes and expectations also allow you and your partner to communicate well. With them, your communication thrives; without them, it fizzles quicker than you can say, "I want to break up." So what are those enormously important qualities again? Without further ado, heeeerrre they are!

Respect and good faith

When you respect your partner, you understand that he or she is not just an extension of you, but a completely unique individual with thoughts, feelings, and desires that are totally different from your own. Instead of assuming that there is one correct set of beliefs — *yours* — that any sane person would agree with, you understand that there are usually many perspectives on any topic. Just because your sweetie holds a different point of view doesn't make that opinion "wrong" or less worthy of consideration than yours.

So when your mate voices an opinion that disagrees with yours, don't immediately shut it out, or assume that he or she is irrational, crazy, or saying something just to bug you. Instead, take the information in good faith. Assume that she sincerely believes her point of view and that she's sharing that information with you because it's important to her. Give your partner the benefit of the doubt, listen carefully and supportively, and try to understand where he or she is coming from.

Appreciation and caring

When you appreciate your partner, you delight in his company. You care that he's happy, and you show it by being emotionally supportive in your words and actions. When resolving problems, you sincerely want your mate to be satisfied by the compromises you draft together. You don't want to win everything at the expense of your partner's happiness.

People tend to be on their best behavior when they first meet someone. For example, they remember to praise their partner and show affection. But as time goes on, they become more and more used to one another, the newness wears off, and they forget to talk about their positive thoughts and feelings for one another. They forget to mention all those endearing thoughts and feelings that once drew them close.

All the love in the world won't help your relationship if your partner isn't aware that you care! So caring isn't enough; you also need to let your partner know that you care through your words and your actions. And when you tell your partner how important he or she is to you, you also remind yourself — and that's important, too.

Honesty, loyalty, confidentiality, and trust

You and your partner must communicate honestly with one another. But you don't have to say everything, and you may decline to reveal information to protect another person's confidence or because you just don't want to share the information. For example, it's OK to say: *"I don't feel comfortable talking about that,"* or, *"I don't want to discuss that right now."* But *don't* lie.

Why? Because you and your partner must trust that you'll both protect each other's best interests, even when you're not present to see the job done. You trust that your mate is being loyal to you, and you're loyal to him or her as well. If you receive information that seems to imply that your honey has done something against you, don't immediately assume that the information is true. Instead, stay calm and wait until you've had a chance to discuss it with him or her — before drawing any conclusions. *Give your mate the benefit of the doubt!*

Closely related to honesty and trust, confidentiality is another essential ingredient in good communication. In order to share your intimate thoughts, feelings, and experiences with your mate, you need to feel safe that he'll keep those secrets to himself, and you need to keep his secrets sacred as well.

Of course, sharing the information in a professional relationship with your psychologist or therapist is fine. Sharing some of it with a close friend who helps you process events in your life is also OK — provided your friend also keeps your confidences and tells no one else. Often a close friend can let you talk aloud and help you figure out what to do in difficult situations.

Sharing that information with a bunch of hunting buddies while drinking beer, however, is not kosher. Complaining about your sweetie and revealing all her secrets to the woman you're cheating with is also verboten. (Having an affair in the first place is totally unacceptable, but sharing your mate's secrets with that person is an even greater betrayal!)

If you want to stay in love, treat your partner like the person with whom you have the strongest connection. Look out for each other, make one another a top priority, and show each other steadfast loyalty, honesty, confidentiality, and trust.

Best friends

In a healthy relationship, partners are best friends. Similarly, to communicate well, you need to speak to your partner in a manner that shows you consider him or her to be your best friend. Yet some people show less tolerance for their mate's opinions and statements than they would a stranger's. They tune their partner out, and save their best communication habits for company instead.

Well, if you want to alienate your lover and get closer to the company, go ahead! Otherwise, you'd best treat your partner — your closest friend — even *better* than you would a stranger, acquaintance, or a less intimate friend. Practice your best communication attitudes and skills on the one you love most. Encourage him to share his thoughts, opinions, and feelings with you, and remind yourself often that sharing those innermost ideas and feelings will keep the two of you emotionally and psychologically bonded.

Owning and sharing your feelings

To communicate effectively, both partners must take responsibility for their own feelings. Each person has the right to feel as he or she feels, even if that's not the way someone else might feel in the same situation. There's no need to justify your feelings by saying, "*Everyone* would feel this way in this situation," or, "You know, *you* feel that way." You have the right to feel the way you feel just because you feel it; you don't need a group vote or consensus. Good communication involves acknowledging your feelings and sharing them with another person.

As stated earlier in this chapter in the discussion of relationship myths, both partners have a responsibility to share their feelings with the other. Neither partner should presume, assume, or mind-read the other's thoughts and feelings, no matter how long you've been together or how well you think you know one another.

Determination and perseverance

For any relationship to last and grow, you and your partner must be committed to making it work; you need to be determined. Similarly, to communicate well together, you also need to be determined and persevering.

People tend to learn their communication patterns from their parents at a very early age. Because most people don't communicate perfectly, everyone has to continually work on his or her communication to improve it. Understanding and exploring communication can be great fun, though, because good communication has direct relevance to your life — and you can experience the fruits of your labor relatively quickly to boot. By being determined and persevering in your efforts, you can improve your communication with your significant other — and experience the intimacy and joy that success brings.

Positive attitude

Both partners need a reasonably optimistic attitude toward life and their union to make the relationship thrive. Similarly, to foster good communication, they need to feel reasonably confident that they can amicably discuss and resolve whatever problems come their way. Their statements to one another must be more positive than negative, so they'll feel upbeat and excited around each other — and look forward to more sharing and communicating.

When you and your partner communicate in healthy ways, you *feel* healthier and more upbeat. Just as thinking, feeling, and behaving upbeat draws others to you, communicating with optimism encourages other people (including your partner) to spend time with you. If you think positively and treat problems like challenges to be overcome — rather than insurmountable obstacles ruining your life — your mate is more likely to discuss issues and share his or her feelings with you. And you're both more likely to feel calm and confident, rather than anxious and irritated. So you'll be able to think more clearly, and you'll find it easier to amicably discuss problems and find appropriate compromises.

Then your mate will love being around you, and will reciprocate with positive communication. Then you'll feel valued and find it easier to communicate positively with him or her, too. Your positive attitude and healthy communication helps you overcome any challenges, while bonding you even more closely together. And so the self-fulfilling cycle continues. . . .

Then when problems with other people occur, you're more likely to use your positive attitude and communication skills to solve them, too. And that, in turn, tends to make the rest of your life improve as well! It's all one big circle upward when you think positively and use good communication skills to make friends and keep 'em, too.

Reviewing the Most Common Topics for Argument

People tend to argue about the same handful of topics. Disagreements about these issues happen often enough, become intense enough, and end badly enough that many relationships fail as a result. I discuss these topics in detail in Chapter 9 on cohabiting. However, since most couples break up over these problems, it's good to review them in light of what you now understand about communication. The most common topics of argument between couples are:

- ✔ **Money:** How to make it, spend it, and save it.
- ✔ **Sex:** How much to have, when to have it, and what kind to have.
- ✔ **Kids:** Whether to have them, how many to have, who will discipline them and how, how much time to spend with them, and how to spend it. If the kids are from a previous relationship, issues like jealousy, resentment, and other blended-family problems also occur.
- ✔ **Extended family and friends:** When and how often to see them, activities to do with them, and how they treat you and your partner.
- ✔ **Spare time:** How much you have, how you spend it, and what percentage of that time you spend with your partner versus others.

To avoid arguments, check your attitude and expectations frequently, and readjust them in a more healthy direction as needed. Then be sure to use the communication skills described in Chapters 12 and 13 to discuss disagreements amicably and resolve them with satisfactory compromises. Remember, good communication is Superglue #1, bonding you and your partner tightly together and keeping you there 24/7. So use it generously to keep your intimacy — and your relationship — strong.

❤ ❤ ❤ ❤ ❤ ❤

We're Both Bullheaded!

Dear Dr. Kate,

My age: 44   **My gender:** Female

My husband and I divorced three years ago after 22 years of marriage. We haven't spoken since before the divorce was final. Our family calls us both "bullheaded." I still love him with all my heart. But if he really cared, he'd call and tell me, and he doesn't. Instead, he just tells his son about it. Please help!

Dear Bullheaded,

I agree. You're both bullheaded. And terribly self-defeating.

Let me get this straight: You love this man with all your heart, and he tells his son that he cares for you. But that's not good enough. You want him to tell you. Well, OK, I understand that you want him to tell you. But why make your life miserable waiting on him? Why do that to yourself?

And who do you think you're hurting worse by being so stubborn — him or you?

Having too much *pride* isn't good for you. Nor is being stubborn, bullheaded, obstinate, headstrong, or pigheaded. (Wow! That's a lot of synonyms for one emotion!) After all these years, why not change and grow up a little? Be kinder to yourself and make your life easier — don't make it so hard. Apologize. Yup, *apologize*. What can it hurt?

Respect yourself by having dignity and grace. Tell your husband that you love him and miss him and you don't care, for once, who's "right" and who's "wrong." Because as far as you're concerned, you both suffer when you get into power struggles — like this one. So you've decided that you're no longer going to fight him like this. You want him to know that you love him and miss him, and you'd like very much for him to please come back home. Will he?

If he's a smart man under that pig head, he'll be home in very short order.

Power struggles never benefit anyone; they just hurt everyone. You've suffered enough. Call a truce or, better yet, a total and permanent end to the war, and get back together with your man. It's past time, isn't it?

All the best, and please let me know how it works out.

Dr. Kate

Chapter 12

Good Communication: The Bolts

In This Chapter

▶ Expressing feelings and attitudes through appropriate behaviors

▶ Developing and practicing behaviors that promote, strengthen, and maintain verbal intimacy

▶ Finding compromises that work for you and your partner

*I*n Chapter 11, I mention that good communication is Superglue #1, bonding you and your mate tightly together and keeping you up close and personal. I discuss how healthy attitudes and expectations make up one set of communication building blocks — the nuts. Now it's time to talk about the *how*. How can you show those healthy attitudes and expectations — your respect, good faith, appreciation, caring, honesty, loyalty, confidentiality, trust, friendship, responsibility, reciprocity, determination, perseverance, and optimism — through your behavior?

By regularly using the second set of communication blocks, the *bolts*. In this chapter, I show you how to use these practical techniques to express yourself clearly and respectfully. Then in Chapter 13, I show you how to assemble the nuts and bolts — to use the techniques in this chapter together with the attitudes described in Chapter 11 — to amicably and efficiently resolve disagreements.

Communication Bolts: Behaviors

The behaviors in Table 12-1 represent the bolts — the essential behavioral ingredients in your communication skills repertoire. When used properly, these behaviors demonstrate the healthy attitudes and expectations described in Chapter 11 and remind your partner why he or she is in the relationship. Memorize these communication skills, and practice until you can do them automatically, with ease and without thinking. Make them the staples of your communication-skills repertoire to keep you and your partner close. Then refer to Table 12-1 periodically to help you remember each technique and how to do it.

Table 12-1	Communication Skills/Behaviors
Communication Skill	*How to Do It*
Reflective listening	Paraphrase or repeat part of what your mate has said in a tentative fashion. For example: *"So what you're saying is _____. Is that correct?"*
Facilitative agreement	Agree with whatever part of your partner's statement you can agree with: *"I can see/understand that _____"* or, *"I agree with you that _____."*
Supportive statements	Show empathy/support for your partner: *"I'm so happy for you,"* or, *"I feel so sorry it didn't work out."*
Positive reinforcement/ reward	Reinforce/reward the behavior you'd like increased or small steps in that direction by giving your mate something he or she likes. Verbal rewards: Praise, thanks, words of endearment. Praise nonspecifically (*"Great!"*), or preferably, describe the behavior you like: *"That's great, Babe. I love it when you _____."* Nonverbal rewards: Kisses, hugs, touches, smiles.
The Dr. Kate 20-1 Rule	Give at least 20 positive reinforcements *before* asking for 1 behavioral change in an assertive manner.
Assertiveness	Use only when you have equal or more power. Use "I" statements to respectfully express your feelings (*"I feel _____ when you _____"* or *"when _____ happens"*), and to make respectful requests (*"I would appreciate it if you would _____"*). Ask questions to find out how your partner feels; don't tell him. Avoid power words, name-calling, yelling, interrupting, and assuming. Keep your voice sincere, at moderate volume, speed, and pitch. Use appropriate eye contact, facial expressions, body position, interpersonal distance, and gestures.
Compromise	Grant concessions, and negotiate a middle course to find satisfactory solutions, so you both get some of what you want. Either: 1) Split the difference; 2) Alternate behaviors on some regular basis so you each enjoy what you want sometimes; 3) Alternate 100 percent concessions, giving in on issues you don't care about and getting your way on others you do care about; or 4) Adopt routines to satisfy mate's objections and allow you both to win in all-or-none situations.

Reflective listening

Reflective listening is a technique that lets your partner know you're hearing him and considering his point of view with respect. In reflective listening, you paraphrase, summarize, or repeat part of what your mate has said. You do it in a tentative fashion that implies that this is what you *believe* he's said, but you may not be correct. You don't voice your opinion or thoughts; you stay in the moment with your partner by "reflecting back" what he or she has just said.

Here are five main sentence structures for reflective listening:

✔ *"So, what you're saying is _____. Is that correct?"* For example: *"So, what you're saying is you don't feel comfortable walking the dog late at night by yourself. Is that correct?"*

✔ *"I hear you saying that _____. Am I hearing you correctly?"* For example: *"I hear you saying that you feel angry towards me when I raise my voice to you. Am I hearing you correctly?"*

✔ *"It sounds like you're feeling/saying _____."* For example: *"It sounds like you're saying you're happy you got the work promotion, but you're worried that it will cause trouble between us."*

✔ *"I understand you to mean _____. Is that correct?"* For example: *"I understand you to mean you'd rather visit your parents than go to Anne's party. Is that correct?"*

✔ Or you can simply paraphrase your partner's words in a sincere tone of voice: *"So you'd rather visit your parents than Sue . . . ."*

If you don't understand your partner's message, use one of these four types of questions to clarify what he or she is trying to say:

✔ *"Are you saying that _____?"*

✔ *"Do you mean that _____?"*

✔ Repeat your partner's last few words, ending the sentence with your voice up, like you're asking a question. Say your partner uses several sentences to describe how tense she feels when you speak aggressively. She ends with: "I feel nervous when you raise your voice." But you don't remember doing that or you don't understand what she means, and you want more clarification. You can simply repeat her last few words as a question: "_____?" For example: "When I raise my voice?"

✔ Use a combination of the previous paraphrases and questions. For example: *"I understand that you feel _____. But are you also saying that _____?"* (*"I understand that you feel happy about the promotion. But are you also saying that you're worried it will cause problems between us?"*)

When you use these types of sentences and questions, with their respectful, tentative wording, your partner:

- Feels understood and valued.

- Realizes you're showing respect and making a good faith effort.

- Tends to feel positive about the discussion and friendly toward you, even when the two of you disagree about the issue.

- Is encouraged to continue sharing his story with you; the conversation moves forward.

- And you avoid *power struggles* — unproductive shouting matches where both people speak faster and faster, raising their voices, and choosing more insulting, aggressive words, without adding any helpful information. (For example: "You did that." "No, I didn't!" "YES, you did!" "NO, I didn't!!!" "YES, I'm not blind and YOU most certainly DID!" "NOOO, you JERK! I told you already, and I'll tell you again: I ABSOLUTELY DID <u>NOT</u>!!!" "<u>YOU</u> always think you're RIGHT!" "Oh, yeah, well, <u>YOU'RE</u> NEVER WRONG, huh, MS. SMARTYPANTS!?")

In a power struggle, the focus quickly becomes who's "right" and who's "wrong," and who can get their partner to back down and admit defeat — basically, who can *win* the argument. But when someone "wins" an argument at their partner's expense, both parties actually lose.

When women share information with you, they're often just looking to vent or de-stress. They want *emotional support*, not advice. So don't give advice or tell them what you'd do. If they want advice, they'll ask for it. Instead, just listen with empathy and use reflective listening.

For example, your partner might say: "Boy, did I have a rotten day today. The boss scheduled a meeting at the last minute, and I was hard pressed to get all of the papers ready on time. I had to work through lunch, and then that diffi-cult client came in and was all over me, and . . . and . . . ." And you, being totally enlightened by what you've just read, would: Listen carefully, wait until she's finished talking, then say something like: ***"Sounds like you** had a rough day today, **huh?"*** To which your partner might respond: "Yeah, sure did, and after that, the office manager . . . ." You'll know if you did the tech-nique correctly because if you did, your partner will continue with the story and seem relieved to unload this stuff onto someone who really understands.

Facilitative agreement

In this technique, you agree with whatever your partner has said that you can agree with — before presenting your point of view. You don't have to agree with your partner's complete opinion on anything. Rather, you voice your agreement with any *part* you can agree with. For example, let's say you and your live-in boyfriend greatly disagree on how to spend or save money. He says: "You know, Dianne, I was thinking, the guys and I are going camping in a few weeks, and my camping gear is really old. I'm going to buy a new tent, a sleeping bag, and maybe a new fishing pole. I know the joint account is for household expenses, but I'll work overtime next week to replace what I take out."

You, as Dianne, have a number of choices at this point. You can attack your boyfriend as incredibly immature and irresponsible, reminding him once again that the bills have to be paid before spending money on nonessentials — particularly when he's already got functional, albeit old camping gear. Or you can respond in a healthy way that assumes your partner is bright and usually responsible, mature, and caring. *"I agree with you that your camping gear is pretty old. And I understand that you're really looking forward to having a great time on this trip. And you certainly deserve it; you've been working so hard."*

If your partner has been expecting a fight, he's now surprised that you're not screaming and yelling. Agreeing with him helps him feel respected, cared for, and affectionate toward you in return. He relaxes.

Then you can present your concerns in a polite way, and he's ready to listen: *"But I'm also concerned that we need to pay the bills, and I'm not sure that spending money before we have it is very wise. What if your boss won't OK the overtime, or you get sick, or some emergency arises? It would be cutting everything really close, wouldn't it?"*

Using facilitative agreement in this way shows good faith; it tells your partner that you think he's basically a good guy — intelligent, responsible, mature, and normal. It shows empathy — you care about him and want him to be happy, too. It communicates that you want to have a friendly, respectful, mature discussion, and it appeals to that affectionate, respectful, and mature side of your partner to do the same.

Supportive statements

Supportive statements are direct statements of empathy for the other person. For example: *"I feel so happy for you,"* or, *"I'm so sorry it didn't work out the way you wanted it to."* Like reflective listening, supportive statements show you care. But while reflective listening encourages the speaker to continue venting and/or sharing new information, supportive statements tend to end the conversation. So it's often best to use supportive statements at the end of a long discussion that includes reflective listening and facilitative agreement. For example, if your partner tells you what a rotten day she's had, you can make a supportive statement: *"I'm sorry your day went so badly, Honey."* That's an excellent comment. However, it's better to use reflective listening first, to allow her to vent and get it all out. Then make the supportive comment: *"**I'm sorry** your day went so badly, **Honey. I hope** tomorrow goes much better."* That, together with a hug and kiss, will keep your love strong!

Supportive statements are also appropriate following short statements about happy events:

> Your partner: "I got a promotion yesterday."
>
> You: *"**Good for you! I'm so happy for you!**"*

Or following short statements about unhappy events:

> Your partner: "Mom just called. My father passed away at 3 p.m."
>
> You: *"**I'm so sorry. What can I do** (or **is there anything I can do**) **to help?**"*

If all couples increased their reflective listening, facilitative agreement, and supportive statements, the world would be a more peaceful, happy place, and many more relationships would last long-term.

Positive reinforcement/reward

When you work, you get a paycheck, and that's why you go back to work; you get paid. If you stopped receiving those checks, you'd look elsewhere for work, so you could once again get paid. In that scenario, money is a *positive reinforcement.* Anything that follows a behavior and causes it to increase is called "positive reinforcement." So basically, positive reinforcement is a reward — and anything can be a reward, as long as the person receiving it likes it.

If your mate says he loves the way you kiss, you'll feel good and try to kiss him more often. If your honey takes your car to the shop and you thank him, he'll probably do it again. If you also smile, hug, and plant a passionate kiss on him, he's even more likely to repeat what you liked.

Positive reinforcement can be verbal (like compliments, praise, thanks, and words of endearment), or nonverbal (like smiles, touches, hugs, and kisses). It can be as simple as, *"**Great!**"* or, *"**Thanks!**"* Or it might include more specific information about what you're pleased with: *"**That's great, Honey. I love it when you** rub my back at the end of a long day!"* Saying, *"**I love you,**"* calling your partner pet names, and using other terms of endearment can also be positive reinforcements. Even singing to your mate or reciting a poem can be a reward — provided your mate enjoys it. When you positively reinforce/reward someone for a behavior, that person perks up, pays attention, and generally tries to increase whatever you rewarded him or her for. That's particularly true when that person likes or loves you.

Then you're pleased that your mate has increased the behavior, and the increase acts as a reward for you — you'll be more inclined to reward him more in the future as well. And so the cycle continues — with you and your partner feeling more love and good will toward one another, and becoming more emotionally intimate and bonded.

So it's absolutely essential to bestow lots of positive reinforcement on your mate. Be sure to praise your partner whenever he or she does something you like. If a certain task is difficult for him or her, be sure to praise every little step in the appropriate direction. It lets your sweetie know that you've noticed his effort to change, and it gives him a reason to keep trying. Also, try to describe the behavior specifically so your mate understands what behavior you enjoy.

For example, say you'd like your boyfriend to hold your hand more often in public. One day when you're out and about, he grabs your hand and holds it briefly. Immediately say (with a soft, gentle, sincere tone of voice): ***"That was really nice, Babe. I love it when you*** *hold my hand."* Chances are, he'll hold your hand for a longer period of time next time. If you continue to reward him each time, he'll eventually end up holding your hand most of the time you're out together.

But let's say he grabs your hand, holds it, and then lets it go. If you criticize him instead of thanking him ("Why can't you keep holding my hand? Why are you such a wuss?!"), chances are, he'll hold your hand less often in the future. And if he does hold your hand to get you to stop picking on him, he'll probably feel resentful as well.

And what if your partner doesn't give *you* much positive reinforcement? To help him feel like doing it, start rewarding him whenever he does! When he praises you for something, immediately say (in a sincere tone of voice): ***"Thanks, Honey. I love it when you*** *say you like something I'm doing, because it lets me know to keep doing it!"*

The Dr. Kate 20-1 Rule

People tend to give their mates lots of praise in the beginning of a relationship, when they're excited and feeling oh so lucky that this person has entered their world. They notice details that suggest this person may be compatible, and they comment on it in a positive manner. So the mate feels valued and wants to spend more time together.

Ever heard the saying, "People fall in love partly because of the way they feel about themselves when they're around you?" Well, it's true. If you act like your partner is a wonderful person and he enjoys that feeling, he'll stay much longer in the relationship. Conversely, if you act like your partner can't do anything right, she'll probably make a hasty retreat — particularly if you aren't married and there aren't any children, money, or other complications holding the two of you together.

Unfortunately, as people get to know their partners better, they often start taking them for granted. They stop reveling in how incredibly wonderful this new compatibility is and begin to expect it to be there tomorrow. At the same time, they stop noticing all the "good" stuff and start focusing on whatever they consider to be the "bad" stuff. They stop giving positive reinforcement and start nagging or complaining instead.

But think about that: If you nag your partner all day long, why should he stay with you? If she constantly feels like a failure in your presence, why would she stick around for more?

The Dr. Kate 20-1 Rule says that before you ask your partner for one behavioral change, you must first give at least 20 positive reinforcements. Now, the number 20 holds no magic; I just use it to remind you that the number of positive reinforcements has to *greatly* outnumber the amount of requests for behavioral change. Otherwise, your partner has no reason to want to please you. Your request for change also has to be phrased in a positive, emotionally supportive way — not as criticism. For example, if your live-in partner usually dumps his socks wherever he takes them off, but you'd like him to put them in the hamper instead, follow these steps:

1. **Give him lots of positive reinforcement/reward (at least 20) for everything he does that you enjoy.** Be sure to include both verbal rewards (like ***"Thanks for** taking the garbage out. **I really appreciate it,"*** or, ***"I really love** going for walks with you, **Honey")***, and nonverbal rewards (like smiles, touches, hugs, kisses).

2. **Then using respectful, assertive language, ask him to make the one behavioral change.** For example: *"You know, **I'd really appreciate it if you would** toss your socks in the hamper instead of leaving them on the floor. **Would that be OK with you?"***

Chances are your partner will graciously try to hit the hamper with his socks the next time. If you then give positive reinforcement (***"Thanks for** putting your socks in the hamper. **I appreciate it."***), he'll probably continue doing it most of the time. He'll also feel appreciated throughout the process, so your relationship will stay strong, too.

Note that the effect would be totally different if you yelled, "For heaven's sake, Mark, why can't you ever put your dirty socks in the laundry? They're filthy and smelly, and I trip all over them! What do you think I am, your maid? Did you grow up in a barn? You are *such* a slob!" Mark might then make a slight effort to hit the hamper, but not much, and he'd also resent it. He sees no reason to try, because you've already criticized him severely and labeled him a slob. And after all, if he really *is* a slob, how can he act in any way except slobby?

Don't get caught up in righteous indignation, thinking that he *should* pick up his socks because every decent, responsible adult (including you) does. "Well, he should just put those socks in there. Why do I need to thank him for doing something he ought to do as an adult anyway?" Try taking the same logic and applying it to your performance in the workplace. You're hired to do a good job, and therefore, you should do your best, right? But don't you feel more motivated when your boss compliments you on what a fine job you're doing? Of course you do.

We all work for positive reinforcement, whether we know it or not. And the person who dispenses it generously at appropriate times is a person other people want to be around. Be that person, and watch your life circle upward, just like that self-fulfilling prophecy I keep talking about. Be a negative, complaining, irritable grouch instead, and watch everyone walk — or run — away. The choice is yours.

Assertiveness

Assertiveness is a way to share your feelings, get your point across in a calm and rational way, and stand up for yourself — while also showing respect for the listener and his rights. It's very different from being *passive,* where you let someone walk all over your rights, or being *aggressive,* where you stand up for your rights at another's expense. When you're assertive, you act like an equal and share your thoughts and feelings with the listener — and that draws you closer together.

Assertiveness should only be used when you have equal power and status with someone — like your partner, your friends, and certain members of your family. Or you can choose to be assertive when you have more power over someone — for example, when you're the boss.

However, using assertiveness with people who have more control over you (like your boss, the policeman giving you a ticket, the judge hearing your case) is *not* a good idea. When you have a lot to lose and the outcome, not the relationship, is the focus, it's usually better to use *political* behavior instead, picking and choosing what you say to bring about a successful outcome. When the relationship and keeping it strong are the focus, however, assertiveness is usually warranted.

What you say (the content or your message), how you say it (your verbal delivery), and how you act when you say it (your nonverbal delivery) are all very important. While your partner probably won't break your message down, part by part, as I do in this chapter, he or she will interpret your message based on all these variables. So pay attention to all your verbal and the nonverbal signals — because your mate will. The following sections describe these important elements, and how they can either enhance or impair the way your message is received.

Content — what you say

The words you choose and the order you put them in make a big difference in how your message is received by your partner. Whether you make a statement or ask a question is also important. The sections that follow describe the most important things to remember about content.

Stick to two basic sentences

The first sentence has two forms, and the second has three. Use these two basic sentence structures, with their different forms, to express any feeling or request in a healthy, assertive way:

1. To express a *feeling*:

    "I feel _____ (happy, sad, hurt, angry, confused, overwhelmed, or whatever the case may be) ***when you*** _____ *(tell me how much you care, speak to me that way,* or whatever the behavior is)***."***

    "I feel _____ (happy, sad, hurt, angry, confused, overwhelmed, whatever) ***when*** _____ ***happens*** *(when we're together, when we don't see one another for weeks,* and so on)***."***

2. To make a *request*:

    "I would really appreciate it if you would _____ *(try to keep your voice calm when speaking to me)."*

    "I would like it if you would _____ *(make time in your schedule so we can see one another on Saturday nights)."*

    "Would you please _____ *(do what)?"*

Steer clear of sentence structure no-no's

People are conditioned to hear criticism following the word "you" because that's what usually happens, especially in intense discussions. So when disagreeing, *never, never, never* start a sentence with the word "you." Instead, take responsibility for your feelings by starting your sentences with the word *"I"*: ***"I feel _____."*** For example:

- ✔ *Don't* say: "You're so stupid, you couldn't fight your way out of a paper bag," or, "You never do anything right," or the ever popular, "You made me mad."

- ✔ Instead, say: ***"I feel*** *angry* ***when you do*** *that."* (Note that this simple statement tells your partner how you feel much more clearly than any of the aggressive sentences in the preceding bullet. Expressing yourself in this way allows you to say how you feel while showing respect for your partner at the same time. It's more likely to help your communication, not hurt it.

And for heaven's sake, don't tell other people how they feel or think! Similarly, don't imply that everyone reasonable feels the way you do and anyone who doesn't is crazy.

Know when to ask a question and when to make a statement

Ask a question when you want information. When you want to say how you feel, don't ask a question; make a statement. For example:

- ✔ *Don't* say: "So don't you think we should go to that party on Wednesday?" You're not really asking; you're voicing your opinion.

- ✔ Instead, say: ***"I'd like to _____*** *(go to that party on Wednesday).* ***How do you feel about it?"***

Also, don't ask rhetorical questions in the middle of a heated argument. Instead, stay on track — sincere, focused, and practical.

Avoid power words, labels, and name calling

Avoid power words like *never, always, stupid, dumb, crazy, ridiculous, anyone, anything, no one, nothing, the most,* and *the worst. Don't* say: "You always act really stupid when Donna's around," or, "You're the worst kisser I've ever had!" Similarly, avoid superlatives (like words ending in *-est* or preceded by *most*) when you're using them to say something negative. *Don't* say: "You're the dumbest girlfriend I've ever had," or, "You're the most disorganized person I've ever seen." Last but not least, avoid name calling. *Don't* say: "You're a slob!" or, "You're such an incompetent moron!"

Your verbal delivery — how you say it

The way you say your words also affects how the listener interprets your message. Important elements of verbal delivery include: *timing* (when you say your words), *volume* (how loudly), *speed* (how quickly), *pitch* (how low or high), and *tone of voice* (the mood you convey, like sincerity or insincerity, by the way you accent your words).

Timing — don't cut someone off or speak over him

Nothing's worse than trying to express a point and having someone cut you off — except possibly, both of you cutting each other off and speaking over one another! When you or your partner interrupt each other, you're not listening to the other's message; you're focusing on what you want to say instead. Remember, communication is a respectful *inter*-action — you each take turns. So let your partner finish talking; don't cut him off or speak over him. Show respect by listening intently and using reflective listening, facilitative agreements, and supportive statements (described previously) — *before* stating your feelings.

Volume — keep your voice at a normal conversational level

Don't yell. Yelling makes people tense, and it's difficult for either of you to think under such stress. Plus, you don't want anyone else to hear your conversation; it's private, just between you and your mate. So always keep your voice at a moderate volume level. Listen to your voice as you speak. If you begin to get louder — catch yourself, pause for a moment to switch gears, and lower your voice. Remember, if you want your partner to understand your point of view, he or she has to be able to *"hear"* you. Louder volume makes that harder and *less* likely, not easier.

Speed — speak slowly and carefully, in a relaxed voice

When you have strong feelings about a topic, it's easy to speed up — especially if you anticipate that your mate is going to disagree with you. Unfortunately, both of you will then feel more tense. Your partner will probably speed up, too, and you'll speed up even more, and then he'll speed up even more, and so on. Soon you'll both be talking so fast, you'll word your sentences poorly and become increasingly aggressive. That escalation will quickly defeat the purpose of the conversation. Usually, you'll also get louder at the same time, and you'll probably start cutting one another off and speaking over one another, too.

So always speak at a relaxed pace. When you're saying something you find difficult, speak slowly. Choose your words carefully and phrase them in an assertive, not aggressive, way. Listen while you speak. If you find yourself getting faster and faster — stop! Pause. Take a slow, deep breath. Then start again, speaking softer, lower, and slower.

Pitch — not too high, not too low

Just as people speed up and get louder when disagreeing, they often raise the pitch of their voices as well. Since most people find higher pitches more stressful and lower pitches more relaxing, raising your pitch as you become increasingly upset just adds stress and makes it harder for both of you to *hear* each other. So listen to yourself while you're speaking. If you find yourself morphing into Squeaky Mouse — pause, take a deep breath, then drop your voice and start again at your normal pitch.

Tone of voice — the mood you convey through inflection

You can easily change the meaning of a sentence by accentuating different words and using a different tone of voice. For example, try saying the sentence, "What did you do?" in different ways. Said one way, it's a question asking your mate to describe his or her actions. Asked another way, it's full of anxiety, as if you dread hearing the answer. Asked yet another way, it becomes an accusation, as if you're assuming that your partner did something wrong.

To communicate well, always speak in good faith. Avoid being sarcastic or insincere. Don't speak tongue-in-cheek or cynically, and don't try to imitate your partner's ineffective communication in hopes that he'll get the message.

Chances are, he won't. And if he does, he'll just become angry and reject or even ignore your message and point of view. Instead, encourage your mate to hear your message by using a sincere, respectful tone of voice and by approaching the topic straight on.

Monitor and adjust your verbal messages

When you're speaking, listen to your statements and correct them as needed to keep the discussion productive and friendly. If you catch yourself saying anything inappropriate — stop yourself in mid-sentence, pause, take a breath, then correct your statement. For example: "You are the most . . . (pause). *No, I'm sorry, I didn't mean that. What I mean is:* I would appreciate it if you would _____." Or, *"I'm sorry, I misspoke. What I mean to say is:* 'I feel hurt when you _____. I would appreciate it if you would _____.'"

If you realize that the *way* you're saying something is inappropriate — stop yourself, pause, then correct yourself. *"I'm sorry, I'm starting to sound sarcastic, and I don't really mean to be. I guess I'm just feeling a little defensive about this. Let me start over."* For more on taking responsibility for your mistakes and apologizing to your partner, see the apology sidebar in Chapter 13.

Monitor the conversation — and keep it positive and productive

Listen to the direction of your conversation. Is it going well? Are the two of you practicing these behaviors, or are you starting to become aggressive? If you say one thing and your partner says the exact opposite, resist the urge to come back with a quick retort. Instead, pause, take a slow, deep breath, gain control of yourself, and lower your voice. In a sincere tone, either ask a question, use reflective listening and/or facilitative agreement — or if necessary, agree to disagree and table the discussion.

Nonverbal delivery — how you act when saying your words

Besides the words you choose and the way you say those words, what you do when saying them is also extremely important in determining how your partner will interpret your message. Important elements of your nonverbal delivery include eye contact, facial expressions, body position, interpersonal distance, and gestures.

Make good eye contact

Where you look when saying your message makes a big difference in the mood you convey. If you resist meeting your partner's eyes or look too intently, you'll detract from your message in some way. For example, if you look down, you'll appear timid. If you look to the right or left most of the time, or if your eyes keep darting about, you'll look shifty or disinterested. Conversely, if you look at your partner too intently, you may appear to be glaring or challenging him in an aggressive way.

To communicate effectively, look directly at your partner when he or she is speaking. Don't look down, around the room, or at anyone or anything else. Your partner will then look at you at least half of the time, with periodic glances to the left or right when he's thinking hard. When you're speaking, you should do the same: Look directly at your partner half the time, with periodic glances to the left or right when thinking. Also, make sure that you and your partner are turned toward one another so you can maintain effective eye contact throughout your discussion.

Facial expressions

Your facial expression gives your partner another nonverbal cue about the meaning of your message. When it's appropriate, it adds to the meaning. When it's inappropriate, it detracts. For example, people sometimes smile or laugh when they're feeling nervous, which can lead their partners to overlook the words being said. If you say "No" to a man's advances while grinning at him and making eye contact, he'll probably think you're teasing him — and want him to keep advancing.

So don't smile when you're talking about something serious, or your partner might think you're lying, being insincere, teasing, or just don't mean what you say. Similarly, don't smirk or your statement will come off as sarcastic and aggressive. Instead, keep your facial expressions in sync with the feelings and desires expressed in your message. If you're trying to have a sincere, honest, assertive discussion, your facial expression should also be sincere, honest, and assertive.

Body position

The way you position your body also cues your partner about your message. If you lean backward or look around when he's speaking, you'll look disinterested or even impatient. If you turn your body away, you might even appear hostile. If you cross your arms in front of you, especially if you cross your legs at the knees at the same time, you'll seem defensive or angry. If you stand over a sitting partner, you'll appear aggressive. If you walk up quickly while she's sitting, you'll seem even more aggressive, especially if you get very close. If you're sitting side by side, you'll look away from each other a lot — because making eye contact requires twisting your bodies uncomfortably.

So start by getting on the same height level as your partner. If she's sitting, sit down. If he's standing, stand up or ask him to sit down so you can talk more easily. Then either face each other or sit at a 90-degree angle (perpendicular). Always keep your head and body turned toward your mate, and lean forward. When you're looking away for a second, move only your eyes, not your head. Uncross your arms; cross your legs at the ankles, or not at all. If you're tightening leg or arm muscles, take a moment to relax them, and you'll feel more relaxed. Then monitor and change your body position as needed to consistently gave appropriate, assertive nonverbal cues.

Interpersonal distance — agreeable and non-threatening

How far your body is from your mate's also affects communication. If you sit too close, you won't be able to see his or her face or make appropriate gestures. If you sit too far away or if there's a large object between you, you'll feel more emotionally distant. So keep the distance comfortable. If your mate prefers being closer or farther away, find something you can both live with and try to keep that distance.

Gestures — calm, assertive, appropriate

If you wave your hands around, you'll look flighty or nervous. If you wring them, particularly while looking down, you'll appear shy, anxious, and uncomfortable. If you play with an object or keep clicking and unclicking your pen, you'll add to the tension and distract your partner from your message. If you pound on the table or stick your finger in someone's face, you'll appear aggressive. You'll also increase the stress, and escalate the discussion into an argument. If you throw something, hit the wall or objects, or push, shove, or hit your partner, you're acting in an extremely aggressive and inappropriate manner.

It's *never* appropriate to throw things, hit the wall, or in any way physically hurt your partner or her possessions. If you have problems with these kinds of behaviors, read the sidebar on physical abuse in Chapter 20 and see a psychologist immediately. Also, if you've hit or shoved your partner before, have no more contact with her until you've gotten professional help and have learned to be assertive, not aggressive. See the psychologist on a regular basis for a long time, and then periodically for an even longer period of time, to make sure you continue to behave appropriately in the future.

Remember, use assertiveness only when you and your mate have equal power. Don't speak assertively or even raise difficult topics with a physically abusive partner, because he's always in power over you. If your mate acts abusively toward you, be sure to read the sidebar on physical abuse in Chapter 20 and see a psychologist immediately. The life you save could be your own. If you physically abuse your mate, be sure to follow the advice given in the previous paragraph.

During any conversation, including assertive discussions, it's normal to make some respectful, appropriate gestures. Just keep them within the norm for your culture and respect your partner's interpersonal space. To soften the impact of a statement, gently touch your partner on the hand, arm, or knee, or hold his or her hand while speaking.

Avoid power struggles

Stop any power struggle before it begins. If you say one thing and your partner says the exact opposite — take a slow, deep breath, and lower your voice. In a sincere tone, either: Ask a question, use reflective listening and facilitative agreement, or agree to disagree for now.

Teasing

Teasing is a very complicated phenomenon, and it's important to differentiate between positive teasing and negative teasing. A *positive tease* is a tease in the form of a compliment: "Oh, m'gosh, you look so beautiful, you'll be the prettiest one at the party!" In contrast, a *negative tease* is more like a little jab: "You're such a bad cook, you make carry-out hamburgers sound gourmet!"

Essentially, teasing can be used to become closer, more intimate, and more playful with someone, or it can be used to put people off. What makes the difference are these key variables:

✔ Whether the tease is positive or negative.

✔ How often you tease your partner.

✔ The ratio of negative teases to positive reinforcements.

If you give positive reinforcements generously, then teasing positively is no problem, and teasing negatively once in a while is just fine. However, if you give very few positive reinforcements, but frequently tease negatively, then it's just a matter of time before your mate takes offense.

Also, never tease in front of others to embarrass your partner or get revenge. If you find yourself doing that, stop. Then as soon as you and your partner are alone, rested, and calm, use the techniques in this chapter and Chapter 13 to discuss what's bothering you. Don't pretend that something doesn't matter and make a joke out of it when it really bothers you very much.

The Art of Compromise

When you compromise, you grant concessions to another person and find a satisfactory solution to the differences between you. You negotiate a middle course, where you each get some of what you want. It's a give-*and*-take, not 100 percent give or 100 percent take.

To stay in any relationship, you'll need to compromise from time to time. If you aren't willing to do that, you're either not mature enough for an adult relationship, or you don't care enough about your partner to be in a relationship with him or her.

In most situations, there are many ways to compromise. However, both partners have to believe that they're benefited when they're *both* able to get *most* of their needs met. Then they have to be creative about how to do it. The following sections detail the different kinds of compromises.

To find solutions that work, remember to brainstorm possibilities when you and your partner are both feeling rested, relaxed, and affectionate.

Splitting the difference

You and your partner can agree to split the difference between your positions and meet one another halfway. You can split the difference in time, frequency, and amounts in many situations to achieve a reasonable compromise. If you want to get married in a year and your partner wants to marry in two years, you can compromise and marry in 18 months.

Alternating your choices

Perhaps you enjoy flea markets, but your partner considers them tacky. Or she loves movies, while you consider them a waste of time. Try compromising by alternating your choices. Catch a movie together Friday night, visit the flea market together Saturday afternoon, then do something you both enjoy at other times.

Alternating 100 percent concessions

If you don't care about a particular issue and your partner does, you might opt to give in completely on that issue. Then when you care much more about a topic, your partner could give in to your preferences. As long as you're both compromising about halfway overall, you can occasionally give 100 percent concessions and get 100 percent concessions.

However, keep in mind that some people are just more intense than others, so they care more intensely about everything. That person's partner shouldn't always give in just because he's more easy-going. The concessions should pretty much balance out. Otherwise, the over-giver will eventually feel dissatisfied, the over-taker will simultaneously lose respect, and the relationship will fade away.

Satisfying the objections

It's difficult to compromise on some issues (like whether or not to get married or have children afterward). You can decide when, how, or where to get married, or when to have a child or how many to have, but marriage and children are all-or-none choices. You can't get half-married or have half a baby. These types of decisions are even more complicated because people usually have strong opinions about them.

In such situations, the reluctant partner can discuss why he's reluctant (for example, why he doesn't want to get married or have a child). Then the partners can explore changing the factors involved to satisfy that reluctant partner. For example, if the man doesn't want to marry because he doesn't want to turn down a promotion out-of-town, the woman could move with him to the new city. Then she gets what she wants (marriage), and he gets what he wants (the promotion); it's a win-win situation.

If a husband doesn't want a child because he's heard that sex disappears once the babies come home, he and his wife can discuss his concerns and put certain practices in place to be able to have frequent sex post-baby. For example, the wife could work less hours outside the home, have weekly dates with her husband, maintain a regular roster of babysitters, hire a maid to help with household chores, and enlist the help of extended family members. In addition, the couple could alternate babysitting duties with friends who also have children, so each couple can enjoy some weekends and periodic vacations together alone.

Chapter 13

Good Communication: Putting It All Together

In This Chapter

▶ Communicating effectively with your partner

▶ Using communication skills to discuss and resolve difficult problems

*W*haaaatttt?? Another chapter on communication? You betcha! Faulty communication is the most common reason why relationships break up, and communication is a lot more difficult than it seems. So it's very important that you take the time to really memorize the proper attitudes and expectations to hold regarding communication (the nuts, described in Chapter 11), and the behaviors to use in conjunction with those attitudes and expectations (the bolts, described in Chapter 12). And now, in this chapter, I discuss how to assemble those nuts and bolts together in an effective order so you can discuss and resolve issues productively and efficiently.

Resolving Issues Successfully

To use this information most effectively, I recommend that you also memorize the steps in this chapter. Then, when you're holding a discussion with your mate, go through this checklist in your head. Be sure to follow the steps in the order presented as closely as possible. You probably won't need to use all these steps in every conversation you have with your partner over decisions. But you *will* need every element here for any difficult discussion on any topic the two of you vehemently disagree about, yet must resolve, in the near future.

Besides memorizing the nuts and bolts in Chapters 11 and 12, practice the behaviors outlined in Chapter 12 until you can do them fairly easily as isolated behaviors. You need to become skilled at using the nuts and bolts separately before you can expect yourself to combine them together to make a communication masterpiece. That's particularly true because difficult discussions become stressful, and people tend to forget what they want to say under pressure. The more automatically you can work with each individual communication nut and bolt, the more likely you'll be able to combine them well when you're under duress.

1. Pick your battles

Remember the saying, "Don't win the battle and lose the war?" You can amend that statement by saying, "And too many battles will definitely cause you to lose." Most people shy away from confrontation in the first place, preferring to get along as much as possible. Everyone has only so much capacity to handle confrontation. When you exceed that amount, whatever it is, your partner will begin tuning you out. The more you nag or complain, the more your partner will begin to completely ignore what you say so that he or she can exist happily in spite of you.

So pick your battles. The more things bother you, the more you'll have to restrict yourself. If you have a long list of grievances, write them down, prioritize them, and pick the top three to handle this year. Then put the list away and only revisit it *after* you and your partner have found satisfactory compromises for the top three items, *after* you've put those compromises to work for many months, and *after* you're both satisfied with the result. After you've done all that, you can pick another topic.

To prioritize, ask yourself: Why is this important? Is my discomfort with this problem likely to dissipate over time? What's likely to happen if we don't resolve this issue? Is a compromise necessary by a certain date? What date? What's the best outcome? What's the worst possibility if we don't reach a compromise? Is this issue similar to any other item on my list? Combine the items that are basically similar, and start with the items that require a compromise very soon. If your list includes, "I don't like the way my partner speaks to me," and, "I don't like the way he disrespects me in front of my kids," you can combine those topics as, "Improving communication between us."

If one of the items is, "Deciding who'll pay what bills this month," that item would go before your item about communication — simply because it requires a decision in the near future. On the other hand, if none of the items on your list are pressing, it makes sense to discuss the communication topic first. That way, you can use good communication when resolving the other items on your list.

2. Choose an appropriate time and place

If you're like a typical U.S. citizen, you have important conversations with your mate when you're riding in a car, dressing for work in the morning, or dashing off to some appointment or event. And guess what! Those are definitely *not* appropriate times to hold important conversations.

To have a *productive* conversation with your partner, choose a time and place that will enable such a conversation to occur — a time and place when/where you and your partner:

- ✔ Won't be disturbed, overheard, distracted, or interrupted
- ✔ Can focus on the issue being discussed
- ✔ Can maintain good eye contact
- ✔ Usually feel physically and emotionally comfortable
- ✔ Will have enough time to finish a lengthy discussion and reach a suitable compromise

Discuss problematic incidents as soon as possible when these conditions are met. If that's unlikely to happen spontaneously in the near future, ask for a time and place to get your partner's attention. ***"I'd like to talk to you about something important** — without the TV or phone interrupting.* **How about having dinner with me** *Wednesday night* **around** *7 p.m. at Mario's Restaurant?"*

3. Lay the groundwork

It's very important to have a history of mostly positive experiences with your partner before you try to resolve difficult issues. So use ***The Dr. Kate 20-1 Rule*** (described in Chapter 12), and give your partner lots of verbal and non-verbal positive reinforcement — including praise, hugs, kisses, and touch — *before* you ask for any behavioral change.

If you haven't been getting along or if the mood between you has been strained for a while, practice ***The Dr. Kate 20-1 Rule*** for weeks before having any difficult discussion. It's important to establish a positive context before trying to resolve any difficulties. If you've been getting along, be sure to give your mate lots of verbal and nonverbal positive reinforcement/rewards the day prior to and the day of your discussion. Tell your partner what he does that you truly enjoy. If you don't live together, make sure that your contacts on the phone are positive and rewarding.

Then at your meeting, when you have your partner's undivided attention, raise your issue. Begin by letting your partner know that the topic you're about to discuss is very important: *"Thanks for meeting me to talk. I appreciate it because this issue is important to me.* We've been dating for two years now, and *I'd like to discuss* how it's going."

4. Ask about your partner's feelings first

It's important to ask about your mate's feelings first to show that you care about how he or she feels. You're not obsessed with getting your needs met at his expense. Rather, this is a two-way street. You want to know his feelings and preferences, too. *"How do you feel about _____?"* For example: *"How do you feel* we've been doing the past two years?" Pause and wait for your partner to answer. Never ask more than one question at a time; otherwise, it sounds like you're complaining, not asking for information.

5. Use reflective listening to show that you understand

Now, using tentative language, paraphrase or reflect back what your partner has just said to show that you understand it. *"So what you're saying is _____. Is that correct?"* For example: *"So what you're saying is* you think we're getting along really well. You're very comfortable with our relationship, and you want it to continue, but you don't feel we're ready to get married yet. *Is that correct?"*

6. Continue reflecting if your partner keeps sharing

Sometimes your mate will go on to add new information. Other times, he'll just repeat similar ideas in an attempt to vent. For example, he might continue with: "Yes, I love you and I believe you love me, and we both enjoy each other's company, but I think we're just too young to get married at this time."

Using reflective listening, you could then say: *"You're concerned that we're too young to get married."* To which he might reply: "Yeah, we don't have much money saved up. I don't think we even have enough for a wedding, much less a honeymoon, an apartment together, and moving expenses."

So, you could reflect back again and say: ***"Sounds like you're concerned that** we need more money, **too."*** To which your partner might just nod and say, "Exactly." Or he might continue adding information, which you would then continue reflecting back to him.

By continuing to allow your mate to vent and/or share new information, reflecting it back each time, you allow him to figure out his feelings and thoughts by saying them aloud. You also make it more likely that you'll discuss the most important information about this topic, because you're creating a supportive environment for that to occur. You're continuing to show your partner that you understand and care, and you're not rushing. And by doing all these things, you're helping your mate care how you feel as well.

7. Ask questions if you're not sure what your mate is saying

If you find that you're not sure what your partner means by a particular comment, don't assume that you understand. Instead, ask a question. For example, you might say: ***"So are you saying that** you'd like to get married at some point in the future, just not now?"*** To which he might say, "Yes."

If you review the statements our fictional male has made up to this point, you can see that he hasn't yet made that clear. He's talked about being too young and about practical considerations of marriage, and he's told you that he loves you. But he hasn't really addressed whether he sees you as a potential marriage candidate for the future. Rather than jump to conclusions, it's best to ask. Just make sure that the question is really a question — that you're asking for information, not using a rhetorical question to make a point.

When people discuss their feelings, they frequently use adjectives and other phrases that are vague or have different meanings to them. Listen very carefully to your partner's words, and imagine explaining them to me. Could you really tell me exactly how your partner feels about this issue? If not, or if any part of his message seems unclear or confusing, don't assume you know the meaning. Ask him.

8. Use facilitative agreement

When you understand what your mate has said and have no more questions, and when your mate seems to be finished venting or adding new information and has agreed that you understand what he or she has said, it's time for facilitative agreement. As described in Chapter 12, agree with whatever your partner has said (or whatever *part* of what he or she has said) that you can agree with. For example: *"**I agree that** we're pretty young. We're only 26, and we probably will develop more in the next two years. And **I agree that** we don't have much money, and **it's probably not** enough to pay for a wedding with as many relatives as we both have. And **I would also like to** have a nice wedding . . . ."*

Facilitative agreement reminds both partners that they have more in common with one another — and more agreement with one another's positions — than disagreement. That knowledge keeps both partners feeling friendly toward one another, and it also keeps the communication flowing in a positive manner. In contrast, if you skip over reflective listening and facilitative agreement and jump into presenting your point of view, the discussion will quickly turn negative and may dissolve into a whopping power struggle (see Chapter 12 for more on this).

9. Give supportive statements and positive reinforcement

Besides using reflective listening, questions, and facilitative agreement to show your partner that you understand and care, supportive statements and positive reinforcement are also helpful. *"**I'm very happy that** you want to get married, and that you're being practical and mature and thinking about our financial welfare. **I really appreciate it. I think it's great that** you're thinking ahead."*

By giving supportive statements (*"**I'm very happy that** . . . ."*) and complimenting your partner (*"**I think it's great that** you're thinking ahead"),* you help him feel appreciated and loved. You also make it far more likely that he'll continue to care about you and your needs in the future.

10. Express your feelings assertively

Now it's time for you to present your concerns. Use the assertive sentence structure described in Chapter 12 to express your feelings. For example: *"**But I feel nervous that** we may never get to the goal of marriage. **I'm concerned that** if we don't set some kind of reasonable goal for where we're going and when — if we don't make a plan — we may never save enough money for that wedding. **I don't want** to be single forever."*

11. Your partner reflects back your statements

Just as you need to show your partner that you understand his or her comments by using reflective listening (described in Step 5), your partner also needs to use reflective listening to show you that he or she understands your position. For example: *"It sounds like you're feeling tense about this, like we need to get organized and start saving money for a wedding. Is that correct?"* To which you nod and continue: "Yes, that's how I feel. I feel very uncomfortable when I can't plan my life because we don't have any kind of wedding plan, not even a long-term one. I don't want to be single forever, and I would appreciate it if we could make some kind of plan to prevent that from happening."

By using reflective listening, your partner has shown you that he understands and cares. He's also encouraged you to elaborate on your feelings and desires. And that has carried the communication forward in a positive way.

12. Your partner uses facilitative agreement

Now your partner agrees with whatever you've said that he or she can agree with, just as you did in Step 8. For example: *"Yes, I can see your point. I agree that it would be helpful for us to set a date and make a plan. We can first pick a date for the wedding, then make a list of what we need to do to get there, and how much money we'll have saved by when."*

In his first sentence, your partner has agreed with whatever he can agree with: *"Yes, I can see your point. I agree that it would be helpful for us to set a date and make a plan."* That helps you feel understood and positive about him and this conversation. Then in his next sentence, he is really tossing out the first possible compromise: *"We can first pick a date for the wedding, then make a list of what we need to do to get there, and how much money we'll have saved by when."* Now you're really moving forward, but you're ready to, because you're both feeling understood, loved, and positive toward one another.

13. Brainstorm compromises

Your mate has just suggested a compromise. Discuss the merits of that compromise, and if you don't like it, suggest a different compromise. Be sure to tell your mate what you like about his or her compromise — or at least give some kind of positive reinforcement for offering it — before you say what you don't like about it or offer an alternative compromise. Use tentative language, like you're proposing an idea, not like your way is best and his isn't.

"Well, that's a good idea, and we certainly could do it that way. But it seems like it's going to be tough setting a date without knowing how long it will take us to save the money. How much money we'll need is going to depend on what kind of wedding we want, how many people we invite, and all that good stuff. *So I was thinking it might be better if we* first discussed what kind of wedding we want, and how much it will cost. Then once we know that, we can discuss how much money we can save each paycheck or each month toward that cost. Then working backwards, we can figure out about when we'd have enough money to pay for the wedding. And based on all that, then we can set a date that's realistic. *How does that sound?"*

To which your partner might reply: "Well, that sounds pretty good. But how are we going to know what weddings cost?"

14. Discuss possible compromises

If your partner doesn't like your suggestion, brainstorm an entire list of possible compromises, writing them all down. Be creative and just say whatever ideas pop into your mind, no matter how silly they seem. Don't censor them; just go with the flow and write them down, so you'll think of even more possibilities. After you've thought of every compromise you can think of, go back and discuss the pros and cons of each one, using communication Steps 4 through 12. That is, every time your partner says something, reflect it back, ask questions about anything you don't understand, use facilitative agreement, give supportive statements and positive reinforcement, and then share your feelings assertively. Your partner should also follow these steps with you.

15. Choose a mutually acceptable compromise to try

As you follow Step 14, you'll notice which compromises you both like better. After you've discussed all the possible compromises and how you feel about them, choose a mutually acceptable compromise to try. *"Well, it sounds like we've ruled out _____ and _____, because neither of us likes those compromises. We both seem to prefer _____, so why don't we try that one?"*

16. Write down the compromise

Take a new piece of paper and write down the compromise and any mini-goals you've agreed on that will lead you to accomplishing that compromise, your big goal.

Compromise: We will get married in the not-too-distant future. To accomplish that, we're going to:

- ✔ Decide what kind of wedding we want.
- ✔ Figure out how much it will cost.
- ✔ Discuss how much we can save from each paycheck.
- ✔ Calculate how long it will take us to save for that wedding.
- ✔ Based on all of the above, pick a wedding date.

Read what you've written back to your partner, and ask: ***"Have I written it correctly? Is that what we agreed on?"*** To which he'll probably reply, "Yep."

Give your mate a copy of the compromise, keep a copy for yourself, and if you live together, post another copy where you'll both see it regularly. That will help both of you stay on track — without one of you having to continually remind the other.

17. Set a time to evaluate the compromise

Every compromise needs a checkpoint, a time when you evaluate how well your agreement is working, and whether or not the two of you are still happy with it. The exact date you choose will depend on the compromise. Pick a date that is a reasonable period of time later — one that allows you and your partner to experience the effects of the compromise and whether or not you're still comfortable with it.

For example, if you and your partner agree to do something differently each weekend (like setting Friday nights as your special out-on-the-town date night), you might agree to revisit the compromise in a month. ***"OK, why don't we talk about this again*** *in a month,* ***and see how the compromise is working for each of us?"*** If your mate agrees, you each need to write that meeting date on your calendar or in your datebook. If you live together, write it on a note and stick it to the fridge door or bathroom mirror, so you'll both see it regularly. In the wedding example, however, the compromise is an ongoing plan, with a series of mini-goals, so you'll need to choose a date for each mini-goal.

- ✔ ***"Why don't we set a time period and date*** *for doing each of these things?* ***When would you like to discuss*** *what kind of wedding we want?"*
- ✔ *"How about next week, same time, same place?"*
- ✔ *"OK, sounds good to me."* You write, *"Wed., _____ (date),"* after *"Decide what kind of wedding we want."*
- ✔ *"OK,* ***how about the next one*** *— figuring out how much the wedding will cost.* ***Want to do that*** *two weeks* ***later?"***

✔ *"OK, sure."* Writes *"Wed., _____ (date),"* after *"Figure out how much it will cost."*

✔ *"OK, we have three items left on our list — figuring out how much we can save from each paycheck, calculating how long it will take to save for the wedding we want, and then based on all that, picking a wedding date.* **Do you want to do all of those the** *following week, same time, same place?"*

✔ *"OK, great."* Writes, *"Wed., _____ (date),"* behind those three items on the list.

✔ *"OK, we've got it; this sounds good. Why don't I make a copy for each of us? We can both put one in the bathroom, so we can look at it every morning when we brush our teeth. That should keep us on track."*

✔ *"Great idea."*

18. Evaluate and compromise again as needed

Meet with your partner on the date you've agreed on to discuss the current compromise and evaluate how it's going. If one of you isn't pleased, that person suggests an alternate compromise.

For example, in the Friday night date scenario, if you aren't pleased with the results:

✔ You: **"I like** *going out at least one night on the weekend,* **but I feel** *pretty beat on Friday. Can we make our special night Saturday instead?"*

✔ Your mate: **"OK, let's try it for** *a month,* **then discuss it again and see how it's working."**

So then you try that compromise for a month. Keep going back and forth in this fashion until you find a compromise that works for both of you.

The wedding example is a bit more complicated, because there are several mini-goals to accomplish along the way to reaching your big goal. So you might need to amend the order of the mini-goals or their allotted time frame; you might even add more mini-goals to allow you to accomplish your big goal. Perhaps you meet on the first date you've set aside and decide to have an indoor wedding. OK, one mini-goal down. But there are several halls that might be appropriate, and you've only allowed two weeks to reach the next mini-goal, "Figure out how much it will cost." So you decide to set a different date to give you more time to reach that mini-goal. You might also decide to divide the list of wedding hall possibilities and check them out separately to cover more ground, then get together on certain dates to visit each other's top picks together. So, you've basically amended your plan by adding new mini-goals and changing the dates for accomplishing those mini-goals. However, by staying organized, revisiting the compromise, and refining it as needed, you can eventually reach your big goal in a way that satisfies both of you.

19. Agree to disagree and set a date to discuss the issue again

If you and your partner just cannot seem to find a suitable compromise, it may be best to end the discussion on an amicable note and table it for a later date. Even though you allow two or three hours for a discussion, at some point the discussion would be better off ended — at least for the current time.

If one or both of you are tired, or you're deadlocked and can't even agree to try out a compromise, table the discussion until another time when you can revisit the topic with fresh eyes. End the conversation respectfully: *"Well, it seems like we're not going to find a compromise we can agree on tonight. It's getting late, and we're both tired. Why don't we agree to disagree for now, and get together in about a week to discuss it again? In between, we can each think about it some more, and see if we can come up with anything else that might work. How does that sound to you?"*

Set a time to reopen the discussion: *"How about getting together next Wednesday at 7 p.m. at Mario's Restaurant to have dinner and talk about this again?"*

After you've had time to rest and re-think, you may discover a solution you've overlooked. Or you may realize you feel differently and are now willing to try one of the compromises your partner previously suggested.

20. Summarize your agreements and reward each other before ending the conversation

Everyone receives information from the outside world and processes it through their sense of sight, hearing, smell, taste, and touch. Studies show that the more ways you process information — the more senses you use — the more likely you are to remember that information.

When you write down your compromise, you use your sense of touch and vision. When you read it aloud to your partner, you also hear the information. When you reread your goal periodically, you remind yourself through your sense of sight. And when you summarize your agreements at the end of a discussion, you once again use your voice and your sense of hearing. The repetition also helps you organize, remember, and recall the information. Doing all this also clarifies the compromise and any mini-goals. It makes it more likely that you and your partner are on the same page — and will remember your goals and mini-goals the same way. If one of you has a different impression of your agreement, it should become obvious when you summarize, note, and reread it. You can then correct and clarify your agreement.

In addition, when you summarize what you've accomplished and reward one another for your efforts and/or the outcome, you feel good about yourselves and your relationship. You also end the discussion on a positive, affectionate note, and remind yourselves why you want to be with each other.

"OK, so we've basically agreed that we love each other, and we're going to get married! Yayee!!! We've reached a compromise and set up a beginning plan, with mini-goals and dates. That's a great start. We did good!"

Even if the discussion got a little heated and you didn't agree on any trial compromise, you can still mention something you did agree on, and positively reinforce/reward one another.

"Well, we didn't finish reaching our compromise, but that's OK. We've got a date set up to revisit this, and we did agree that we love one another and want to get married. And we were able to discuss our disagreements without getting aggressive, and that's really good. We're making progress. I appreciate you getting together with me tonight, and all your efforts to discuss this and find a compromise."

And, in fact, you did agree on many things. You agreed that you love one another and want the relationship to continue to marriage. You agreed that this issue is important and needs further discussion. You agreed that it's important to find a solution that is satisfactory to both of you. You agreed that you'll get together at a certain time to revisit this and try again to find an appropriate compromise. That's a lot of agreement! So now you can go to bed next to one another and feel good about each other. You may not agree on everything, and you certainly don't agree on everything right at this moment, but you're in enough agreement to know that your partner values you, the relationship, and your comfort in the relationship. And that's really pretty good, isn't it?

A wise man and terrific friend once told me, "My wife and I have some issues we resolve right away. With others, it takes us a few months to settle them. And we have one or two that we still don't agree about." This man has been married for over 30 years. Can you tell why?

Once you have memorized each communication skill step listed in this chapter and have used them in the proper order in various situations, try using the more abbreviated *Dr. Kate's MAKE-A-DEAL Technique* as a handy reference guide. It's described on the Cheat Sheet in the front of this book.

DR. KATE SAYS

Mastering the art of apology

Remember that old movie line, "Love means never having to say you're sorry?" Well, forget it. When you love someone, you'll need to say "I'm sorry" often — and mean it — or you can kiss your relationship bye bye! To keep your love thriving, you and your partner will need to work through problems in a direct, respectful way. And to do that, you'll both need to take responsibility for your own behavior — your strengths and your "in-need-of-improvements" — the whole shebang.

When someone refuses to apologize, it's generally a sign of insecurity — that person is afraid to admit to any fault lest something terrible should happen. Of course, he or she usually can't explain what that terrible thing might be. Sometimes men have a harder time apologizing because they were taught never to show vulnerability. Both men and women can become "apology avoidant" if they were frequently criticized and blamed growing up — told what they did "wrong," but not what they did "right." The person then becomes shell-shocked and hypersensitive. At the first hint of a criticism, his mind shuts off, and he either changes the topic, defends himself vehemently — or goes on the offense, blaming his partner. For him or her — whoever the person might be — apologizing is too big a threat. It's like admitting he or she did something *truly awful* and *unforgivable*.

But the bottom line is: No one is perfect. Everyone makes mistakes, and in any relationship where partners interact frequently and intensely, it's usually just a matter of time before both of them make a mistake. Usually the errors are small, relatively insignificant, unintentional faux pas — like saying something insensitive when fatigued or stressed. And sometimes the mistakes are much bigger. There are also times when it's kinder to your partner just to fix your mistake without divulging it. (For example, if you've been cheating, don't lie about it, but don't hurt your mate further by bringing it up. Just end the affair and vow to always be faithful in the future.)

When you've done something your partner knows about and experiences discomfort about — like all those little stupid, yet hurtful, mistakes of everyday life — just apologize and commit to doing better: *"I'm sorry I* _____ (did what). *I know you feel* bad about it, *and I can understand* that. *I wish I hadn't* done it, *and I'm sorry you feel/felt* _____ (hurt, frustrated, angry, whatever). *In the future, I'll try hard to do* _____ *instead."*

Saying you're sorry in such a direct, clear, non-defensive manner usually helps the two of you make up and grow closer. In contrast, failure to take responsibility and apologize can quickly drive you apart. Your inability to apologize quickly becomes a huge stumbling block. If you let your partner take responsibility for everything that goes badly between you, the relationship will become very uneven, and will either end or become very unhealthy. Even if your mate doesn't fill in for you in the apology department, blaming her for your mistakes — or squirming around every which way to avoid apologizing — will quickly lead her to lose respect for you.

So if you have trouble apologizing, see a psychologist to work on your thoughts and your self-esteem. Concentrate on accepting and loving yourself as the imperfect mortal you are. Look at your mistakes as unfortunate, but inevitable facts of life. By seeing them in a more realistic light, you'll actually be able to face them and fix them. In doing so, you'll free yourself up to be happy and healthy — and the best partner you can be.

Part IV
Feeding the Flame — Physical and Sexual Intimacy

The 5th Wave   By Rich Tennant

"I KNOW WHAT A ROMANTIC GETAWAY IS. IT'S WHEN MY PARENTS TELL ME TO GET AWAY FROM THE HOUSE FOR A FEW HOURS."

In this part . . .

People stay in love and nurture that bond in two major ways: A) Psychologically and emotionally, by sharing thoughts and feelings with one another through verbal communication; and B) Physically and sexually, by staying close through sexual communication. In Part III, I talk about "A," staying close to your mate through verbal communication. In this part, I consider "B" — how to stay close to your mate through sexual communication.

First, I examine some of the common myths about sex, and explain why the reality of sex is more satisfying than the myths. I discuss how important sex is in a committed relationship — how it brings you closer and keeps you there. I also answer the what, when, where, why, how, how much, and with whom questions about sex in a long-term relationship. Then I discuss various sexual disagreements couples encounter — the ones that can be compromised, and the ones that shouldn't be. Finally, I give you specific, practical tips that you can immediately use to keep the romance and spark alive in your relationship.

Chapter 14

Sexual Baloney

In This Chapter

▶ Examining six common sex myths

▶ Replacing those misconceptions with rational sexual expectations

*W*hen's the last time you had coffee with your parents and discussed your orgasms? Or chatted up your in-laws about fellatio over a good Italian dinner? Right, you've got it — sex is still the topic nobody really talks about.

As a result, there are a lot of strange ideas about sex floating around out there. Of course, sex isn't as taboo as it used to be. It's a wonder people actually figured out which body parts went where in the old days. No, we're more educated now. All we have to do is turn on the TV or visit a magazine stand, and our education is promoted. Yet talking about sex in many settings and situations is still inappropriate, so it still carries a "hands-off" aura. And just like men who worry when they can't go an hour like a porno star, or the women who fret because they don't look like airbrushed centerfolds, people who get Sex 101 training from movies and porno rags often acquire some strong misperceptions about sex as well.

In this chapter, I examine six of the most pesky sex myths — and how they make sex even less user-friendly. Then I tell you the good news — how and why the realities about sex are so much more enjoyable than the myths.

Squashing Six Sex Myths

As I discuss the following myths, review your ideas about sex. What strange ideas do you hold, and how do those beliefs cause you difficulty? Then consider the realities, and how you can incorporate those beliefs into your lovemaking, to make it a whole lot more fun for you and yours.

Myth #1: Achieving orgasm is the goal

Many people believe the myth that you and your mate should both have an orgasm during each episode of sex — and if you don't, there's something wrong. When a man believes this myth, he presses his girlfriend to have an orgasm every time. He tries and tries and tries and becomes quite frustrated when she can't; he may even feel like a failure. Usually the woman tries to reassure him, but if he believes sex is not good without her orgasm, or that he's less of a man for not being able to give her one, he becomes increasingly frustrated and determined to "make" her climax.

In cases like these, sex becomes increasingly stressful, more like a tedious chore than playing. The big question hanging in the background is: Will she have an orgasm, or won't she? Finally, the woman feels too tense to orgasm. Sex stops being fun, and instead, becomes the quest for "The Big O."

The same thing can happen if the man can't ejaculate. The woman wastes a lot of time feeling inadequate, and presses him to have an orgasm. If she keeps pushing, he can become so tense that he has trouble getting an erection.

But all that tension and grief are just wasted energy! Sex is the giving and receiving of pleasure between two people. It's the most intimate act you can share with your partner. As long as you're giving and receiving pleasurable sensations, orgasm is not required.

In addition, it's very important to *feel* during sex. When you get caught up in the performance — watching yourself like you're on a stage and wondering whether or not you'll be able to climax *this* time, your anxiety makes it difficult to enjoy any of the sensations — much less reach orgasm. Orgasm just naturally occurs when the pleasurable stimuli reach a certain level, but anxiety/tension/stress (all one and the same) can block the enjoyable sensations from getting through to your conscious awareness.

So the best way to have good sex is to take the pressure off. Just get into the sensations and *feel* them. If an orgasm occurs, fine. If not, that's OK, too.

Myth #2: Experience is necessary

You have to have a lot of experience with sex to be good at it, right? After all, practice makes perfect, doesn't it? Wrong-o! If you believe in this myth and are new at sex, you'll drive yourself nuts worrying about not being able to please your partner. And if you've been having sex for a long time, you may become cocky and overconfident, taking it for granted that you're a regular stud-muffin, while proceeding to use the same moves on everyone, as if your new lover should enjoy exactly what the last one did. Nothing's worse than treating your partner like she's a member of the harem.

In reality, every new partner is a new sexual experience unlike any other. There's a vast network of neurons traveling from your skin and sexual organs to your brain, and everyone is wired differently. No two people ever feel sensations exactly the same, even when the stimulation originates at the same place in their bodies. And no two brains are ever completely alike either; there's always some variance. What one person finds highly stimulating, another may find irritating, painful, or just boring. Everyone's reactions are different during and after sex, and everyone orgasms a bit differently. Some people orgasm quietly, some very loudly, some laugh big belly laughs, and some cry happy release tears — all different, but normal, reactions. On top of that, how you perceive sensations is also somewhat learned. Your automatic physical responses, along with your learned/conditioned psychological and emotional responses, combine in any sexual experience to determine how much pleasure you receive.

So it's a real mistake to do to your new partner as you did to your last, without checking to see if this new person prefers different movements, pressure, timing, and strokes, in slightly different places. Experienced people sometimes forget that. They also have a tendency to skip over much of the foreplay — the hugging, kissing, and stroking of other areas besides the genitals — to go right to the "main course." Many women complain that after they've had inter-course, their mate no longer kisses them as much.

In contrast, a novice sexual partner usually takes time to smell the roses . . . and the gardenias . . . and the lilies . . . and . . . and . . . and . . . ! And how enjoyable playing in the garden can be! Because everything is new, the neophyte often spends a great deal of time in foreplay, loving every minute. It's like having a new toy to play with. There's no pressure to go forward; the moment is to be enjoyed, and that is precisely what good sex is all about.

So, if you've had a lot of experience, remind yourself to view every partner as unique. Learn what yours likes, and don't skip the foreplay! If you're new, don't worry. The enthusiasm and joy you bring to sex can be a blessing. Just learn what your mate likes, and you'll be as good as any lover ever was.

Myth #3: Size is necessary for good sex

The myth of "size is necessary for good sex" states that the larger the man's penis, the better the sex. Since it's the penis that makes the man a man (and not a woman), many people think that the bigger the penis, the bigger the man. The man with the smaller penis who believes this myth feels he's less of a man because he doesn't have enough to play with, and the man with the larger organ who believes this myth often exerts less effort to please the woman with foreplay. After all, if he's large, and large is important, then he doesn't have to concern himself about using his fingers, mouth, and foreplay, right? He assumes his woman will get plenty turned on just by seeing him.

In the end, it's not the size of the penis that matters; it's what you do with it. The guy who has a big penis may feel like a powerful guy — a Sexual Samson deriving his power from his penis — and may consequently feel very comfortable sexually. And if so, good for him. But that large appendage and feeling does not automatically translate into pleasure for the woman.

Sure, many women like the sight of a large male organ. However, once they look at it, what the man does with it becomes much more important. Besides, women aren't nearly as drawn to visual stimulation as men are. (Compare the sales of *Playboy* to *Playgirl* if you doubt this in any way.) Instead, women tend to prefer a man who pays attention not just to intercourse, but to the entire context of sex — the romance and emotional stimulation, as well as foreplay that includes kissing, touching, oral sex, and manual stimulation. Many women don't have orgasms through intercourse alone — they need added manual stimulation and/or oral sex. So if the man overemphasizes the power of his size and consequently shorts his partner manually and orally, his partner may not receive as much stimulation as she'd prefer.

If you're smaller, learn to give the woman lots of kissing, touching, manual stimulation and oral sex, and help bring her to orgasm that way. Experiment with different intercourse positions to figure out which ones feel best to each of you. Then combine the oral, manual, and intercourse stimulation with emotional and psychological stimulation, paying attention to the context of the sexual act (the romance) and your relationship. If you do all of the above, as well as tell her how much you care and show it in your everyday behavior, the two of you should enjoy truly exciting and satisfying sex.

If you're larger, the same advice holds true. Give your sweetie the foreplay she needs — kissing, touching, manual stimulation, and oral sex — before you try to enter her. Make sure she's extremely lubricated. Pay attention to what she enjoys: which positions, what movements, speed, and intensity, and how deep she likes you to thrust. Incorporate those preferences into your lovemaking, and make sure she's always comfortable during the act. On rare occasions when you need more lubrication, go ahead and use a lubricant. Just be sure to choose one that doesn't eat through latex condoms! And *don't* use lubricants as a lazy substitute for good lovemaking.

Myth #4: Achieving orgasm one way is better than another

This myth, made popular by Sigmund Freud, says that one kind of orgasm is better than another. Freud believed two kinds of orgasm existed: "vaginal orgasm" and "clitoral orgasm." He taught that vaginal orgasm was healthier, more mature, and vastly better than clitoral orgasm. Because vaginal orgasm was, of course, reached through intercourse, this view made intercourse the focus of sex. Freud also believed that oral sex was perverted. (Read Freud's *Three Essays on Sexuality* for some amusing sexual myths.)

If you're female and believe in the vaginal-orgasm-is-better myth, you'll try to have an orgasm through intercourse alone (with no manual or oral stimulation before, after, or during intercourse). If you then find it difficult or impossible to climax that way, you'll find yourself feeling inferior. And if your lover believes this myth, he'll tend to push you to have orgasms through intercourse alone, with little or no foreplay, manual stimulation, or oral sex. He may devalue you for not being able to climax through intercourse, and may feel like a failure himself for not being able to give you that experience.

Freud's view on orgasm proliferated until the '60's, when Masters and Johnson arrived on the scene to save us all. By directly observing, measuring, and filming sex in the laboratory for the first time, those famous sex researchers proved that there is only one kind of orgasm. No matter how the sensations are delivered to the woman — manually, orally, or through intercourse — the orgasm itself (the muscular contractions, physical changes, chemical changes, and a whole series of spontaneous, complex psychophysiological interactions) remains the same. An orgasm is an orgasm is an orgasm. Any stimulation she receives — through any method of stimulation to any body part — adds up. When she receives enough pleasurable stimulation, she crosses a certain point and has an orgasm.

During intercourse, the man moves his penis back and forth, which causes indirect stimulation of the woman's clitoris. However, if he also uses oral and manual stimulation, he can directly stimulate the woman's clitoris. He can also control the exact location, pressure, speed, intensity, and rhythm better, so that the woman receives more arousing stimulation. Because of this difference in direct and indirect stimulation, degree of control, and amount of stimulation, many women find it easier to orgasm through oral sex and manual stimulation. So they prefer that oral and/or manual stimulation be in the couple's sexual repertoire. Yet they would *never* want to give up intercourse. While they may find oral sex and/or manual stimulation more sexually arousing per se and want it to be a regular part of their lovemaking, many find intercourse more emotionally stimulating and romantic — because it involves getting as physically close as they can get to their partner.

See the Sex file on my Web sites (www.drkate.com and *AOL Keyword: DrKate*) for more on this topic. *Sex For Dummies* by Dr. Ruth Westheimer, published by John Wiley & Sons, Inc., also contains more detailed information.

There's no one right way to stimulate someone. Oral sex, manual stimulation, and even anal sex are all A-OK — provided the sex is healthy (occurring between two consenting adults, and involving only positive, healthy feelings, with no pain or harm involved.) See Chapter 15 for more on this topic.

Myth #5: "Faking it" is bad

This myth states that you should never pretend to have an orgasm if you're not really having one. Because you should be honest with your partner and true to yourself, this myth says that faking it is a no-no.

But this is really a chicken-or-the-egg which-came-first situation. Feelings can come before behaviors, but behaviors can also lead to feelings. After all, you cheer at a ball game, don't you? And when you jump up and down, clap, and cheer with the crowd, isn't it more fun? You're getting into the action, and you feel more excited when you do. And if you're having a less than stellar day, but you start jumping up and down, clapping, and cheering with everyone else anyway, you'll usually find yourself lightening up little by little — until you're in a more upbeat, cheery mood. In contrast, if you just sat there watching everyone emote, you wouldn't enjoy yourself nearly as much.

Sex is similar. Nothing's worse than a partner who plays dead during sex, laying flat as a board, and saying and doing nothing. It's much more fun to moan, make noise, move, pull your honey's bod where you like it, and *get involved* in the action! That's also how your mate can figure out what you like — by noticing your verbal expressions and physical movements when he or she does certain things. If you show your excitement or pleasure when your sweetie touches you a certain way, he'll know that you'd like more of that in the future! In contrast, if you just lay there, he won't have a clue.

Don't be shy! Give your partner verbal and behavioral feedback when he stimulates you. For example, make noise, move your hips, press your pelvis against his, and use your hands to press him even more tightly against you. Say in a low, soft voice: *"Softer," "harder," "faster," "slower," "That feels great,"* or *"Stay right there,"* to let him know when he's doing something that feels especially good. Don't have conversations (they'll break the mood); just use short phrases. And *never* ever say anything negative (*don't* say, "I don't like that") unless you absolutely have to. Instead, if he's doing something that irritates or even hurts, just shift position or gently guide his hand, head, or torso to a slightly different place, and say: *"That feels better right there."* Or: *"I'm really delicate, but it feels good gentle, right there."*

Men, volunteer similar feedback when your woman is pleasuring you. Be sure to guide her in a positive way. If she's making you tingle head to toe, let her know. Say: *"Ummm, everything you're doing is just great."* When you desire something different, gently let her know.

Everyone wants to be a terrific lover, so everyone appreciates knowing when their pleasuring efforts are having good results. Your moaning and moving are really types of positive feedback/reinforcement, rewarding your mate for pleasuring you. They also stimulate him or her sexually. Also, when you move and make noise, you hear yourself, and it helps stimulate you, too! You might even have an orgasm when you least expect it. And even if you don't, you'll have much more fun by getting into it and acting "as if."

Don't lie and tell your partner that you had an orgasm. Just move, make noise, moan, and act *as if,* while giving positive feedback and guiding him into pleasuring you better. If you do this and have a good time with sex, your partner probably won't even ask if you've had an orgasm — because he can tell you've enjoyed it. However, if he does ask, just say: *"I really enjoyed it. It was wonderful,"* and give him a slow, sexy, satisfied kiss. He'll be happy and the subject will end there, with both of you feeling good about it. Then you'll continue to have fun together in the future, and you'll stay emotionally bonded in the process.

Myth #6: If one of you isn't in the mood, you should skip sex

This myth says you should be receptive to how you and your partner feel, and if either of you isn't in the mood for sex, you should just skip it completely and wait until you are. Of course, if you believe this myth, you'll tend to have less and less sex with your partner as time goes on because two people are hardly *ever* in the same mood at exactly the same time! Another problem is that this myth emphasizes your mood *before* any foreplay or sexual stimulation. Unless you already know that you definitely want a roll in the hay and your partner also knows he's up for a hayride, you'll just skip a trip to the old barn! If you buy into this irrational practice, you'll find yourself having less and less fun in the bedroom or the barn as time goes on — and drifting further and further away emotionally, physically, and sexually.

Many partners are hardly ever in the same mood at the same time. Most people work long hours inside or outside the home, so they need time to relax and change gears before they can get interested in sex. If you wait until you and your mate are both in the mood, you can kiss your sex life goodbye!

In addition, as you have sex less and less, several disadvantages occur:

- ✔ Because sex is a drive and a stress reducer, you'll probably feel more irritable, depressed, and stressed when you don't have it. In time, you'll become increasingly alienated from your own body and your mate's.

- ✔ Because being sexually close to your partner also encourages you to verbally communicate and become more emotionally intimate with your partner, not having sex makes it more likely that you'll end up holding grudges longer, become more frustrated and angry with your partner, and grow emotionally more distant as well.

Sex is way too important to leave it up to a chance — those few occasions when you and your partner will feel "in the mood" at exactly the same time. Sex helps you and your partner stay physically and sexually intimate with one another — and that helps you stay emotionally and psychologically intimate as well. So if you're not in the mood, allow your partner to give you foreplay and *get* you in the mood. And if you're in the mood and your partner isn't, give him the foreplay he or she needs to get there. Have fun, play, enjoy! And get closer to one another in the process.

Reviewing the Myths and Realities

Use Table 14-1 to remind you of each sexual myth and reality mentioned in this chapter. Then in the future, when you catch yourself entertaining one of these irrational ideas, use the reality to squelch that myth quick!

Table 14-1	Six Sex Myths and Realities
Grief-Causing Myth	*Saving Reality*
M1: Orgasm is the goal.	R1: Having fun is the goal, not orgasm.
M2: Experience is necessary.	R2: Every new partner is a new sexual experience, unlike any other.
M3: A large penis is necessary.	R3: It's not the size that's important; it's what you do with it that counts.
M4: One type of orgasm is better than another.	R4: An orgasm is an orgasm is an orgasm. Many women need manual and oral stimulation to reach orgasm.
M5: Faking it is bad.	R5: Acting *"as if"* helps you get into it, and can be a self-fulfilling prophecy.
M6: If one of you isn't in the mood, you should skip sex.	R6: If either partner wants it, he or she should help the other get in the mood.

❤ ❤ ❤ ❤ ❤ ❤

I Cry after Sex!

Dear Dr. Kate,

My age: 19   **My gender:** Female

I've been really emotional and started crying right after sex. But I've never had a bad experience, so I don't know what my problem is! Any advice?

Dear Waterworks,

Many people cry after having an orgasm. In addition to being a physical release, orgasm is an emotional release. Whatever feelings are there can come out, and that's good. Just explain to your partner that this is part of your normal sexual response, and it means that things went well. But it doesn't mean that if you *don't* cry, things didn't go well. (That way, he won't think he has to make you cry to know you enjoyed it!)

Some people cry after sex; some people laugh. The brain is at the center of everything we do, and it's wired somewhat differently in everyone. If you feel good after sex and you cry, don't worry about it. There's probably no problem. On the other hand, if you think very sad thoughts when you're crying, you can use the experience to pinpoint what's bothering you down deep. You might even find that you cry for different reasons at different times. Some people just cry because they think lovemaking is so beautiful!

Crying doesn't always mean that something is bad. Crying is very good for cleaning out stress. Tears release stress chemicals, and that can help you feel much more relaxed. So have fun, but do tell your partner not to worry when you cry. Some men may not believe you, but those who are compatible with you will.

Best wishes and enjoy!

Dr. Kate

She Just Won't Have an Orgasm!

Dear Dr. Kate,

My age: 29 **My gender:** Male

My girlfriend and I have been together for three years, but she still can't relax enough to orgasm. She's 23 now, and none of her previous partners were able to achieve an orgasm out of her either. In the beginning, we had great sex, lots of foreplay, and oral sex followed by two to three hours of sex in many positions, followed by afterplay and snuggles. She'd feel as if she'd almost have one, but then she wouldn't. Now it's difficult to go nearly as long, and she cries when she gets close. She won't see anyone, read any books, try anything new, or talk to me about it any more. What can we do — diet, artificial stimulants, special/other G spots, anything else?

Dear In Search of The Big O,

Yes. I suggest you stop trying to "achieve an orgasm out of her." The whole bedroom scene has become way too tense. You're trying too hard, and it's putting way too much pressure on her. Most people would eventually wear out after three hours of sex, especially if it's fairly frequent. If she doesn't feel that she can please you, that's like three hours of hell. She's probably feeling very inadequate, because deep down inside, you feel that way about her — and your actions show it.

Instead of thinking, "She *won't* have an orgasm," try thinking, "She's *just not ready* to have one yet." Not because she doesn't want to please you or enjoy herself, but because she really can't. Her anxiety and tension are interfering with the pleasurable feelings. The closer she gets, the more pressure she feels, until she starts crying. She's tired of trying to be a good sexual partner, and she feels your frustration.

Back off. Forget about her having orgasms. Tell her you love her and you're sorry for pushing her too hard. Limit your lovemaking to about 30 to 40 minutes, unless she spontaneously asks you to continue. Don't ask her if she wants to, or she'll feel pressured to continue.

Give her a long time to relax — about a year. Or forever. She does not have to have an orgasm to enjoy your lovemaking. The sooner you stop pressuring her, the sooner she'll start enjoying it again.

Best wishes, and write me back if you need more direction.

Dr. Kate

Chapter 15

Superglue #2: GOOD SEX!

In This Chapter

▶ Understanding why sex is important

▶ Defining good sex, great sex, and maintenance sex, and why you need all three

▶ Exploring the *when, where, why, how, how much*, and *with whom* questions of sex in a committed relationship

▶ Understanding which sexual differences can be compromised

▶ Fixing sexual problems that can be fixed and avoiding those that can't

In Chapter 11, I discussed how good communication is like Superglue #1, bonding the partners tightly together through emotional and psychological intimacy. Similarly, good sex is Superglue #2, bonding the partners tightly together through physical and sexual intimacy. In fact, not only does sex help couples stay physically and sexually close, it also helps them stay emotionally and psychologically intimate as well.

In this chapter, I discuss good sex, great sex, and maintenance sex, and why they're all important for your relationship. I answer questions about the who, what, when, where, and why, as well as the how's — how much to have, and how to have it. I talk about when to compromise, and when not, and which problems are fixable and which to avoid. In Chapter 7, I discussed the pros and cons of sex early in the relationship. In this chapter, I focus on sex in the longer-term relationship, where both partners feel like they have a relationship with one another.

Defining What Healthy Sex Is And Isn't

Sex is a natural, normal, biological drive, like eating, drinking, and sleeping. Sex is inherently good and healthy. As with all good things, however, you need to use it in an appropriate way and in the proper context to keep it that way. In Chapter 1, I define *"good relationship"* as a relationship that is both healthy and fun. Similarly, *"good sex"* is sex that is both healthy and fun. The "fun" part is usually easier to figure out than the "healthy" part. So what exactly is healthy sex?

Healthy sex is any kind of pleasurable sexual activity that occurs between two consenting adults and doesn't cause tissue damage or psychological confusion. As an inherently good and healthy thing, sex must always be accompanied by healthy thoughts, feelings, and behaviors. It must never be paired with unhealthy thoughts, feelings, and behaviors because otherwise, orgasm — an incredibly powerful reward — can make those unhealthy thoughts, feelings, and behaviors increase.

In Chapter 12, I explain that *positive reinforcement* is anything that follows a thought, feeling, or behavior, which causes that thought, feeling, or behavior to increase; it's basically a reward. And when you reward a behavior, it increases. Because orgasm is so pleasurable, it's a natural positive reinforcer/reward. It's like a shot of pleasure — Zap! — right to your brain. For that reason, it's especially important that you only orgasm after healthy thoughts, feelings, and behaviors. Otherwise, you may end up experiencing more of those unhealthy thoughts, feelings, and behaviors in the future. Just like love, sex should only be accompanied by pleasant, positive thoughts, feelings, and experiences to avoid psychological confusion and unhappiness.

So sex that includes negative thoughts and feelings (like humiliation and embarrassment) is unhealthy. Similarly, sex that includes negative behaviors (like inflicting tissue damage — bruises, bites, burns — and real pain) is unhealthy. Sex that is forced on someone, or sex that occurs between an adult and a child/adolescent under legal age is also not healthy. And all of these unhealthy forms of sex should be avoided.

For the rest of this chapter, I will address healthy sex, according to this definition.

Enjoying the 3 S's: Great Sex, Good Sex, and Maintenance Sex

To have a wonderful sex life, incorporate three types of sex in your life: great sex, good sex, and maintenance sex.

Great sex is like a peak experience. It's extra-special and only happens once in awhile — when you and your mate are both feeling smitten with one another, and the occasion is also exciting or special in some way. For example, some people have great sex after a terrific, romantic date, when they're unusually emotional and attentive to one another. Some people have great sex when they've spent the day or weekend relaxing together and forgetting about everyday stresses. Some people find it easier to have great sex on vacation in foreign locales, away from their usual responsibilities. They might have great sex when they've just finished some major project and are feeling on top of the world. Or they might have great sex when the emotional current between them is extra high, perhaps following the celebration of an anniversary, engagement, or wedding. Some extra variable adds to the pleasure and makes it a peak experience.

Every episode of sex simply can't be a peak experience. To have a peak, you have to have a valley — at least a little one. Peak experiences are "peaks" because they're different from the usual experience.

Good sex is the kind of sex you probably have most often with your partner. It's the giving and receiving of pleasure between two adults, and both of them enjoy it. Good sex includes exploring one another sexually, learning what you each like and don't like, then giving and receiving pleasure during each episode of sex. As I discuss in Chapter 14 on sexual myths and realities, you don't have to orgasm to have good sex; it's neither a requirement nor the end goal. As long as you and your partner enjoy one another and the sex is healthy (as defined previously), the sex is good.

Maintenance sex is also extremely important to relationships. Maintenance sex is the kind you can have every day with your partner. Perhaps there's not enough time for a date or even extended foreplay; you've got to sleep and get up early tomorrow. There's no time to laugh, cuddle, and talk endlessly for hours. Yet it would be nice to connect with your partner, even briefly, and have some physical and emotional release. At those times, it's maintenance sex to the rescue! It might take only 20 minutes, but it includes enough pleasurable giving and receiving to help one or both parties feel better sexually, physically, and emotionally.

Women usually love great sex, and generally prefer good sex over maintenance sex. However, to stay close to your partner, it's also good to have maintenance sex. Maintenance sex alone is not enough to keep a relationship thriving, but when there is occasional great sex and lots of good sex, maintenance sex can help you and your partner stay in touch when life pressures are just too demanding for more connection at that time.

WHEN to Have Sex

So when should you have sex in a longer-term relationship? In my opinion, whenever either of you are in the mood. The more healthy sex you can have, the better. If you're not in the mood, your partner should help you get there, and vice versa. The person not in the mood should do his or her best to get in the mood with the mate's help.

People often disagree on when to have sex. Some like it in the morning, while others prefer the evening. Some people like it only in the dark, while others love the daylight. Discussing the "when" of sex with your partner is a good idea. Discover when you each like to have it most. If you differ, take turns having sex at different times you each prefer.

WHY to Have Sex

Sex is a very effective superglue, helping you stay physically and emotionally intimate with your partner. By sharing this uniquely intimate experience with one another that you don't share with anyone else, you become tightly bonded, and physically, sexually, and emotionally closer. You feel like a team, so you tend not to argue as much; you can sense how much your partner cares about you and tries to give you pleasure. When disagreements arise, you're far more likely to discuss and resolve them, then get back to snuggling and lovemaking. And those calm, secure, loving feelings and expectations then trickle down to every part of your relationship.

Sex is also an incredible release from the everyday stress that you and your mate experience and tend to bring home to each other. The sexual sensations and orgasm help calm you, and they also distract you from your problems. Sex offers a natural emotional and physical release, followed by physical and emotional relaxation. So most people are easier to live with after sex, too!

HOW MUCH Sex

The less sex you have, the less you'll want it. Eventually, you'll fall out of touch with your body. In contrast, the more sex you allow yourself, the more you'll want it. You'll get back in touch with your body and your mate's. You'll remember how pleasant those sensations are, and come back for more.

Some people grossly underestimate how much their lack of sex affects them physically, mentally, and emotionally — and how it affects their relationship. Keep in mind, however, that sex is a natural drive, like eating, drinking, and sleeping. So ignoring it doesn't make it go away. When you have healthy sex with a partner, you both feel more relaxed, calm, and confident. When you don't, you both feel stressed. And the more relaxed, calm, and confident you are as individuals, the more relaxed, calm, and healthy your interactions — and your relationship — will be.

In addition, partners who have sex frequently are more likely to bring up and resolve problems in a more timely way. Getting naked with someone you can't stand is kind of difficult, so frequent sex encourages partners to discuss and work out their problems.

No matter how much someone is or is not consciously aware of the beneficial effects of sex, the fact is: Most people benefit greatly from frequent, healthy sexual release. So be sure to view lovemaking with your mate as a priority, and make time for it. As discussed in Chapter 14, if you or your honey isn't in the mood, that person should help the other get in the mood.

WHERE to Have Sex

Most people have sex in the bedroom, while others "christen" every room of their house or apartment. Some people like to have sex in places where they might get caught; the risk makes the sex more enjoyable to them. A certain amount of relaxation is necessary, however, to be able to feel the stimulation. Anxiety can get in the way of experiencing pleasure. In addition, most women like a lot of foreplay, which doesn't lend itself to sex in public places. And, of course, there are laws against displaying too much flesh or interaction in public.

People often find it easier to have sex in foreign locales, when they're on vacation from routine stresses. If you haven't had sex with your partner in awhile, try starting again when you're on vacation — provided you're going away soon. If not, perhaps a weekend getaway is just what the doctor ordered! The vacation provides an excuse to break from routine and gives you permission to act differently. You may also find that your sex drive increases — along with your spontaneity, sense of humor, and play — after you're relaxed and well-rested. So take advantage of opportunities to jump-start or enhance your lovemaking. Then be sure to continue those new behaviors when you get back home!

WITH WHOM to Have Sex

It's important to have sex only with your partner. Sex with someone outside your relationship will hinder the development and survival of your union.

In my observation, there's been a greater curiosity about swinging and ménage à trois (threesomes) since more and more people have started using computers at work and home. More people are gaining access to the Internet, and suddenly, every possible sexual perversion is accessible online.

Just because there's more curiosity, however, doesn't mean that having sex with someone other than your partner is healthy for you or the relationship. Just as sex between you and your partner builds intimacy, sharing sex with more than your partner will inhibit it or even damage your relationship beyond repair. One of the reasons sex becomes an intensely intimate, bonding experience between you and your mate is because you're sharing it only with each other. You're a team, and those very private sexual experiences are special and unique to the two of you. The minute you invite another person into your sex life, that bonding starts to erode.

If you choose to open Pandora's box, you may get a disappointing surprise. Your partner may develop a preference for the third person or threesome experience and want more in the future — when you don't. Conversely, he or she may find it difficult to forget the sight of you making love with someone else, and that image can damage your sex life together. Or the third party may talk and damage your reputation in the community.

If you want to keep your relationship strong, I highly recommend keeping sex between you and your partner. Period.

The HOWs of Sex

Your preferences and those of your partner largely determine how the two of you have sex. The only rule of thumb is that sex should always be fun for both of you, and it should be healthy. As I define it earlier in this chapter, that means the sex is between two consenting adults, and includes only positive feelings, thoughts, behaviors, and experience — not real pain, tissue damage, or any other negative thoughts, feelings, behaviors, or experiences. As long as the sex fits this definition, and both people enjoy it, it's fine.

Most women are able to feel the more direct sensations given in oral sex and manual manipulation better than the more indirect sensations from intercourse. Most of those women, however, still enjoy intercourse, and would never want to do without it. Some women are not able to enjoy the sensations in oral sex or digital manipulation because of unfortunate lessons they were taught growing up, either by their family, their religion, their culture, or even people in the neighborhood. If someone was raised to believe that their body is dirty, or that some sexual practices are dirty, that person is more likely to feel dirty and inhibited when he or she tries to have sex. The more rigid the ideas, the more difficulty the person has; the ideas inhibit the person's ability to feel the pleasurable sensations.

People who experienced the sexual freedom of the '60's and early '70's and those who were raised in the more liberal sexual times that followed are usually far more open about all forms of sex, while people raised before that time hold more conservative views.

Each person has his or her own preferences, and each couple has to discover what they enjoy together. However, because women are able to have orgasms better when intercourse in different positions is combined with oral sex and manual stimulation, it's better if the woman tries to become more open to participating in oral sex, manual stimulation, and various positions — just so that she and her mate can experience more satisfying sex together. If she has a very big inhibition in this area, talking with a clinical psychologist/sex therapist can gently open up her mind. In contrast, however, if the woman finds anal intercourse uncomfortable or painful, the man should back off and respect her wishes. Remember, in the final analysis, any sex that causes physical pain, tissue damage, or psychological discomfort should be avoided.

DR. KATE SAYS

If you choose to have sex with your partner, use a latex condom along with another highly effective form of birth control to help prevent sexually transmitted diseases (STDs) and unwanted pregnancies. As I discuss in Chapter 7, the *only* birth control method that is 100 percent effective in preventing pregnancy is abstaining from intercourse. That means no matter what method you use, there is always a failure rate. And even though it may be quite small, do you really want to end up in that small margin of error? So the best way to protect against pregnancy is to use not just one, but *two* very effective methods of birth control. Since you need to use two birth control methods anyway, making one the latex condom is helpful — because then you'll also be protected from many STDs by the latex condom.

Avoiding STDs and unwanted pregnancies

Sexually transmitted diseases (STDs) are a major problem in society. Latex condoms offer the best STD protection to date other than abstinence. But be aware that latex condoms can't protect you from all STDs. For example, crabs, mites, lice, genital warts, herpes, and others can be spread by contact with other parts of the body not covered by the condom, some STDs can be passed orally and through touch, and acquired immunodeficiency syndrome (AIDS) can also be passed on through infected needles and infected blood. However, when used properly, latex condoms are very effective in preventing the transmission of STDs carried in semen, so they should always be used. In addition, use your head, and limit your sexual partners to limit your risk. Also, educate yourself about the details of STDs. You can find a wealth of information on the topic at various sites on the Internet or in *Sex For Dummies*, by Dr. Ruth Westheimer (John Wiley & Sons, Inc.).

Many couples do not continue to use latex condoms once they're in a committed relationship together. If you do away with the condoms, however, you're trusting that your partner doesn't currently have any STDs. It's not just a question of whether or not your partner is honest; many people don't even know they have a STD until they pass it on to someone else. Many don't have clear symptoms, some can have no symptoms, and symptoms can be very difficult to see in women. You're also trusting your partner not to pick up any STDs during the time you're sexually involved together. Yet in the real world, many people cheat on their partner at one time or another, and any outside sex can bring STDs into your relationship. If you or your partner uses drugs, you can also bring AIDS into your relationship by sharing needles with others who are infected with the HIV virus. So take those facts into consideration before making a decision to do away with the condoms.

In addition, before you lose the condoms, you and your partner should both be tested *twice* for AIDS, with the second check following the first test by about 6 months. It can take that much time for the HIV virus (the virus that causes AIDS) to be detected by the test, so a person can have it and still come out clean on the present tests. That's why checking for the virus at least twice is always recommended. To protect you and your partner from both STDs and unwanted pregnancies, use two methods of birth control, with one being the latex condom and the other being another highly effective method of birth control (such as the pill, IUD, or diaphragm). If you decide not to use the latex condom, always use two other forms of birth control anyway, and keep in mind that you are then not protected against STDs.

Shedding Light on Sexual Differences

Every couple is different with regard to what they enjoy most in sex. What one person finds enjoyable, another may find irritating or even painful. Besides their physiological differences in how they perceive sensation, their psychological and emotional learning may have caused them to prefer one type of stimulation or position over another. It's always best to look at each sexual partner as a unique person, with unique preferences.

Most sexual differences can be worked out through compromise, but some can't. It's very important to understand which can be compromised, which shouldn't be, and why.

What can be compromised — and what shouldn't be

You can compromise on most elements of sex. Going back to our "Ws" and "Hs," you can compromise on:

- *When* you have sex
- *Where* you have sex
- *How much* sex you have
- *How* you have it

If you and your partner differ on these issues, working out a compromise is best. For example, depending on each partner's preferences, you might vary:

- The *time* of day
- The *place* you have sex
- The *positions* you use
- *How much foreplay* you have
- How much *oral sex* versus how much *intercourse* you have
- *How much time* you actually spend in the sex act

 If you have fairly different preferences (for example, if one of you prefers reaching orgasm during intercourse, while the other prefers reaching orgasm through oral sex), you can satisfy both partner's preferences in the same sexual episode. The man can bring the woman to orgasm through oral sex, then they can have intercourse, where he orgasms, and she may orgasm again. Or you can *alternate*, having sex one way on one night, then having it another way the next night to please the other partner.

All of these issues can easily be compromised, and doing so is usually good. That way, both partners get more of what they want on a more regular basis. It's a win-win situation.

But some sexual differences should not be compromised. Basically, you should never compromise with your partner if compromising means having *unhealthy* sex. So going back to our definition of healthy versus unhealthy sex mentioned earlier in this chapter, *never* compromise if compromising means pairing negative thoughts, feelings, behaviors, or experiences with sex, or opening up your relationship to another person.

So applying this definition, roleplaying can be fun and can add variety to your sex life. However, the roles played should not be negative or humiliating to either partner because those feelings can increase when followed by orgasm, the ultimate positive reinforcer/reward. If you or your mate have to be submissive or dominant to experience sexual excitement, those roles will tend to transfer to real life, making the relationship (which should be a 50-50 equal partnership) unhealthy. Similarly, sadomasochistic sex (also known as S/M), pairs pain with pleasure, so it's not healthy. If you occasionally dress up and *pretend* to do S/M, but it's just light-hearted roleplaying and no real pain or tissue damage is inflicted, that's OK. But if you or your partner inflict or receive real pain or tissue damage, that is *not* OK.

Sex with children, underage teens, the mentally impaired, or anyone who can't understand and refuse sex is always abusive and unhealthy. It's also illegal. Just as you don't want to have those kinds of unhealthy sex, it's also important to avoid pornography depicting such actions, to avoid increasing sexual fantasies about those unhealthy forms of sex.

If you notice yourself experiencing any unhealthy sexual fantasies or desires, avoid those images in the future, use thought-stopping (see Chapter 10), and see a psychologist for additional help if needed. If your partner wants you to indulge in unhealthy sex, voice your objection, and refuse to compromise on the issue. Read what I've written here to him or her. Then check out Chapters 16 and 24 for more healthy ways to keep your home fires burning. Using those ideas as starting points, brainstorm even more fun, healthy ways to spice up your love life. You can also visit my Web sites at www.drkate.com or *AOL Keyword: DrKate* for more tips to keep your passion alive and sparking.

What to use in moderation

Sex toys, vibrators, and roleplays can be fine as adjuncts to lovemaking. However, although there's nothing inherently wrong with using them, and they can sometimes be helpful and fun when paired with positive feelings and experiences, the frequency with which you use them is important. If you overuse a vibrator, you may find it difficult to enjoy your partner's tongue or hands instead. If you *always* use a sex toy, porno film, or roleplay prior to orgasm, you may eventually find it difficult to have sex without the toy or roleplaying. So be sure to use them in moderation, and have sex often without the props to reinforce the union between you and your partner. Sex should always remain the most important physical way you show your love for each other. It should always reflect the caring and respect you have for one another as people and partners.

Examining Sexual Problems

Sexual problems come in many varieties. Some are purely mechanical — which tend to be easier to treat — and some involve communication and relationship problems carried into the bedroom — which can be treated, but take a bit longer. Other problems, like sexual addictions, can and should be treated, but are very resistant to change and require a highly motivated patient and years of therapy. And other sexual differences — like sexual orientation — cannot be changed. If you or your partner have sexual problems or find it difficult to change unhealthy sexual practices, consult a psychologist with experience in sex therapy.

Fixing the mechanical problems

Sexual problems that are mainly mechanical problems — occurring in a relationship where the partners are happy and positive with one another — usually improve fairly quickly with professional treatment. Treatment begins with a thorough physical checkup to rule out or correct any physical problems that might be contributing to the problem. Once the physical problems are taken care of, a psychologist skilled in sex therapy can provide psychologically oriented sex therapy. Usually the couple is seen together, and treatment can be accomplished in a very short time period. And of course, the couple is usually overjoyed with the results!

For example, premature ejaculation and other erection, ejaculation, and orgasm problems are usually fairly easy to fix. *Vaginismus* — a contraction of the outer third of the vagina that prevents or impedes entry of the penis and causes pain — can also be treated. If you find sex painful, you should get treated for the condition as soon as possible. Often, a gynecologist and psychologist can work together to resolve the physical and psychological mechanisms involved, allowing you to share fun-filled sexual adventures with your honey.

If you've had trouble feeling sexual due to things you were taught growing up — perhaps you were raised to believe that sex was evil or sinful — changing those thoughts can take a bit longer. However, as long as you continue treatment long enough to replace those problematic thoughts with healthy, positive thoughts, you should be able to reduce your anxiety and let more pleasurable feelings through.

For some couples, all that's needed is to clear up their misconceptions and mis-expectations about sex. Perhaps they suffer from believing in one or more of the sexual myths discussed in Chapter 14. If so, discussing the problem with the psychologist may quickly fix the problem. Their "attitude readjustment sessions" may also include getting the couple back into a "playing with one another" frame of mind, rather than the "ESO — Eternal Search For Orgasm" mode!

Sexual misconceptions still proliferate!

Because sex is still a semi-taboo subject, there are still an amazing number of misperceptions and misunderstandings floating around out there.

During a radio show, for example, I was once asked if oral sex caused cancer. When I told the woman it didn't, the board lit up with misinformed callers phoning in to disagree with me. At my AOL site (*AOL Keyword: DrKate* or `www.drkate.com`), I have received hundreds of letters asking if masturbation really causes blindness, hair loss, impotence, insanity, incompetence, and permanently reduced sperm count, among other problems. Judging from the amount of mail and the incredible variety of disorders people worry about in association with masturbation, it's clear that masturbation myths are in no danger of dying out any time in this century! Even after the sexual liberation of the '60s and '70's, our culture still instills a lot of guilt about this simple little solo activity!

Many a young male has gleaned his ideas about sex from reading his dad's girlie magazines. And if anyone bases a sex education on porno movies and magazines, he or she is likely to pick up some rather strange ideas. For years, some people — including women — actually thought other women really looked like the very buxom, very airbrushed *Playboy* models shown in the magazine. Now that late-night cable has more than its share of exposed female breasts and amateur porno films have appeared in video stores, the full range of possibilities — from small and perky, to huge and saggy, and everywhere in between — is more evident.

Views of the male body and its mileage demonstrations have also confused some folks. One very bright man asked me to treat his premature ejaculation problem. His symptoms? Recently, he'd only been able to have intercourse for 20 to 30 minutes before ejaculating — instead of his usual 40 to 60 minutes! He'd been watching a lot of porno movies, and thought all men were able to "last" for an hour! (For the record, 20 to 30 minutes is *not* premature ejaculation.) The bottom line is: It's good to realize how much our ideas about sex — and those of our partner and our children — are influenced by the media and our peer groups. If you or your partner have some strange ideas, talk about them and clear them up.

Carrying communication and relationship problems into the bedroom

Sometimes, when a couple goes for sex therapy, they really aren't there to fix a sexual problem per se. Whatever is going wrong in the bedroom is an extension of the problems going on in their relationship, including their communication. If the woman feels angry or hurt with her partner, it makes sense that she wouldn't be able to feel the positive sexual sensations he gives her. Their verbal communication is tense, so she can't relax and sexually communicate well either.

While such relationship-based sexual problems take a little longer to fix than the purely mechanical type, most can still be fairly easily resolved with therapy. Once the psychologist determines that the problem lies in the communication and the relationship, not the sexual mechanics, treatment shifts to that arena. After the couple learns how to communicate well with one another and resolves their current list of problems through satisfactory compromises, the sexual problem usually takes care of itself. If not, it can usually be quickly and easily remedied then. Progress is almost always assured if both parties continue to attend therapy and work on their behaviors.

People sometimes stall and go through all kinds of gyrations to evade treatment — especially when they're worried that therapy will shed light on something they can't handle. For example, rather than admitting to an impotence problem, a man might let his partner think he's been avoiding sex because he's having an affair. If your mate shows this type of fearful avoidance, gently and patiently nudge him toward therapy. See Chapter 20 for more on how to do this.

Tackling sexual addiction

Sexual addiction is a very frustrating and resilient problem. In sexual addiction, as with all addictions, the addict uses an inappropriate method (sex) to try to fill a void in his or her life. Just as an alcoholic or drug addict consumes more and more of the drug to reach the same high, the sex addict takes increasingly larger risks to fill his addiction.

Sexual addicts may be peeping toms, exhibitionists, public masturbators, or strip joint regulars who blow their weekly paycheck on strippers and prostitutes. The addict becomes obsessed with witnessing or performing some lewd act, and becomes consumed by the fantasy, until he finally indulges in it. Once he has experienced orgasm, however, he feels terrible about himself, and the low self-esteem and self-loathing increase until the addict once again feels the need to act out by indulging in his sexual addiction behavior to relieve the pressure. And so the cycle continues.

If you have a sexual addiction, see a psychologist with experience in treating sexual addiction. If you're also addicted to drugs or alcohol, that addiction must also be treated. If you're not married and your partner has a sexual addiction, it's probably best for you to just cut your losses and say goodbye. As with any other serious addiction — like drugs, alcohol, and gambling — the relationship can't improve until your partner conquers the addiction. You have virtually no control over that, other than refusing to be an *enabler* (someone who covers for the addict, inadvertently rewarding the addictive behavior). See Chapter 20 for more on addiction and relationship problems.

Acknowledging unfixable problems

Unfixable problems include such issues as gender identification and differences in sexual orientation. Don't kid yourself into thinking that your gay, lesbian, or bisexual friend could suddenly change his or her sexual orientation to be more compatible with you. Instead, respect his or her choices and sexual preferences, and if you're heterosexual, don't push for romantic or sexual involvement. Don't take it personally that your friend isn't able to love you romantically or become sexually attracted to you; he or she can't change sexual orientation any more than you can change yours.

If you're heterosexual and your bisexual friend is willing to commit to you and only you — and won't feel stifled by not indulging in same-sexed or opposite-sex affairs, the relationship can work. (But expect some stress if that person has previously been known in the community as gay or lesbian.) On the other hand, if the bisexual is not willing to commit to you, or you don't think that he or she will actually be happy long-term that way, then you're better off looking for someone who does share your sexual orientation.

Just as you need to avoid dating married people because they can't really give you what you want, you also need to avoid romantic relationships with people whose sexual orientation is different from yours. Being friends is fine. Being more romantically or sexually involved is not wise, and in the end, you'll probably both get hurt. For more on these topics, see Chapter 4 on compatibility.

❤ ❤ ❤ ❤ ❤ ❤

Don't Open Pandora's Box!

Dear Dr. Kate,

My age: 20   **My gender:** Female

I'm married, but I sometimes wonder what it'd be like if we had a third party in our bed. I've asked my husband, but the idea of me having sex with another man bothers him. So I said it'd be OK if we had a female in bed with us, but he still says, "No." What do I do?

Dear Ménage à Trois?,

Forget about it, and be happy that your husband doesn't want another man or woman in your bed. If you search the advice archives at **AOL Keyword: DrKate** or www.drkate.com, you'll find lots of examples of people who've tried it, much to their chagrin. Opening your marriage bed to others can unleash a host of problems. For example:

- You may find that you don't like it or want to do it again, but your husband really gets into it and decides that he's bisexual. Or vice versa.

- Your husband may start an affair with the third person behind your back.

- Your husband may decide that he can't have sex with you any more because you cheated with another man — or another woman.

- Your husband may lose his ability to have an erection with you because the memory of you with another person bothers him so much.

- You and your husband may end up playing games, bringing home different partners to annoy or "get back" at each other.

- Your husband may blame you for "ruining your marriage," and pay you back by seducing your best friend or doing something even more hurtful.

- If you continue to play group grope, you may eventually find yourselves unable to enjoy lovemaking the old-fashioned (one-on-one) way.

- The third person may tell others in the community about your interactions. If someone takes pictures, you may end up the slut of the neighborhood. You might even have to leave town to escape your new-found fame.

- You or your husband may contract a sexual disease.

All of the above and more has occurred. Conversely, I've heard of nothing beneficial that would make all these risks worthwhile. Don't ruin your love-making and your marriage just to try out a sexual whimsy. Instead, use thought-stopping (see Chapter 10) to dump this fantasy, and try more constructive ways to jazz up your sex life!

All the best. Please let me know what you decide to do and how it works out.

Dr. Kate

Shrimp Sex — He Prefers Masturbation to Her!

Dear Dr. Kate,

My age: 26   **My gender:** Female

I've been in a relationship for three years. Last summer, we became engaged. Since then, our sex life has dwindled down to nothing. I'm a very sexual person; I like having frequent sex with my fiancé. He's also sexual, but he'd rather masturbate than have sex with me. We've talked about this many times. He says he likes to masturbate because he can be with any woman he wants in his imagination — without cheating on me. He gave me an analogy, comparing me to shrimp: "Shrimp is my favorite food in the world, but if I have it every day, I get tired of it." Our lovemaking went from daily to once a month if I'm lucky. Should I call it quits or what?

Dear More Than Shrimp Cocktail,

Unless you want to live the rest of your life with a guy who compares you to shrimp and prefers having sex with himself as opposed to you — and who doesn't have the sensitivity and empathy to understand that he's being enormously unfair to you in the process — it's time to bail. Besides, I'll bet he's even dining on shrimp more than you! Masturbation is fine, but when a partner prefers masturbation to having sex with a mate, something's very off in that partner and/or your relationship.

Ordinarily, I encourage people to try therapy before terminating a serious relationship. And if you want to do that, fine. But you're 26 and will soon be entering the prime of your dating life (see Chapters 4 and 5 for more on dating in the prime of your life). So don't spend more than six months to a year on therapy. There are plenty of other fish in the sea, and from the sound of it, you can certainly find yourself a more compatible fish — and fisherman.

All the best. Please let me know what you decide to do and how it works out.

Dr. Kate

I Want to Get Naked

Dear Dr. Kate,

My age: 33   **My gender:** Female

I've been married to a wonderful guy for 11 years. But I've always enjoyed men wanting me, and I've always wanted to be naked around them. That hasn't happened since I've been married. But we recently met a couple who are swingers, and the husband seems very interested in seeing me naked. I'd love to do it, but I don't want to have sex with him or his wife. I'm such a flirt, but I don't want this to go beyond pure flirtation.

Dear Naked Nelly,

Get a grip, woman. Do you really think you can get naked in front of this man and his wife without anything happening? In layman's terms: Fat chance. Don't delude yourself.

You have the right to get into swinging if you want to. You also have the right to ruin a perfectly good marriage if you want to. (Many women would love to be married to a wonderful guy for 11 years, so they'll be lining up for your hubby in short order.) Maybe things have gone so well for you in your marriage that you just want to stir them up a bit — make them a little crazy?

I encourage you to resist the urge. A good marriage is nothing to take for granted. I'm sure there must be some happy swingers out there. However, there are many, many *un*happy swingers.

Ask yourself: Why do you flirt? What do you get out of it? Do you feel insecure about yourself in general, so you want to get approval for your physical attributes? Playful teasing and flirting must have boundaries. You shouldn't flirt at your husband's expense. If you feel compelled to do it, then it's coming from something stronger than playfulness. In general, the more intense the feeling, the more likely it's being fueled by some kind of psychopathology or marital problem.

You may also have a tendency to take risks, to live on the edge, to stir things up when they're going too well, and indulge in other rebellious, impulsive behaviors. A small amount of these qualities can be useful, but too much can easily mean disaster for you and your family. Even if your husband initially goes along with your exhibitionism or swinging, he may later become angry, resentful, and blaming. You may find that no amount of apologizing erases the problem and returns your relationship to where it was prior to your indiscretion.

If you feel an intense need for extrinsic (external) approval from others in order to feel good about yourself, consult a psychologist to learn to value yourself and develop your intrinsic (internal) worth. Be sure to avoid alcohol and drugs to avoid losing whatever judgment and control you do have. Keep this letter and review it periodically during the course of your therapy. By treating the underlying reasons and being motivated, you should be able to stay faithfully — and happily — married.

All the best. Please let me know what you decide to do and how it works out.

Dr. Kate

Chapter 16

Light That Fire!

In This Chapter

▶ Changing the way you think, feel, and act to enhance your sensuality, romance, and fun

▶ Energizing your relationship with romance, passion, and spark!

I've been asked a lot of interesting questions on radio and TV, but the most common one is, "How can I put more romance in my relationship?" The person asking is usually female. Often she and her partner began their relationship with romantic habits, but these quickly bit the dust in a year or two or more — or less. For many, the life expectancy of romance is even shorter. Some people find that passion takes a hike after they move in together. Others complain that they've never had many sparks in their relationship, but they'd certainly like to ignite some now.

In Chapter 2, I discuss how the early intense feelings of infatuation can grow into a more relaxed, loving feeling. But that doesn't mean that romance and passion have to go out the window.

In this chapter, I suggest ways to keep your spark alive and kicking. And if the flame is already cold, I suggest practical ways to re-light it. Remember, everything of value requires attention and care. If you never give your car maintenance, it isn't going to run for long. A relationship is much more complex, so it needs attention, energy, and a lot of enthusiastic maintenance! If your partnership is due for a tune-up, try the suggestions in this chapter.

Spppaaaarrkkkinnng!!! Your Thoughts, Feelings, and Behaviors

I frequently talk about how thoughts lead to feelings. And although your feelings don't *make* you act a certain way, they certainly make acting in a particular way more easy or difficult. So when something isn't going well in your life, break the problem down and figure out where you can improve your thoughts, feelings, and behaviors.

If your relationship lacks spark, chances are, you're not treating your partner with passion. If you were, he or she would probably get into the passion, too. And if you're not *behaving* sparky, then chances are you're not *feeling* very sparky toward your partner or your life either. And if you're not feeling passionate and romantic, you're probably *thinking* in ways that inhibit those feelings. So to fix the problem, you need to examine your thoughts, feelings, and behaviors to see how you can make them more passionate, more romantic, and more *alive!*

First, ask yourself some important questions: Have you been thinking negatively about your partner and his or her idiosyncratic behaviors? Have you failed to appreciate those habits as the adorable quirks they are? Have you been shorting your special someone on quality time? Have you been acting like someone you'd never want to be with? Do you feel like you're not communicating well with your mate? If so, read on for ways to liven up your relationship.

Appreciate each other's quirks

Life would be pretty dull if everyone ended up with his or her clone. So dumping on your partner for every way in which he's different from you doesn't make a lot of sense. In my opinion, women have a lot more in common with women, and men have a lot more in common with men. If you are heterosexual, however, you're interested in a relationship with the opposite sex. So it doesn't make a whole lot of sense to dwell on your partner's differences as though they're the worst things in the world, particularly when many members of that gender tend to act similarly.

In *My Fair Lady,* Henry Higgins moans, "Why can't a woman be more like a man?" Similarly, women and men both complain when their partner doesn't act like they do, because, of course, their way is the *proper* way to act. When a woman comes into my office and launches into a lengthy tirade about how her boyfriend isn't romantic, intuitive, communicative, and aware of details — basically rattling off a long list of traits more commonly found in females than males — I don't console her. Instead, I look her straight in the eye and say, "Well, if you want to marry a woman, you can, you know."

My suggestion generally produces a small episode of surprise/shock before the woman quickly realizes what I'm getting at — men and women are very different in many ways. It makes no sense at all to date a man and then complain about the ways in which he acts more like a man than a woman. Similarly, it makes no sense for a man to date a woman and then complain when his girlfriend acts more like a woman than a man.

Try to look at your partner's idiosyncrasies with a sense of humor. If your boyfriend has a habit of leaving cabinet doors open after searching for something, don't get irritated. Instead, take a step back and lighten up. It's not like he went on a murderous rampage. No. He didn't even steal all your money and leave town with your dog. He just left some cabinets open! Try thinking of his somewhat goofy behavior as an endearing trait, something nonsensical that makes him unique.

Similarly, if your girlfriend has a habit of sweeping the floor and leaving the dirt in a pile that you invariably step in later, don't rant and rave about how inconsiderate she is. What difference does it make if you step in a little dirt? She's probably not doing it deliberately; she just has a strange little habit. So instead of frustrating you and her, watch where you walk. If you notice a pile, take the broom and sweep it up. Focus on how *nice* it was that she swept most of the floor, not how *awful* it was that she didn't quite finish. View her behavior as something endearing, rather than a monumental problem.

With so many serious problems in the world, little quirks — like being messy, throwing clothes on the floor, leaving the toilet seat up, being late, squishing the toothpaste tube haphazardly, setting and resetting the alarm three times before getting out of bed, piling up mountain after mountain of magazines that somehow never get read — are in the end, just little quirks. They're not important in the grand scheme of things. If you approach these idiosyncratic behaviors with a sense of humor and laugh — rather than nag, moan, and complain — your mate might even make a bigger effort to become housebroken.

Remember, no one is ever perfect — not you or your partner. So if you allow yourself to become upset by every imperfection, you'll just drive yourself nuts, won't you? You'll also make your partner miserable, until he or she eventually leaves, and you get to be miserable all by yourself!

See Chapter 24 for exercises to help you think rationally and positively toward your partner. When you stop being irritated and annoyed by silly behaviors — and instead, focus on and appreciate your mate's wonderful qualities — you'll feel more passionate and alive. And you'll find it easier to treat your partner that way as well.

Practice being upbeat, warm, empathic

Most people are not masochists; they want to be around someone who is upbeat and positive, not someone who's constantly complaining, nagging, and critical. Ask yourself: If you're not fun to be around, why would anyone want to be around you? Yet when couples are at war, they often don't stop to think about that. Everyone has problems, but you can be positive, warm, empathic, and affectionate in spite of them.

Take a moment to imagine yourself in your partner's shoes. If you were to switch places with your partner, how would you enjoy your own behavior? Try to act like someone you'd enjoy being with, and chances are, your sweetie will enjoy you, too. If he or she has special preferences, how else can you show that you care? Practice this empathy technique often, switching places with your mate in your mind. Then your mate will enjoy you and your relationship more — and so will you. See Chapter 24 for other techniques to remind you both why you're in this relationship together.

Make special time together a priority

Anything worth having is worth working for, and your relationship is important. So don't just give your partner whatever time you have left after you satisfy everyone else. If you want your sweetie to treat you like you're special, try treating him or her that way, too. Make your mate and your relationship a top priority. If you do, your relationship will thrive for a much longer period of time. If you don't, expect your union to die from neglect — and your mate to pursue someone else who does make the partnership a priority. See Chapter 24 for ways to make your time together special.

Keep communicating

Partners become close by communicating their thoughts, feelings, dreams, and desires, and to keep the spark alive and kicking, you must continue to communicate in a healthy, enjoyable way. Be sure to read Chapters 11 through 13 on how to communicate with your partner in a respectful, positive, assertive manner. Read and reread those chapters until you have them memorized, then follow those suggestions to keep your relationship satisfying and close. Remember, you can disagree with your mate and still get along beautifully — as long as you discuss your disagreements with respect.

Remember the Three Most Important Times of the Day

Although your actions, interactions, and communications are always important, there are times when they're more likely to be noticed by your mate. So pay special attention to what you do and say at those times. To keep your union strong, engage your mate in upbeat, emotionally supportive, enthusiastic talk for 10 to 15 minutes at three particular times of the day:

 ✔ The first time you see one another in the morning

 ✔ The first time you see each other after being at work or away for awhile

 ✔ The last time you talk before bedtime

For example, if you spend the night with your mate, don't wake up reciting a litany of the problems you're going to solve that day. People vary with regard to how fast or slow they wake up, but who wants to hear bad news first thing in the morning? It's enough to make someone go right back to bed! Instead, give your partner a big hug and kiss and a warm *"Good Morning!"* Then you'll both get the day off to a good start.

Similarly, pay attention to the first 10 to 15 minutes you spend with your mate after any long absences. If you live together, that would be the first 10 to 15 minutes after work each day. Don't come in complaining about what a rough day you've had. Bond with one another instead. Give your partner a big hug and kiss, and act excited to see him or her. Psych yourself up; let yourself feel enthusiastic. If you're home when your mate arrives, stop whatever you're doing and meet him at the door with a big hug, kiss, and some upbeat, emotionally supportive conversation. If he doesn't like to talk right away, just be there physically with your kiss, hug, and smile, and allow him to de-stress in the way he prefers.

If you're not living together, make sure the first 10 to 15 minutes you spend together on a date are positive and emotionally bonding. Don't start complaining the minute you get in the car. When you speak to each other on the phone in between dates, consider those your first 10 to 15 minutes of that day. Reward your honey for calling you by being pleasant. Act enthusiastic, and let him remember why he called you in the first place.

The third critical time is bedtime. Remember, whatever you say to your mate right before bed is likely to sit in his or her memory until morning. Do you want to be the star of your sweetie's nightmare? I think not. So cuddle up and give your partner some pleasant conversation and a reason to think loving thoughts about you as he or she drifts off to sleep.

If you spend a great deal of time with your partner — for example, if you live with one another or see each other several times a week — you'll have more opportunity to practice these behaviors. If you don't, follow these suggestions on the phone and in person whenever you do interact. In general, the less time you spend in person together, the more your mate will notice what you say during that time, and the more important it will be to talk in a positive, enthusiastic, emotionally supportive manner.

Don't take your mate for granted, or one day, he or she won't be there when you get home. In contrast, if you use that mere quarter hour to bond with your sweetie three times a day, several wonderful things tend to happen. You'll find it easier to handle any stresses that occur later that day. You'll find it easier to remember that you're a team. And when conflicts occur, you'll find it easier to assume that you each have the other's best interests at heart. And while you're doing all this, you'll both enjoy yourselves more in the process!

Laughing All the Way to the Bedroom

When you find joy and humor in life and the world around you, you embrace life. The humor needs to be positive, not sarcastic or cynical. Laugh with your partner. Share funny stories. Visit comedy clubs together. Look at the lighter side of life. Yes, you have problems to solve. Yes, they're important. But when you laugh, you lower your stress (including the stress chemicals in your body). You reduce your blood pressure and heart rate, and promote your health and well-being. You're even likely to live longer! So what are you waiting for? *Laugh it up!*

In Chapter 10, I talk about how to think so you'll feel happier and healthier. I mention that when you think in a healthy, happy way, you attract healthy, happy people to you, and you keep their interest. Try thinking of life as an adventure. Practice the five steps to happiness in Chapter 10, including changing your negative thoughts and statements to positive ones, selling yourself on life, and making every day count.

Don't get into a rut. Everyone needs some routine in their life, as well as some spontaneous change. If you have too much of either, life becomes stressful. Pay attention, and if you find yourself falling into the same routines, add some new love traditions (see Chapter 24). Have fun together.

Play together sensually and sexually

One of the most important ways you play with your partner is through sex. When people begin a relationship, they usually relish their lovemaking. They get into touching, holding hands, wrapping arms around each other, kissing, hugging, sitting close, walking hand in hand down the street, and touching each other frequently for any little excuse. They're physically comfortable with one another. That comfort is reinforced when they make love and become sexually close as well. The more physical you are with your partner in nonsexual ways, the easier it is to feel sexually comfortable together, and vice versa. They go hand in hand; one is an extension of the other.

In contrast, if you stop having sex, you begin to shut your body off. As you lose touch with your body, it gets easier and easier to stop touching your mate in nonsexual ways as well. Gradually, you become more sexually distant and removed from one another, until eventually, it seems like there's a wall between you.

So making love is extremely helpful to keep you and your mate sparking. It helps you de-stress and keeps you both in touch with your bodies. It helps you trust one another and your relationship, and encourages you to feel like a team. It reminds you that you each have the other's best interests in mind and creates good will that gets you through ambiguous situations until you have time to talk and clear things up. Making love also helps you overlook small issues that aren't important, so you can resolve important issues sooner. It makes it easier for the two of you to communicate with one another in a respectful, positive, manner. And, above all, it helps you and your partner stay physically, emotionally, and psychologically intimate and bonded.

For more on how to make your sex life more fulfilling and fun, be sure to read Chapters 7, 14, 15, and 24. But what if you don't *feel* sensual? Read on!

Get in touch with your body and your partner's

If you've lost contact with your body somewhere along the line, getting that connection back is important. Perhaps you've gained weight, had a baby, or just put other priorities ahead of your physical self for so long that you've kind of lost touch. How do you get it back?

Well, don't wait around for your partner to make some kind of miracle. You're not going to suddenly wake up and feel like Viagra personified. And don't procrastinate until your body connection grows even weaker. Instead, take steps to improve your mind-body connection. See Chapter 24 for how to restructure activities to enhance your sensuality and surround yourself with an environment that encourages you to feel sensual.

When You Meet Resistance

If you try various methods to jumpstart your romance and continually meet a wall, consider whether or not there's more there than meets the eye. Is your partner angry, resentful, or hurt about some unresolved issue? Have the two of you been having power struggles? If you have unresolved issues, it can be difficult to jump-start your spark. Most people find it difficult to act loving when they're feeling hostile.

The problem may be outside your relationship. Is your mate stressed out by work or other responsibilities and problems? Is he worried about money or health? He may be emotionally drained and temporarily unable to focus on your relationship. Does he have any sexual concerns? Men often avoid their partners if they fear that they've lost some sexual ability.

Of course, your mate may avoid getting romantic with you to avoid being emotionally intimate with you. Perhaps he or she doesn't see this relationship as long-term. Maybe he's dating other people as well. Or maybe her reluctance has nothing to do with you; she's just stressed out by life.

The bottom line is: If you try to add romance, spark, and fun to your life, but your mate keeps resisting, there must be a reason. That reason may or may not have anything to do with you, and he may or may not be consciously aware of why he's acting the way he is. Use the communication skills outlined in Chapters 11 through 13 to gently discuss your mate's reluctance to interact with you, including any underlying reasons. If you find that difficult, consider taking an assertiveness class or a couples workshop together.

Use Professional Help As Needed

If you and your partner have been together awhile and/or you consider this relationship serious, but your partner refuses to do any of the suggestions given in this chapter or offer any of his own, it's time to see a psychologist. That's particularly true if your mate used to act in a more romantic, motivated manner toward you. A psychologist can help you and your partner address any motivation and communication problems. And if the battery is really dead in your relationship and no jump-start can fix it, you'll find out sooner rather than later by attending therapy together. It's better to get some movement going than to just sit around, becoming more and more frustrated and resentful, while you watch your partnership and *joie de vivre* rot away.

❤ ❤ ❤ ❤ ❤ ❤

How Do You Affair-Proof a Marriage?

Dear Dr. Kate,

My age: 45   **My gender:** Female

Any ideas on how to affair-proof a marriage?

Dear Thinking Ahead,

The average man cheats when he doesn't feel emotionally supported by his partner, when he's not happy with the sex at home, or when he stops having fun with his mate. So the best way to "affair-proof" a marriage or any committed relationship is to stay intimate with your partner, both psychologically/emotionally and physically/sexually.

To keep your relationship psychologically and emotionally intimate:

- **Be sure to show your affection, respect, and support verbally.** Use reflective listening, supportive statements, and *The Dr. Kate 20-1 Rule* (all described in Chapter 12), giving him far more praise/positive statements than requests for behavioral change. The requests also need to be assertive (not aggressive) — stated in a way that shows respect. So don't demand, nag, blame, or criticize.

- **Give your mate at least 10 minutes of undivided positive attention at the three most important times of the day.** Those three times are first thing in the morning, when you first see one another after being apart all day (or after a long absence), and right before bedtime.

- **When problems arise, use good communication to discuss issues and reach compromises you both find satisfactory (see Chapter 13).**

To keep your relationship physically and sexually intimate:

- **Keep your sex life thriving.** Make love often and in a manner that keeps your partner satisfied. Be sure you frequently kiss and touch in nonsexual ways as well. Touching breaks through a lot of emotional walls. So act like you did when you first met, when you couldn't wait to touch one another.

- **Keep the fun in your relationship.** Be positive and upbeat, and keep the joy in your relationship. You'll feel better and your partner will feel better around you, too.

- **If your partner does cheat, see a psychologist immediately to work on your marriage.**

Best wishes, and please let me know how you're doing from time to time.

Dr. Kate

Mirror, Mirror . . . Yikes! It's Mom!

Dear Dr. Kate,

My age: 28   **My gender:** Female

Growing up, I saw my mom take things out on my dad for no reason. She'd start an argument at the drop of a dime. My dad told me he loves her, but he had to tune her out, so he stopped having sex with her. I got married this past year, and I now find myself acting like my mom. I look in the mirror and see her! How can I keep my marriage happy and avoid driving my husband away?

Dear Mirror Image,

People often take their loved ones for granted and pick on them when they're unhappy. And as you've noticed, that behavior ruins many marriages. So now that you've recognized this unhealthy pattern in your behavior, take action to reverse the pattern and keep it reversed. The do that, see a psychologist specializing in cognitive-behavioral techniques. Discuss your history first, to understand the patterns you learned at home. Then use that information to avoid recreating them. When you begin to act or speak in an unhealthy way, remind yourself to stop. To help you remember, try the following:

Keep a relationship notebook. First, draw a line vertically down the page. On the left, list your unhealthy behaviors. On the right, note what you'll do differently for each item. Every night, review your list and note improvements, as well as what you still need to improve. If you do this every day, you should make considerable progress. Use sticky notes to remind yourself.

To think more positively, put masking tape over your watch. Each time you look at it, say: *"I'm a positive, loving woman, with a terrific husband, and I love him."* Or cue the positive thoughts to getting coffee or going to the bathroom — any behavior you do several times a day and never forget to do.

Be sure to give your mate lots of positive reinforcement, and use **The Dr. Kate 20-to-1 Rule,** as well as reflective listening and supportive statements (see Chapter 12). Also, follow the suggestions in the preceding letter, including supportive talk at the three most important times of the day.

Once you've improved, review your behavior at least weekly so you can fix any nasty behaviors before they become a problem.

All the best, and please let me know how you're doing from time to time.

Dr. Kate

Part V
Moving Forward Together

The 5th Wave By Rich Tennant

ⒸRICHTENNANT

"I knew they were writing their own vows, but I expected quotes from Robert Frost poems, not The Geneva Convention."

In this part . . .

Relationships never stay static. They either continue to grow or move backwards. As time goes by, the partners need to make decisions about whether to continue the relationship, how long to continue it, and in what form. Whether they move toward marriage will depend on how they see their relationship in the context of their lives. Their decision will also be influenced by age, marital status, relationship goal, life goals, and how they feel about marriage — especially given their history with previous marriages and relationships.

In Part V, I examine common myths about marriage and present the saving realities. I also talk about when you're ready for marriage and when you're not. I fill you in on marriage phobia — what causes this irrational fear of marriage, and how to fix it. I also describe how to know if your relationship can be fixed, when it can't, and when it's just time to quit trying.

Chapter 17

Marriage: The Magic Wand?

In This Chapter

▶ Exploring six marriage myths that lead to unrealistic expectations about marriage

▶ Understanding the realities — and how they're healthier and more enjoyable than the myths

▶ Exercising the power you do have to make yourself happy

*I*n a magical kingdom far, far away, there lived a tall, dark, Handsome Prince with raven hair, big brown eyes, and even bigger biceps. One day, while riding about on his Silver Steadfast Steed, the Prince met a Beauuutiful Princess, with long blonde hair, big blue eyes, and bodacious bod. As soon as he saw her, he was consumed by Endless Love and Enchantment. The Beautiful Bodacious Princess soon felt similarly, especially when she found out about his daddy's fortune, and she and Prince planned a very, very large wedding. But before the calligraphy was even dry on the wedding scrolls, the Horrible Hairy Evil Sorcerer kidnapped the Beautiful Princess and locked her in his Dirty Dungeon Tower. The Beautiful Princess cried and cried, waiting for her Heroic Handsome Prince to save her. She also refused the repeated advances of the Horrible Hairy Evil Sorcerer, until in a fit of rage, he placed the Beautiful Princess under the Sleeping Spell of a Thousand Years. If he couldn't have her, nobody would. Meanwhile, the Handsome Heartbroken Prince searched for his Beautiful Bewitched Princess — day after day, month after month, year after year.

Then one day, acting on a tip from MTV — the Magic TV Station — the Handsome Prince found the Horrible Hairy Evil Sorcerer hiding behind the Wobbly Warped Woodshed. With one fell swoop of his Mighty Merciless Sword, The Handsome Prince sliced through Horrible Hairy Evil Sorcerer and reduced him to So Much Kindling. The Handsome Prince then raced to the Dirty Dungeon Tower, kissed the Beautiful Be-snoring Princess, and broke the Sleeping Spell of a Thousand Years. And so they were married in the Magic Kingdom, in front of all the loyal subjects and 7 bridesmaids, 6 caterers, 5 bugle blowers, 4 chocolate wedding cakes, 3 clergymen, 2 white-winged doves, and a pear tree. And then they all lived Happily Ever After.

Cut! OK — end scene! Hey, I'm all for the joy and creativity that goes with an active imagination. I love romantic tales, handsome princes, and magic kingdoms as much as the next guy. I support the rights of fairies, elves, and wee people too, but they're more likely to appear on the side of a cookie package than waving magic wands at your front door. I also love Rocky and Bullwinkle, but I don't expect to find a flying squirrel or Moose-With-Attitude around the next corner either. But sometimes it's hard to remember that "happily-ever-afters" exist only in books. Most people would like to believe in magic. Yet it's important to keep your feet firmly planted in reality, especially if you'd like to enjoy a relationship and keep it working.

Interacting closely with someone for years and keeping an emotional and sexual commitment long-term — being married, in other words — is usually challenging, even when the spouses love one another and are realistic about their expectations. When they're not realistic, however, the marriage road goes from challenging to impossible. If you hold unrealistic expectations about marriage, you'll place unrealistic demands on your partner, and you'll get upset when those unrealistic expectations aren't realized. Your unrealistic demands and irrational feelings can then lead to divorce.

In this chapter, I discuss six common marriage myths and how they lead to unrealistic expectations and grief. I also discuss six saving realities, and how believing in them instead can keep your marriage thriving.

Demystifying Six Marriage Myths

As I discuss six marriage myths common in our society, review your beliefs and assumptions. Do you hold any of these misconceptions? How do they affect your relationship right now? How might they affect you in the future? Then reflect on each reality and how believing it could change your life.

Myth #1: Marriage is a miracle — it'll cure what ails ya

Some people believe that marriage conquers all. It's a miracle! Like a magic wand, it wipes out all grief and unhappiness! Get married and suddenly, all your problems disappear, and you live happily ever after — just like the fairy tale. All the arguments you've been having with your mate will suddenly end. Your money problems will disappear. Your personal problems and those of your partner, your interpersonal problems with family and friends and your partner's family and friends — and all your worldly stresses — will magically vanish as soon as you're wedded in marital bliss. Well, at least that's how the myth goes.

We grow up on fairy tales and marriage myths. Then those myths are reinforced through movies, novels, poems, and songs that imply that this is the process: You meet someone, fall in love, marry, and everything works out so you "live happily ever after." No particular training or effort needed — it's magic; when it's time, it just happens. Because people learn this myth when they're very young, they don't question it; they just accept it as fact. And then they expect the fairy tale to come true for them, too.

Unfortunately, it doesn't. And when the miracle doesn't happen, those people who expected it quickly become disillusioned. Why isn't life getting better? It's a rude awakening. If they don't realize that the problem is the unrealistic expectation, not their mate or the relationship, they soon blame their spouse. And that can lead to serious marital problems and divorce.

But fairy tales are fairy tales, and marriage is real life, not a miracle. You and your partner are mere mortals, not superpowers, and you're short on magic wands. So marrying one another can't possibly solve all your problems. In fact, marriage often adds some problems and increases others. The biggest question marriage answers is, "Where is our relationship going?" If you've been dissatisfied with your partner's lack of commitment, and he then marries you, you'll no doubt be happy about that. And if your partner *is* afraid of commitment, then he should vastly improve when you get married (read more about marriage phobia, an irrational fear of marriage, in Chapter 19). And living with someone is sometimes cheaper. You can consolidate some bills, and share a home, furniture, car, and certain other possessions.

However, marriage can't *make* you happy. As I discuss in Chapter 10, only you can do that. After your married, you'll still experience most of the same problems you've always experienced. If you have a happy marriage, you can talk to your spouse about your difficulties and feel better, but don't expect your problems to magically disappear just because you're wed.

In fact, some problems can even increase. If you don't have enough money, you and your spouse may end up disagreeing about how to spend or save what little cash you have. And that can put enormous pressure on your marriage. Similarly, if your sex life hasn't been going well, marriage usually makes it worse. If you've been bothered by religious taboos against premarital sex, you'll feel better once that taboo no longer applies to you. But many couples experience less frequent and less satisfying sex after they're married. Once they know they can make love whenever they like, many don't want it as often. If you don't get along with each other's friends and family, spending time with them over the years can increase the strife. And everyone has to be careful not to take his or her partner for granted.

Marriage can be a wonderful experience. However, in order for it to be wonderful, each spouse has to accept responsibility for his or her own feelings, behaviors, and happiness. Marriage is a work-in-progress all the time, something both partners have to try hard at *every day* so they can continue to experience that stability and happiness. When you approach marriage realistically, without false expectations, you're more likely to enjoy the experience, and your marriage is likely to last longer.

Myth #2: Marriage is forever

This myth is based on the "happily ever after" fairy tale, and it's reinforced during the marriage ceremony when the partners promise to keep their vows "'til death do us part." When you believe in this myth, it's easy to believe that the hardest part is the "getting married." After all, that part *can* be difficult. But this myth implies that after you get that commitment from your partner, you're in like Flint and you'll always be together. You'll always have a best friend and partner, and because you can count on your spouse to be there, you can finally relax and enjoy yourself. You can focus on other priorities at the expense of your marriage. You can count on your spouse to understand, so why not work more hours to buy that great house or vacation? And if you really believe the marriage-is-forever myth, you'll be in shock when your spouse dies. You assumed you'd have a partner for life; you never expected to be single again.

Nothing lasts forever, including marriage. Roughly half of all marriages still end in divorce. You can't completely control what happens in a marriage; you're only one of the two people involved. And neither of you can control some outside events. So even though you try, your marriage may end for reasons beyond your control. People vary in their ability to work hard to overcome adversity and keep commitments. They also vary with regard to how long they can delay gratification to achieve a common goal. Your spouse may change his or her mind and decide he or she doesn't want to be married to you. Or one of you could develop a physical or psychological illness or experience another emergency that causes havoc with your marriage. And even if your marriage is happy and healthy, one of you will eventually die first, leaving the other partner single again — at least for awhile.

To keep your marriage going as long as possible, choose a reasonably compatible partner, be realistic, and work on your relationship in a positive, productive manner. Take care of your appearance and health. Make your mate a top priority, and give your relationship quality time and energy. Realize that even though you try, your marriage will eventually end when one of you dies. Use that information — not to feel depressed ahead of time, but to help you appreciate your partner and feel joy today. Don't take your marriage for granted. Instead, savor every moment and feel it. Instead of always thinking about what isn't "right" about your partner, focus on what *is*. Continue to be the best partner you can be, and put energy and effort into your relationship 24/7. Live every day enjoying what you have now; make it special for both of you. And when you do that, your marriage will last as long as possible — and you'll be able to handle whatever life throws at you.

Myth #3: Having kids will bring us closer

Similar to the marriage-cures-all myth, people often think that having children together will bind them together and solve their relationship problems. When you believe in this myth, you're inclined to have babies sooner — perhaps before marriage or at a very young age. And if you have a baby to save your relationship, you'll feel a tremendous postpartum letdown when you discover that your fantasy doesn't come true. If your partner cheats or leaves you, you may feel betrayed and resentful, short-changed by life.

In reality, kids don't save relationships; they almost always *add* stress. For example, you need sleep to survive, but the baby won't sleep on schedule. Instead, he or she will need a breast or bottles, burping, and diaper changes around the clock — including the middle of the night. Over the years, you'll need money for clothes, food, doctors, meds, school supplies, field trips, and a million other things. If you're young and inexperienced or somewhat impatient and tense, a baby's cries or the sound of your child playing can easily get on your nerves. If you don't have psychological, emotional, and financial resources, the support of family and friends, or even the mate who co-made the child, parenthood is a very rough road to travel.

It's *always* a mistake to have a baby to accomplish some other goal. So don't do it to trick your partner into marrying you; it probably won't happen, and if it does, you'll probably get divorced anyway. Don't have a baby because you already have a baby by someone else and your new partner wants you to have his to show how much you care. There's no guarantee that this partner will stick around either, and having a baby for that reason is abusive to the baby. And don't have a baby just to have someone to call your own. That's not fair to the baby, who isn't a toy, but a real human being, with needs and feelings. Instead, have a child together only when you've met *all* these conditions:

- ✔ You and your partner are mature and psychologically healthy (see the next myth, and Chapters 4, 8, and 18 for more on maturity).

- ✔ Your relationship is stable and long-term (preferably, you're married).

- ✔ You and your mate usually communicate and resolve problems well.

- ✔ Your relationship is going very well and can handle the extra stress.

- ✔ You and your partner have the financial, emotional, and psychological resources to give that baby the best in life, and you both can raise him or her to be a happy, healthy adult.

Myth #4: Marriage should automatically follow dating

This myth says that marriage is a logical extension of any romantic relationship. If the relationship stays together long enough, you just naturally progress to marriage, regardless of age or life stage. This myth is also a byproduct of fairy tales. After all, the prince and princess *always* get married.

It's important to experience life and be emotionally mature before you marry. Bringing that emotional maturity and life experience to the marriage can help you stay happily married much longer.

I define *emotional maturity* as first experiencing life, growing and developing emotionally, and then using all that experience to make wiser, healthier, more consistent life choices. You see the "big picture" — and have a more realistic, rational view of life, other people, yourself, your actions, and how they all fit together in the world. You avoid many problems by thinking them through in advance and choosing your behavior wisely. In addition, you have experienced enough and changed so much that your rate of change now slows. You'll continue to change a little all the time, but nowhere near as much as when you were growing up and frequently changing your mind about life.

At **AOL Keyword: DrKate** and www.drkate.com, I get many letters from people who are engaged at 18 and even younger. They'll graduate high school soon, they've dated their mate awhile and get along, and all their friends are getting hitched, so why not? Many people *feel* mature at 18, but when they look back at 28, they realize how immature they were ten years before. Looking back even one year can amaze when you're growing, changing, and learning valuable lessons about life, love, and how you fit into it all.

It takes awhile to become emotionally mature. So if you marry before you and your partner are done maturing, there's a higher risk that you'll change in incompatible directions.

In Chapter 8, I discuss the ages at which maturity is likely to occur, and how important it is to consider your maturity level before becoming exclusive with someone. It's even more important to be mature before marriage. In Chapter 9, I recommend living with someone if you're not mature enough to marry.

Think back. When you first dated the opposite sex, didn't they all look pretty good? That's because you didn't have the skills to differentiate between them yet. A teenage female might date a guy because he's captain of the football team, or because he has a cool car. A teenage male might date a girl because she's cute, or because all the other guys want to date her. If those two people marry and 20 years later, I ask them why they married one another, they'll say: "All our friends were doing it, we were dating each other at the time, and it seemed like the right thing to do." But are those reasons — having a cool car, being an ex-football star, or marrying when your friends do — good ways to ensure a long-term, fulfilling marriage and family? Hardly.

As you experience more people through dating, you start to notice differences in people, how you get along with them, and what you need in a relationship.

You start choosing mates for better reasons — like who's more compatible long-term. All of that comes in handy when you finally choose a spouse. If you choose without that info, you're more likely to choose unwisely.

Similarly, if you marry without enough dating experience, you may find yourself wanting to date again in your 40s. Think about it. If you marry at 18, you'll be married for 22 years by the time you hit 40! That's most of your life! Many people who marry without much experience regret it later, wishing they could have had more fun before settling down. They often end up having an affair or going through a mid-life crisis later. Having fun and sowing your wild oats are appropriate when you're a teen and young adult, but they're *not* appropriate when you're married, with a spouse and 2.2 children.

Myth #5: We should wed after graduation

This myth says that life events should dictate your marriage schedule, and getting hitched should just naturally follow other rites of passage — like graduating from high school or college or joining the armed forces. A suspiciously large number of people marry after high school (if their education ends there), after college (if they end their education there), or before they go off to war (if they go to war). Think about it: What's the probability that the person you're dating at those times is one of the most compatible people you'll ever meet in your life?

Graduation from high school or college is a wonderful accomplishment, but it doesn't make you a mature adult ready for marriage. Joining the service may be right for you, and going off to war may be appreciated when the need is there, but neither makes you fit for marriage. No one is emotionally mature at age 18 or 21 — that's normal. Yet that's the age when those events usually occur. If you commit to someone then — hardly meeting anyone beforehand — how do you know you're making a good choice?

Today's world demands advanced training and education, and that demand is likely to increase, not decrease. So if you're under 25, instead of getting married, finish your advanced training and firm up a career. It's easier to do that when you're not supporting a family at the same time.

Marriage is a rite of passage unlike any other. To be successfully married requires more than just loving one another. It requires social, emotional, and psychological maturity, as well as communication skills and the ability to work out the inevitable problems that will arise between you. Those skills are not required in or automatically conveyed by any other rite of passage, like graduating, joining the armed forces, or going off to graduate school. It's important to get married only if you're truly ready to get married — not because you have or are about to experience some other rite of passage.

Myth #6: My wife is an extension of me

This myth basically states that the wife is kind of like an addition. The husband's the building, and she's his wing or annex. He's the main event; she's the sideshow. Basically, he's more important than she is.

While somewhat less common these days than before the sexual revolution, this myth is still going strong in families where the husband is wealthy (he may have even dumped the first wife for a better looking arm piece now that he can afford it). This myth thrives in conservative families who believe the Bible ordains man as "chief" and woman as "subordinate." And it's assumed in countries where women are regarded as lower-class citizens without rights.

When you believe in this myth, your marriage isn't equal. The wife is like a trusty servant — valued, but not at the same rate of exchange as the husband. Believing that he is smarter and better able to make decisions, the husband may overlook his wife's feelings and preferences, while his wife finds herself in a very unfulfilling marriage with an egocentric, selfish man. If the wife believes her husband is superior, she may stay married, but they both lose the fulfillment they could otherwise enjoy if the wife was equal. If the wife grows to believe in herself instead, the marriage will probably end.

There's no reason why a husband is any smarter or better at decision-making than his wife. It's far healthier for both of them if they discuss their opinions, feelings, and preferences, and then draft satisfying compromises together.

And even a husband who enjoys power loses a lot when he doesn't treat his wife as equal. An empowered woman, with good self-esteem, is more intellectually stimulating, spontaneous, and fun. She's also better at initiating and enjoying sex than a woman who regards herself as secondary to her husband.

Reviewing the Myths and Realities

Use Table 17-1 to remind yourself of each marriage myth and reality. Review the table before you marry to make sure you're thinking rationally. Then reread it periodically to remind yourself to make the most of your marriage experience.

Table 17-1	Six Marriage Myths and Realities
Grief-Causing Myth	*Saving Reality*
M1: Marriage conquers all.	R1: Marriage can't take away all your problems. In fact, it often adds some and increases others.
M2: Marriage is forever.	R2: Nothing lasts forever; marriages end through divorce and death. Instead of taking your marriage for granted, savor it, and make it a priority. Then you and your mate will enjoy it more, and it will last as long as possible.
M3: Kids will bring you closer.	R3: Children almost always add stress to a relationship.
M4: Falling in love and getting married should automatically follow dating.	R4: It's important to experience life before you marry. The emotional maturity and experience you bring to the marriage can help you stay happily married longer.
M5: Life events should dictate our marriage timetable.	R5: Outside events should not be used as a marriage-readiness marker.
M6: My spouse is an extension of me.	R6: The husband and wife are equal in importance and should have equal rights in the marriage. Decisions should be made together and include compromises fair to both.

Controlling the Things You Can Control

Many things in marriage can't be controlled. You can't control your partner, the actions of people around you, a lot of the stress that happens to you, and when either of you dies. But if you try, you can control yourself. To stay happily married for as long as possible, exercise that power in your own life. Incorporate the marriage realities into your thinking, then change your behavior to be in sync with them.

The choice is yours. You can be mature, thoughtful, and fair. You can think rational thoughts, hold realistic expectations, and be as happy as possible — or cling to erroneous beliefs and make yourself miserable.

So always exercise your choice to be rational and healthy. When you marry, do it only for appropriate reasons. Then after you're wed, review your thoughts and actions periodically to be sure they're still realistic, positive, and healthy. Exercise the power you do have to be happy, and you and your spouse will reap the benefits for as long as possible.

❤ ❤ ❤ ❤ ❤ ❤

Baby Won't Solve Problem — Just Complicates Life!

Dear Dr. Kate,

My age: 22   **My gender:** Female

I can't get over my son's father. We were never really "involved," to be truthful, but I held out hope that he would come to see me in a different light after the baby was born. Well, he sure does — as the enemy! He's now living with a woman and says that they're "in love." He's even talking marriage with her. He's at least making an effort to see our son, but each time just brings up the pain even more. Our son is 9 months old, and after all this time, I still ache like we broke up yesterday! How can I get on with my life?

Dear Disappointed Mama,

I'm sorry you're hurting. Babies don't solve problems; they don't save relationships. They generally put stress on romance, even when the people are happily married. So stop expecting your baby to save your life. Stop expecting this man to change his mind. He wasn't really emotionally involved with you to start with, and he's not going to become so now. You need to make yourself face reality.

So you've learned a valuable lesson. Now you have to be the best single mother you can be for your son — while also balancing a career and making sure that you can support your son for the rest of his life. Don't count on the father to be there. It's great if he continues to be, but I can tell you from experience that he may bolt if/when his girlfriend/wife no longer approves of his association with his son.

You also have to learn to be happy on your own. Don't expect anyone else to make you happy. Don't look for a man to save you from your life. It won't happen, and you'll just end up complicating your life even further. Plus, when you're needy, you draw needy, unhealthy people to you. And you certainly don't need that, do you?

Use thought-stopping and *The Dr. Kate Quick & Dirty Grieving Technique* to help you deal with the pain (see Chapter 10). Sit down and write up a list of goals, and how you'll reach each. (For example, you might finish college in night school, apply for a better job so you can afford day care for your son, and/or do better at your current job so you can ask for a raise.) Then focus on reaching those goals. Once you've improved your personal situation — perhaps by the time you're 26, for example — then start dating again. To find a compatible mate, use an efficient method (like a reputable introduction service, the personal ads, or both), and look for someone who is compatible with you. Be sure that you start looking by age 27, because it will be easier to find someone before age 35, all other things being equal, than after that.

Best wishes, and please let me know how you're doing from time to time.

Dr. Kate

Married After Dating the Same Man My Entire Life!

Dear Dr. Kate,

My age: 24   **My gender:** Female

I've just married a man after dating him since age 15; I've never dated anyone else. He was my entire world. His friends are my friends, and our families were joined a long time ago. But I've changed. I long to be independent and experience other people — through dating and sex. I miss the excitement. I wish my parents had stepped in and suggested that I not get so serious so young. My husband is still very much in love with me. Everyone says they've never seen a man more in love. But I can't seem to look the other way at his shortcomings, and I no longer find his idiosyncrasies cute. My dreams are different now, but his remain the same. We've grown apart. I've always been the responsible/dependable one; this is unacceptable behavior for me. I wish I could change the way I feel so everyone would be happy, including me. What should I do?

Dear Newlywed Blues,

Thank you for writing. Every time I publish a letter advising young people to date around and delay marriage, other young people write to say that they *are* old enough to get married, thank you, and how dare I imply that people who marry young may want to explore their freedom later on? I'm very sorry you're not happy, and I'm posting your letter to help others who are contemplating marriage at a young age. It's good to know that you wish your parents had tried to intervene, because many people automatically ignore their parents' advice.

It's always best to meet someone special after dating around to find out what other men are like and who fits you best. But timing can be very off, and life is never perfect. It sounds like your husband is a good guy. If you'd met him after dating a lot of other guys, you'd probably be happy that you'd found him. The problem is that now you're not sure, because you met him so soon. You've also matured and grown a lot since you met him, so your needs have changed. Plus, you've been together for nine years, so you're experiencing the same problems people face when they've been with anyone for nine years — how to keep the romance alive. And on top of that, the first year of marriage can require tremendous adjustment. Women often dream such great fantasies about what marriage is going to be like — how can the reality measure up?

Take *The Dr. Kate Compatibility Quiz* and *The Dr. Kate Communication Quiz* (found in the appendixes) to find out more about the compatibility and communication between you and your husband. Read my suggestions on marriage and try some of my ideas for jumpstarting your spark (see Chapters 16, 20, and 24). Then see a psychologist for marital therapy. Evaluate your expectations for marriage, and be sure you aren't blaming your hubby for not making your life perfect. Discuss your feelings privately with the psychologist for at least a few sessions. Try to pinpoint what you'd like to see different in your marriage. Then in joint sessions, see if your husband is willing to make those changes. But don't bring up any reservations about marriage until you've spent two years following these recommendations and have pretty much decided to divorce. Your husband will probably feel betrayed, so it would be difficult to rebuild the trust after that.

Best wishes! And please keep me posted on your progress.

Dr. Kate

P.S. Be sure to settle this issue before having any babies!

Chapter 18

Move Forward to Marriage?

Relationships are not static entities. They either move forward — or backwards. If you and your partner are happy, enjoying one another, and working on the relationship, you're progressing. If you're arguing and disrespecting one another or cheating and breaking your commitments, you're regressing. And if you're just ignoring one another, you're stagnating — and that means you're really moving backwards, too.

So every relationship eventually begs the question: "Where are we going with this?" Is marriage on the horizon? Or is status quo the way to go, at least for now? If that's unsatisfactory, will anything improve? Or would it be better to break up?

In this chapter, I discuss how to know when you're ready for marriage. I give you a framework by which to examine your relationship, your motivation for marriage, and your behavior. I also talk about the shelf life of relationships — how long you have to make a decision about marriage before your relationship begins falling apart. Compare notes with your partner to see how you feel about marrying one another, and whether you agree. If you do want to marry, review your reasons why and whether they're appropriate. Discuss your behavior to see if you have a reasonable chance of staying married if you do marry. Then, using all that information, decide what to do about your relationship.

When You're Ready

It's important to understand the behavioral signs that suggest you're ready — or not ready — for marriage. Here are ten behaviors and attitudes that commonly occur in people who sustain happy marriages. If you lack any of these, opting against marriage is a good idea — at least at this time and/or with this particular partner, depending on which sign you do not have.

You've both dated around enough

It's very important to date a number of people before you marry. Dating is the process by which you get to know people. When you first meet members of the opposite sex, they all seem quite interesting. In time, you begin to notice differences between them and which kind of people you tend to get along with better. You also get a better idea of what you're like in a relationship, and how you tend to act and react to certain conditions. All of that information is important when you eventually choose a spouse.

Marriage, while not forever, should last for a very long time. When you're young, it's important to get to know a lot of people, date casually, and have fun. So when you finally do marry, you won't have any regrets about leaving the single world. Have an adolescence when you *are* an adolescent.

You're both emotionally mature

To become emotionally mature, you must first have life experiences, see the big picture of life, then use the knowledge you gain from those experiences to avoid mistakes and make wiser choices in the future. In my opinion, women tend to mature around ages 26 to 28+, while men often mature later, around 30+. Some people, on the other hand, *never* mature. When you're in the process of growing and maturing, you'll change in many directions and make many mistakes. You'll grow as a result of your association with different people, different experiences, and changing responsibilities. If you marry before you or your partner is emotionally mature, you're taking more of a risk that the two of you may change in different directions and eventually grow apart. Or one of you may grow while the other doesn't, causing you to feel less compatible in time.

This phenomenon is so common, when asked why an early marriage ended, most people say, "We grew apart." While growing apart can happen at any age because you can always develop new behavior and interests, it's far more likely to occur when one or both partners are young and still developing into the people they will become.

After you're emotionally mature, you'll still change over time, but the changes will be less dramatic. Waiting until then can increase the chance that your marriage will succeed. Also, it takes a fairly mature person to handle the stresses and responsibilities of marriage in a healthy way. If both of you are mature and insightful with good judgment, you can enjoy a much happier marriage for a much longer period of time. If you just can't wait that long, however, try waiting as long as you can. For example, it's much better to marry at age 26 than at age 21. If you marry early, you will essentially be growing up together, so you'll need to be exceptionally understanding and forgiving to be able to stay together. And you'll have to work even harder than most couples to avoid growing apart. See Chapters 4, 8, and 17 for more on emotional maturity and relationships.

You're both ready for and want marriage

It's possible to be emotionally mature, but not desire marriage at this time. Perhaps you have other goals that you want to accomplish and feel that marriage would impede your ability to do so. Perhaps you want to remain single longer because you haven't dated around enough. Or maybe you need to recover from a divorce and gain more dating experience first.

Marriage is not easy. To make it work, both parties have to be dedicated and work hard at it. If you're psychologically healthy, but other goals consume so much of your time that you can't make your relationship a top priority, it's best not to rush into marriage. If you're suffering from a fear of marriage, however, get treatment *now* so you can eventually move forward toward marriage. (See Chapter 19 for more on marriage phobia.)

You and your spouse are compatible

No matter how mature or ready for marriage you are, you can't force a square peg into a round hole. Living with someone is a challenge, so you must have a high degree of compatibility for your union to last for any significant length of time. So don't marry unless you and your prospective spouse are highly compatible.

To determine how compatible you and your mate may be and to understand the elements of compatibility, try taking *The Dr. Kate Compatibility Quiz* in Appendix A and reading Chapters 3 and 4 on compatibility.

You both love one another deeply

Because no compatibility is ever perfect and living with someone can be difficult even under the best of circumstances, the two of you must love one another deeply. You don't have to have that heady excitement you felt during The Infatuation Stage, when you first got to know one another, but you need to love one another in a stable, deep, enduring way. And you need to recognize that feeling as love.

That way, when the inevitable problems occur, you'll hang in and work on the relationship, even though you're uncomfortable. You won't jump ship just because you're not enjoying yourself so much today. Also, when you realize how much you love your partner, you'll be able to act in ways that show your appreciation. You'll give more positive reinforcement and praise, which will, like the self-fulfilling prophecy, help the marriage go more smoothly. You'll consider your partner's preferences, and make concessions and compromise so both of you can get your needs met. That willingness to compromise can see you through a lot of problems together.

You've known each other long enough in person to know

As I mention in Chapter 2, it takes time to know if the strong feelings you have for your partner are really love or just infatuation. To get to know someone well, you have to experience that person in different situations (at work and home), interacting with a variety of people (coworkers, family, friends, and strangers), under different conditions (fatigued, stressed, sick, and so on). And to do that, you need to interact with your partner frequently (at least three times per week) for at least three to four months.

If you meet online, get to know one another offline before deciding to cohabit or marry. You're taking a huge risk if you just pick up and move halfway across the country to marry someone you've known mostly through letters, e-mail, phone calls, and very occasional visits. When you finally see that person in the flesh every day, you may find that the two of you are not compatible after all.

You're both healthy and happy

Marriage is a challenge for people who are healthy and happy. If one or both of you are unhealthy or unhappy, your marriage will be very strained by those problems. If you suffer from any major psychological or personal problems, you'll bring those into the marriage. Besides making your own life difficult, those problems will create stress for your spouse and your marriage. If you have any addictions (like alcohol, drugs, sex, or gambling), they will color all your interactions together and your relationship will suffer. To solve your marital problems, you'll first have to solve your own.

Give serious consideration to resolving such problems before you marry, when motivation is much stronger. If there's no motivation before marriage, don't delude yourself into thinking that your mate will perk up after you're married. Instead, most existing problems get worse after marriage, because the spouse has already achieved what he or she wants (marriage) and is less motivated to change.

You want a spouse, but you don't need one

Never marry anyone because you can't bear to be alone as a single person. Your mate can't make you happy; you have to do that yourself. For a marriage to be successful, both parties have to enter the union as independent, stable, happy individuals. Otherwise, the unstable partner becomes a real drain on the more stable one. A healthy marriage is an interaction between two equals, not one partner pulling the other along. It should not be a father-daughter, mother-son, or adult-child relationship. When you're healthy, you don't *need* a spouse to survive; you just *prefer* that companionship. Sharing your life with a loving spouse then becomes icing on the cake.

You're able to earn money and live well

Young couples often underestimate how much money a life together will cost. Fueled by the marriage-conquers-all myth (see Chapter 17), they overestimate how much love can compensate for the lack of creature comforts. They lack the foresight to imagine the full range of things that can "go wrong" — for example, how layoffs and other crises can curtail financial independence.

When people go directly from living at home to living with a spouse, they're even more likely to underestimate the amount of money they'll need. Yet money is the most common topic couples tend to fight about — not having enough money to pay bills, how much money to save or spend, and how to spend what they spend.

After you're married, start a family, and have financial responsibilities and other demands on your time, you may find working on your education and career difficult to impossible. Or you may have to do it part-time, greatly adding to the length of time and expense. Also, many industries prefer hiring younger people, who can presumably be with them long enough to justify the training expense and pension payout.

Since it's easier to get your education and career in order when you're young, and because you'll need the money you earn from that career in your marriage, it's best to finish your education and career before you wed. The more training you have, the more job descriptions you can fill. Then if something happens to your usual field (economic recession and layoffs, for example), you'll be more likely to find another position.

You're able to support yourself and your kids if you get widowed or divorced

Thanks to the marriage-is-forever myth (described in Chapter 17), many people don't consider what they'll do if they end up widowed or divorced. A woman often gives up her education and career to marry and raise a family. When the marriage doesn't work out, that same woman usually ends up with a much lower standard of living than her ex-husband. And because a woman is more likely to be awarded physical custody of the children, she has less opportunity than ever to further her education and career post-divorce. Since she hasn't worked outside the home for years, she finds it difficult to compete with others who have been continuously employed.

Sure, alimony and child support are supposed to take care of the problem and help the woman get back on her feet. But some deadbeat fathers don't pay their child support, much less alimony — and forcing them to do so is difficult.

And when the employed spouse dies, there may or may not be enough money for an unemployed spouse to get on his or her feet. The surviving spouse will also be grieving the loss and taking care of the kids; she won't be at her best to start looking for a job.

Due to unpredictable factors such as death or divorce, it's best if both the man and the woman finish their education and develop careers. That way, if they end up divorced or widowed some day, they'll both be able to support themselves and their children, despite negative changes in the economy. If the woman wants to stay home for years to raise children, she should finish her education and establish a profession beforehand. Then she'll be better able to return to the workforce if tragedy occurs — or after her children are grown and out of the house.

When NOT to Marry

Just as there are signs that you *are* ready to marry, there are also signs that you're *not*. A surprising number of people are able to look back on their marriages and say why they weren't ready to marry at that time, and how that lack of readiness contributed to their divorce.

Read the following list of signs, which represent the flip side of the signs I mention in the previous section. Review your motivation for marriage *before* you wed to help you avoid making these mistakes. If you fall into one of these categories, it might be best to avoid marriage at this time. Instead, follow the suggestions listed as an alternative remedy. At the very least, you should understand the risk you're taking if you choose to get married for the following irrational reasons, or while in one of these situations:

- **To escape a poor, chaotic, or unhappy home:** Consider going away to school or even the armed services. Focus on developing as an independent, psychologically healthy person, so you can live a happy, healthy life. The more dysfunctional your home, the more work you'll need to do to avoid repeating the mistakes of your parents. If you do marry young to escape your home, keep in mind that it may only be a transitional marriage — to get you out of the house. Delay having children until you've found another, more compatible spouse, or until you've fixed the current relationship so it's happy and healthy.

- **When you're too young or immature:** Enjoy your adolescence, and delay marriage until you're older and more mature.

- **When you lack dating experience:** Start dating a variety of people casually (no sex) to get the experience you need. Learn what you're like, what you need in a relationship, and how to differentiate a compatible partner from someone who isn't healthy or compatible. Delay marriage until you've learned to choose wisely and gained enough experience that you're ready to settle down and make a healthy marriage.

- **When you've just graduated, are not self-sufficient, have never been on your own as an independent single person, have no stable career or means of support, are afraid to be alone, or your partner is leaving soon for a long time:** Finish your education and advanced training for your field. Forge a career that has some flexibility and can support you and a family for the rest of your life. Live on your own as a single person and learn how to pay bills, balance your checkbook, save money, and become self-sufficient and independent. Learn how to be alone without being lonely, and how to be happy single. Enjoy this relatively carefree time in your life, because it is a very special time — one that will all be over very quickly.

- **To make someone else jealous:** Read books and see a psychologist to become more emotionally mature. Don't marry anyone until you have matured, and have also acquired a variety of adult behaviors and coping skills to rely on when you're hurting. Take assertiveness and communication skills classes to help you talk through problems amicably, rather than resorting to manipulation.

- **To supply self-esteem:** Seek cognitive-behavioral psychotherapy with a psychologist. Read Chapter 10 in this book, and replace your low self-esteem thoughts with positive self-thoughts. Don't marry anyone until you feel confident and comfortable with yourself. Be sure you're choosing someone who really is compatible, not just someone to fill in because you're needy. Read Chapters 11 to 13 on communication, and take assertiveness classes to add to your psychology medicine chest and give you the confidence to handle stressful situations.

✔ **Because everyone else is doing it:** Read books and see a psychologist to learn, grow, and become more emotionally mature. Date a variety of people casually (no sex), or your current flame exclusively, but do not marry anyone until you have matured. Finish your education, develop your career, and enjoy being young and carefree for now.

✔ **When you're pregnant:** *Don't* assume that your boyfriend will be there for you and the baby if you carry it to term and keep it. Consult an impartial psychologist immediately and review your options carefully and completely before making your choice.

✔ **When your relationship is not compatible or fun, but you're growing older and you're afraid you won't find anyone better:** Take *The Dr. Kate Compatibility Quiz* and *The Dr. Kate Communication Quiz* for each relationship you've had — to learn more about the compatibility and communication in each relationship. Discuss your relationship history with a psychologist, and explore how compatible you and your partner really are. Don't marry until/unless you're fairly sure that you are compatible and could sustain a happy marriage. If your current partner isn't very compatible, consider joining an introduction service or placing a personal ad to efficiently meet people who may be much more compatible with you.

✔ **When you haven't spent enough time together to know if you're compatible:** If your partner has just been too busy to make the relationship a priority, use the communication skills outlined in Chapters 11 through 13 to discuss the problem with him or her. See if you can come up with a compromise that is satisfactory to both of you.

If you've just met someone recently, relax and give yourself time to get to know one another. If your partner is long-distance and you've communicated mainly through e-mail, letters, phone calls, and occasional visits, don't marry until you've gotten to know each other better in person and the relationship is very strong. In the meantime, take the whole thing with a grain of salt, so you won't be upset if it ends.

✔ **When one or both of you haven't been broken up, divorced, or widowed long enough, or one of you is on the rebound:** Read Chapters 21 and 22 and follow my suggestions for grieving efficiently, getting closure, and moving on. Enjoy your current relationship while it lasts, but understand that it could end at any time. When the jilted partner heals, you may find that you're not compatible enough to sustain the relationship long-term.

✔ **When one or both of you suffer from serious personal or psychological problems:** See a psychologist to resolve your problems. If your partner is the one with the problems, invite him to couples counseling with a psychologist. Rely on the therapist's judgment as to whether or not the two of you can progress. If your partner is addicted, not motivated to pursue treatment, or abusive, terminate the relationship with the psychologist's help. When you've healed enough, use an introduction service to efficiently meet healthy single people who share your relationship goal (marriage or marriage and children). Read Chapter 20 to help identify which problems are fixable and how to get help, and Chapters 21 and 22 for more help on moving on and starting over.

✔ **When one or both of you have committed physical, sexual, or child abuse:** This relationship has very little potential. If you're the abuser, you need urgent treatment by a psychologist. Seek treatment *immediately*, and let the psychologist know that this is an emergency. See Chapters 12 and 20 for more information on abuse. Also, read the letters at my Web sites (`www.drkate.com` or *AOL Keyword: DrKate*) for more information.

If you are the abused person, you also need to see a psychologist immediately for help. Check into local services for abused people and take measures to save yourself. Be sure to reach the sections on abuse in Chapter 12 and the sidebar on abuse in Chapter 20. Also, read the advice I've given to abused people at my Web sites (`www.drkate.com` or *AOL Keyword: DrKate*). Use the *Dr. Kate Search* function there to locate the letters. Stay in therapy until you have broken free of your abusive partner and your pattern of being attracted to abusive people. Read Chapters 21 and 22 for more on recovering from a relationship and starting over. Remember, your relationship isn't worth saving, but you are. Act now to change your present and future.

Considering Special Marital Situations

Certain situations can affect how much a couple wants to marry. It's not good to be afraid of marriage, and in my opinion, marriage is usually preferable to living together. However, depending on the situation, marriage may not be necessary to attain the relationship quality you desire. In Chapter 9, I discuss situations where people might be better off cohabiting instead of marrying. Here I discuss other circumstances that may affect your desire to wed.

Older couples

Marriage is more important when neither person has been married before, when the couple is younger, when there are children involved, or when the couple wants to raise a family. Men and women 50+ often want a long-term, compatible, intimate relationship, but may not care as much if they marry their partner or not.

Sometimes people who come from large families don't remarry. If you have brothers and sisters living with you, or an extended family, you might not ever lack adult companionship. Or maybe you don't want to sell your house to move in with a spouse after all these years. It may be easier to just date and see people as friends.

Maybe the man you're dating wants to move to Florida or travel around the country in his motor home, and you don't want to be gone that far from home. He's OK to date, but you don't want to leave your entire family behind for months or forever.

Maybe the woman you're dating has older children still living at home and many family problems. You enjoy her company, but don't want to get in the middle of all the family squabbles. She doesn't really care to remarry, so you're both happy with the arrangement. You see one another for dating, but you separate out the rest of your lives.

As long as you and your partner are *both* happy with the situation and the relationship is healthy, you don't have to get married. If you're not going to have any more children, there's no one to get confused by your arrangement. You can each maintain your independence, while enjoying companionship at the level you desire it.

After one or two spouses

Some people don't choose to marry again after they've been married several times, or been continuously married from a young age. They've raised their children — maybe even two sets — so they have no desire for another family. They may even have grandchildren. They've worked very hard in a family setting, and now that their kids are out of the house, they want to enjoy life by taking long trips and doing things independently.

For example, if you were married to your husband for 50 years and took care of him through his illness and death, you may now prefer to be independent and on your own. Perhaps you've been married most of your life, and you'd like a change. Maybe you're reluctant to marry someone who might also get sick and die. You'd rather play the field with male friends, and there's certainly nothing wrong with that.

A person who has experienced a lot of turmoil in marriage (for example, someone who was married to an alcoholic, drug addict, or a physically, sexually, or emotionally abusive partner) may be reluctant to remarry. A man who has lost a lot of money in a divorce may avoid marriage to prevent that from happening again. If he has a lot of self-built wealth and has come to hinge his self-esteem on that power and position, he may be more concerned with that issue than the average man who isn't used to having much money or power anyway.

If two people who don't want to marry somehow find each other, they can have a healthy, long-term relationship — because neither of them wants to get married. However, if either one secretly wants to get married, but is trying to accommodate the other, they're not compatible together. In addition, if any reluctance to marry is temporary (as it might be with someone trying to recover from an unhealthy marriage), it would be better to work on the issues in therapy than to try to avoid marriage altogether.

Money problems

As I mention in Chapter 9 on living together, money issues sometimes dictate whether or not a couple should get married. If one person would lose a pension, social security, public assistance, alimony, or other funding when marrying, and the situation she'd marry into wouldn't be as financially comfortable, then she might opt not to marry. It's sad when marriage is penalized and when money dictates who marries whom, but this is the real world, and it happens.

The Shelf Life of Relationships

So now you understand when you're ready for marriage and when you're not, and how to examine your motivation for marriage. But what if you and your partner disagree on this goal? What if one of you feels ready to marry now, and the other doesn't? You understand why it's best not to marry too young or too soon after meeting a partner. But is there also a time when it becomes too late to marry a particular person — when not marrying or moving forward in that direction becomes a problem for your relationship? You betcha. Read on!

A relationship is a living thing. When it's not moving forward toward greater commitment, it's generally moving backward — unless both of you really and truly don't want to get married. If one or both of you ever want to get married, then your relationship has a type of shelf life. You and your partner need nurturing on a regular basis, and so does the bond between you. If it doesn't get that nurturing, the relationship dies out gradually over time. Because men and women differ in their attitudes toward marriage, it's especially important to understand how certain factors can alter the timing of the relationship and its shelf life. That way, if you want to keep your relationship thriving, you'll have some idea of the time limits involved.

The *shelf life of a relationship* — how long you have to make a decision about marriage before your relationship begins falling apart — depends on several factors, including the chronological age of the people involved, whether or not they've had sex, how soon and how often they've had sex, whether or not they've been married before or had children, and whether or not they want to get married or have children.

Younger people can date longer without getting married, as long as they believe that marriage is unrealistic at this time. That's particularly true if they haven't had sex yet. In contrast, older couples tend to become sexually involved sooner, which tends to speed things up.

Women who have never been married tend to be most driven to get married, while a divorced woman is often more patient, particularly if she isn't interested in having any (more) children. A woman who has recently been divorced may feel like grabbing someone immediately to fill the void. However, once she gets past that anxiety and has been single awhile, she usually doesn't feel as pressured to get remarried. As silly as it may seem, the previously married woman has a stamp of approval on her; someone loved her enough to marry her. In contrast, a woman who hasn't been married has no outside sign that anyone found her desirable. And because women are judged by whether or not they have a relationship, the never-married woman has a tough load to carry. If the woman runs into man after man who doesn't want to marry her, even if it's due to a fear of marriage in general and not a personal rejection of her, her self-esteem may begin to suffer.

The woman also needs to be aware of two important factors that are outside her control:

- **There is a difference in the pool of available men and women at different ages.** There are more men born than women, but they die faster all the way through the lifecycle. When the woman is less than 30, she's outnumbered by men. But when she's in her mid to late 30's, she begins to feel the pinch, especially if she tends to date men a little older than her. When she's in her late 30's, she'll begin to experience rejection from men who want to marry a younger woman who can make babies longer (see the next bullet for more). When she crosses 40, she's definitely competing with other women for the available men.

- **Chances of having a healthy baby decline after age 35.** After 35, the risk of having a baby with genetic abnormalities increases. After 40, the number of eggs may be getting sparse, and the woman may not ovulate every month.

So while you should never give up trying to find a compatible mate, a woman should be especially careful to use the time before age 35 productively. A woman has about 8 prime years — from age 27+ when she matures, until 35, when the odds get tougher. So don't waste any of that time on a man who is afraid of marriage, particularly if you want to have a family. Instead, restrict your dates to men who are single, emotionally available, and compatible — including with regard to your relationship goal. They should be willing to say they want marriage or marriage and children (whatever your goal is) in a straightforward, enthusiastic way, without any vacillation. And they should behave in a way consistent with that goal. They should also live close enough to allow you to see them often and to enjoy a regular, intimate relationship leading to marriage in the near future. See Chapters 4 and 5 for more on this topic.

Keep your options open by dating more than one person at a time, subtly allowing the men to compete with one another. That's especially true if you are 27+ or if your preferred partner is fearful of marriage. If he then perks up and approaches marriage on a compatible timetable, you can still marry him. But along the way, you may also find someone else more compatible — in timing, relationship goal, and other ways. If not, at least you've kept your options open. And if you don't find someone to have children with before your time runs out, you won't feel resentful toward your partner for taking up all that time.

Try to understand where the woman is coming from, and factor that into your behavior. For example, if your girlfriend is between 27 and 35 and single/never-married, with no children, understand that she'll probably become annoyed and resentful if you don't propose after about 18 to 24 months of exclusive dating. If she's 35+ and wants children, she may be even less patient and more resentful and upset when the relationship doesn't move forward in 12 to 24 months, even if she has been married before. She's running out of time to make babies, and she can't afford to waste it on someone who doesn't share that goal. She doesn't know how long she'll be able to get pregnant, so every year wasted is another year she may not have to reach that goal.

Even if your girlfriend tries to be patient with you, the two of you may end up arguing about little, seemingly meaningless topics. If that happens, keep in mind that the real issue is that she wants to get married and thinks you should already be married, and she's frustrated by your reluctance. See a psychologist to try to resolve the problem in a productive way. If you don't care enough about your girlfriend to do that, then be considerate enough to break off your relationship in a kind way (using the methods described in Chapter 21), so that she can move on to more compatible opportunities as soon as possible.

For more on *marriage phobia*, an irrational fear of marriage, and what to do if you or your partner suffer from it, see Chapter 19.

❤ ❤ ❤ ❤ ❤ ❤

Missed Out? Married Second Girlfriend — Midlife Crisis!

Dear Dr. Kate,

My age: 48   **My gender:** Male

I've only had two girlfriends in my life — one of whom I married at age 22. Although I've been faithful all these years and still care about my wife, I now find myself obsessing about other women, and I'm tempted to do something about it. I've really missed out in life. What should I do?

Dear Making Up for Lost Time?,

You've spent 26 years with your wife; that's a long time. I don't think you would have been able to do that unless you and your wife shared a lot of compatibility and love. If you have an affair, you'll be throwing all of that away. It really isn't worth it. You'll be 50 soon; many people would call this your "midlife crisis." You're examining your life and trying to figure out where you've been, where you wish you'd been, where you're going, and what you want to experience before you die.

But the question is: What exactly are you missing? Great sex with a lot of women? I doubt that it would make you happy for long. True, dating a lot of women would be a novelty for a while, and you might have some great sex along the way. But I can guarantee that you'd also have some rotten sex and find that many of the women aren't nearly as compatible for you as your wife.

Of course, by that time, you probably would have lost your wife, so you'd also be upset that you threw away "the best thing you ever had." Your kids (if you have them), and of course, your in-laws, would also resent you for throwing it all away, so you'd lose part of your extended family as well.

How's your career going? Have there been any recent disappointments in your life? Sometimes, people blame their spouses when they're unhappy. A man might feel that he should have accomplished more, so he projects that feeling onto his marriage, blaming his wife rather than himself. Are you feeling depressed? If so, that can also cause you to think negatively about your life.

Consult a psychologist for individual therapy; explore your thoughts and feelings. If you find that you really are dissatisfied with parts of your marriage, ask the same psychologist to see you and your wife together for marital therapy. Fix the problems. If your sex life isn't as fulfilling as you'd like, add the passion. But don't go outside your marriage. Also, be careful about making any big decisions while depressed because your judgment could be faulty.

I agree that it would have been better if you'd dated more women before settling down. Then when you eventually chose your bride, you would have felt that you made a good choice. As it is, you're wondering. But don't forget: No partner is ever perfect or perfectly compatible with you. So don't take your wife for granted just because you didn't suffer enough before marrying her. Ask any long-time single person who hasn't found a compatible spouse; they'd love to be in your shoes. Often, the grass is *not* greener on the other side.

All the best. Please let me know what you decide to do and how it works out.

Dr. Kate

Older Mother Fares Better — Maturity Helps!

Dear Dr. Kate,

My age: 51   **My gender:** Female

I want to join you in encouraging women to wait until they're older before having babies. My husband and I had our daughter when we were 36, and our sons when we were in our early 20s. In many ways, we've been much better parents with our daughter. Being older and more emotionally mature, as well as more financially secure, has helped immensely. We've been calmer, wiser, and more content, so we've been able to pass that on to her. We've also had greater financial resources, so we've been able to provide her with more experiences and opportunities.

Dear Older Mom,

Thank you for your comment. I take a lot of heat from young women who are absolutely, positively sure that they're ready to be mothers, even though they haven't finished maturing yet. They don't have the years of experience to see the big picture; they don't understand what lies in front of them, or how much they still need to learn about life.

There's no question that life isn't perfect. Even though a woman's body may be in the best shape for childbirth in her 20s, she's not as emotionally ready as she will be when she gets a bit older. Young women are naturally very self-absorbed, and when people age, they tend to become calmer, wiser, and happier. Studies show that older people report being happier, even though biologically, they're not as fit as they were when they were younger.

That happiness and maturity translates into more effective, more consistent, and happier parenting. And that makes for a psychologically healthy kid. So while it's possible to raise a healthy child at an earlier age, I advocate being a child yourself when it's appropriate to be one, and having fun as a teen and young adult when you're a teen and young adult. Then, when you're a bit older, more emotionally mature, and ready to settle down — get married (around age 28+), and have your children (age 30+). Use appropriate medical care and testing as needed to help. You'll still have plenty of years to enjoy family life, and your kids will enjoy you better as well.

Thanks again for reading my Web site and for your comment. All the best, and please let me know how you're doing from time to time.

Dr. Kate

Chapter 19

Mmmmmmarriage: The M Word

In This Chapter

▶ Exploring the definition and causes of marriage phobia

▶ Treating marriage phobia effectively

▶ Improving your partner's motivation to marry

*P*eople come with histories, and sometimes those histories include *"emotional baggage"* — problems that inhibit the formation and growth of new, healthier relationships. One of the biggest forms of emotional baggage is marriage phobia. A *phobia* is an irrational fear of something that causes you to avoid that thing. For example, if you were wary of and avoided poisonous snakes, that fear would be rational — poisonous snakes are dangerous and life-threatening, especially when there's no anti-venom nearby. On the other hand, if you are afraid of nonpoisonous garter snakes, even though you know they aren't poisonous, then you have an irrational fear of garter snakes. You know on a cognitive level that those particular snakes are safe, but emotionally, you react as though they aren't.

When people are afraid of other people, objects, or experiences, they go out of their way to avoid them. While that avoidance is wise when the people, objects, or experiences are harmful or life-threatening, that avoidance is unfortunate when there's no danger. And when you avoid something that isn't harmful out of an irrational fear, you never get a chance to find out that there's nothing there to be afraid of. Because you don't allow yourself to come in contact with whatever you're afraid of, you never get the chance to get over your fear. While avoiding snakes may not seriously compromise your life, avoiding safe people and experiences can cost you a lot of joy.

For example, some people develop an irrational fear of intimacy that causes them to avoid intimate relationships (an *intimacy phobia*), an irrational fear of commitment that causes them to avoid making any kind of emotional commitment *(commitment phobia),* or an irrational fear of marriage that causes them to avoid marriage *(marriage phobia).* However, avoiding intimacy, commitment, and marriage out of irrational fears would prevent you from enjoying all that life — and other people — have to offer. Of these, marriage phobia is arguably the most harmful, since it causes considerable pain for the partner, as well as the person with the phobia. Because the issue of marriage doesn't usually come up until later in a relationship, you could be very much in love before realizing that your mate's marriage phobia will inhibit your future together (or vice versa).

In this chapter, I focus on marriage phobia — what causes it, how to overcome it, and what to do if you become involved with someone who has it.

What Is Marriage Phobia — And What Causes It?

Marriage phobia is an irrational fear of marriage that causes people to avoid getting married. It's a fearful reaction to the institution of marriage, not a response to a particular person. For example, if your boyfriend *would* marry someone else, but doesn't feel compatible enough to marry you, he's not phobic — irrationally fearful — of marriage. Rather, his hesitancy is a rational reaction to the incompatibility (as he sees it) between the two of you.

On the other hand, if your boyfriend is afraid to marry anyone, even women he has loved intensely, because of some irrational idea he holds about marriage that really isn't true of most marriages or doesn't have to be true of his marriage, then he has a marriage phobia. For example, maybe he believes he'll lose his individuality when he becomes one with his wife, or that he'll cheat on his wife because his father always cheated on his mother. Whatever his irrational belief about marriage, it's about the institution of marriage — marrying anyone; it's not about you personally. He may not admit that he's afraid of marriage, and he may not even realize it himself. But he will show a pattern of *never* being able to marry anyone. He may even go along with the idea of marriage up to a certain point, then break up with you when wedding details are discussed and/or the marriage seems imminent.

So how does someone become irrationally afraid of marriage? The following sections examine a few of the more common causes.

Approach-avoidance conflict

I'm not into Freud's ideas about psychotherapy, but he did have some really good theories about why and how men learn to fear intimacy. And of course, a fear of intimacy can translate into a fear of marriage later in life.

According to Freud, the mother feeds the baby most often in most families. So most babies, male and female, identify with the mother first. They look up at their mother's face while she gives them the wonderful bottle or breast, and they associate positive, warm feelings of attachment with the mother.

The female baby never has to stop being attached to the mother; she grows up emulating her. So the female learns that getting close to someone is always good. The closer, more intimate you get, the better it gets.

But the situation is different for the male baby. When he reaches a certain age, adults encourage him to emulate his father's behavior instead of his mother's. He is pushed out from behind his mother's skirt and encouraged to act like his dad. But frequently, he doesn't know his dad that well because Mom has spent more time with him. Dad may also seem a lot scarier, with his bigger size, rough beard, and deep voice. He's a little boy in a big world run by grown-ups, so asking him to stop being so close to Mom and get closer to Dad is a big stress in his young life. And so begins the male intimacy conflict. The little boy learns that getting close isn't always good. You can get so close, then be rebuffed; intimacy can suddenly end or change form on you. So instead of learning the little girl's straightforward lesson that the more intimate you get, the better it gets, the little boy learns a more confusing message — that intimacy isn't all pleasant; sometimes it's painful. And that pain happens outside your control, when you least expect it, too.

And so the groundwork is laid for the male *approach-avoidance conflict*. The man becomes emotionally intimate with a woman and feels fine up to a point. Then he becomes afraid of getting any closer, so he backs off. When he's far enough away, he gets comfortable again and moves closer. Then when he gets too close, he gets uncomfortable again and backs off. And so it goes, back and forth, back and forth, back and forth, like a seesaw.

Early socialization

Girls and boys are socialized differently. Girls are rewarded for thinking and speaking about relationships, while men are not. Girls "play house," roleplaying the wife and mother role. In contrast, boys are rewarded for thinking and talking about competition, achievement, and aggression — competing with other boys and winning in outside activities like games, sports, and races. Girls grow up to be women who are judged by their relationships and whether or not they have a husband and family, while boys grow up to be men who are judged by how successful they are in the outside world. So females are rewarded more for relationship-oriented thoughts and behavior, while males do not receive this positive reinforcement/reward. As a result, we would expect women to be more drawn to relationships than men.

Adult lessons

As an adolescent, the male feels the same pain from rejection that the female adolescent does. But if Freud's theories are correct, the male started out with a more problematic relationship with intimacy. And unlike females, he is not simultaneously receiving positive reinforcement for his relationships. So when he gets rejected, it has a different impact. While women may hurt, they also feel a great drive to find another relationship. That keeps them moving forward. In contrast, the male may sit on his relationship aspirations for awhile. He is interested in the sexual side of those relationships, but already sensitized by his intimacy conflict, he can do without the emotional pain. He often focuses on his career instead, for which he typically does receive a lot of positive reinforcement.

When the male grows into adulthood, his feelings toward marriage are much more conflicted. He doesn't have the confidence and motivation the woman has to move forward. He often vacillates, moving forward as long as he feels comfortable, then backing off when he gets too close and feels uncomfortable, then moving forward again until he feels uncomfortable . . . back and forth, back and forth, in the same old approach-avoidance seesaw pattern. So he ends up in long-term relationships where his girlfriend wants to get married, but he's reluctant to take the risk.

If he goes through with the marriage and it ends in divorce, he learns to become even more fearful of marriage. He overcame his fear to marry the first time, and look what happened!

When a couple is divorced, the man often loses custody of the children. In addition to the pain of not having their children at home, men *hate* to lose — much more than women — because they're trained that they should always compete and *win*. Because he usually loses half his finances and material possessions as well, the man who judges his worth by how much money he makes and how much he has accomplished in the material world also feels his self-esteem and manliness threatened. So the marriage phobic man usually becomes even more phobic after a divorce. He may avoid remarriage for years — or forever.

Adding up all these elements and recapping our equation of how a man theoretically becomes phobic of marriage: As a toddler, he learned that intimacy can be wonderful or painful, and it's often very confusing, unpredictable, and out of his control. As a child and adolescent, he wasn't rewarded for talking about or roleplaying relationships; he was rewarded and consequently learned to compete and win in outside activities, especially against other males. As an adolescent, he learned that intimacy comes with even more losses when relationships break up. As an adult, he learned that marriages often end in divorce, and the loss of children, finances, material possessions, self-esteem, and manliness. So he's been punished for being intimate, and he hasn't been consistently rewarded for pursuing it. At the same time, he's been rewarded for skills that are almost "*anti*-intimate," like how well he "wins" in the outside world.

In contrast, the female toddler learns that intimacy is wonderful. She is rewarded for thinking about, talking about, and roleplaying relationships and marriage in childhood and adolescence. While she also feels the pain of rejection when relationships don't work out, her early intimacy lessons, strengthened by all the reinforcement she receives for relationship thoughts and behaviors, motivate her to keep trying. When her marriage ends in divorce, she also loses, but the loss that is most important is the loss of the intimacy she craves. So she has much more motivation to seek remarriage than the man.

And that, in a nutshell, is why women tend to be more motivated to get married, and why men can be skittish or even phobic about it.

Irrational ideas about marriage

In the beginning of this chapter, I explain that a *phobia* is an irrational fear that causes someone to avoid the feared object. If the fear was rational (if there really was a reason to avoid that object, in other words), then it wouldn't be a phobia. So marriage phobias are irrational fears — they're based on ideas about marriage that are out of proportion to reality. Someone has *associated* irrational ideas with marriage that really don't go with marriage — or don't *have* to go with a healthy marriage. The irrational idea underlying marriage phobia can be almost anything.

The idea may be linked to something the man or woman heard or learned in the past. For example, a mother frustrated by her husband's cheating might admonish her son, "You better not grow up to be like your dad. Cheating and divorce always runs on his side of the family!" So the man begins to believe that he is somehow genetically predisposed to ruin marriages, and he may subsequently avoid marriage to avoid cheating. Similar comments from a frustrated mother or father can stick in a kid's mind and fester into adult problems.

The idea may also be an inappropriate lesson learned at an older age. For example, if you're a woman who was previously married to a man who controlled and beat you and you subsequently learn to avoid men who control or abuse you, that would be an appropriate lesson, not a phobia, and you would be acting wisely. However, if you subsequently become fearful of and avoid *all* men, then you have developed a marriage phobia.

Both men and women can hold irrational ideas about marriage, but because of all the other factors described in previous sections, men tend to develop more of them.

If we ask a marriage phobic man what marriage means to him, he might say, "Having to become one person. Being consumed by marriage and losing my identity." Or, "Having to make my wife happy; having to like everything she does." Or, "Having to succeed at marriage when I have failed before, giving up all my possessions, and starting all over again." An abused woman might say, "Marriage means letting a man control me and beat me whenever he feels like it." Or she might voice some other idea about marriage that isn't really valid.

But if marriage really meant all those things, then it *would* be rational (not irrational) to avoid it, wouldn't it? Fortunately, marriage does *not* mean those things. For example:

- ✔ While the myth is spread through movies, songs and novels, two partners don't really become one person in marriage.

- ✔ No one can ever *make* anyone do anything, so nobody can ever *make* anyone else happy. As I discuss in Chapter 10, everyone is responsible for his or her own happiness.

- ✔ Spouses never like *everything* the other spouse is doing, so it's definitely *not* a condition for successful marriage.

- ✔ Just because someone has divorced before does not mean that he or she will "fail" in remarriage.

- ✔ Being married and living closely with a spouse is difficult, so no matter how long the marriage lasts, divorce should never be viewed as *failure*.

- ✔ In the future, you can draw up a prenuptial contract to avoid losing more than half your finances in a divorce.

- ✔ All men do not abuse and control their wives, and no one should tolerate abuse. Instead, follow the suggestions in Chapter 20 to make your life better.

The person who is afraid of marriage really needs to examine his or her irrational ideas, and change them for more realistic, healthy ideas. However, because marriage-phobic people also avoid marriage and talking about it in any meaningful way, they don't learn that there's nothing to be afraid of. Instead, they usually go through life avoiding marriage, causing a lot of pain for themselves and others, and missing out on a lot of joy.

Curing Marriage Phobia

So how can someone cure his or her phobia? The best way to cure any phobia is to see a psychologist for treatment. With the psychologist's help, the client talks about what marriage means to him, discovers which ideas are irrational, and replaces those ideas with more rational beliefs. Once he's fixed his irrational beliefs, he then needs to fix his behavior to stop avoiding and instead, do whatever he's afraid of. So basically, the marriage-phobic client needs to get married. That can be done in either of two ways:

- ✔ **Gradually, using a hierarchy of steps:** The marriage phobic client makes a list of the actions that cause anxiety (for example, telling his family about the impending marriage, looking for halls, booking the church, sending the invitations, and so on). He completes the item that is easiest for him, then the next, and the next, seeing the psychologist in between to help relax. He continues to complete each step in ascending order of difficulty until he has finally gotten married and feels just fine about it.

✔ **Quickly, doing the step that causes the most anxiety first:** The client gets married in a quick, civil service. Then once he's married and the irrational fears don't materialize, he relaxes, and the phobia is cured. The client can then get remarried in front of family and friends, enjoying the celebration himself as well.

If the client is motivated, treatment for the thoughts/cognitions and behaviors, or *cognitive-behavioral therapy,* as it's called, does not have to take long at all. However, clients are sometimes so afraid of marriage (or whatever they're phobic of) that they avoid therapy rather than dealing with the problem. In so doing, they reinforce the idea that marriage is really something to be feared and make the problem worse.

If you're the person with the phobia, consult a psychologist who uses cognitive-behavioral therapy to fix phobias. Treatment can be successful in weeks or months, not years, and you'll feel much, much better — like a weight has been lifted from you.

If you're involved with a phobic partner, invite your mate to accompany you to "relationship therapy." Avoid use of power words like, "You have a problem," and, "You need therapy," which will effectively put off most people. Instead, treat this like it's a joint problem that you can solve together. (See Chapter 20 for more on how to invite your partner to couples counseling.) Your partner will probably be more comfortable initially attending therapy with you. After he has rapport with the psychologist, he can go alone or you can sit in the waiting room for moral support. Be sure to give him praise and hugs (positive reinforcement) when he emerges from a completed session. Reward small steps, and eventually, he will finish treatment.

But what do you do if your mate won't agree to therapy? Read on!

Encouraging Your Mate's Marriage Motivation

Earlier in this chapter, I explain that it's usually the man who is marriage phobic. So in this section, I'll focus specifically on how a woman can encourage her man's motivation for marriage. If you're a man dating a marriage-phobic woman, however, applying similar techniques should help.

To help your partner get over his fear of marriage, don't nag, complain, and criticize. It won't help, and it will only ruin your relationship. When someone is afraid, pushing him to do something just encourages him to bolt. It certainly won't keep him coming back to weekly therapy sessions. Instead, try using healthy communication as described in Chapters 11 through 13 to discuss his irrational ideas about marriage. If your partner can tell you the history leading up to his phobia, the two of you might better understand how the fear became engrained in his psyche, and he might better understand how the thoughts are irrational.

But you can't be your partner's therapist. For one thing, you have a vested interest, so it's difficult for him to believe you're being objective. Also, because our culture teaches men that they need to be big and strong, they usually avoid admitting that they're afraid of anything. Your mate might admit it to the psychologist, but not to you. In addition, by the time you discover that your partner is afraid of marriage, you're probably so invested in the relationship, you won't be able to remain calm, patient, and objective during the discussion. Instead, you'll tend to come on too strong and push too hard. So what can you do? Read the following sections and follow the yellow brick (marriage) road!

Understand what you're doing and why

When someone has a phobia, he or she can miss out on a lot of what life has to offer. For example, if you were irrationally afraid of traveling, and never treated your phobia, you would miss all the joy that discovering new places and people can bring.

Similarly, man is a social animal. We're innately wired to love companionship. So normal people enjoy sharing life with a close, emotionally supportive partner. When someone is marriage phobic, however, he spends a lot of energy avoiding marriage — and a lot of energy dealing with his partners' hurt feelings along the way. In addition, walking around with all that anxiety is a constant drain on anyone's energy. Remember Roosevelt's statement that, "The only thing to fear is fear itself?" That's really true. You only have so much energy. If you waste it worrying about irrational fears, you have less to spend on enjoying all that life has to offer.

While you can't *make* anyone do anything, what you do and say can make it easier or more difficult for your mate to act in a certain way. When you allow someone to have an intense relationship with you but not marry you, and you continue to date him and only him, you basically *enable* him to remain phobic. By staying in the relationship, you're rewarding him for his sick behavior and making it easier for him to stay sick.

On the other hand, if you can alter your behavior, avoid rewarding your mate for sick behavior, and instead, reward him for well behavior, you will be helping him and you. It's a win-win. In Chapter 4, I explain why spilling your guts is not the same as honesty, and how you need to use discretion when choosing what to share with your mate. Similarly, the techniques I will describe in the next sections involve using discretion when choosing what to share with your mate — verbally and behaviorally — to help your relationship progress in a healthy manner.

You're not going to manipulate your sweetie in an attempt to control him and make him do something you want at his expense. Rather, you're going to alter your behavior so that instead of enabling your mate to stay sick, you encourage him to do something that is healthier and in his best interest. Those behaviors will also help your relationship improve, and you will profit as well. However, keep in mind that the focus is on *healthy behavior, honesty with discretion,* and a *win-win* resolution of the problem.

Avoid ultimatums

Many a woman has tried giving her mate an ultimatum: "Decide to marry me by _____ (date), or we're finished." There are four big problems with that approach:

✔ **If your mate decides not to marry you by ultimatum time, you have to break off the relationship or you'll lose all credibility.** If you say one thing and do another, it won't take long for your mate to ignore your statements, so never "cry wolf."

✔ **It underestimates the intensity and irrationality underlying marriage phobia.** Remember, marriage phobia is *not* rational, so it doesn't have rational boundaries either. It's larger than life in his imagination, and often, the unknown is much more frightening than the "known." So although he probably loves you and doesn't want to lose you, the big, black, unknown hole of marriage can be much scarier, and he may choose breaking up as the lesser of two evils. He might come back after he's lost you and is feeling the pain from that loss — or he might not.

✔ **Men often rebel against ultimatums.** They're raised to be strong and stand up for themselves; they're not supposed to be wimpy and give in to threats. If a man ends up getting married after your ultimatum, he may later resent you for it. Even though the marriage will end his phobia, the resentment can cause problems. He might even pick fights to show you he was right — marriage doesn't work for him! He might unfairly throw the ultimatum in your face during arguments: "Well, I didn't want to marry you, and you made me!"

> ✔ **If the man is afraid of being controlled and consumed by you, issuing an ultimatum is *not* a great way to convince him that it won't happen.** He's going to feel like you're forcing him into marriage, which may just reinforce the phobia. Even though marriage doesn't mean that you *will* control him, and you can do all you can after you're married to show him that you won't, he may still feel controlled anyway. He may spend hours ruminating about how you pushed him into marriage, and your marriage will either suffer or end as a result.

So, although an ultimatum might work on some men, it would probably back-fire on a lot of them, particularly if they are intensely phobic.

Why buy the cow . . . .

Another mistake women make when trying to convince a phobic man to marry them is they decide to live with him. Of course, a man who is phobic of intimacy and commitment won't want to live together either, but someone who is mostly just phobic of marriage can get to the point where living together is possible and even preferable. After all, it's just living together; they can split whenever they want to, right?

You might think it's a step in the right direction when your man agrees to live with you. But it isn't; it's actually making the problem worse. When you give him your company, emotional support, undivided loyalty, attention, and sex — everything he wants — without marriage, you're basically rewarding him for not marrying you. And remember, whatever you reward is likely to increase — he's likely to want to marry you even less after that. Meanwhile, you don't get a marriage license, legitimacy in the eyes of the world, or his committed attitude. When you bring up the topic of marriage, he'll probably change the subject. After awhile, you'll realize that you're back to square one, giving him an ultimatum and threatening to move out.

Read Chapter 9 on cohabiting. Most couples who live together go on to marry other people instead, and cohabiting isn't a good test of whether you should marry one another anyway. When you live together, your partner also sees you at your worst, which can quickly boomerang.

There's an old saying: "Why buy the cow when you can get the milk for free?" If you sell yourself for cheap, you won't get a higher price later. Instead, you've just lowered your price with that person for the foreseeable future.

Be smart: Reward a competing drive

Say you're at an auction, and there are two vases up for auction. You were planning to bid on the one you thought was a rare, valuable vase. However, when it's time, very few people bid on it, and the bidding price is very low.

Don't you question your assessment of the vase? Of course, you do. Now, say everyone seems to be bidding on the vase you weren't going to bid on. Don't you want to re-examine that vase to see what you might have overlooked — what makes it so special?

Similarly, when a man chooses a mate, he's frequently influenced by "auction behavior." He appreciates the woman who isn't so available — the one who makes him work a little harder for her attention and companionship — and he takes for granted the woman who comes too easily. Then once he's in a relationship, he often relaxes, gets comfortable, and takes his mate for granted. But if a suitor suddenly comes along, vying for the woman's attention, the man perks up and gets interested. He's at least going to take another look, and consider what losing her would mean — and how much it would hurt.

Earlier in this chapter, I mention that men are rewarded for competitive behavior from the time they're children. They're rewarded for achieving and being successful, and they're trained to compete with other men and *win*. So although the man may have an approach-avoidance conflict toward commitment and marriage, he also has a strong drive to compete. One of the best ways to alter your behavior to encourage your man to overcome marriage phobia is to reward his competition drive. Start dating other people — or at least let your boyfriend suspect that you are by not being so available. Once he figures out that another man may be interested in you, he may compete with that man for your attention and get so caught up in it that his phobia goes right out the window. Instead of irrationally worrying about being consumed by marriage, he's rationally worried about losing you to some other guy.

So keep dating that other guy. When your boyfriend asks you out, say: *"I can't make it Saturday; how about Friday night instead?"* Do *not* say what you're doing on Saturday, and don't — repeat _don't_ — ever describe or give any details about other men. If you do, most men will either become so jealous, hurt, and angry that they break up with you to avoid the pain, or they'll temporarily become more comfortable, knowing you aren't yet moving toward marriage with the other guy. Instead, be subtle, and let your mate's mind start working. Help him conquer his marriage phobia by not rewarding him when he takes you for granted. Stop enabling him and in a subtle way, let him learn that his actions have consequences. Yes, you love him. But if he isn't ready to marry you, then you can't just date him alone. You have to explore your other options. When he understands that, the man usually continues to compete, without breaking off the relationship.

In actuality, to be fair, you should stop dating anyone else as soon as you set the marriage date with your partner. However, continue to turn your fiancé down for dates periodically, and don't tell him whether or not you're dating anyone else — just avoid discussing the issue, and let him wonder if there's another man in the picture. If your fiancé thinks he's the only one, he may totally relax, become phobic again, and quickly lose his drive to marry you. Trust me on this one; *never* underestimate a phobic man's drive to avoid marriage. Many women have relaxed too soon, thinking that a ring and a wedding date means the wedding is actually going to take place. Yet as soon as the woman stops dating the competition, the fiancé finds excuse after excuse to permanently postpone the wedding. So help your man conquer his phobia by not giving him too much information in advance.

If he presses you, you can simply say: *"I love you, and I fully intend to marry you on _____ (date), and I will be faithful to you and keep my vows after we're married. But I also know that you've had mixed feelings toward marriage, so I have to marry you before I totally cut off my other options."*

If your fiancé really hates the situation, offer to marry quickly in a civil service, then remarry months later in the wedding you've always wanted — with a party that you *and* your husband can enjoy.

The goal of this technique is a win-win: To help your mate overcome his irrational fears and enjoy life to the fullest, so you can enjoy a healthy relationship together. You're altering your behavior and instead of rewarding him for sick behavior (taking you for granted and avoiding marriage out of fear), you're rewarding him for healthy behavior (realizing how much he does want you in his life and overcoming his phobia). Once your mate marries you, the phobia should quickly end. It may end once he actually goes through with the marriage, or it may end shortly afterward, when he realizes that his fears have not materialized. Yet when you use this method, you also allow your mate to choose his own behavior. You're not making him marry you; you're helping him see the consequences of his actions and non-actions more clearly, so he can choose to be healthier. See "The Wedding Bell Blues" letter at the end of this chapter for more on this topic.

Spotting Commitment Phobics Sooner Rather Than Later!

Dear Dr. Kate,

My age: 37   **My gender:** Female

Are there typical ways to tell if a guy fears commitment — before you've wasted years?

Dear Proactive Woman,

Sure. To spot a commitment-phobic man sooner rather than later, consider the following:

- **What happened to his previous relationships?** If he's never dated anyone for long, he may be addicted to the early adrenaline rush and beat feet from a "normal" relationship. If he dated several women for years but always had a reason not to marry, perhaps no reason will ever be enough. If women always break up with him, maybe it's because he refuses to marry them.

- **How does he deal with commitment in general?** If he never likes to be pinned down (for example, if he *rents* rather than *buys* a house, or always waits until the last minute to confirm plans), he'll probably want to keep his relationship options open as well.

- **How easily does he make up his mind?** Does he have difficulty making decisions in most areas of his life? Does he usually procrastinate? If so, he'll probably find it very hard to decide if your relationship is good enough for marriage. On the other hand, he may be able to move millions around in business, but fall apart at personal decisions and any mention of the "M" word.

- **What is his family history of marriage?** Has he seen more healthy or unhealthy unions? If his parents have a dysfunctional marriage or none of his adult siblings are married, be careful.

- **What kind of comments does he make about the marriages of his friends and family?**

- **What does he say about your future together?** Some men deliberately say positive things to "hook" a woman into continuing the relationship — for example, "If I were ever to marry someone, it would be you." These teasers really mean: "I have a problem with marriage. I might consider changing my mind someday, but not in your lifetime."

- **If he's anti-commitment post-divorce, how long has he felt this way?** It's normal for someone to go through an anti-marriage phase right after divorce. However, if he's still running from commitment more than four years after the ink's dried on his divorce papers, he may never change.

The most important thing to remember is: Don't count on him changing for you. If he's been anti-commitment in the past, assume he'll be the same with you. If he really wants to marry you, he'll ask you. So if he's over 30, heterosexual, and not recently divorced or widowed, but hasn't proposed by about 24 months, then he probably doesn't love you enough to marry you — or he has a phobia.

Hope this helps. All the best.

Dr. Kate

The Wedding-Bell Blues

Dear Dr. Kate,

My age: 41   **My gender:** Female

Two years ago, I broke off a relationship with my boyfriend of three years. He's divorced, and said he wasn't interested in marriage with anyone at that time; he wanted to be able to see other women. Although my heart wasn't in it, I joined a dating service and dated several men. Within weeks, my boyfriend called, saying that I was the best person for him and he wanted to get married. I was afraid to believe it, but after he repeated it for a month, we became mutually exclusive again. We set a wedding date for the following year and began making arrangements. Then a few months later, he suggested we postpone the wedding due to some family problems. Now the problems are over, but he says he's afraid of making another marriage mistake. What do I do? We're highly compatible in many ways, we enjoy spending time together, and our sex life is still terrific.

Dear "I Don't Want to Give Up,"

Is your dating service membership over yet? If so, buy another one.

I've seen this situation many times over the past 20 years. One woman had a boyfriend who wouldn't marry her. She joined my introduction/dating service, and while we were getting the first match ready, her boyfriend popped the question.

Another client had a very similar experience to yours. After her partner got cold feet, she met a new man, who then competed with the old boyfriend for her affections. Once the old partner won out, she made the mistake of not getting marrying quickly. Instead, she became exclusive with her partner again. The heartbroken second man left the state. When she told her mate, he promptly cooled his heels again. It was only when she became involved with a third man that the first man finally married her. And guess what? Once he did, his phobia was broken, and he was very happy!

Your boyfriend is afraid of marriage. It's called an *approach-avoidance conflict*. He feels comfortable approaching you until it gets too serious; then he backs off until he feels comfortable again. Then he approaches again until he becomes uncomfortable, and the pattern repeats. But when you're dating others, his fear of commitment is eclipsed by his fear of losing you. His drive to compete with other men is stronger than his drive to avoid commitment, and he moves toward you. However, once he wins you back and the fear of losing you has subsided, the old seesaw behavior and phobia return.

This time, tell him: *"It sounds like you're not ready to marry me yet, and I can't wait forever. You have a right to take as long as you like. However, I will have to date other people, so I can keep my opportunities open."* Then rejoin that introduction service. If your boyfriend proposes again, tell him you'll marry him — as long as it's right now. Then marry in a civil ceremony in the next one or two days and don't break off your other relationships until you tie the knot. The phobia should end at or shortly after the "I Do's" are exchanged, and you can then celebrate with friends and family at another time. And if he never perks up and proposes again, don't fret. Just keep dating others, and you'll eventually find someone else who is compatible with you — and also shares your relationship goal.

All the best, and please let me know how it works out.

Dr. Kate

Why Buy the Milk When You Can Get the Cow for Free?

Dear Dr. Kate,

My age: 21   **My gender:** Female

My long-distance boyfriend of one year has asked me to move in with him soon. He wants to buy a house in his hometown (where I know nobody) but only live there with me for five months. Then he'd go overseas with the military for six months straight. I love him, so I brought marriage up. He said he doesn't need a piece of paper to prove that we're committed to each other. He thinks we should just live together for the rest of our lives. My first thought was, "Why buy the milk when you can get the cow for free?" I told him I needed security, and he said he'd set up a $2,000 bank account for me. If we break up, I could use that money to move back home!

I told him I wasn't about to live with him without marriage for the rest of my life. He's a man and can always find a younger woman, but I won't have that option when I'm older. Help!

Dear Cow to Be (?),

You've only dated a year, and it's been long-distance. After five months, he's going to leave you all alone in a new city. I don't think that sounds like a good deal, do you?

There are really three questions here: 1) Should you live with someone without being married? 2) Should you get involved in a long-distance relationship when you know that you'll be apart more than together? 3) How will you adapt to living in another city without anyone you know?

You're only 21, so you're still too young to get married. It'd be better to wait until you're about 26 to 28 and he's about 28 to 32. So, there's no rush. However, once you pass 26, you'll need to date only men who desire marriage and children. You'll then have about nine great years to find someone compatible and settle down. Have you dated a lot? If not, you really should get more experience under your belt before playing house with anyone. On the other hand, if you've had a lot of experience, I wouldn't be opposed to you trying to live with someone for awhile. It can be a great learning experience. Just remember that most people who live with people end up getting married to other people — not each other.

Cohabiting is like experiencing each other at your worst (when sick, irritable, looking frumpy) — without experiencing the best of marriage (like people recognizing you as a legitimate couple). People tend to try harder when they're married, and commitment-phobic people only become more phobic when allowed to avoid what they fear — commitment. In other words, there really is something to that *cow* thing.

Why not just rent for five months and live together, then move home while he goes away? It's no fun waiting on your soldier to return. You'll miss him, and you'll miss him even more if you have no friends and family around. Instead, take a temporary work position in his hometown while you live with him; then find permanent work when you return home. When your boyfriend is done traveling for the military, you can get back together. In the meantime, you can work on your career and build your future. If the relationship is really compatible, it will still be good when he develops a more stable, local career — and when he decides that marriage is really worthwhile.

All the best, and please let me know how it works out.

Dr. Kate

Chapter 20

Relationship Rx

. . . .

In This Chapter

▶ Keeping your relationship healthy and enjoyable

▶ Recognizing when your union is in trouble

▶ Differentiating problems that can be fixed from those that can't

▶ Getting professional help

▶ Deciding when to throw in the towel

. . . .

*I*n Chapter 16, I talk about how important it is to recognize and appreciate what you have in common with your mate and the ways that you're compatible. Similarly, it's also important to recognize what's happening when things don't go well. How serious are the arguments? How bad are your problems? If you keep trying, are you likely to fix them? Or are you just batting your head against the wall? And when is it time to end the whole thing?

In this chapter, I suggest ways to keep your relationship well. I discuss how to recognize when your relationship is in trouble — before you get into so much trouble that it's extremely difficult to fix. I discuss problems that can be fixed, and how to differentiate them from those that can't. I also give you advice on seeking professional help. And finally, I discuss how to tell when it's time to throw in the towel and end the relationship for good.

Your Relationship Wellness Action Plan

Although infatuation can disappear overnight, established relationships don't fall apart that quickly. The disintegration takes awhile, and along the way, there are usually many opportunities to make your union more healthy and satisfying.

Yet many people spend years doing nothing about their relationships. They can't conceptualize what's happening; their thoughts are disorganized and confused. So they just avoid thinking about the problems and hope for the best. But of course, problems that don't get worked on don't usually improve.

Instead, they tend to get worse and worse, until both partners are upset over any number of things. Communication continues to cycle downward, and heated discussions and power struggles become routine. Saying one small phrase can remind partners of the entire argument that went with it, so discussions quickly escalate into communication chaos.

To keep your relationship happy and healthy, follow this logical *Relationship Wellness Action Plan:*

- ✔ **Daily wellness Rx:** Give your relationship daily care and maintenance. Expect this to be part of any healthy relationship, and remember to keep doing the things you've done in the past that brought you so close together.

- ✔ **Add healthy new routines:** Institute new behaviors to draw you and your partner closer.

- ✔ **Do daily/frequent checkups:** Review your relationship on a frequent (preferably daily) basis and note any problems that exist.

- ✔ **Sort out the problems:** Differentiate problems that can be fixed from those that can't.

- ✔ **Fix the problems you can fix:** Act to correct fixable problems as soon as you notice them.

- ✔ **Get professional help to fix the ones you can't:** If you can't fix a problem on a reasonable timetable, consult a psychologist as soon as possible — well before any serious damage occurs.

- ✔ **Decision time:** If you can't fix the problems even with help, decide if you need to end the relationship — or if you can overlook the problems and still enjoy a satisfying, healthy partnership.

- ✔ **Take action:** Follow your decision with appropriate action.

The following sections examine these steps in more detail.

Daily Wellness Rx

It's easy to stop paying attention to something that *is* going well to focus your energy on something that *isn't.* Unfortunately, you can't ever afford to stop paying attention to your relationship, or it will stop functioning.

For example, everyone knows that a car needs regular maintenance. If you get the car checked periodically, give it gas, change the oil, and maintain it on a regular basis, you can keep the vehicle running better for a much longer period of time. If you don't, your car will eventually stop running, and you'll need to shell out a lot of money for another one. Cars are expensive; they're paid for with money that takes time and energy to make. So most people take care of their cars.

At the same time, many people overlook the care and upkeep of their relationship. They don't pay attention to the relationship oil, gas, or any other kind of maintenance; they just expect the relationship to keep humming without it. But as complicated as a car *isn't,* a relationship *is.* Cars are metal objects without feelings; they react to what you put into them in a fairly predictable fashion. But people have thoughts, feelings, desires, motivations, and actions of their own that complicate any interaction considerably. Cars wait where you put them, whereas people can cause much more trouble in much less time, interacting with other people as well as you. No matter how much you paid for your car, a relationship is more expensive — it costs you a lot of time, energy, emotion, and money to build. So doesn't it make sense to give it the attention, care, and maintenance it requires and deserves?

In the early days of your relationship, you and your partner became close by sharing many thoughts, feelings, and experiences with one another that you didn't share with anyone else. Be sure to keep those behaviors in your relationship repertoire to keep your relationship special.

People sometimes feel guilty nurturing their relationship when they have so many other pressing responsibilities — like work, a house, and children. Yet you owe it to yourself, your mate, and your relationship to give your special someone top priority. Yes, you need to work, pay bills, and do other tasks that come with being an adult. But you also need to be nourished as a person and lead a balanced lifestyle — and that's where your relationship comes in. So always make time to do the things that will keep you and your mate closely bonded and intimate. If you don't, you'll spend a *lot* more time, energy, emotion, and money breaking up and starting over.

Add Healthy New Relationship Routines

Don't just get into the fix-it-once-it's-broke mode. Instead, institute a plan for increasing the positive interactions in your relationship as well. For example, use the suggestions in Chapters 14 through 16 and Chapter 24 to add or jump-start the sparks and romance in your relationship. Use the suggestions in Chapters 11 through 13 to become closer through healthy communication.

It's vitally important to keep the bond between you and your partner strong. When it deteriorates, you'll have increasing problems over everything — no matter how big or small the issue.

Do Daily/Frequent Checkups

Catholics have a lovely tradition called *examination of conscience*. I recommend that you do an *examination of relationship* at the end of every day when you're drifting off to sleep: Review the events of the day. How did your interactions with your partner go? Are you satisfied? If you had an altercation, how could you have handled it differently? What can you do to correct it tomorrow?

If you do this daily, you'll notice any problems a lot sooner than if you don't. And noticing a problem that is brewing is the first step to correcting it.

Sort Out the Problems

It's very important to know the difference between problems that can be fixed and those that can't. That way, you'll be less likely to bail out of your relationship over a difficulty that could have been fixed — and less likely to waste time trying to fix something that isn't likely to be fixed within an acceptable time frame.

Problems that can easily be fixed

As I discuss in Chapter 9 on cohabiting and Chapter 11 on communication, most couples tend to argue about *money, sex, kids, family and friends,* and *spare time*. Disagreements about these everyday topics can be fixed and are also fairly easy to fix if the partners are motivated to compromise. That's because these issues have many possible compromises, and usually the couple can find one they're happy with. The only issue related to these problem areas that often cannot be fixed is whether or not to have children. That particular decision causes a lot more trouble and is discussed in the following section.

Most problems *can* be fixed if both partners want to fix them and are motivated to do what it takes to find a compromise. That's particularly true if the couple is willing to consult a professional and learn better forms of communication when needed.

In Chapter 4 on compatibility, I mention how honesty, trust, loyalty, monogamy, maturity, psychological health, a shared relationship goal, and timing are extremely important in any relationship and also very difficult to change. Keep these qualities in mind as I discuss problems that can't be fixed in the next section.

Problems that can't be fixed

Unfortunately, some problems can't be fixed, no matter how much you try. It's important to recognize them so you don't waste time and energy trying to fix something that has little chance of improving.

When your partner refuses to compromise on any issue

If your partner refuses to compromise on any or most issues, you have to decide if you can live that way. Usually, doing so isn't healthy. If you almost always give in, your partner is controlling too much of the interaction and the relationship. Instead of being appreciative of your accepting nature, your mate will take you more and more for granted while he or she respects you less and less. If your partner disrespects you and is not willing to compromise on any or most issues, it's probably best if you just move on.

When your partner doesn't share your relationship goal

It's vitally important for your partner to share your *relationship goal* (your end goal for the relationship — like marriage and children), because these issues are "all-or-none." For example, you can compromise on when, how, and what kind of wedding you'll have, and how many children to have and when, but you either get married and have kids or you don't. You can't get half-married or have half a child.

As I discuss in Chapter 12, if your partner is opposed to marriage or children, you can discuss his or her reservations, try to put practices into place to try to satisfy those objections, and see if he or she is then satisfied and willing to move toward marriage and children. However, this often doesn't work because the decision is a big one — permanent in the case of children and relatively long-term in the case of marriage — and people often hold very strongly to their own preference. So if you and your partner cannot see eye-to-eye on your relationship goal even after working on it with a psychologist's help, then you'll need to end the relationship and move on.

When your partner is immature and not ready for a relationship

If your partner is less than 26 and not emotionally mature, he or she has a good chance of getting there in time. However, if your mate is plenty old enough (30+) to be mature and still isn't, that's a serious problem. If he's willing to seek professional help, he can make progress. But making progress will take time, and if you're a woman over 26 who wants to have children, you don't have that kind of time. Also, if he doesn't share your relationship goal (like he has no intentions of ever marrying or having children), then he's not likely to make any significant progress in any period of time acceptable to you. In contrast, if you're male, under 35, and your girlfriend is willing to go to counseling, you could give it a year or two before throwing in the towel.

When you and your partner are diametrically opposed on major life goals, and neither of you will compromise

You can compromise with your partner on some life goals, particularly if you use the help of a psychologist. For example, you can compromise on when to buy a house, when and how to go back to school for a degree, when and how to go on an expensive vacation together. The more expensive the goal in terms of money, time, or energy, and the more sacrifice required on the part of both partners, the more difficult it can be to compromise. If the two of you aren't married, you may not wish to put in that kind of investment. For example, it would be unwise for a single person to put another single person through medical school. Similarly, if your life goals are diametrically opposed and you can't alternate periods of time satisfying each partner's goal (for example, if you want to spend your life as a relief worker in third world countries and your honey wants to be a news anchor in New York City), you're better off moving on separately. Your life goals are just too opposite, and they require a continuous period of time in different parts of the world.

When your partner is in a different relationship stage, and you feel you can't wait

In Chapter 2, I discuss *The Love Cycle* and its relationship stages. If you and your partner are in different relationship stages, the problem may not be fixable at this time. For example, if your partner is grieving a broken relationship or the death of a former partner, you can speed up grieving and make it more efficient (see Chapter 21 for how to do that). However, no one can completely skip the grieving and recovery process, and there is only so fast the healing can go. For example, if your partner hasn't even gotten divorced yet, and you're feeling pressure to get married and have children, chances are you'll be very dissatisfied about the amount of recovery time your partner needs. In this situation, it's usually best to move on to a more suitable partner.

When your partner is sexually or physically abusive toward children or adults

When your partner has been physically or sexually abusive to you, another adult, or a child, maintaining the relationship is very risky. If the partner is unwilling to get therapy or drops out, there's absolutely no reason to take that risk. Even if your partner attends therapy regularly, the recidivism rate is quite high. Physically and sexually abusive people generally get more abusive when they relapse, which can lead to the death of you or your children, or to your partner molesting kids in the neighborhood. If you want or have children, living with someone who has abused kids is also extremely unwise. So before you stay with an abusive partner, carefully consider how a relapse would affect your life and whether it's worth taking such a big risk. Since there are other people out there who are compatible with you, why not move on to someone else who doesn't have such a serious problem? For more information, see the sidebar on abuse in this chapter.

When your partner is severely mentally ill and refuses to take medication and other needed treatment

If your partner is *psychotic* (out of touch with reality), he or she will always need to take antipsychotic medications. The problem is that all medications have side effects. Psychotic people often stop taking their medication, because they think they don't need it or because they greatly dislike the accompanying side effects. Then they revert to psychotic behavior. Depending on the type of psychosis, this might include hallucinations, paranoia, delusions of persecution (thinking someone's out to get them), or delusions of grandeur (thinking they're Jesus or the devil), all symptoms of *schizophrenia*. Or it might include sleeping around, acting impulsively, giving away lots of money, and staying up for days thinking they're writing something brilliant when they're actually writing nonsensical junk — then crashing into despair and not taking care of themselves *(symptoms of manic-depression bipolar disorder)*. Also, a child born to a parent with either of these disorders is more likely to develop the disorder than someone with no incidence in the family.

When your partner has a personality disorder and refuses to get help because he's not uncomfortable

People with *personality disorders* cause grief to others, but they themselves don't feel uncomfortable, so they rarely seek treatment. Instead, it's the victims — the people on the receiving end of his behavior — who become uncomfortable and seek help. When someone with a personality disorder does go to therapy, progress can take years. One particularly common personality disorder that causes havoc in relationships is the psychopathic/sociopathic/antisocial personality disorder, where the person lies and cheats repeatedly, always putting himself before you or anyone else. People with this disorder are usually intelligent, verbally skillful, and extremely charming. They pretend to be whatever you want so they can get what they want from you. Many women become attracted to men like this, only to have the man use them and dump them. See the letter about con artists at the end of Chapter 21 for more on this.

When your partner suffers from severe characterological problems and refuses to get help

Honesty, trust, loyalty, monogamy, and empathy are extremely important in any relationship. They are also deeply engrained and learned at a young age, so they are very difficult to change. In normal development, people learn to be honest and empathic, to care about others as well as themselves. When someone doesn't develop in this way — when he or she is cold, heartless, disloyal, selfish, and doesn't feel for others in a normal way — that person doesn't usually change. Empathy can be developed in therapy. However, when someone really feels alienated from others and has felt that way all his life, he's not likely to make progress and become a good partner. These problems can occur in the psychopath described in the previous paragraph.

However, they can also occur in people who do not have the psychopath's charm, intelligence, and verbal skill. So if your partner isn't honest, trustworthy, loyal, monogamous, and empathic, with a normal amount of warmth and ability to care for others, you're better off looking for someone more compatible who does.

Problems that can be fixed or controlled with therapy

Many problems can be fixed or controlled with psychotherapy. Some of these problems are easier to fix than others, and with professional help, the person or couple can experience a complete recovery from the problem. Other difficulties cannot be completely cured, but they can be controlled through a combination of therapies.

Problems that are easier to fix with therapy

The following problems are fairly easy to fix with professional treatment. Therapy doesn't have to take a long time, and it doesn't have to cost a great deal. Just be sure that you find a psychologist who has expertise in your problem area to ensure that you're getting the most efficient, effective treatment.

Sexual problems

Sexual problems, as annoying and frustrating as they can be, are relatively easy to fix with the help of a psychologist. Premature ejaculation, difficulty with orgasm, ejaculatory dysfunction, difficulty maintaining erections, and painful sex — are all fairly mechanical, and treatment is usually short-term and successful. However, many sexual problems are not really sexual in nature, but a result of other problems in the relationship. You can't expect to have great sex if you and your mate are busy arguing and thinking nasty thoughts about each other all the time. When the relationship and faulty communication are the culprits, not the mechanical aspects of sex, therapy quickly shifts to relationship counseling rather than sex therapy.

Communication problems

Therapy should focus on teaching the couple how to use healthy communication skills to amicably resolve current disagreements. Therapy is not over and should not be terminated until the couple has amicably resolved the current problems *and* learned the process — how to work out problems by discussing them assertively and negotiating satisfactory compromises. That way, when problems arise in the future — as they will in any relationship — the couple can successfully resolve them without returning to the psychologist.

Neuroses

When a person suffers from a *neurosis,* he or she is in touch with reality and uncomfortable — and often very amenable to treatment as a result. *Anxiety* and *depression* are two of the most common neuroses. If you or your partner suffer from a neurosis, you should attempt to solve the problem before marriage, if possible; otherwise, the anxiety, depression, or other neurosis will also affect your partner and your marital relationship. However, many people become anxious or depressed over time in response to various life stresses. Depression can be treated most efficiently with cognitive-behavioral therapy and medication as needed. Anxiety is also treated with cognitive-behavioral therapy, as well as relaxation techniques and hypnosis. *Phobias* (irrational fears) are easy enough to treat if the person will continue with therapy. *Obsessive-compulsive problems* — ruminating thoughts and repetitive behaviors — can also be treated with shorter-term therapy.

If you see a psychologist for help with these problems, but don't see any progress after four months, discuss your lack of progress with him or her to see if you're overlooking signs of improvement. If you still don't see any progress after six months of weekly therapy sessions, consult another psychologist — someone who approaches your problems differently.

More difficult problems that can be overcome in time with therapy and hard work

Some problems are more difficult to treat and therefore usually take longer, but they can be fixed in time with professional help if the partner or couple is willing to work hard. Two of the most common problems in this category are cheating and jealousy.

Cheating

Cheating is a serious problem, because it involves betrayal and weakens the couple's sexual and emotional bonds. Many relationships do not survive an episode of cheating. In Chapter 6, I discuss how partners become close by sharing thoughts, feelings, and experiences with one another that they don't share with others. The emotional and sexual exclusivity are Superglues #1 and #2. When someone cheats, he or she weakens both of those bonds: Sharing sex with a third party weakens the sexual bond, and sharing private thoughts and feelings with that person, while simultaneously lying to the mate, weakens the emotional bond. The more the cheater lies, the weaker the emotional bond becomes.

Most people assume that their partner is honest, loyal, and trustworthy — until he or she does something that demonstrates the opposite. Once that happens, however, it throws the relationship a severe curve ball. How does the faithful partner know if he or she can ever trust the other again? If the mate betrayed her once by putting his own needs first, why wouldn't he do it again if/when it was convenient?

If your partner has cheated on you, see a psychologist together for couples therapy. Your mate will need to take responsibility for his or her transgression and the pain caused by it. You'll need to express your feelings, which usually include hurt, anger, resentment, humiliation, embarrassment, betrayal, and low self-esteem. You'll both need to explore any other problems that may have contributed to the betrayal. Often the man who cheats is dissatisfied with the quality or frequency of sex at home, and the woman who cheats frequently craves romance and doesn't feel appreciated by her mate. There are usually numerous communication problems. Sometimes the cheater is angry and acting out in passive-aggressive (indirectly aggressive) ways by having sex with another person.

While it is very difficult to work out problems and rebuild the trust, it can be done if both parties are invested in the relationship and really try. As long as the cheating has stopped, it's better if you forgive one another, because it will give you closure and help you heal. If you're married to one another or if there are children involved, it's definitely worth trying to fix the problems and stay married. If you marry young, expect that your partner may stray if he or she is not really ready to settle down. One of you may also end up cheating years later, when you have a mid-life crisis and feel dissatisfied that you've only been with one (or very few) sexual partners in your life.

If the cheating was only a brief, time-limited event (like a "one-night stand"), it will be easier to repair your trust. Everyone makes mistakes sometimes, and it's in the offended partner's best interest to forgive and move on to better times together. However, the more long-term and pervasive the cheating, the more lying involved, and the more it reflects disrespect and the general tendency of that partner to put himself before his mate, the more difficult and long-term the treatment becomes. If that person is not willing to stop the cheating, at least temporarily, to give the problem his or her best shot in therapy, then the problem will not be fixed. When the problem is long-term and involves a lot of lying, a lack of remorse, and no real desire to be faithful, it probably reflects a characterological problem like the psychopathic personality discussed in the earlier section on problems that cannot be fixed.

If you're the one who's been cheating, stop the cheating immediately, and see a psychologist to sort through your feelings. Do *not* tell your partner about your cheating. While you may feel better for a moment getting it off your chest, your mate will feel lousy for a very long time afterward; it will only cause more problems and pain. If your partner knows, don't lie about it. But don't volunteer the information. Just stop the cheating and fix your problem, so you don't do it again. If you find that you're not able to keep your exclusivity agreement with your partner, use ***Dr. Kate's MAKE-A-DEAL Technique,*** outlined on the Cheat Sheet, to tell your mate that you want to change your status to non-exclusive. Always try to treat your mate the way you'd like to be treated; don't say one thing and do another.

Jealousy

When someone is jealous, that person is chronically suspicious that the mate is cheating — or in some serious way, taking attention away from him or her and giving it to someone else instead. The jealous person becomes hyper-vigilant, watching every move the partner makes for a sign that he or she is cheating. If that mate really is cheating, the situation is more rational, but still very intense. If the mate really isn't cheating or violating any promise (which is often the case), then the jealousy is irrational. While the jealous partner may think the intense feelings are a sign of love, jealousy is not love. What that person thinks is acting in a loving manner is usually acting in a possessive and controlling fashion.

Jealousy is usually a long-term, chronic problem. Fueled by low self-esteem, the jealous person is possessive and controlling, or hyper-dependent and clingy. He or she may even be having an affair or fantasizing about having one. But instead of accepting those thoughts and behaviors in himself, the jealous person imagines that his mate is doing the cheating.

Jealousy is extremely destructive to any relationship because it damages the trust between the partners. The jealous partner basically accuses the mate of lying, cheating, and being untrustworthy. If it's true, the constant criticism without resolution just makes things worse. And if it's not true, as is often the case, it severely damages the trust and intimacy between them. No one likes to be accused of doing something wrong — especially when he or she is not really doing it. Instead of being emotionally supportive, the mate is being critical and accusatory, and the constant put-downs make the other partner feel very maligned. In fact, she may begin to wonder if she really should have an affair, since she's being punished for it anyway.

If you are the jealous partner, see a psychologist for individual sessions to overcome your irrational feelings. Discuss lessons learned growing up or any events in your history that may have made you more sensitive to this issue (like a partner cheating; things your parents or peers may have said about not trusting people; or your culture or age group espousing possessiveness as normal behavior). Change your irrational beliefs about love to more rational beliefs, so you can feel more rationally. In particular, review how love includes giving your partner the freedom to choose and grow, and trusting him or her to protect your best interests without being watched. Learn how to give your mate praise and positive reinforcement and act like someone he or she enjoys being around. Concentrate on the positives your mate gives you, rather than what you lack. Like cheating, jealousy will take some time to treat. If you are the jealous partner, you absolutely must go to therapy and fix this problem, or it will continue to haunt you and destroy your relationships — one after another.

If you're the partner of the jealous person, trying to figure out whether or not to hang in, consider how serious the jealousy is, how much you love your partner, how much the positives in the relationship outweigh the negatives, and your relationship timeline. If you and your mate are married or there are children involved, it's usually worth it to wait awhile if your mate gets treatment; you can also have joint sessions whenever the psychologist feels it's helpful. On the other hand, if you don't have that much time because your relationship goal of marriage and children is closing in, if you're not that invested in the relationship, or if the negatives in the relationship outweigh the positives, you should probably move on instead. Successful treatment will take time, and even after the problem has vastly improved, your mate will still relapse from time to time and need additional sessions. If the jealousy is a symptom of more severe problems (like paranoia or physical abuse), or if your partner refuses to get help or blames the problem on you, then the problem is not fixable. If your partner is also physically or sexually abusive, follow the suggestions in the sidebar on physical abuse located in this chapter.

Long-term problems that can be controlled through therapy

The following problems are examples of disorders for which there is no known cure. Without treatment, they can make any relationship a real mess. However, if the person with these problems receives regular professional care as needed over the lifecycle, he or she can enjoy a relatively normal life, including a happy, healthy relationship and marriage.

Addictions to alcohol, drugs, or gambling

If the addicted partner accepts responsibility for the addiction, seeks help, and continues to get the help needed to maintain abstinence, he or she can have a happy, healthy relationship. However, addiction is usually accompanied by denial. If the addict denies having a problem, it's unlikely that the problem will be resolved in any satisfactory time frame. The addict has to "hit bottom," realize that he or she has a problem, and get the help needed. Unfortunately, hitting bottom sometimes includes losing a much-needed job, spouse, and family.

If your mate has a drug or alcohol problem, do not marry before he or she is well on the way to recovery. The addict has to focus on getting well, and marital stress will not help. In addition, the addicted partner is generally a little more amenable to treatment before marriage (when he or she is more concerned about losing you) than afterward (when you're more of a sure thing). If you're already married to an addict, go to Narc-Anon or Al-Anon to learn how to live with your partner in a way that does not escalate the problem. Then decide if you want to continue the marriage in spite of the addiction.

If your mate has a gambling problem, you may not be able to live with him or her — simply because you can't live without money. If your partner cannot be trusted with money, it puts enormous strain on the relationship. Your mate might even sell off your possessions right under your nose! And if you marry that person, you may be responsible for half the debts. So don't get married until/unless your partner has resolved the gambling problem, kept clear of the addiction for a significant period of time, and either continues treatment or is willing to as needed. If you're already married to a gambling addict, consult an attorney and try to organize your life in a way that limits your financial and legal liability as much as possible.

Attention Deficit Disorder (ADD) or Attention Deficit Hyperactive Disorder (ADHD)

If your partner has ADD or ADHD, two forms of the same brain dysfunction, your life will be very affected by the disorder. Your partner will have limited ability to focus, concentrate, prioritize, follow through, or succeed at any task. He (there's a higher incidence in men) may jump from job to job, run up huge credit card bills, act out very impulsively, and take off when problems become serious. People with ADD or ADHD vary with regard to the severity of their symptoms, but they usually need medication (at least for awhile) and counseling/coaching by a psychologist. Most psychologists, physicians, and other health care workers were taught that ADD and ADHD burn out in childhood. Only in the last 10 years have we discovered that over a third of childhood cases grow into socialized adult forms of the same disorder.

So be sure to consult a psychologist with experience treating adult versions of the disorder to ensure proper diagnosis and treatment. People with ADHD often rely on alcohol to treat their hyperactivity and restlessness, so they can appear depressed or addicted instead. Many do not receive the therapy they need, and their wasted lives are a travesty. There is also a genetic factor: If either partner has ADD/ADHD, your child may be born with it.

If the ADD/ADHD mate continues to receive coaching, therapy, and medication as needed, you can stay together with that person. If he or she doesn't, your life together will be so chaotic that you can easily fall into a parent-child relationship rather than an adult-adult partnership. You'll end up taking care of everything, including your mate and the mess he leaves behind. There's nothing anyone can do to make another person accept treatment. If your partner isn't willing to pursue treatment, your relationship will be as skewed as his symptoms. On the other hand, ADD/ADHD people can be very intelligent, talented, charming, affectionate, delightful, and easy to love. So you don't have to avoid someone with this disorder — *if* he or she is willing to get professional help as needed.

Fix the Problems You Can

Fix whatever you can by yourself. For example, if your communication is faulty, try reading Chapters 11 through 13 with your partner, and practice the steps outlined in those chapters. If your sex life is a problem, read Chapters 14 and 15 together. Then practice the behaviors discussed in Chapters 16 and 24 to add more romance, pizzazz, and fun to your relationship. If you or your partner are suffering from a belief in myths — whether relationship, compatibility, intimacy, happiness, communication, sex, or marriage myths — talk about it. Reread the chapters in this book that apply.

Discuss your problems together, using the steps outlined in Chapters 12 and 13 and on the Cheat Sheet, and draft compromises you both find satisfactory. You can also attend assertiveness classes and communication skills workshops at community colleges, adult learning centers, YMCAs, park districts, and community centers.

Get Professional Help to Fix the Problems You Can't

If you do as I suggest in the preceding section and can't fix the problems yourselves, then you need professional help. It's always best to get help for the following situations:

✔ If you and your partner can't resolve a serious issue or personal problem that is affecting the relationship.

✔ If every discussion becomes a battle instead of amicable negotiation because one or both of you lack healthy communication skills.

✔ When you must compromise and make a joint decision fast (for example, deciding whether you should accept a job that would require a change in your joint lifestyle or a relocation that could keep you from marrying soon; deciding whether to invite your mother to come live with you when she's discharged from the hospital).

How to invite your mate to counseling

To invite your partner to counseling, follow these simple steps:

Use *Dr. Kate's MAKE-A-DEAL Technique* listed on the Cheat Sheet. Make a date to talk to your mate, ask him how he feels your relationship is going, keep reflecting back his responses as long as he vents or shares new information, express empathy and support, and agree with whatever you can agree with.

Then state your feelings assertively: *"I've been thinking about seeing a psychologist to try to make our relationship the best it can be. How would you feel about that?"*

Again, reflect back his or her responses, express empathy and support, and agree with whatever you can agree with.

Express your position in a gentle, but assertive manner: *"I love you, and I'd like you to come so the psychologist can understand your point of view. If you don't want to come, I respect your choice, and I'll try to tell your side of the story as fairly as I can. But I'd rather you came to tell your side, because you know it better than I do, and it's important for the psychologist to get an accurate perspective."*

If your partner agrees, great. Just thank him or her, reward with praise, and clarify the logistical arrangements: *"**Wonderful! I'm so happy** that you'll come. If you like, I'll pick you up on Tuesday after work so we can drive over together."*

If your mate disagrees, back down so you don't get into a power struggle: *"**OK, I respect your decision. I guess I'll go by myself then. But if you change your mind, you're always welcome to come.**"* Then pick a regular appointment time when your mate can come if he or she wants to. Go to sessions by yourself and talk to the psychologist about your relationship.

Wait a month. Then gently tell your partner the day and time of your standing appointment: *"**I just wanted to let you know that I'm seeing that psychologist every week on** _____ (Tuesday), **at** _____ (6 p.m.). **Just wanted to let you know, in case you ever want to come. You're always welcome.**"*

Do *not* tell your partner what's happening in the sessions. If/when he asks, just say: *"**We talked about you and me, and it was helpful.**"* Don't go into detail. If your mate asks what you said about him or her, don't give any details. Just say that you tried to present his side of the story as well as you could.

Your mate may become concerned about what you're telling the psychologist when he's not there to defend himself. He may eventually see the psychologist just out of curiosity or to make sure the doctor understands his viewpoint. If he goes, the psychologist should try to make rapport with him, help him feel comfortable, peak his interest, and gently motivate him to keep coming.

Whatever happens, keep going to therapy, and keep the door open. Allow your partner to change his or her mind without losing face. If he says that he'll go as a favor to you, or because he thinks that *you* have a problem, say: *"**OK, thanks! I'd like that.**"* Don't take his attempts to save face personally. Just focus on the big picture: You need him to come with you to therapy.

When your mate does go, be sure to give lots of positive reinforcement/reward like hugs, kisses, thanks, and praise *("**Thanks for coming with me, Honey. I really appreciate it**")*. Remember, if you give positive reinforcement, your mate may continue to come. If you criticize him, why would he? Try to make the sessions end on a positive note, and use *Dr. Kate's MAKE-A-DEAL Technique* to resolve your disagreements with healthy, win-win compromises. Once your partner realizes that he can benefit from the sessions, he'll be much more willing to accompany you. And when he sees how well good communication works, he'll be much more invested in learning how to do it with you.

DR. KATE SAYS There is an optimum time to get professional help. Unresolved issues don't really go away; they just fester and get worse. When people become resentful, they also avoid sex, which in turn, creates a physical distance between them that begins to match the emotional distance. If you continue to avoid confronting and fixing problems, you'll eventually grow apart. So get help as soon as possible — before it hurts your relationship. The sooner you get help, the easier and faster you can fix the problem, and the less pain, grief, and money you will be spend.

Starting all over with a new partner would also take time and pain. You'd probably take your problems, especially any communication problems, with you to the new relationship — ending up right where you are now with your new partner. On the other hand, if you pursue therapy and fix your communication and other problems, you might be able to make your relationship healthy and happy again. If you end up breaking up anyway, that energy, time, and money won't be wasted. Instead, you should be able to transfer what you've learned to your new relationship to make it more successful.

If your relationship is important to you, especially if you've been together for many years or are married, don't give up based on your experience with one professional. Every psychologist uses somewhat different techniques, some therapists are better than others, and sometimes your personalities just don't mesh. However, if you've tried a number of psychologists, including more efficient, shorter-term treatments (such as cognitive-behavioral techniques and communication skills training), and you still haven't made significant progress in a year or two, it's usually best to stop therapy, heal, and move on.

On the other hand, if the relationship is not that important to you, you may decide to terminate it rather than pursue therapy. If you're a 40-year-old woman who wants to have kids, you may not have a year to spend in therapy with your current mate. If the relationship ends, you'll be back at square one looking for a compatible partner. So you might want to give your relationship six months of therapy, and then, based on your progress, decide whether or not to stick it out. Or you might want to change the status of your relationship and start seeing other people as well, opening up your options.

I believe it's always best to seek out professional help before divorcing or ending a long-term, previously satisfying relationship. (The only exception is any relationship that has included physical or sexual abuse.) Compatibility is difficult to find, and if you've spent a lot of time with someone, there's probably a lot of compatibility there. If the problems can be resolved, the relationship can return to being satisfying. When the couple is already married or if children are involved, separation and divorce are always difficult. So unless abuse is involved, it's usually best to consult a psychologist to determine if the relationship can be sufficiently improved for you and your mate to be satisfied. See the sidebar in this chapter on how to invite your mate to counseling.

When physical or sexual abuse of children or adults is involved, the abused party is usually more at risk when she leaves, during separations, and if she ever returns. If you return to an abuser, the abuse continues and usually gets even worse because the abuser basically got away with it the first time (you took him back). Returning to the abuser rewards him for the abuse, and makes it far more likely that the abuse will increase in intensity and frequency. So I am definitely *against* trying to salvage any relationship in which physical or sexual abuse has occurred. See the sidebar on abuse in this chapter for more on this topic.

Decision Time: Stop Loss?

Stop loss is a term normally applied to trading. When the price of your stock is falling, you need to decide whether to stay put and hope that it goes back up, or designate a point at which you will sell it off, no matter how much loss you have incurred up to that point. You basically decide that you will stop the loss by selling the stock at a loss.

I find this term wonderfully applicable to the world of human relationships. When you invest time, energy, and emotion into a relationship, that's a significant investment. You make that investment because you assume that it will pay off — that you will be rewarded with love, support, and companionship that more than compensates you for your time, energy, and emotion. But sometimes, it doesn't work out that way. For example, your partner cheats on you, you have arguments, or the relationship suffers in some way. At that point, you need to decide whether it's time to stop loss.

When you can't fix the problems even with professional help, you either need to decide to overlook them and appreciate what you have in the relationship — or stop loss, end the relationship, and eventually look for another partner who is more healthy and satisfying.

How long can you live with someone despite your differences? It depends on the degree of the differences and the effect that your partner's problems have on the relationship. So although physical or sexual abuse is so harmful that I never suggest trying to fix the relationship, you can certainly be more patient with a partner who is anxious or depressed.

Sure, the anxiety and depression will affect your relationship, but it is bearable, and the good times may be good enough to warrant staying in the relationship until your partner makes more progress in therapy. That may be especially true if you're in no hurry to get married or if you're already married.

On the other hand, if your partner is not willing to get help over a period of time, if you're in incompatible life stages, or if your partner's treatment will take years, you may not be able to spend much time at all together before moving on.

It's time to stop loss when:

- You experience any of the unfixable situations described in this chapter.
- You and your partner have spent years in therapy and still can't live amicably with one another.
- You and your partner have seen more than one psychologist (preferably more than two), without any significant progress.

✔ You're in a committed relationship, but not married, and fixing the problems with this partner will mean that you'll run out of time to reach your relationship goal.

When deciding whether or not to end your relationship, follow this convenient checklist:

✔ Start with the proper attitude. Look at each situation, including yours, as unique. Don't jump to conclusions or break off your relationship impulsively because you're angry right now. Instead, think everything through when you're more relaxed and calm.

✔ Review your relationship goal and your partner's, and whether they're in sync.

✔ Define the problem at hand. Try to differentiate whether the problems are mostly communication problems or difficulties with immaturity, addictions, or serious psychological problems.

✔ Consider the severity and type of problem, how quickly it needs to be fixed, and what would happen if you weren't able to fix it.

✔ Consider how motivated you and your partner are to fix those problems. Notice what your partner says and does, and when there's a discrepancy, pay more attention to steps he's actually taken to change his behavior.

✔ Consider whether you have time to fix the problems and still reach your relationship goal.

✔ Based on your responses to this list, decide to continue therapy with your mate, or stop loss by ending the relationship.

✔ If you're not sure, visit a psychologist for a few sessions to talk it through.

✔ You might also discuss your observations with your partner — and see if he or she becomes more motivated to change. However, as discussed previously, do *not* do this if your partner is abusive.

Take Action on Your Decision

Once you decide that your relationship is hopelessly unhealthy and not worth trying to save, don't waste time wallowing in indecision, anxiety, or depression. Instead, take effective action to end the relationship in a humane way and get your life back on track. See Chapter 21 on how to break up with less pain.

When you review your relationship and take action in an organized fashion, as outlined in this chapter, you'll probably spend a lot more time in healthy, supportive, satisfying relationships — and a lot less time in unhealthy, frustrating, dead-end unions.

A few words about physical abuse

Both men and women can be physically abusive — to each other and to their children. They can also be abusive to their parents or other humans or animals in their care. Abuse, including the abuse of animals, is always very abnormal. It should always be taken seriously and given psychological treatment. Women can certainly abuse men, using various weapons to assault. However, in most abuse cases, it's the man who abuses the woman. And because he is usually stronger physically, the abuse is often much more dangerous. If the man is much taller or bigger than the woman, a slight shove can send her flying across the room into walls or objects, causing bruises, cuts, concussions, and other trauma. If the man actually hits the woman, he can slice her with a ring and open up her face. If he punches her, he can cause even more damage.

Physical and sexual abuse are *never* OK. *Never!* There is no excuse for any kind of abuse. Often, the abuser blames the abusee, telling her that it is her fault that the abuse is happening. If she didn't act in a certain way, he wouldn't have to hit her. Such protestations are totally unfounded. No one deserves to be physically or sexually abused, no matter what they've done. It is simply the abuser's way of disavowing responsibility for his or her aggressive behavior.

The damage caused by abuse is both physical and psychological. The more the abusee allows the abuse to continue, the more the abuser will escalate the abuse. If children witness the abuse or receive the abuse themselves, they are far more likely to grow up to abuse others or be abused by others. While not all abused people go on to abuse others, most abusers were abused themselves or witnessed it in the home while growing up.

Besides blaming the victim, the abuser generally attempts to control the victim in more and more ways over time. He will usually attempt to cut the victim off from supportive family and friends so she can't be influenced by them. The victim may also begin to withdraw from others to hide her bruises and embarrassment. As she spends more time with the abuser and less time with normal people, she loses her ability to see reality in an objective light. Because the abuser is so convinced that it's her fault, she starts to believe him. But no matter how hard she tries, she can't ever please him. It's impossible.

If you suffer from abuse, get help in your community as soon as possible. Services vary from place to place, but you can locate them by contacting abuse hotlines, by calling women's services and governmental agencies located in the front of your phone book, or by calling your police department, community mental health center, or even the local hospital emergency room. Do not tip the abuser off to your actions; just get in touch with people who can help you. Have those people inform you of your rights and help you exercise them, including filing any orders of protection. In addition, protect yourself by going to a women's shelter. To protect the safety of those who use them, these shelters are not advertised. But the people working at community agencies can hook you up with them.

If you're abused, you're most in danger right before and after you leave the abuser. So don't tell the abuser about your plans either. Just use the help of your community network and carefully make a plan, then follow through. Be careful; take every threat and action the abuser makes seriously, and follow through with legal procedures available to you. And *never, never, never* return to the abuser. If you do, you will be rewarding him for everything he did to you before that point, and you can count on the abuse to increase in frequency and intensity. If it escalates enough, you and/or your children may die.

He Beat Me and It's MY Fault?

Dear Dr. Kate,

My age: 32   **My gender:** Female

Eight months ago, my boyfriend was sent to jail for beating me. My son witnessed it for the first time and phoned the police. At the time of the beatings, I was using drugs. I'm clean now, and my ex wants me back again. But he says the beating was all my fault; if I hadn't done drugs, he wouldn't have beaten me. Yet each time I change for the better, he finds something else I need to change.

My age: 24   **My gender:** Female

My husband hit me this past week. He broke my hand, gave me a hairline fracture in one of my cheekbones, and blackened my eye. I love him, and he loves our 4-year-old daughter with all of his heart. He says he loves me, that he'll never do it again. But I was always told, "Once a hitter, always a hitter." Is that true?

My age: 25   **My gender:** Female

As a child, I witnessed my dad abusing my mother — emotionally and physically. I eventually met someone who treated me like an angel, and I quickly became dependent upon him. I felt like I needed him to be happy. We married six months later, and he's been abusing me for the past six years — mostly bruises. But the last time he abused me, our children — ages four and two — saw it. I tried for an entire month to tell him that there's a serious problem with our relationship, that I wasn't going to stand for him hitting me anymore. He just joked around and told me that things weren't as serious as I made them out to be. He said if I didn't say or do things to upset him, he wouldn't have to hit me. When I told him I was planning to leave after the holidays, he told me, "OK, leave now." So, I left. Now he calls me all the time, drops by my office, and is driving me crazy, begging me to come home. He implies that I'm the bad guy for leaving.

Dear Confused Ladies,

If your ex is gone, thank your lucky stars. Don't let him come back. Unfortunately, the abuser obsesses about whatever woman he's with at the time, until his attention becomes dangerous for her. So before you can ever really be safe, he has to forget about you. As much as you wouldn't want anyone else to experience abuse, the sooner he stops attending to you and starts attending to someone else, the sooner you'll be safe. You need to get out of his thoughts and feelings so you can get your life back.

It's very common for a man who beats a woman to act like — and even believe — that it's *all* her fault. It's a way to control and manipulate you. While not all abused people grow up to be abusers, most abusers were physically or sexually abused or observed abuse in their homes. They believe that it's their God-given right and privilege to control you. And as you have observed, they'll never be happy with you, no matter how much you improve. They will never accept responsibility for their own actions. And no matter what you did in the past, it does not justify anyone beating you. No one has the right to do that to you.

And yes, most hitters go on to hit again. If you take them back, it's like rewarding them for the abuse. The abuse becomes more frequent and intense, until it becomes life-threatening. In addition, the times right before and after an abused woman leaves are also very dangerous. So be careful. Rely on the police, shelters, and other agencies to protect yourself. Take it seriously.

Many abused women go on to other abusive men. See a psychologist to find out why you chose an abusive man — and how to choose more wisely in the future.

All the best,

Dr. Kate

He Sexually Abused His Daughter Years Ago

Dear Dr. Kate,

My age: 40   **My gender:** Female

My boyfriend, 39, was convicted of sexually abusing his daughter five years ago, when she was 12. She's now 17, and he says that he's "cured" of his obsession. Yet the relationship between them has always seemed bizarre — she acts jealous of me, wears skimpy clothing around him, and dances very suggestively. He also has porn movies starring girls who resemble her. Advice?

Dear Girlfriend of Ex-Con Child Molester,

I think you should get yourself a new boyfriend. Here's the bottom line: No one is perfect. No relationship is perfect. However, some problems you can work with — and others, you should just avoid.

In general, totally avoid men who are currently involved in or have any history of sexual abuse, physical abuse, child molestation, sexual addictions, paranoia, violent tempers, and psychopathic behavior. Also, totally avoid current alcoholics, drug abusers, gambling addicts, convicts, and psychotics (people who are out of touch with reality). Be very cautious of anyone with past alcohol or drug abuse, gambling addiction, jail or prison time, psychosis, bad judgment, lying, infidelity, an inability to commit, or intense family pathology.

In contrast, men who are "workable" include those who are shy and need help opening up; those who basically want commitment, but need a little help learning to express their feelings; overweight men or those who smoke; men who dress badly; and those who basically have good intentions and treat others well, but who have a few issues (for example, low self-esteem, anxiety, non-psychotic depression) that don't threaten or malign other people.

Your boyfriend has a history of bad judgment, sexual abuse, sexual addiction, and child abuse. He was 34 when he molested his own daughter. How many others did he molest or consider molesting before that? It takes a lot for an adult to completely throw away his judgment and cross the line to molest a child. Don't underestimate the pathology involved.

You've noticed his bizarre relationship and daughter obsession. So trust your gut. With someone like him, you'll never have a stable future. Why do that to yourself? You can find a man who is much healthier.

All the Best. Please let me know what you decide to do.

Dr. Kate

UPDATE:

Dear Dr. Kate,

I just wanted you to know that I've left my boyfriend. He suddenly realized that I was right — he still lusts after his daughter and he needs help. I wish him well in his future counseling. But I don't believe a word he says anymore. Boy, did you ever wake me up! This is the first time in my life that I've ever lived alone, but life is wonderful. Thank you for the wonderful wakeup call!

Motivating the Two Slobs

Dear Dr. Kate,

My age: 46 **My gender:** Female

My husband of 25 years is a good man and excellent father, but he's a slob. He does nothing to help around the house. I know he's tired, but I work, and I'm tired, too. I do taxes, bills, cleaning, cooking, repairing, and so on. To make matters worse, his mother has moved in, and she's a slob, too. I've asked, I've begged; my husband "understands." So why won't they do anything? I'm tired of moaning and groaning. My son does more than the two of them put together!

Dear Maid/Butler/Accountant/Handyman/Chef/Domestic Goddess,

Your husband and his mother aren't going to help until you stop enabling them to be slobs. As long as you're all talk and no action, they're going to continue to let you do everything. Instead, try this action plan:

- **Get a computer banking program, and set it up so it routinely pays all your regular bills.** For bills that vary, make the amounts paid a little higher than the average due. Every few months, review the statements and ask the companies to send you refund checks for any credits.

- **Hire a maid to do once-a-week cleaning.** Depending on where you live, six hours should run about $50 to $90. Have the maid do all routine heavy work.

- **Hire a handyman for repairs.** Make sure your husband sees the bills.

- **Leave your husband's clothes, mail (other than bills), and other possessions exactly where he hangs or drops them.** Do *not* do his laundry or take his clothes to the cleaner. Follow the same procedure for his mother. If the pile gets too big for you to get through the doorway, take two big garbage bags (one for each of them) and put their clothes in them. Throw your mother-in-law's in her bed, and your husband's on his side of the bed — so they have to move their bags to sleep. If anyone complains, say you understand.

- **Do not cook dinner for your husband or his mother.** Buy frozen microwavable food, paper plates, and plastic cutlery. This situation can't last, so take your son out for some discounted specials for his dinner. When your hubby or his mother ask what's for dinner/lunch/breakfast, tell them where they can find the food, paper plates, and cutlery, and *Let Them Do Microwave!* Your son should load the dishwasher with the dishes you and he use, but leave his father and grandmother's right where they put them. They'll eventually have to clean up their places at the table to be able to eat. If they haven't moved anything in a few days and it's getting really rank, pack the mess in plastic bags, and leave each bag on that person's chair. When taking out the trash, dump only what's actually in the trash can.

- **Make only your side of the bed.** Don't make his mother's bed. If she has her own room, just keep the door closed. When you straighten up the house, don't move their stuff.

- **Stop complaining and nagging immediately.** Your husband will get the hint. If he doesn't, hang a sign in the kitchen: *"Wife/daughter-in-law on strike. The maid doesn't live here any more."*

- **As soon as your husband or mother-in-law does anything to help, give generous praise.**

- **Do your taxes or give them to a professional.** You don't really want your husband to do them, do you?

Be consistent in following the above tips, and you'll get results. It may cost a little money, but it will save your sanity. If your husband improves a lot, sit down and divide chores in a more intelligent way. If you can't get anywhere, see a psychologist for couples counseling.

All the best,

Dr. Kate

Part VI
Moving Forward Separately

The 5th Wave   By Rich Tennant

"When we met we seemed to be on the same track, so we hitched up. Then, just when I thought the relationship was gaining a head of steam, something derailed it. I don't know—maybe I was sending the wrong signals."

In this part . . .

In Part V, I discuss how to move forward together. In this part, I talk about how to move forward separately. If your relationship can't move forward, it's best to break up, grieve your loss, then live through the pain and recover with as little suffering as possible. It's also important to learn the best lesson from the experience, so you can apply that knowledge to make your future relationships more enjoyable and healthy.

In this part, I give you tips for doing all of that and more. I also suggest ways you can take the next step — starting over. I show you how to tell when you're ready to begin again — and how you can move on and build a new, more satisfying relationship for yourself.

Chapter 21

Breaking Up with Less Pain

. . . .

In This Chapter

▶ Breaking up in a respectful way

▶ Handling the breakup with class and dignity

▶ Grieving efficiently and productively

▶ Using practical, effective techniques to live through it, cope, and recover

. . . .

*B*reaking up is never fun. It's usually quite painful, depending on how much you've cared about your partner, how long you've been together, how long you expected to remain together, and whether you wanted the relationship to end. But even though emotional pain is usually involved, you can suffer less if you know how to break up with class, how to grieve more effectively, and how to recover more fully, in less time.

In this chapter, I give you tips on how to do all of these things. I talk about how to break up with the least amount of suffering for both parties, and how to live through the breakup and recover. I also describe helpful techniques and practical exercises that you can immediately put to work to make your breakup less painful.

Breaking Up with Class

The following information does not apply to physically abusive relationships. Those are special cases that need to be handled entirely differently. For how to break up from an abusive relationship, see the sidebar and letters on abuse in Chapter 20.

There are better and worse ways to break up with someone. How you break up will largely affect how much pain you and your partner feel from the breakup. If you break up badly, you may create a lifelong enemy and a lot of pain. If you break up with class, you can leave with more pleasant feelings, and eventually, after years have passed, you may even become platonic friends. Even if you never desire to see your partner again, breaking up well will help both of you recover with less pain, which is a worthy goal — no matter how the relationship transpired.

Adjust your attitude

I'm a firm believer in the saying, "What goes around comes around," particularly when you are dishing out garbage. So no matter what your partner did or didn't do to you, there's no reason to treat him or her badly when the relationship ends. How you react to people under stress is a sign of character and class. If you burn your bridges with everyone throughout your life when things don't go as you'd like, you'll end up a very lonely, unhappy, and bitter person.

When breaking up with anyone, be honest and straightforward, but also kind and empathic. You are causing your partner discomfort and emotional pain, and the more sincere and kind your tone of voice, the better.

Switch places with your partner in your mind before the breakup to develop more empathy. If your mate was breaking up with you, how would you feel? How could he or she make it easier on you? Then imagine that you are your partner, and your partner is you. How would your partner feel? How could you make it easier on him or her? Try to keep those feelings and preferences in mind when you break up.

Break up in person

Your partner deserves to be treated with respect. Just because the two of you didn't work out to be a compatible couple doesn't mean that you should treat him or her in a hurtful way in your final actions together. Breaking up with someone via letter, e-mail, phone, by using another person to convey your message — or by dropping out of sight, never to be heard from again — is unbelievably insulting. Plain and simple, it's a coward's way out. You owe it to yourself — and your mate — to act with more class.

Forget about taking the easy way out. If you want to break up with your mate, be sure to arrange a face-to-face meeting, in person, where the two of you can talk and interact without being overheard or disturbed.

Your partner may cry or get angry, and it's important to let him or her vent with dignity and privacy. Give your mate time to interact with you — to ask questions and respond to your comments. It's OK if the two of you don't agree on things; just let your mate comment and express his or her feelings.

Use healthy communication skills

When communicating your feelings to your partner, it's important to use the communication skills described in Chapter 12, especially *reflective listening, facilitative agreement, supportive statements, positive reinforcement/reward,* **The Dr. Kate 20-1 Rule,** and *assertiveness.* However, if you are set on breaking up, you probably won't be using *compromise,* unless it's regarding the details of your breakup (like when and how to tell people).

Of course, it's helpful to use these communication skills in a certain order. So when breaking up with someone, follow a slightly revised version of the steps listed in **Dr. Kate's MAKE-A-DEAL Technique** (described on the Cheat Sheet). Start by following Steps 1 through 5:

1. <u>M</u>**ake a date to talk about the problem, choosing optimal time and place**. At your date, lay the groundwork and prepare your mate for what is coming. For example: **"I have something important I'd like to discuss with you."**

2. <u>A</u>**sk about your mate's thoughts and feelings first.** For example: **"How do you feel our relationship is going?"**

3. <u>K</u>**eep reflecting back (use reflective listening) as long as your mate shares new info**: **"It sounds like . . . ."**

4. <u>E</u>**xpress empathy with supportive statements** (**"I'm so _____ for you; I hope** *everything goes better tomorrow"*), **and facilitative agreement — agreeing with whatever you can agree with** (**"I agree that . . . ."** or, **"I can see that . . . ."**). Similar to using **The Dr. Kate 20-1 Rule** (covered in Chapter 12), first tell your partner what you've enjoyed about the time you've spent together. Give a lot of praise and positive reinforcement. Even if you didn't enjoy the relationship very much, you can still thank your mate for his or her time, energy, thoughtfulness, and anything else you appreciated along the way. For example:

   "I've enjoyed *a lot of the times we've spent together.* **I appreciate your** *thoughtfulness and all the energy you've put into making our dates special and unique.* **I love** *so many things* **about you** *— your sense of humor, your drive to succeed, your energy and ambition.* **I feel very** *physically and emotionally attracted* **to you."**

5. <u>A</u>**ssertively (not aggressively) state your feelings, and deliver your breakup message.** Be sure to speak calmly and slowly, with a modulated, sincere, gentle tone of voice. For example:

   "But I feel *disappointed* **with** *where our relationship is going.* **I want to** *eventually get married and have children — that's always been my relationship goal. When I met you, I mistakenly thought that you shared that goal. But as we've gotten to know one another, we've talked more, and* *you've made it clear that you don't see yourself settling down in the near future. **So, as much as I hate to change the great relationship we have, I'm going to have to** start dating other people. **I can continue to** see you as well, if you like, on a more casual basis. **But since you** don't share my relationship goal, **I'll also have to** meet other people and keep my options open. That way, I'll have the opportunity to settle down if I find someone compatible who does share my goal."*

Now, at this point, you'll deviate a bit from **Dr. Kate's MAKE-A-DEAL Technique** by inserting a new step:

6. **Give more supportive statements to help ease the blow and end your message on a positive note:** *"I hope you can understand where I'm coming from. **I do love you, and I have loved** the time we've spent together. **I think you're** a great person, and if you eventually decide to settle down, **you will make** someone a great spouse."*

And then just as you would normally alternate Steps 2 through 5:

7. **If your partner asks questions or wants to discuss the breakup further, answer his or her questions and use Steps 3 through 6 as needed.** In other words, use reflective listening and supportive statements, agree with whatever you can agree with, deliver your assertive answer, then give more supportive statements.

If there are aspects of the breakup that are open to compromise, then *Deal Time* (discussing and choosing a compromise) would follow. If not, then the conversation ends there.

Avoid the blame game

When breaking up with class, it's important not to blame anyone for the outcome of the relationship. Remember, just because a relationship doesn't work out romantically, it doesn't mean that it's anyone's fault. It doesn't have to be your fault, your partner's fault, or anyone else's fault. It just means that the relationship was incompatible, and there's another person out there for you who *is* more compatible. Breaking up your current relationship isn't the end of the world; it's the first step to finding that other person.

So take the pressure off yourself and don't waste any time ramming yourself or your partner into the ground with blame. Yes, you wanted this relationship to work out long-term, and yes, you're disappointed that it didn't. But this is life, not heaven, so many things don't work out in ways we prefer. The best thing to do when life doesn't work out the way you want is to learn what you can, then move on in a way that's as positive and classy as possible.

So do you and your partner a favor by not phrasing sentences in a way that blames either of you. For example, *don't* say: "*You* don't want to get married, so we can't make this relationship work." As I explain in Chapter 12, never start a sentence with the word "you" if you can avoid it. Instead, talk about your feelings and start with *"I feel."* For example, say: *"I feel uncomfortable that we're not moving toward marriage."* Or, *"I feel disappointed that we don't seem to communicate better."*

Talk about the breakup in mutual terms. *Don't* say: "You're not compatible with me." Instead, say: *"We don't seem to be compatible enough with one another to continue dating at this time."* Or, *"We seem to have different relationship goals."*

It's also good to use a more tentative sentence structure by including phrases like, *"seem to," "appear to," "it seems like,"* and, *"it sounds like."* This can help avoid power struggles that occur when you act like your opinion is fact. ("You're not compatible with me." "Yes, I am." "No, you're not." And so on.)

Keep the secrets, and give your partner space and respect

After you break up with your partner in a kind, empathic manner, give your mate time to adjust. If your mate wanted to stay together, the breakup will be painful, and he or she will need time to recover. Be respectful of your ex's needs and privacy. For example, don't bring a new date to the same places that your ex frequents. Don't talk about your ex, and don't reveal any secrets entrusted to you when you were getting along.

Agree on how to tell other people

Treat your partner with the same respect you'd want if you were the one being broken up with. Your mate may be embarrassed about the breakup. The relationship was between the two of you, and although others will eventually need to know that you're no longer a couple, it's nobody else's business what happened. You can confide in a good friend, provided that person keeps your secrets confidential. However, don't spread stories about your mate, blame him or her, or make negative, critical remarks when your ex's name comes up in a conversation.

If you and your ex share mutual friends, you can ask if he or she wants to inform those friends; then try to follow those wishes. It's the least you can do after breaking up. You each should tell your respective families, unless you have some other preference that you both agree on.

Helping your kids through a breakup

It's important to help children through a breakup. If you and your mate have children together, sit down with him or her and discuss how you're going to tell the kids. Keep the breakup confidential until you have time to do that — you don't want the kids to find out from other people. Then, when you're ready, talk to the children as a united front, and be careful not to blame one another. Make sure the kids understand that they did *not* cause the breakup. Children frequently worry about this, even if they don't mention it, so go out of your way to address the issue thoroughly. Also, reassure them that you will both continue to be their parents and love them very much. You will live in different houses now, but you will always be their mommy and daddy, and you will always love them and see them, no matter what.

Then after the breakup, continue to say only positive or neutral things about each other to the kids. Studies show that this is a very important factor in helping children adjust well to their parents' breakup. Whatever went wrong between you and your mate should stay between you and your mate. Remember, your kids' welfare is at stake, and they should never be put in the middle or feel pressured to choose between the two of you. So go out of your way *not* to speak negatively about your partner, and never interrogate your kids about your ex's behavior.

Realize that your children have just suffered a terrible loss; they experienced a breakup, too — and they had no control over it at all, so it's very stressful for them. Give them lots of extra attention and positive reinforcement (like praise, hugs, and kisses) to help them through this difficult period. Spend extra quality time with them. Watch for any signs that they are suffering (a decline in school performance, spending more time alone, or drawing pictures with aggressive or sad themes, for example). Talk to them about their fears and other feelings in words appropriate for their age level. If they still seem to be having difficulty despite your intervention, see a psychologist together with them, and use that family therapy to help you grow closer as you work through this difficult time together.

Receiving a Breakup with Class

When someone breaks up with you, it's always best to respond in a classy, adult fashion. Most people don't break up very well with others, and often, they don't give enough information to help their partner understand what motivated the breakup. So feel free to ask your mate about his or her motivation.

If your partner uses adjectives in the description, go ahead and ask about the behaviors involved. For example, if your mate tells you that you're just "_____ (too intense)" for him, ask: ***What is it that I do that you find to be _____ (too intense)?***

Sometimes, partners balk when asked questions because they're afraid that you'll try to talk them out of their decision. If that happens, just say: ***"I'm not trying to talk you into staying with me. That's your choice, and I respect your decision. I don't want to be with anyone unless that person wants me as much as I want _____ (him/her). But I would like to understand your decision better, so I can get closure and heal faster . . . ."***

At that point, your partner will probably give more details. If not, just ask the same kinds of questions about the behaviors that bothered him or her. ***"It sounds like you're saying that I'm _____ (not giving enough for you). What would I have done differently during our relationship if I had been _____ (more giving)?"*** Or, ***"It sounds like you're saying you prefer women who are _____ (less pushy). I'd like to understand this better. Can you give me an example of what I would have done differently if I had been _____ (less pushy)?"***

Of course, you don't have to ask any questions, but you should get some kind of understanding about why your mate no longer considers the relationship fun and desirable. You can use that information later to help you get closure and heal. Instead of talking endlessly with friends and trying to figure it out when you don't have a clue and can't possibly read your ex's mind, ask the questions.

Use a soft, gentle, sincere tone of voice — not sarcastic, argumentative, or insulting. Keep the volume steady, at conversational level, and speak slowly. Avoid power words, name-calling, yelling, interrupting, assuming, and yelling. Use good eye contact, appropriate facial expressions, body position, interpersonal distance, and gestures. In other words, pay attention to the verbal and nonverbal cues that are always important in good communication (see Chapter 12 for a full description of these cues).

Avoid the blame game

Just as you shouldn't blame your partner when breaking up with him, don't blame your partner for breaking up with you. When girls are young and their boyfriends break up with them, they usually reassure one another that it wasn't their fault. It was the boyfriend's fault; he was an insensitive, insightless "jerk" (or some other pejorative term) who couldn't tell how wonderful she was.

Although that kind of thinking might make you feel better temporarily, it's really not the most mature, healthy way to think. Maybe your ex is insightless and insensitive, and maybe it would have been healthier if he'd realized your value. Or maybe your ex wasn't any of those things at all.

The breakup does not have to be blamed on anyone — not you or your ex. It doesn't have to be anyone's fault. It's usually better to take the view that *if someone doesn't appreciate you, it means that the relationship isn't compatible.* If it had been compatible, your ex would have appreciated you as much as you appreciated him or her. And since that didn't happen, it's better that you found out now — before you put any more time into a relationship that wouldn't have worked out anyway. There *are* many more compatible people out there for you, because there are many more compatible people out there for anyone. So when someone isn't compatible for you, it just means that there's someone else out there who *is*. After you're done healing, you can get started on finding one of those people.

Keep the secrets, and give your partner space and respect

Women tend to discuss their relationships with female friends who keep their confidences. It's fine to tell a trusted friend about your breakup and try to get closure. It's even fine to tell two or three of your trusted friends. But it's a mistake to "bad mouth" your ex to anyone who will listen. Just as you kept each other's secrets when you were together, it's important to keep those secrets after you break up as well. Instead of emoting all over the place, see a professional to help you weather the storm. I talk more about this in the next section.

Living through It and Recovering

If your partner has broken up with you and you're not happy about it, there are better and worse ways to get through it. What are the better ways?

See a psychologist to vent

Most people in the midst of a breakup need to vent. They need to say how they feel, and they need to get a little irrational about it. They need to voice their deepest fears and anxieties ("Will anyone ever love me again?"). They need to be able to do so without worrying about the other person's feelings, and with absolute trust that the information will be kept confidential.

For all those reasons, it's best to consult a psychologist whenever you're experiencing a serious breakup. Your friends can be good listeners when you're between therapy sessions or it's 10 p.m. But friends have a limited base of relationship knowledge from which to extrapolate when helping you figure out your relationship, so their opinions may be subjective and less than helpful. Friends don't usually have the time, energy, or stamina to give you their full attention for extended periods of time either. And you need to look at your relationship in an organized way. Friends have informal, casual conversations; they don't do therapy.

In contrast, a psychologist has a lot of training and professional experience to draw on. In addition to personal experience, he or she has treated many different kinds of couples under many different kinds of conditions. The psychologist also sets aside specific time for you every week. Your time together is all about you, and it's goal-oriented — helping you vent and get closure in a thorough and organized way. It's professional therapy, not a two-way social conversation. As a result, the conclusions you reach about your relationship are often more valid and helpful.

Try to get closure

To close this love chapter in your mind and be able to move on, you need to *get closure* — to review, summarize, and come to some understanding about *what happened* in your relationship and *why*. Without closure, the questions will just kind of hang there, continuing to bother you. You may begin to doubt whether you can ever have a successful relationship. In fact, if you don't get closure, you can end up repeating the same pattern over and over again. You may continue to choose inappropriate people who remind you of your ex, and you may experience the same painful outcome over and over again, without even realizing the similarities in your choice of partners and your unproductive behavior.

To get closure, ask yourself: What can you learn from this experience? Why did you choose this partner? In what ways were you compatible? Incompatible? Whom does your partner remind you of now? In what ways? Whom did he or she remind you of in the beginning of your relationship? In what ways? Were there any signs along the way that suggested what would eventually happen? What were they? Why did your partner break up with you? Could you have seen that coming? What mistakes did you make? What mistakes did your partner make? If you could go back in time, what would you do differently? What will you do differently in your next relationship to prevent this from happening again?

Keep in mind that everyone makes mistakes; no one is ever perfect. The reason for asking these questions is to learn the "right" lesson from this experience, so you can apply that knowledge in the future to make your relationships healthier and more satisfying.

When you keep repeating things about your breakup, either aloud or in your head, you're trying to get closure. You're trying to make some sense out of what happened so you can feel better. People generally feel better when they understand what happens to them, especially when they don't like it.

Be kind to yourself physically and psychologically

Splitting up with someone you love is an extremely painful and stressful process. Stress is cumulative; every individual physical and psychological stress adds up to equal how stressed you really are. And besides making you feel miserable, that total amount of stress also determines how vulnerable you are to disease. So if you're breaking up with your mate — a powerful emotional stress — try to take care of yourself physically and emotionally as much as possible. By reducing the stress you receive from other sources, you can reduce the overall amount of stress you receive.

For example, to reduce your physical stress, make sure you get enough sleep, and eat a healthy diet. Get out of the house, and take a walk if you can. The sunlight and fresh air will help raise your spirits, and the mild exercise will stimulate your endorphins and make you feel less depressed. Also, limit your consumption of alcohol. Alcohol is a depressant drug, so although you may initially feel more relaxed and euphoric when drinking, you'll eventually feel more depressed.

To reduce your psychological and emotional stress, try to limit your contacts to friends and family who are positive, emotionally supportive, and easy to be with. Avoid problematic people as much as possible right now; you're not up to it. Be careful not to take on any additional responsibilities. Instead of accepting new work assignments, cut back on work tasks if possible. Don't watch any sad movies or read any sad books.

Avoid making any big decisions if you can. One of the symptoms of stress is faulty judgment. Everything seems important and larger than life, and you may have difficulty prioritizing. If you make large decisions or life changes during this time (for example, changing jobs, moving, or marrying someone), you may end up regretting it. The changes may initially feel good — partly because they distract you from your pain — but they can cause you more problems down the road. So delay any decisions that you can put off without difficulty. If you must make a major decision, discuss the pros and cons in detail with your psychologist, and then make your choice.

Take it a day at a time

Things always look worse when you view them cumulatively. For example, if you have to clean a really messy house and you think about the entire project, you'll probably feel overwhelmed and avoid it. In contrast, if you focus on cleaning one closet or room every day or so, you'll probably clean it without difficulty. And within a very short period of time, you'll end up with a totally clean house.

The same is true of life stresses. If you're in the midst of a breakup and you start reflecting on your whole life, worrying about how you'll manage to get through Christmas, New Year's, or Valentine's Day without your mate, and what you're going to tell your family, and how you're going to make any relationship work when this one didn't, and how you're ever going to get married and have children, and so on . . . and so on . . . and so on — you'll soon be completely overwhelmed. If you continue to think about everything bleak and miserable en masse, you'll end up feeling massively bleak and miserable as well — until it's just too much trouble to get out of bed.

So save your bleak musings for therapy. In between sessions, concentrate on getting through one moment at a time. Don't think about what you're going to be doing next month, next year, or five years from now. Don't even think about next week. This is no time to be planning your future anyway. Instead, just focus on getting through the day. Get up, put one foot in front of the other, take a shower, change your clothes, put on your usual makeup (if you wear makeup), and get out of the house.

Stress usually plays havoc with memory and concentration. So make yourself a schedule and Things-To-Do List and follow them like a robot. As you complete each task, draw a line through it and say, *"Good Job!!!"* to yourself. The reinforcement/reward will be good for you, and you'll stay more focused and productive as well.

Now having a list doesn't mean that you should work all day. Au contraire! Include relaxing social activities on your list. For example, schedule yourself for a noontime walk, or some evening phone or in-person time with family and friends you enjoy. Just use the list to help you focus on what you're doing *right now* at each moment of the day. The days will then lead to weeks and months, and before you know it, you'll heal and be able to move on to a positive, healthy future.

Use thought-stopping

Use thought-stopping (described in Chapter 10) to help you stop ruminating, worrisome thoughts, so you can focus on the task at hand. Whenever you need to concentrate on anything, use thought-stopping to help you.

When you're trying to recover from a breakup, try not to see your ex at work or other places. Also, be sure to put away whatever reminds you of him or her (like photos and memorabilia). Otherwise, you'll think about your ex every time you look at the object, and it will take much longer for the thought-stopping to work. Don't throw the object out unless you really want to. Just put it where you won't see it unless you deliberately look for it. Then forget it for awhile, until you're able to look at it without a problem.

People sometimes say, "Dr. Kate, the technique didn't work." That's impossible. Every time you use it to stop a thought, it's working. Just keep using it each time — until it becomes automatic. And then all of a sudden, one day, you'll say, *"Wow! I remember when I used to think about _____ every day and cry myself to sleep. I haven't thought about him for months now!"* And that's when you'll realize that the technique worked. The nature of thought-stopping is that you can only realize that it's been successful by briefly remembering what it is that you tried to forget! By using this simple technique, you can control your thoughts and make them work for you, not against you. You can also get through your breakup with less discomfort and less disruption to your life.

Read Chapter 10 for more on how to make yourself happy, and follow those tips as well.

Expect yourself to have fluctuating emotions

When recovering from a significant stress, it's normal to have various, frequently changing emotions on different days — or what psychologists call *vacillating emotions.* One day, you're hurt; the next day you're angry; the next day, you're sad. You may even have *conflicting emotions* or *mixed feelings,* feeling two somewhat contradictory emotions at the same time. For example, you might feel sad about breaking up, but excited about moving on — all at the same time. Then one day, you wake up and feel good, so you think you've finally gotten over your grief. But then the next day, you again experience another negative emotion.

When this roller coaster happens, just remind yourself that these emotional swings are normal. Sure, that realization won't take away the pain. But it will help you feel saner, which will certainly help you feel better about yourself.

Your feelings are caused by your thoughts, so your feelings will vary as much as your thoughts vary. When you're in the midst of a breakup, you're thinking about the many different perspectives on your relationship and trying to get closure. Because there are so many angles to consider, it's just natural to experience a number of emotions as you cope with the stress.

To understand this grieving process, it's helpful to understand the stages people go through when dealing with death. Dr. Elisabeth Kübler-Ross described those stages in her famous book, *On Death and Dying* (Simon & Schuster reprint, 1997). First, you may experience denial, where you try to convince yourself that the breakup isn't really happening. You tell yourself that your partner will see the light, and change his or her mind. Next, you may get angry when you realize the situation isn't changing. You may be angry with your partner, God, or life; you want to place blame. Then in the next stage, you bargain with God — you pray and make promises that you'll change some behavior if only He will change the breakup. Then you may feel depressed, feeling overwhelmed and out of control. Finally, you will eventually find acceptance. Of course, instead of accepting it and dying like the person does in Kübler-Ross's last stage of acceptance, you just quietly accept the breakup.

The order of the stages you experience may vary, and you may not experience them all. But it is common to experience many or all of them when grieving any significant relationship. It doesn't feel good to be in these stages. But being able to identify when you're in them usually helps you feel more sane and "in control" — and that helps you find closure and cope better with your loss.

Change irrational thoughts to rational thoughts

Most people find a breakup stressful, even if they wanted it. But in the final analysis, how you *think* about the breakup makes a big difference in how you *feel* about it. As I explain in Chapter 10, it's not the actual event that causes you to be upset; it's how you think about it that does. If you think irrational, exaggerated thoughts about your breakup, you'll make whatever happened much worse. For example, if you walk around thinking, "I can't take this; I'm devastated," or, "Nobody will ever love me again, and I'll never love anyone again either," you're going to feel really awful, like a devastated, unlovable, total failure at life.

Of course, those thoughts really aren't rational; they're very exaggerated and out of proportion to reality. For example: "I can't take this; I'm devastated," is irrational, because you *can* take it, you *will* take it, and you *are* taking it. The only thing that will change is whether you'll take it better or worse, and that really depends on how you think about it. So this statement isn't accurate, and it becomes a self-fulfilling prophecy only because you convince yourself that it's true.

Similarly, "Nobody will ever love me again, and I'll never love anyone again either" is also irrational. You are lovable just because you exist; everyone is. And I can pretty much guarantee that someone will love you again, even if the relationship doesn't work out exactly the way you want. Now, it's perfectly all right if you don't feel like going out and finding someone now, or if you don't think you could ever love anyone again. That's a normal stage of recovery from a breakup. Believe it or not, many people feel that way right after a breakup and then surprise themselves later when they fall in love again. In fact, if this isn't your first breakup, you've done it yourself before, too. You've broken up with someone and gone on to love and be loved again. The only way to avoid that love is to believe these kinds of thoughts and wall yourself off from other people.

So when you find yourself saying or thinking irrational comments, write them down. Then under each statement, write why that statement is irrational and inaccurate, as I've just done. Then once you understand why and how it's irrational and inaccurate, practice saying an appropriate version of the following: ***"I'm disappointed about the breakup. I would have preferred to continue that relationship, but I can and __will__ be happy in spite of it."***

Making this statement will help you relax and feel more confident about the future. You'll feel disappointed, but you won't be devastated.

If you like, you can also include the thought that is opposite of whatever is bothering you: ***"I know it seems like*** *I'll never love and be loved again,* ***but*** *it's only a stage I'm going through.* ***I know*** *from my history and from what I know about psychology* ***that I will*** *love again,* ***and I will be*** *loved again, too.* ***But even if that doesn't happen, I'll be happy anyway."***

You can also combine thought-stopping with this technique. Whenever you get an irrational idea, say: ***"Stop It!"*** to stop the irrational thought. Then tell yourself the opposite, rational thought: ***"I will*** *find someone else to love who will love me back."*

Use The Dr. Kate Quick & Dirty Grieving Technique

But what if you're doing thought-stopping, and the irrational thoughts seem to be winning? The lump in your throat is so big, it's difficult to swallow or talk. Something small happens (your cat knocks over his food dish, for example), and you get teary-eyed. Or you're so irritable, you start screaming at your coworker for no reason.

That's when it's time for ***The Dr. Kate Quick & Dirty Grieving Technique*** (detailed in Chapter 10). This technique is a way to control your grieving; you choose the time, place, and how much you grieve. It allows you to get irrational for an evening, think the awful thoughts nagging at you, let the emotions out — and then return to thinking rationally and feeling better the next day. See Chapter 10 for step-by-step instructions on how to do this technique.

While not a substitute for therapy, you can use this technique as an adjunct — to help you get some of the stress out in a controlled fashion so you can heal more quickly.

I'm not making light of your grieving. Grieving is serious stuff, a necessary stage of healing and moving on. If you use this technique, however, you can shorten your grieving while making it more productive. You're not repressing thoughts and burying them; you're bringing them up, facing them, and coping with them. Confronting your fears head-on in this way can greatly decrease the time you suffer — and allow you to live the days in between with as much dignity, grace, and comfort as possible.

Forgive your partner and yourself

Just as it's important to avoid blaming your ex in statements to him or other people, it's also important to avoid blaming him in your thoughts. If you continually tell yourself what your partner *should* have done or how he *should* have treated you, you're going to wallow in suffering for a *very* long time. The fact is, you're not God, and you don't have any right to tell anyone how they *should* live. In addition, if you go around making those kinds of judgments about people, you're only setting yourself up for failure. You can't control how other people think and behave, and every person has to do what he or she thinks is best. Trying to dictate what that *should* or *shouldn't* be, and acting as if people *should* do what you want is only fooling yourself. When those people inevitably don't act as you like, you'll end up feeling upset.

Instead, try to think in terms of **prefer: "I would have preferred that** *we not break up,* **but I will be happy in spite of it."** Similarly, forgive your ex for not being perfect. No human being is ever perfect. You're not perfect, your ex isn't perfect, and no partnership is ever perfect or fully compatible. Besides, what "perfect" means to one person is almost always different from what it means to someone else.

If your ex behaved in a way that you found hurtful, *let it go.* Forgive him or her. If you don't, *you* will be the one who suffers, not your ex. And if you believe that your ex wanted you to suffer, then in refusing to forgive, you're actually giving him what he wanted.

Instead, act in a healthy way: Examine your irrational ideas about your partner and his or her behavior. Change those irrational ideas and expectations to rational ideas; then release the angry, resentful feelings. When you do, you'll open the way to heal more quickly, and you'll probably feel like a weight has been lifted off your shoulders.

Learn the "right" lesson

I'm always amazed when I hear someone saying, "Men are all jerks!" "Women are all nuts!" or, "I swear, I'm never going to trust anyone again." Or even, "I will absolutely, positively never love anyone again; it's just not worth it." There are many different variations on this theme. Some people just say these angry types of thoughts when venting, but they understand that the thoughts are irrational, and they don't make decisions based on them. On the other hand, some people actually go forward and make relationship and life decisions based on those ideas. And that's when the situation becomes unhealthy.

Just because this one relationship didn't work out as you would have preferred does *not* mean that you can never make a happy, healthy relationship. Don't exaggerate, stereotype, or generalize. Just because your boyfriend or girlfriend acted a certain way does *not* mean that *all* men, or *all* women — or even *all* men or *all* women who share a particular quality with your ex — will act like your ex did. Therefore, it would be ludicrous to avoid all men or all women because this one particular relationship didn't go as you would have liked. And even worse — while you're walking around thinking these irrational kinds of thoughts, you're also avoiding opportunities that could be enjoyable.

Ask yourself: *"What would I do differently if this situation were to occur again?"* But answer that question with a rational, healthy answer. You might say: *"I'll try to choose my partner more wisely." "I'll pay attention when my partner hints that she's not happy."* Or, *"I'll be empathic and use reflective listening to find out how he's feeling; I won't assume I know."*

You can usually learn many good lessons from each relationship. If you write these down and review them periodically, you can use the information to make your future healthier and happier. You can also talk these issues through with your psychologist. Once you vent and get closure, and you understand what happened in your last relationship and why, the appropriate lesson to apply to future relationships should just naturally flow from there. If it doesn't, be sure to raise the issue and discuss it with your psychologist.

Understand that this is only a stage

Nothing makes people more miserable than thinking that they're out of control of their lives. But it's easy to get tunnel vision when you're weathering a breakup. Your misery may seem like it'll never end; you can't grasp the big picture because you're focused on this one particular time in your life.

If you find yourself in this position, step back. Try to see your life as one big *Love Cycle,* a series of relationships stages that you go in and out of during your lifetime. (See Chapter 2 for a description of the phenomenon I call *The Love Cycle.*) First, you find love, then you try to make the relationship work, then you let go and feel loss, and then you start all over again. So if you don't like your current stage of loss and letting go, don't think about it like it's the end of your life. It's not forever; it's just a time-limited stage. When you're ready, you can heal and move on to a stage you prefer. You can start over and find love again. When you think that way, you'll feel more hopeful and optimistic. So you'll be able to do the work you need to do to heal — and that will help you move on sooner.

There are many people out there who are compatible with you; there are many people out there who are compatible with everyone. Don't allow yourself to die inside because this one relationship didn't work out as you would have liked. Instead, look toward the future and know that when you're ready, you can find someone more compatible for you. You can forge a healthier, happier relationship. Then before you know it, you *will* heal and start over again.

Reward yourself

Don't blame yourself for getting upset about your breakup. Don't expect yourself to not feel anything or to bounce back as if the breakup didn't really hurt. When you act that way, you're just kidding yourself. You also risk burying the pain rather than really facing it and coping with it. And that just means the pain will continue to be there, just under the surface, for a very long time.

Instead, reward yourself for everything you do well. When you practice one of the tips in this chapter, tell yourself that you did well: ***"You took a walk today; that's great! I'm proud of you!"*** Write it down in a diary or on a list. Or write it on a sticky note, tack it up on your bathroom mirror, and read it every day while brushing your teeth.

If you feel your confidence fading, do some self-esteem exercises. For example, make a list of ten things that are "good" about you, like ten behaviors you do well or ten qualities you like about yourself. Then memorize the list. Put a green dot on your wrist right next to the dial of your watch. Then every time you look at your watch, let the green dot remind you to say one of the items from your list: ***"I am kind to** children and animals." "I write well." "I have **beautiful** green eyes." "I have a **warm heart." "I have** many loyal friends."* When you get tired of that list, make up another. Use thought-stopping to stop all self-denigrating thoughts, and replace each one with one of your self-affirming thoughts.

Then you'll soon find yourself thinking — and feeling — much better about yourself and your life. And you'd really like that, wouldn't you?

❤ ❤ ❤ ❤ ❤ ❤

Can Exs Really Become Friends?

Dear Dr. Kate,

My age: 27   **My gender:** Female

My boyfriend broke up with me, saying that he still cares about me and hopes we can "be friends." How can I recover from a breakup and "be friends" when I still love him? Can people really become friends after it all? Can it happen when he's dating others, but I'm not ready to yet? Is it advisable? I've been having a hard time with this. Please help.

Dear Stressed and Confused,

People vary in their opinion on this. Some people think it's better to cut all ties, but I don't. In my opinion, you can't be platonic friends immediately after a breakup, especially one that wasn't mutual, because you're still romantically involved — you just don't feel platonic toward your ex. However, after you've found another romantic interest — one that excites you as much as your ex did — and he's done the same, your romantic feelings for one another should fade and morph into platonic affection. Then the two of you can really become friends.

I believe it's good to keep your former loves as platonic friends — provided they'll treat you with respect and friendly affection. I don't think it's healthy to expect yourself to stop loving someone completely. Besides, just because you can't live with someone or be romantic lovers any more doesn't mean that you don't respect and care for one another as people. Old lovers can make some of the best friends you'll ever have — especially when they continue to be buds after years have passed. After all, they've known you way more than other people. So when they choose to remain pals, you can feel very supported and valued.

In contrast, if you cut off all ties every time you disagree with someone or fail to marry that person, you'll probably find yourself a very old, lonely woman some day.

To help you recover from your loss, use thought-stopping and **The Dr. Kate Quick & Dirty Grieving Technique** (both described in Chapter 10), and take it one day at a time.

I'm sorry you're hurting, and I wish you the best in your recovery.

Dr. Kate

Con Artist Ruins Fairy Tale . . . How to Trust Again

Dear Dr. Kate,

My age: 29   **My gender:** Female

I'm a very confused young lady who wants to believe in the fairy tale, yet at the same time, believes that there are no good men out there. I ended a three-year relationship about four months ago. The man I was dating turned out to be a real con artist. He slept with everything he could get his hands on, stole my money, and was still able to look me in the eyes and tell me that he loved me. How am I ever supposed to trust a man again?

Dear Confused Young Lady,

I'm very sorry that you had this experience. One way to trust again is to learn how to differentiate people you can trust from those you can't. It's important to learn from this experience, but it's also imperative that you learn the "right" lesson, not something that will make your life more difficult.

The first lesson is how to recognize a con artist/psychopath — a user/ gameplayer who always puts himself first. Cold and calculating, he views others as objects to be manipulated for his own ends. He doesn't mind lying, so he can really play into your romantic fantasies, pretending to be your ideal man. As a result, you may find a psychopath much more enchanting and irresistible than normal, honest men. However, once you've been burned by such a man, it becomes much easier to value someone who tells the truth — even if he's not as charming *because* he tells the truth.

In the future, if something seems too good to be true, ask yourself if it really is. Talk to the man's friends. If he doesn't have any long-term or close friends, if he refuses to introduce you to his family or friends, if they make references to him making up stories or tease him about being really good at manipulating people, or if they don't treat you as very important (because he's introduced them to so many women before), then there's most likely a problem. If you catch him in any small, seemingly meaningless lies, that's also a warning sign.

To get over such a man, simply imagine that he's saying the same romantic things he says to you to all the other women he beds. That should break the romantic bubble.

Although there are many psychopaths out there, there are also many nice men who say what they mean and mean what they say most of the time, and who do not manipulate, steal, or intentionally lie. If you allow this one experience to color your whole approach to men, you will, in effect, be allowing your ex to hurt you more than he has already. So don't distrust all men because of this one person. Instead, calmly and objectively evaluate each man's character. Differentiate the honest from the dishonest; then act accordingly.

I'm sorry you're hurting. Learn what you can from this experience, and use it to find a healthier, more compatible mate.

All the best,

Dr. Kate

Learn to Forgive, but Don't Ever Take Him Back!

Dear Dr. Kate,

My age: 33   **My gender:** Female

I was married to an extremely abusive man for almost seven years. When I told him I was pregnant, he threw me over a chair, screaming that there was no way the child was his; I had to be cheating. Of course, my son was his, and I later found out that my husband was the one who was cheating. The abuse got worse and worse and also escalated when he drank. But each time I tried to leave, he put a loaded shotgun to my temple. So I'd lie awake nights fashioning fantastic ways to "off" him. My mom has remained friendly with his family, and she recently told me some news: My ex fell through a rotted-out bathroom floor and hurt himself. I nearly laughed myself sick over it, and the incident sparked a whole new spate of fantasies about him meeting his demise. So am I deranged? Just angry? Do I need professional help?

Dear Formerly Abused, Vengeful Ex-wife,

I'm very happy that you were able to get out of your situation with your life intact. Many women don't, and the time right before and after they leave tends to be the most dangerous. Many women need to rely on shelters and community agencies to protect them.

Now to answer your questions: No, entertaining "revenge" thoughts isn't normal. It's one thing to have them flit briefly through your mind, and quite another to have them rest there. Yes, you're also very angry, and yes, you should get professional help. Consult a psychologist for therapy, and talk through your anger and hostility. You're wasting a lot of energy feeling so negative.

In saying this, I don't mean to negate your experiences in any way, shape, or form. No one has a right to abuse anyone, and your husband treated you very poorly. You did the best thing in divorcing him. The abuse would have grown more dangerous over time, until one day you might have been killed. And your son might have grown up watching the abuse and gone on to abuse his wife, too. However, those things can be in the past — *if* you allow them to be. But when you keep them alive in your mind, you basically continue the abuse in the present.

That's why you have to forgive and move on — for you, not him. Every time you think a negative thought, you remind yourself of the past and keep it alive — and you continue to suffer. While you're busy thinking in such an unhealthy way, you're also far more likely to attract negative people — including other abusive men. In contrast, if you think positively about life, you'll feel happier and healthier, and draw healthier, happier people to you. I personally think you've suffered enough negative, unhealthy men. Don't you?

So learn to forgive your ex, but never take him back. Avoid him as much as possible, and be (quietly) pleased when he gets involved with someone else and forgets about you completely. (As much as you don't wish bad experiences on anyone else, your ex has to consider you unimportant and "forget" about you before you will be truly safe.) If he has visitation, try to use your mother as a go-between so you don't have to see him. If your ex ever becomes abusive with you again, file a restraining order and use community agencies to help you. Plan your strategy with the help of your attorney and therapist. If your ex ever shows signs of being abusive with your son, consult an attorney and take appropriate steps. Otherwise, make your future better by letting go of the past, forgiving, and moving on. The life you save could be your own.

All the best,

Dr. Kate

Chapter 22

Starting Over

• •

In This Chapter

▶ Recognizing when you're ready to begin each stage of Starting Over

▶ Using appropriate activities to make new acquaintances and begin dating again

▶ Pacing yourself to make your return to single life as healthy and enjoyable as possible

▶ Avoiding rebounds and people exactly like or unlike your ex

• •

*L*osing a love is the number one stressor for most people. Whether you've broken up, divorced, or been widowed, no one likes rejection or the loss of a loved one — or the flood of emotions that it brings. However, if you follow the tips for breaking up with less pain in Chapter 21, you will eventually heal. As you do, you'll get to the point where you again desire companionship. At first, just mixing with people you don't know may be a struggle, but in time, you'll get used to it again. Then you'll eventually want to meet more interesting people, and finally, you'll eventually desire another compatible relationship.

In Chapter 2, I describe the four stages of *The Love Cycle: Finding Love, Making the Relationship Work, Letting Go,* and *Starting Over.* In this chapter, I outline steps you can take to traverse the fourth stage, *Starting Over,* with maximum efficiency and comfort. I describe how to know when you're ready to begin the process, and how to tell when you're ready to progress from one step to the next. I also suggest ways of meeting people, depending on where you're at in the *Starting Over Stage.* I tell you how to look at the surf (step out of the house with family, friends, and maybe a support group), stick your toe in the water (meet strangers casually), wade in (meet singles when you're better), and slowly, but surely start swimming (date singles more efficiently when you're a *lot* better). I also tell you how to avoid the *DRR* — The Dreaded Rebound Relationship — and how to find a more compatible honey this time around.

For a full description of each "meeting people" method mentioned, including how to find it, be sure to check out Chapter 5. That chapter covers the *Finding Love Stage,* and all the various methods you can use — when you're emotionally ready — to find love again.

Starting Over

When are you ready to start over? As soon as you can get out of the house without sobbing continuously or getting intoxicated, you're ready to get started. The breakup is very fresh, and you're going through many vacillating emotions. You're grieving quite frequently and using thought-stopping (described in Chapter 10) all day long to rid yourself of thoughts about your ex. But you need something to distract you other than work. You've begun talking to your psychologist to try to get a handle on what happened and why. In between, you may pray a lot, asking for your ex to return. Your self-esteem is hurting.

Looking at the surf — Getting out of the house with your support group

In Chapter 21, I point out that while you're going through the extreme stress of a breakup, it's best just to mix with supportive family and friends. When you're raw and hurting, it's good just to get out of the house. So the first step to starting over is doing just that. Get dressed, take a walk, and do something outside. Don't sit home drinking and feeling sorry for yourself or, conversely, hitting the bars and having sex every night. Although you don't have to mix with others a great deal, it's often helpful to join a support group, or ask your psychologist about group therapy. This is particularly true if you had to split up because your partner had a serious psychological problem or was addicted to drugs, alcohol, gambling, or sex, or if you lost your partner to a traumatic accident or unexpected physical illness. You can frequently find support groups online, through your psychologist, or through a hospital that treats patients with the same disorder.

Sticking your toe in — Meeting strangers

When are you ready? As soon as you've mastered the previous step (leaving the house to take a walk or attend a support group), are comfortable with it, and feel ready for more, you're ready for this next step. You're still going through many vacillating emotions, and may still be grieving at night on a frequent basis. You're still talking to your psychologist to try to get closure on your relationship. You may periodically entertain thoughts that you and your ex may get back together again. You're still clinging and not ready to move on yet, even though you consciously want to. Your self-esteem may be hurting, and you're definitely not ready for dating yet, but you're over the initial shock and looking for more distraction. You're ready to mingle with new people on a *very* casual basis.

Use the most casual methods outlined in Chapter 5 for meeting people. For example, attend community and church activities and events open to the general public. You might try church and community events or join your local gym or YMCA. Or take a fun, not-for-credit class at a local community college or park district. Learn to samba and get those endorphins firing, or go cross-country skiing, so you can see the sunshine and breathe the fresh air while you're firing your endorphins. Visit any nearby historical museums and parks (like those at Greenfield Village, MI, Williamsburg, VA, or Busch Gardens), and zoos — and stretch your mind, legs, and endorphins at the same time you're enjoying the sunshine and air. See Chapter 5 for a full description of these activities and how to find them.

Bring a friend with you, or go by yourself, whatever you're up for. You'll tend to mix better if you're alone, and you'll meet other single, same-sexed people who may eventually become friends. Because you're not ready to date anyone yet, don't worry about the person's sex, marital status, or age. Just mix with people as people, without sexual interest.

If you're feeling sorry for yourself or suffering low self-esteem, consider volunteering. When you help those more needy than you, five things usually happen: 1) The people you're helping really appreciate it, so they reward you with all kinds of praise, which you can use right now. 2) You put your own grief into perspective and realize that your problem isn't so bad. It's hard to feel sorry for yourself because your boyfriend left you when you're building a house for a homeless family or holding AIDS babies in the hospital. 3) You're temporarily distracted from your grief while you tend to a noble cause. 4) You get to laugh and interact with other volunteers, and laughter can be great medicine. 5) Instead of feeling so alone, you feel connected to that group of volunteers — which usually consists of happy, caring people — and to the world.

Choose a project that serves a purpose and people you care about — and also includes fellow volunteers you can enjoy. Then pace yourself.

Wading in — Meeting singles when you're better

When you've mastered the preceding step, are comfortable meeting strangers again, and are ready for more, it's time to start meeting singles. You're still experiencing some vacillating emotions, but your feelings have leveled off quite a bit from their previous rollercoaster level. Your grieving sessions are getting less intense and further apart. You have consciously realized and accepted that your mate wasn't compatible with you, and you now believe that there's someone else out there for you who is.

Your self-esteem is still in recovery, and your newfound independence is a little tentative. You're not ready for anything heavy, but you are ready to start meeting and casually dating other singles. Remember, though, I'm talking about *meeting* them — *not* sleeping with them, having sex with them, or running off and marrying them. You're nowhere near ready for a steady, intense, or sexual relationship with anyone right now. You're just ready to practice talking to single people without feeling threatened.

Start by going to events that tend to draw other singles, but are usually less intense. For example, you could join a tennis, running, or ski club, or an organization that has a mostly singles population. Or take a class that appeals mainly to singles in your age range. Once you're more comfortable with those activities, you could also explore some singles dances or dinners for singles, or start meeting people in online chat rooms. See Chapter 5 for a full description of these methods and how to find them. Just remember that the goal here is *friendship* with other singles, nothing more intense. You're still healing from your breakup and you're really not ready to commit to anyone — emotionally or physically.

If someone asks you out or you meet someone you'd like to ask out, go ahead. Just don't think about it like you're checking out his or her compatibility for a romantic relationship. Don't let yourself wonder whether he or she would make a great mate. Instead, keep the relationship more distant, as though you're just two people having casual fun together. You're still very vulnerable, so it's best not to have sex with anyone you meet. You might end up feeling more than you bargained for, only to discover that the other person is just looking for fun. And you certainly don't need that, do you?

Swimming — Meeting singles more efficiently when you're really better

Once you've mastered the previous step, are comfortable with the friendships you've made with other singles, and want to do more, you're ready to meet singles more efficiently. You've pretty much recovered from your breakup, and you no longer have to use thought-stopping (see Chapter 10) 200 times a day to get rid of thoughts about your ex. In fact, you can sometimes go days without thinking about him or her, and no longer feel the need to discuss your ex with friends. Your emotions have leveled off to fairly normal levels, and when you grieve, it's much less intense. You've gotten closure on your relationship — you understand what happened and why.

You're sure now that you and your ex will not be reuniting; you've resolved to put that relationship behind you and move on. Your self-esteem has recovered, and you're feeling healthy and happy. You're ready to get into more efficient dating and gradually and slowly start a new relationship without clinging, becoming a basket case, rebounding from the chandeliers, or feeling threatened. In short, you're again functioning as a healthy, happy single in charge of your life. When you can do all of this, it's time to target more efficient ways to meet new people.

Consider using the most efficient methods for finding a partner, outlined in Chapter 5. Try placing an online or offline personal ad, and watch the responses flow in. Love@AOL has a huge selection of free online ads (look for "Basic Personals" at *AOL Keyword: Love*), where you can place a free ad and search for compatible people by age, location, and sex. Or for a small fee, you can use www.match.com for more targeted searches. See Chapter 5 for more on dating through the personal ads, including valuable tips for running and responding to personal ads, online and off.

Be aware that if you answer ads (as opposed to running one), many people will not respond. It's nothing personal. Most people who place ads get many responses. They can become overwhelmed by the sheer number and stop communicating with everyone, or they might burn out after meeting a few people. So the fact that someone doesn't answer your note or e-mail does not necessarily reflect on you or his or her opinion of you.

If you're ready to meet a compatible partner for a more long-term relationship or marriage, consider joining a professional introduction service. Visit several in your community and then out of those who can accommodate you (including someone your age, background, education, and so forth), pick the one that feels most comfortable. Follow the recommendations on how to choose a dating service in Chapter 5, including questions to ask and how to compare answers.

Try visiting matchmaking services where someone makes the matches for you (as opposed to you choosing the people yourself), and give special consideration to any services that give you feedback after your dates. You'll probably find the feedback particularly helpful at this time in your life — especially if you're re-entering the single world after having been involved with your ex for quite a long time. You'll probably find boutique matchmaking services more personal, soothing, easy, and effective than the less personal, franchised library services, where you have to do all the research, too.

Everyone burns out when they do too much of anything, and looking through stacks of profiles and tapes, screening potential matches, and meeting them all can quickly become overwhelming. That's true for everyone (even flaming extroverts!), but especially if you're a more private person or someone who's starting over after losing a loved one. You may burn out quickly if you try to do too much of the work yourself. The good boutique services cost a bit, but they do all the interviewing, screening, and matching for you, while you concentrate on meeting your matches. So they can ease your transition back to single life — especially if you have more money than time and emotional energy.

Avoiding the DRR — The Dreaded Rebound Relationship

When people are healing from loss, they're usually quite fragile. Their judgment is often faulty due to the stress. So it's not a good time to get quickly and intensely involved with another person. If you do, chances are you're *on the rebound* — that is, you're choosing that partner impulsively and reactively to fill your emotional void, not because that person is really compatible with you long-term. You could end up in a *dreaded rebound relationship* (DRR). In other words, you're acting out your need for a partner. You don't want to be alone right now, so having a partner is more important than how compatible you are with him in other ways.

For example, you may become intensely involved with a man because he reminds you of your ex. Perhaps he has a similar smile or the same color hair. But that person could be very incompatible or even unhealthy for you. Or you may do the opposite, becoming very intensely involved with someone because he seems to be the direct *opposite* of your ex. Perhaps you always wanted to marry and have children, but your partner never could commit. Then you meet someone who is more than willing to commit in a hurry, and you quickly become involved. After your sense of urgency has diminished a bit, however, you realize that you're not really compatible in other ways. Yes, you're both able to commit, but you're not compatible enough to enjoy being committed to one another long-term. After your neediness is met, you'll be able to see those incompatible qualities and become bothered by them. At that point, you may have to break up all over again.

Just as you should resist making any big decisions right after a painful breakup, apply that same caution here. Try not to make any big relationship decisions quickly, and, if you need to, discuss the situation first with friends or, preferably, your psychologist. Talk everything through before deciding whether to become involved and to what degree. Keep your expectations realistic. Try to use what you've learned from your last relationship to make your new relationship healthier and happier. Ask yourself: Given what you've learned in your last relationship, what kind of qualities do you want in your next partner? What kinds of qualities and behaviors seem most compatible with yours?

But be careful to apply the "right" lessons. Don't avoid all men or women — or conversely, choose men or women — just because they're so much like your ex. Instead, get closure on your relationship with your psychologist's help (as I describe in Chapter 21), and use that rational, healthy knowledge when choosing friends, dates, and mates.

There really is someone out there for everyone. People come in all combinations and permutations. If you use effective methods and stay warm, upbeat, and realistic, you'll be able to find a reasonably compatible, healthy, happy partner, and build a reasonably healthy, happy relationship together. Being happy and healthy helps you draw happy and healthy people to you. So think happy, feel happy, and enjoy the ride. *I wish you all the best on your journey!*

Male-Female Odds . . . Thanks for the Info!

Dear Dr. Kate,

My age: 42   **My gender:** Female

I just read your letters about the male-female odds and how women start to outnumber men when they're older. I felt such relief. I thought I was going crazy. When I divorced at 30 with two young children, I had no problem dating quality men and forming healthy, serious relationships. Then, suddenly, I hit age 40. Now I can't even find a suitable date, let alone a long-term relationship. I was starting to feel very ugly. I feel much better now, knowing that there are real reasons (outside of me) why I can't attract men my age the same way I used to. Thanks for the info!

Dear *NOT!* Crazy,

Happy to be of service, my dear! I try to mention this problem frequently for two reasons:

- **To inform younger women that their romantic life has a limitation of sorts.** Many women, especially today's career-minded women, spend years finishing their education. Although that's good, it's also important not to delay your social life completely, because you can be in your late 30s by the time you finish an advanced degree and set up a business. And it also becomes more difficult to find a suitable husband in the late 30s. So while women don't have time to date inappropriate men (for example, married or abusive men) at any age, that's even more true after age 28.

- **To encourage older women to be especially careful about the criteria they use to rule men out.** Because the pool of older men is limited, it's extremely important that older women focus on what's really important in compatibility (like honesty, loyalty, monogamy, trust), and work with or overlook areas that are either unimportant or fairly easy to change (like how the man dresses).

As women age, they get better at noticing details in other people. So if they simultaneously get too picky about unimportant details, they can lose out on a lot of fun with an otherwise compatible mate.

All the best, and please let me know how you're doing from time to time.

Dr. Kate

Part VII
The Part of Tens

The 5th Wave   By Rich Tennant

"My wife and I were drifting apart. We decided to go back to doing what we used to do when we were first married. So we called her parents and asked to borrow money."

In this part . . .

There's a great tradition in tens: The Ten Commandments, the perfect-ten score in Olympics competitions, and, of course, the ten beautiful fingers and toes you sport even as we speak. *For Dummies* books also have a great tradition in its Part of Tens chapters. And so, without further ado, I contribute two top-ten lists to help you enhance your relationship.

One list includes ten tips plus one bonus tip that you can use to successfully pace a new relationship. The second list details ten ways to rekindle your romantic flame. Use these suggestions to strengthen your love ties with your partner. Then don't be shy! Brainstorm more ideas of your own and add them to these.

I've also included a special treat for you in the appendixes. Take **The Dr. Kate Compatibility Quiz** in Appendix A to discover how compatible you and your mate may or may not be, and to remind yourself about what's really important in compatibility. Then take **The Dr. Kate Communication Quiz** in Appendix B to get an idea about how you and your mate communicate, and helpful tips for improving that communication. You can also take the quizzes for previous mates, to help you understand those relationships, and to monitor your love life progress. Review the Part of Tens chapters and quizzes from time to time and remember to take action to make, keep, and nurture a healthy relationship that's also alive, kicking . . . and fun!

Chapter 23

Ten (+1) Tips to Successfully Pace a New Relationship

. . . .

In This Chapter

▶ Pacing your relationship by pacing your thoughts, feelings, and behaviors

▶ Avoiding some common pitfalls online and off

. . . .

*I*n Chapter 6, I discuss how fragile new relationships are, and how important it is to slowly and gradually increase your emotional and physical intimacy. It's important to keep your thoughts, feelings, and behaviors in sync with your partner's — and with the time you've actually spent together. If you rush through important intimacy stages instead, the relationship takes a hit — and often ends prematurely. So how do you keep yourself from moving full-steam ahead? By following the tips in the following sections! Here's how to slow things down and keep your new relationship on a healthy track.

Don't Jump into Bed on the First Date

This might seem like a no-brainer, but it's actually one of the most common mistakes — becoming sexually intimate too soon. People get caught up in the passion and wanting to please. Buuttt . . . *if* you have sex early in the relationship, you're sharing the most intimate behavior you can possibly share with someone you hardly know. Talk about getting your feelings, behaviors, and time spent in the relationship out of sync! Because your partner hasn't had time to get to know or care about you, he or she may neglect to inform you about a sexually transmitted disease (STD), fail to take appropriate pregnancy and STD precautions, and/or even disappear after the act.

So avoid sex on the first several dates — or until your emotional intimacy and the relationship have had a chance to catch up. I know you're only human, but try to keep your emotions, behaviors, and time spent in the relationship in sync as much as you can. You'll feel better. And you'll also help your partner respect and value you, and make it more likely that you'll see one another again in the future. See Chapter 7 for more on this topic.

Don't Spend the Entire Weekend Together

If you've been seeing one another once a week, it can be too much, too soon to suddenly spend the weekend together. Your relationship just isn't ready for it. So instead, have dates that gradually increase in length and frequency.

The same advice applies if you initially meet online. Communicating via e-mail is fast and easy, so you and your partner can begin to feel close very quickly. But when you live in different cities or states — or even farther away — it's difficult to have a normal first date. Instead of spending a relaxed three hours together, for example, your first date might last the entire weekend. After all, you've both spent a lot of time, money, and energy to travel some distance to meet. When you finally get together, after all that build-up, it seems natural to spend the entire weekend together.

Buuutttt — don't do it! And don't let that great build-up of excitement convince you to hop into bed together either. (See the previous section.) If you do, you might very well break up shortly after the weekend, and one or both of you could get hurt. So no matter how you meet, online or off — pace yourself. Leave your new friend wanting more of you — not less. You'll be glad you did.

Don't Go On Vacation Together

If you've been seeing one another casually or even spending an entire week-end together every once in awhile, and you suddenly go on a two-week cruise together, kiss the relationship good-bye. Just because you enjoy three days together doesn't mean that you can suddenly enjoy 14 days of 24/7 contact. Better you should take a same-sex pal with you on your cruise and return home to find a lover who's missed you dearly!

Don't Move In Together

When you begin spending more nights with your sweetie, there usually comes a time when you wonder why you're maintaining two households. And every-one likes to save money. So if your lease comes up a little early — before you and your partner have really gotten that intimate — you might try to convince yourself that the two of you should move in together.

Resist the urge! When you live with someone, he or she gets to see you at your best and your worst. And you're probably not at your best a lot of the time, are you? Once you know you can have sex any time you want, you may suddenly not want it any more. Or you may put more and more activities ahead of sex, until you end up making love infrequently. You may even go from having great sex to having none at all. And since most people who play house together do *not* go on to marry one another, cohabiting can mean the end of your permanent future together. (See Chapter 9 for more.)

So spend the money for the extra lease, and let your partner miss you a bit. In the end, it's well worth it.

Don't Say, "I Love You," Too Soon

If you say those three little words to your partner too early in the relationship, you may frighten him or her off. Or he may take you for granted and devalue you because you care more than he does. Besides, the reality is that you don't know yet if that wonderfully powerful feeling you have inside will end up being real love, or just lust or infatuation.

I don't advocate playing games, but in the beginning of a relationship, it's extremely important that the power be approximately equal. (See Chapter 1 for more on this.) There needs to be some challenge, mystery, and intrigue to motivate the other person to pursue you with interest. So give your partner the opportunity to reciprocate your attention and affection.

The woman is usually ahead of the man in this department because men are often more conflicted about relationships. So Ladies, don't say, "I love you," until he does — and until you sense that he really means it, he's not just saying it in the heat of passion to convince you to have sex with him. For more on this topic, see Chapters 7 and 19.

And if you're a guy who tends to come on too strong, this advice applies to you, too. Whatever your sex — if you tend to be emotionally intense, let your partner set the pace for your relationship.

Do Keep Your Sense of Self

Every few years, another book appears on the market, saying that a woman can snare the heart of the man by manipulating him. The woman is encouraged to get what she wants by either imitating the man's actions, acting like his fantasy of a woman, or in some way pretending to be exactly what he wants. And every time one of these books appears, they sell like hotcakes.

Well, I'm campaigning for health. Sure, if you pretend to be someone's ideal, you might hoodwink that person into marrying you. On the other hand, you'll also end up married to someone you're not compatible with. So although you do need to watch the balance of power early in the relationship, be careful not to lose your sense of self — your individuality — in the process. There is an appropriate middle ground; you don't have to become a shapeshifting doormat with no discernable personality of your own. Feel free to improve behaviors you think need improving, and make appropriate compromises when you and your mate disagree (see Chapters 11 to 13 for more on how to do this). But don't change everything about yourself — including your likes and preferences — just to please someone. If you do, he'll probably lose interest in you in short order — and you won't have any fun either!

Do Keep Your Own Life

Just as it's important to keep your sense of self, it's also important to keep your own life, even as you allow someone new into yours. People sometimes make the mistake of dropping their friends when a new love enters the picture. This is especially true of young women, who are so eager to see the man they crave, they break plans with others when the opportunity arises. For heaven's sake, *don't do that!* It's not a good way to treat your friends and family. And your date will respect you more if you aren't always available.

Many men become uncomfortable when they think they're dating someone, and all of a sudden, they've inherited a slave. That's too much responsibility for anyone — especially so soon in the relationship. Whether you're male or female, it's best to maintain your friendships and family ties, and keep a healthy, balanced amount of activities with those people, even when you're dating someone special. Remember, your romantic mates will come and go before you finally settle in with a long-term partner. On the other hand, if you show loyalty and nurture them properly, your friends and family will almost always be there for you. So treat them with care; don't blow them off.

Do Keep Dating Other People Casually

Just as you don't want to ax your family and friends to dive headfirst into a new relationship, don't cut off all your other dates either. Some people feel disloyal if they date more than one person at a time. However, not doing so means betting on one relationship to progress over another — and making that bet before getting to know the person very well. And since you really *won't* know that new person for at least three to four months of seeing him or her several times a week, you're taking quite a risk when you put all your eggs in one relationship basket. That's also a lot of pressure on the basket!

As I mention in Chapters 7 and 19, men like to compete. And most men and women like to date someone who is also desired by others. So don't turn down other dates just to have the evening free in case a new interest calls. And don't cancel a date with one person to date another. Instead, if you already have a date when someone else asks you out, simply say: ***"I'd love to get together. But I can't make it _____ night. How about _____ instead?"***

If you tend to be emotionally intense, dating more than one person allows you to spread your intensity around, reducing the stress on any one person. Give your new date time to get to know and desire you, and give yourself time to figure out if he's really a good fit — before you change your dating habits for him. Allow your new friend time to catch up to you emotionally, and give some subtle competition to encourage him or her to keep moving forward.

Do Keep Your Thoughts, Feelings, and Behaviors In Sync with Reality

To keep yourself from chafing at the bit in the early stages of a relationship, keep a tight reign on your fantasy life. Women tend to think about a man after the date, especially if the date went well. If it went really well, the woman might fantasize about marrying him; she might even — heaven forbid! — imagine her name in front of his. Do you think the man is doing the same thing? Naaahhhh — if anything, he's thinking about *bedding* you, not wedding you!

Whatever your gender — if you tend to get ahead of yourself with fantasy, control your thoughts. Since thoughts lead to feelings (as discussed in Chapter 10), pace your feelings by pacing your thoughts. Use thought-stopping (same chapter) to get rid of any fantasies about your new friend in between dates. Limit thoughts about him or her to when you're actually talking on the phone or getting together in person. That will help you slow down and keep your thoughts, feelings, and behaviors in sync with the time spent in the relationship. It will also keep the balance of power between you more even — and make it far more likely that the relationship will grow.

Be Careful When You're Needy

If it's Christmas (or New Year's Eve, or Valentine's Day, or the anniversary of your last breakup, or . . . , or . . . , or . . . !), and you usually feel alone and needy around this time, be careful. Avoid bars, curb your drinking, and keep in touch with your common sense. Don't spill your guts about your ex or your loneliness, and avoid jumping into bed with someone just because he or she is there. Spend time with buds rather than someone too tempting to resist.

If you're feeling like you need sex, avoid situations where you might get sexually pushy. For example, drop the lady off at her front door, rather than going in for a nightcap. Or spend time with platonic friends instead.

If you're feeling like you need to be loved, avoid situations where you might have sex to win someone's approval or affection. Don't be alone with him when you're feeling vulnerable. If you give in to sex and the man leaves, you'll feel even more alone, lonely, and desperate for affection.

Take It with a Grain of Salt When Someone Else Is Needy

People often make emotional statements they don't mean. A friend or child might yell, "I hate you!" when angry. An adult might profess to be in love when he or she desperately wants to love and be loved. When that person later calms down and feels less needy, he realizes he doesn't feel that way after all.

If you meet someone online who quickly becomes intense about you without even meeting you in person, or if she says she loves you after knowing you for only a few weeks, take it with a grain of salt. Understand the comments *in context;* factor in the person's state of mind before responding. Be respectful, positive, and polite, but keep realistic expectations about your friend and the relationship. The odds of any one relationship working out long-term are very low, so chances are, this one won't work either. When you're realistic in your expectations, you're not hurt and shocked if your date does a 180-degree turn. And if the relationship lasts, you can be pleasantly surprised. For more on pacing your relationship, be sure to see Chapters 6, 7, 8, 9, 18, and 19.

Chapter 24

Ten Ways to Rekindle Your Flame

In This Chapter

▶ Enhancing your sensuality, romance, and fun

▶ Jumpstarting the passion in your relationship

*W*hat do you do if you've neglected your relationship, and it's lost the romantic attraction? How do you jumpstart a partnership that has gone from exciting to ho-hum, booorrriiing? Well, good news! There are hundreds of things you can do to breathe life into your relationship.

As you read these ideas, you'll think of others. Jot them down, and refer to them often. Try the best ones and note which work best, so you can do more of them in the future. Also, check out the letters, articles, and my advice at **AOL Keyword: DrKate** and `www.drkate.com` for more on how to put the flicker back in your love flame. Use **Dr. Kate Search** at those sites to search for "romance" and "spark." You can also see *Rekindling Romance For Dummies* by Dr. Ruth Westheimer and Pierre Lehu (John Wiley & Sons, Inc.).

Recreate the Early Days — What Worked Before

If your partner is now treating you differently from the way he used to treat you, you're probably treating him differently, too. You can't make anyone do anything, but you can certainly influence someone's behavior through your actions and reactions. So, the best way to jumpstart your spark is to think back to when your relationship was exciting. What kinds of things did you do with one another when you first fell in love? What did you do for fun? Where did you go? What did you talk about? How did you dress for one another? How did you show your partner that he's special? Jot down everything you remember your partner enjoying in the early days. Then try to recreate those experiences.

Act "As If"

Moods are contagious. Because partners are together so frequently, they can really infect one another positively *and* negatively. So if you'd like your partner to feel more sensual toward you, you need to feel more sensual towards him or her. Even if you don't feel very positive about your mate at the current time, act "as if." Remember back to when you thought he was Romeo Personified or she was the Gorgeous Goddess, and psych yourself up. Remember how it felt when you were crazy in love — and *pretend that you still are.* Then you'll become more excited, which will help your partner become more excited, and so on, and so on, until you both "bring back that loving feeling." If that's difficult, try this: Close your eyes and imagine that it's the last day of your mate's life. Now can you enjoy him or her with enthusiasm? Go for it! Cherish each moment, and the excitement will come back to you a hundredfold.

Talk about Positive Thoughts and Feelings

In Chapter 10, I explain that *thoughts* lead to *feelings,* and while feelings don't cause *behavior,* they certainly make it easier or more difficult to behave a certain way. So when you're with your partner, spend most of your time thinking and talking about fun, uplifting ideas in an enthusiastic, full-of-life way. Then you'll feel more fun and full of life, your partner will tend to see you that way, and your relationship will become more positive and fun. In other words, your enthusiastic *thoughts* will lead you to *feel* more enthusiastic, and feeling that way will help you *behave* more enthusiastically. Then your partner will *feel* better around you, and *act* more enthusiastically towards you, which will then help you *think, feel,* and *act* more enthusiastically, and so on, and so on.

One way to keep your conversations more positive and fun is to limit problematic discussions to certain time frames, so you don't continually bring up stressful topics the entire time you're together. For example, if you want to discuss a minor problem at work, set a time limit of 30 minutes. When that time is up, spend at least double that amount of time in more playful, fun talk. Be sure to tell your mate what you're doing and enlist his cooperation. Chances are, he'll welcome the idea. For a more intense or complicated discussion, follow the steps outlined in Chapters 12 and 13, make a special date to discuss the issue together, and spend the time you need to either find a mutually satisfactory compromise, or table the issue until a certain date. Then once you've done that, be sure to spend time talking about positive, uplifting ideas.

By restricting the negative talk time, you'll focus better, and resolve any problem more efficiently. And then you'll be able to de-stress by having fun. In the end, you'll feel more upbeat, organized, energized — and in control of your problems as well!

Make New Love Traditions

Everyone needs a balance of some routine, automatic activities, and some new, light-hearted activities. If you and your mate have fallen into a rut, doing the same things together week after week (dinner and a movie?), try making new love traditions together. For example, celebrate spring with picnics, botanical garden walks, or a ferryboat ride. Welcome summer with white-water rafting, canoeing, tubing down a river, barbecues, and picnics. Make fall special with haywagon rides, carving pumpkins, and visiting cider mills. Kiss winter hello with ice-skating, tobogganing, or cross-country skiing. Use any season or holiday as an excuse to sample a new tradition and make a new custom.

Become an expert on activities taking place in your community and the surrounding countryside. Follow the advice given in Chapters 5 and 22 to locate events. In cities that feature them, buy an inexpensive coupon book that offers discounts at local restaurants, boat rides, theme parks, and more. The coupon acts as a special invitation, so you'll end up sampling activities and adding to your play repertoire.

Store your best ideas in a box or file (or "favorite place" it in your computer), so you can easily retrieve them and plan your next trip. You can also repeat that activity — same time, next year — as a love tradition. By varying your activities between brand new and tried and true, you'll maximize the *fun* in your relationship.

Say "Where Ya Been?" to Your Sensuality

Acting in a romantic, sexy way is easier if you surround yourself with things that help you feel romantic and sexy. Start by paying attention to your own senses. Think about each sense and how to stimulate it to help you feel more sensual. Here are just a few ideas:

- ✔ **Smell:** Experiment with colognes, bath oils, potpourri, the smell of apple, vanilla, cinnamon, and pine. Burn some candles or incense, put some cologne on a light bulb, and look for ways to bring pleasurable scent into your world. Pay attention to natural scents, too. Take a walk, and breathe the fresh air. Notice how it smells outside after a rain or on a crisp winter morning. The mild exercise will also fire your endorphins, get oxygen to your brain, and help you feel more energetic and frisky.

✔ **Touch:** Everyone has to bathe, wear clothes, and sleep. But instead of doing these activities in perfunctory manner, why not get into them? Take a warm, relaxing bath (rather than a quick shower), and enjoy the sensations. Do you like the feel of satin, silk, or velvet? Pay attention to the color and feel of your clothes, underwear, and sheets; choose materials and colors that help you feel sensual. If certain colors bring out the *lust* in you, wear them. I personally love deep purple, burgundy, and black velvet, but everyone is different. Just think about the effect certain colors have on you, and wear what makes you feel good. Don't worry about what's "in." Dressing for *feel* will help you stay in touch with your body, and you'll bring that sensuality into your relationship.

✔ **Hearing:** Notice how certain sounds affect you, then try to spend most of your time listening to sounds that help you feel good. One of my former editors swears that hard rock can make cleaning a breeze. Slow jazz may help you feel relaxed and oh-so-sexy. Experiment! Notice! Then do what you can to control your environmental sounds so they're more conducive to the mood you want.

✔ **Sight:** Pay attention to your sense of sight as well. When you're taking that walk I mentioned under "Smell," pay attention to the beautiful sights as well. Notice how beautiful the world is: the people, the trees, and the flowers. Notice the people, the flowers, the trees, the sunshine, the shadows, and the squirrels. There's a world of beauty out there to be enjoyed, just for the taking. And when you're inside, surround yourself with things you like to look at. Take some time to make your home and work space comfortable and relaxing. Invest in some clothing that looks good on you, and enjoy the view in the mirror, too.

✔ **Taste:** Everyone has to eat, but there's a difference between chowing down like there's no tomorrow, and taking the time to really taste and appreciate your food. If you're eating a salad, make it a great one! Notice the colors, textures, and tastes. Use a great goblet and ice cubes when you drink water. And periodically, let yourself have some tempting food as a special experience. Unless you have a food allergy or some other condition that warrants complete abstinence, you don't have to totally avoid treats. Studies suggest that for many people, a glass of red wine or moderate chocolate intake from time to time can be beneficial. But when you indulge, make it special. Eat and drink very slowly. Pay attention, think about the taste — and savor it. You'll get more pleasure from that one savored mouthful than a whole lot of mouthfuls gulped down when you're tense and distracted!

Keep the sensual parts of you in working order by regularly taking care of some aspect of your body: a medical checkup, eye exam, hearing test, dental check, pap smear, mammogram, blood pressure check — whatever upkeep you require. Also, bleach your teeth, have your nails done, get a new hairdo, indulge in a pedicure, get a massage — allow yourself some simple pampering and aesthetic upkeep, too. Rather than letting everything go for as long as possible, schedule some kind of appointment every week or two. If you enjoy this kind of thing, you'll be in heaven. And if you don't, it will become less bothersome. Plus you'll always be at your best — or at least most parts of you will be!

Just as women are more touched by all their senses, men are more influenced by the visual. Rather than lament this fact, get in tune with your body, and help your man stay tuned into you. To stay in shape, pick some exercise you actually enjoy. Concentrate on enjoying it and being healthy, and your body will get in shape with your mind.

Women are usually more influenced by context; they notice more of the details. So help your woman feel sensual and sexy by making your environment sensual-friendly. Invest in candles, strawberries, champagne, bubble bath, and relaxing music — and wear some cologne yourself! Many women get turned on by smell, and very few men truly use that asset to their advantage. Have your sweetie choose a cologne for you. And never, *never,* underestimate the effect that for-no-reason, just-because-I-care flowers have on a woman.

Move from Physical to Sensual to Sexual!

In Chapter 16, I discuss getting in touch with your body and your partner's, and learning to play together. But what if your connection has really lapsed? How can you break down the wall that's come between you and jumpstart the sex?

The items in the previous section will help you get in touch with your body. Then you need to get in touch with your partner's, he or she needs to get in touch with yours, and both of you need to get comfortable interacting physically with one another again. One of the best ways to do that is to start by getting closer *physically*, then leading into *sensual* interactions, and from there, into *sexual* interactions. So to begin, look for ways to touch your honey in non-sexual ways. Touch him on the hand, arm, or leg when making a point in conversation. Hold her hand or put your arm around her when walking down the street. Wrap your legs around each other and snuggle up when you're watching TV. Sit perpendicular while dining, so you can give good eye contact, play footsie, and touch when you gesture.

If you came from a family that didn't touch much, you may have to desensitize yourself gradually. Make a list of ways you can touch your partner and then number them from the easiest to the most difficult. Set a goal to master one behavior each week. Start with the item you find easiest (for example, touching your mate during conversations). After you've mastered that, add another behavior to your list while still maintaining the first one. Keep doing this until you're able to do all the behaviors on your list with ease. If you find a behavior more difficult and are unable to finish it in one week, take another week, but don't avoid doing it.

In addition, try adding more physical activities to your life together. Take walks together, go bike riding, take a "massage for couples" or dance class, attend an aerobics session together, or go to the beach and swim together. When you sweat with your partner without becoming embarrassed, it gets easier the next time. You're getting in touch with your body and getting in shape at the same time. You're also getting used to sweating with your partner in a nonsexual workout — and that will make it easier for you to sweat together sexually as well.

When partners have a terrific sex life, they almost meld into one person physically. As one of my clients describes it, he and his mate touch one another so often, there isn't a clear distinction between being together and making love; it just kind of blends. It's easy to go from affectionately chatting on the couch, with legs and arms entwined — to kissing, making out, and making love.

If you find a particular behavior extra difficult to change, try initiating it on a weekend trip together (described in Chapter 16). It's often easier to change a behavioral pattern when you're in a different context — one that doesn't remind you of the context in which the problem occurs. So use those weekend trips to practice all your new and improved behaviors, including making love! Then keep that passion in your repertoire when you return home!

As you do all of these things, you'll find the walls crumbling between you. You'll get back in touch with your *physical*, then your *sensual,* and then your *sexual* life together. And that will, in turn, strengthen your emotional and psychological intimacy, which will in turn, then also stimulate your physical/sexual intimacy. And so it continues, with one enhancing the other, as you and your partner grow more physically/sexually and emotionally/psychologically bonded.

Remind Yourself Why You're Together

Take a piece of paper and write down everything you like about your mate. You should be able to list at least 10 to 20 items, and if you're detail-oriented, you'll probably fill both sides of the page. Think about everything, from the physical to the emotional to the way your honey treats you to how he or she interacts with the world and other people. Think back to the beginning, and don't overlook anything. Don't qualify your statements. For example, don't say "I kind of like his eyes," or, "She's somewhat attractive." Just write: "I like his eyes," or, "I find her attractive."

If you have trouble, close your eyes for a moment; imagine that someone else is pursuing your mate — someone attractive, charming, sexy, and really, really smitten with your partner. Is it easier to recall your partner's good qualities now? Don't waste time resenting your mate because he or she isn't perfect. Instead, focus your energy in a positive way, appreciate your sweetie for gracing your life, and remember why you're in this relationship.

Remind Your Partner Why, Too

When you do the preceding exercise, reminding yourself of your mate's positive qualities, you'll find it much easier to treat him or her with proper respect. And when you do that, your mate will have an easier time reciprocating and remembering why he or she is involved with you, too! Remember, your partner is not a masochist. He'll only stay in the relationship if he's mostly having a good time.

Don't take it for granted that because you said, "I love you," in 1971, your mate should remember. Tell her often, and show it through your emotional support. Women love to be appreciated as much as you do, but they're more attuned to verbal expressions of appreciation. So even though you may not need her to tell you she loves you, if she needs to hear it and you do love her, why not give her that gift? It's simple, quick, and inexpensive — and it can help her give you what you need as well.

Close your eyes for a minute and imagine that today is the last day of your life. Would you continue sparring, or would you want to make sure she knew how truly special she is?

No one knows exactly what day will be the last. So don't wait. Enjoy every minute as though it *is* your last. Find the joy and happiness there, and share it with your partner. Don't wait for your mate to perk up, and don't blame him or her for not dragging you along the path to happiness. Perk up yourself, and you'll infect your sweetie with joy and wonderment as well.

Put Fun and Play Back in Your Relationship

Don't take yourself too seriously. Don't get all bogged down by your responsibilities and lose your sense of humor. Pompous people are boorrrrrring! If you tend to do too much and worry when you don't, remind yourself that in the significance of the universe, you're just one little drop. You don't have to save the world; have some fun, too. People who have fun and demonstrate joie de vivre attract others, while chronically serious, anxious, and self-important people repel others quicker than bug spray!

If you have trouble finding fun in anything, get some sleep. Watch a kid play — they get such a bang out of everything they do. Observe your cat, dog, birds, or other pets exploring and experiencing the miracle of each day. Animals are so happy just to be alive. Take a vacation to the country, and get a better perspective on everything. Wake up your sense of humor. It may be asleep, but it's still there.

Find Your Smile

Try this experiment: Look in the mirror and think about your problems. Notice your facial expression. You might have a little crinkle between the brows or a wrinkle all across your forehead. Now walk down the street, looking down, with a big ol' frown on your face, and notice what happens. Chances are, everyone will leave you alone.

Then walk down the same street with a big smile on your face. Think about something charming and humorous a child or pet has done, or some other funny thing that made you laugh. Look at everything around you — the grass, trees, sky, birds, squirrels, buildings, and people — and think about how beautiful your world is. People will actually smile back at you! And as you practice more, they'll also approach you to ask for directions, the time, whatever. You *look* friendly and approachable, so they're *treating* you that way. Reconnect with your smile, even if it's been buried awhile, and you and your partner will both benefit. And if you don't currently have a honeybunny, your smile may even attract one to you! It can't hurt!

Appendix A

The Dr. Kate Compatibility Quiz

· ·

Are you compatible with your partner? Take this questionnaire and find out. As with the communication quiz in Appendix B, this is a *fun* questionnaire, not a psychological test. But what have you got to lose? You just might learn something and have fun in the process. (For convenience sake, I use the pronoun "he" to refer to your partner throughout. However, this quiz applies to both men and women.)

The Quiz

Choose the answer that comes closest to describing your situation.

1. **When I'm around my partner:**

    A. It doesn't matter what we do, everything is just more fun, and the time just flies.

    B. It's really fun sometimes, but at other times, we just don't seem to connect.

    C. I find myself thinking of other people and what might have been.

    D. I can't stand it. I try to get away as soon as possible.

    E. Most of the time, we don't connect.

2. **I've been with my partner:**

    A. Less than 3 months

    B. 4–12 months

    C. 1–2 years

    D. 3–7 years

    E. 8 or more years

3. **If I relax and allow my partner to do anything he wants:**

   A. He would walk all over me. I really have to protect myself.

   B. He would go out of his way to look out for my interests. I don't ever have to worry about that.

   C. Sometimes he'd manipulate and use me. Other times, he's selfless.

   D. I haven't caught him yet, but I just sense that he wouldn't be faithful for long.

4. **With regard to intellectual stimulation:**

   A. My mate and I are intellectually on the same wavelength. We enjoy talking about all kinds of things, and it excites me.

   B. My mate takes off on issues I know nothing about and don't really follow.

   C. I don't expect my partner to stimulate me intellectually. I get that from my coworkers.

   D. My mate is fun, but not as intellectually stimulating as I would like.

   E. We are very different intellectually.

5. **Physically:**

   A. I am extremely attracted to my partner.

   B. I am mostly attracted to my partner.

   C. I am somewhat attracted to my partner. If he would just have that plastic surgery . . . .

   D. I'm kind of turned off by his looks, but I find other things more important, so it's OK.

   E. I'm really turned off by his looks and it bothers me.

6. **Sexually:**

   A. I enjoy him completely. It's always great.

   B. Sometimes sex is great, sometimes it's good, and sometimes it's just maintenance sex, but I always enjoy it because it's with the one I love.

   C. We don't really get into sex much, but it's OK.

   D. I abhor sex with my partner, but I do it to please him.

   E. I try to go to bed before my partner does, so I can sneak out of it. When I have to make love, I try to get it over with as soon as possible.

7. **When it comes to money:**

   A. My mate and I always disagree on how to spend it. Money causes many of our fights.

   B. We sometimes disagree, but we talk it through and make compromises.

   C. My partner and I almost always agree on how to spend our money.

   D. My mate and I have separate bank accounts. We divide up any joint activities and, if living together, our expenses.

   E. My partner hides bills and checks from me. I never know what's going on.

8. **With regard to our goals and plans:**

   A. We talk about our goals and plans, and they seem to fit well together.

   B. We sometimes talk about our goals and plans, but I sense that we're not in sync there.

   C. We sometimes talk about our goals and plans, and I'm hopeful that we can make a future together.

   D. We never talk about goals and plans. We just live day to day.

   E. My partner is a planner and I'm a day-to-day person (or vice versa), but we negotiate on things, and even each other out in the end.

   F. My partner and I vary greatly on how we approach things, so we don't talk about it unless we have to.

9. **With regard to our future together:**

   A. My partner and I are in agreement that we are going to get married and have children (or get married without children). We are both sincere about this.

   B. My partner and I can't agree on our relationship goal. We fight about it often.

   C. My partner and I can't agree on our relationship goal, so we focus on the present and don't discuss it.

   D. My partner and I are both single, but agree that our relationship is just temporary. We're not ready for anything permanent.

10. **My partner and I:**

   A. Share a lot of cultural, ethnic, and religious similarities. Our families and friends would (or do) like each other, and are usually supportive of what we do.

   B. Are very different with regard to culture, ethnicity, and/or religion. However, our family and friends have met and are supportive, and they usually pull through with support in times like this.

    C. Are very different with regard to culture, ethnicity, and/or religion. We're afraid to tell our family and friends, so we keep our relationship our little secret.

    D. Are very different with regard to culture, ethnicity, and/or religion. Our family and friends have met and they are most definitely against our union.

    E. One or both of us come from a dysfunctional family who are constantly fighting with people and/or cutting them off.

11. My partner and I:

    A. Never have any problems. We never disagree on anything.

    B. Communicate regularly, with great success. We have conflicts sometimes, but we calmly work them out through negotiation and compromise. I love talking to my partner.

    C. Limp along. Sometimes we communicate well, sometimes not.

    D. Try to keep things light. But if we have disagreements, we may not talk to each other for days. Then we just pretend that it never happened.

    E. Try to talk, but always end up yelling and screaming at each other.

    F. Communication? What's communication?

12. My partner and I:

    A. Love to do the same things. We enjoy doing them together.

    B. Love to do some of the same things. But we also take time alone to do separate activities with others.

    C. Really don't share many of the same interests, but we go along with each other anyway, so we can be together.

    D. Really don't share many of the same interests, so we spend quite a bit of time apart.

13. My partner and I:

    A. Are ordinarily very honest, trustworthy, and loyal.

    B. Try to be honest, trustworthy, and loyal, but sometimes are not as honest, trustworthy, or loyal as we would like.

    C. Make a lot of mistakes.

    D. Have had a lot of affairs on each other.

    E. Are not very honest with one another; we keep a lot hidden.

14. Once my partner and I commit to something:

    A. We don't give up easily. We work very hard to accomplish our goals.

    B. We give everything a good shot, but don't try to excess.

    C. We figure relationships should be fairly easy. Otherwise, it just isn't compatible.

    D. We don't really try very much at anything. Life is too short to work too hard.

15. With regard to friendship:

    A. My partner is my best friend.

    B. We haven't been friends for a long time.

    C. We have ups and downs, but we're still closer to each other than to anyone else.

    D. I feel my mate tries to please other people (like family and other friends) more than me.

    E. I don't believe mates have to be friends.

16. With regard to our marital status:

    A. Both of us are either single/never-married, widowed, divorced, or separated pending divorce (and the divorce papers have been filed).

    B. One or both of us is married to someone else and has not yet filed for divorce.

    C. One of both of us is a priest or other clergy who is not allowed to ever marry.

17. With regard to our interactions:

    A. My partner has physically abused me — or I have physically abused my partner.

    B. My partner has never physically abused me and I have never physically abused my partner.

You've finished the quiz! Great! Now score your results!

Your Score

Using Table A-1, score your responses by drawing a circle around the appropriate number of points for the answer you chose. Note the relationship characteristic/compatibility feature measured by each item to the right of the scoring.

Q	A	B	C	D	E	F	Compatibility Feature
1	10	7	2	0	0		Overall fun and chemistry
2	0	1	2	6	10		Length of time
3	0	10	5	2			Trust, loyalty
4	10	2	7	3	0		Intelligence/intellectual interests
5	10	7	2	4	0		Physical attraction
6	10	10	4	1	0		Sexual attraction
7	1	10	10	3	0		Financial agreements/practices
8	10	2	4	0	8	0	Shared goals and plans
9	10	0	2	2			Shared relationship goal
10	10	8	1	0	0		Culture/religion/ethnicity; Support of family/friends
11	5	10	4	1	0	0	Communication
12	10	8	6	0			Similar interests
13	10	6	2	0	0		Honesty, loyalty, monogamy, trust
14	10	6	2	0			Perseverance
15	10	0	7	2	0		Friendship, solidarity
16	0	-500*	-500*				*For B or C, score negative 500 and see Affair Results
17	-1000*	0					*For A, score negative 1000 and see Abuse Results

Add up your points:

- If you marked A of #17, score yourself as a total score of *negative* 1000 (*-1000*), *no matter how you scored on #1 through #16.*

- If you marked B or C of #16, but not A in #17, score yourself as a total score of *negative* 500 (*-500*), *no matter how you scored on #1 through #15.*

Write your total compatibility score here: _____

Now, read on to discover how compatible you are!

Your Results

Look for your total compatibility score in the following sections. Note that these results address compatibility features measured by the questions in the quiz. The sections are ordered from the highest possible score to the lowest possible score. So if you scored -500 or -1000, you can find your results in the last two results sections.

Highly compatible: Score of 130–150

You have a really compatible relationship. You share many levels of compatibility with your partner. You probably feel close intellectually, physically, sexually, and with regard to shared goals and interests, including the goal of this relationship. You probably believe in communication, and try to resolve your problems together. You tend to work hard at most things, including this relationship, and you probably have support from family and friends. You probably view each other as best friends and feel a strong bond to one another. You enjoy each other's company and have lots of fun together. You trust each other; you believe in monogamy, honesty, and loyalty, and you practice them with each other. Congratulations! You're very fortunate! Keep that in mind, and live every day intimately connected, no matter what stresses befall you in the future. Never take each other for granted. Many people never even experience a relationship like this. Value what you have and make your relationship a priority, so it will continue to thrive.

"Work-in-progress" relationship: Score of 100–129

You and your partner are somewhat less than ideally compatible, but then most things in life aren't perfect. You have a normal, "work-in-progress" relationship. You probably feel some features of your relationship could be more in sync, but many could also be a lot worse. You usually value what you have, although you may take each other for granted from time to time. Some aspects of your relationship feel really good and others don't. You may get along on a number of variables, but fall flat regarding your goals, your sex life, or some area of your life together that causes conflict.

However, with hard work and tenacity, you can probably keep this a workable and satisfying relationship; you might even improve it. You both could benefit from a psychologist's help from time to time — for example, when you are unable to reach compromises together or when you occasionally need to jumpstart your relationship. But therapy does not need to last a long time to produce benefits, and overall, your prognosis is good.

If you and your partner disagree about your relationship goal, try reading Chapters 11 through 13 and using those techniques to see if you can come to a workable compromise. If one of you wants to get married or get married and have children and the other does not, you will need to come to some kind of agreement if this relationship is going to work long-term. This is particularly true if you: are over 28; are either never-married, or divorced or widowed more than three years; and have been with your partner awhile (18 months or more). See a psychologist for extra help. If you're not able to reach a satisfactory compromise, even through therapy, then you should probably look for another partner. You do find many parts of this relationship satisfying, however, so seeking out a new relationship may be difficult. If you're not sure whether or not your relationship has enough positives to warrant staying, given your particular age, marital status, relationship goal, and life goals, see a psychologist to help you figure it out.

Mediocre compatibility: Score of 60–99

There's quite a bit lacking in this relationship. You may be compatible in some ways, but very incompatible in others. Or you may just have a lower level of compatibility across the board. You realize that there are a lot of differences between you and your partner. These differences may be physical, sexual, intellectual, and/or with regard to goals and shared interests. You may lack the social support of family and friends. You may also disagree greatly with regard to your relationship goal. If you have known each other less than two years, you may not have enough in common to make a relationship work. If you have known each other for many years, you may be drifting apart. See the suggestions in the next section (score 0 to 59) and use those that seem appropriate for you.

Need a psychologist: Score of 0–59

You and your partner probably have issues of honesty, cheating, and trust, and you both need a lot of help learning to be a better partner. You may have a lot of disagreements about money and/or doubt your partner's fidelity or honesty. You may often be dishonest with your partner. You and your partner don't communicate well, and there are probably many things festering beneath the surface. You really aren't enjoying this relationship very much. It will take a lot of effort to fix what ails you — and you'll probably need the help of a psychologist to do it. You both have a lot of learning to do, and without help, there's little hope that the relationship can be satisfying for you. Depending on the nature of your relationship — your marital status, how long you've known one another, and how much history you have together — my suggestions vary:

✔ **If you and your partner are married to one another:** See a psychologist together to jumpstart your relationship. Try to work out your differences in therapy, while you also learn to communicate better with one another. Give therapy a good try before throwing in the towel.

✔ **If you are married, but young or newly wed:** You and your spouse may have a lot to learn about how to communicate with each other and what constitutes reasonable expectations for your marriage. Communication skills are not inbred, but therapy can help you develop skills necessary to continuing your relationship.

✔ **If you have been together many years, married or unmarried, and have a lot of history (including good history) together:** There's no way that either of you could have behaved perfectly toward each other all this time. Couples who have been together a long time need to learn to forgive and "re-birth" the relationship. They also need to learn to communicate better so that they can negotiate and compromise regarding any present and future disagreements. Go to couples counseling together, and stay in therapy until you have made significant progress and can retake this questionnaire and score in the top one or two categories. If you don't improve in six months, try another psychologist. Don't throw in the towel until you've tried your best in therapy for several years.

✔ **If you and your partner have just recently met, are long-distance, are not married, or have less shared history together for any reason:** You may be better off just looking for another partner. Why not try a quality introduction service or run a personal ad? See Chapter 5 for more on using these methods to find a compatible partner. It's unlikely that your current relationship will be saved, and in the long run, it will probably be less frustrating if you look elsewhere. You may want to consult a psychologist to learn more about what you need in a relationship and for encouragement to keep looking. Review your current and past relationships with your psychologist. Why are you staying with your current partner when you don't enjoy him very much? Perhaps you're with your mate because he or she is a hook from your dysfunctional past. Apply what you learn to your future relationships, so that you can make them better. That way, the time and energy you've spent, and the experience you've gained through this unfulfilling relationship will be put to good use.

AFFAIRS: Score of negative 500

If you and your partner are having an affair with one another — in other words, if either of you is married to someone else and have not yet filed divorce papers — you're not being realistic with yourselves about the relationship. You're romanticizing about your current situation.

✔ **If you're married, you need to wake up and get your life organized.** If you don't want to stay married to your spouse, file the papers and move forward with divorce. If you want to stay married, stop cheating on your spouse and see a psychologist to repair whatever problems you originally had, as well as the damage that's been done to the trust between you.

- **If your partner is married and you're fantasizing about your future together, you need to wake up.** There's little likelihood that he will suddenly divorce, marry you, and live happily (and faithfully) ever after with you. He's cheating on his current spouse, so why do you think he'd treat you any differently?

- **If both you and your partner are married to other people, it's probably just a matter of time before the situation blows up in your faces.** You probably feel attracted to one another on a variety of levels, but the bottom line is that because one or both of you are married, the relationship will probably not grow into anything permanent or fully satisfying. Even if you have a plan to divorce your respective spouses, one or both of you may not follow through. And even if you do follow through, you may end up with different partners anyway.

The longer you stay in any of these cheating relationships, the more it will hurt when you inevitably break up. And the more likely it is that your spouse or spouses will find out about the affair, causing more stress and strain for everyone involved.

For more on the topic of cheating, browse through the Cheating File at my `www.drkate.com` and *AOL Keyword: DrKate* Web sites. Or use the *Dr. Kate Search* at the sites to target letters even more specifically about your situation.

ABUSE: Score of negative 1000

If you or your partner is physically abusive, your relationship has very little potential for success. The abuser does not respect the abused partner, and both of you probably have long-standing psychological problems.

- **If you are the abuser:** You have a host of long-lasting character problems that require urgent treatment by a psychologist. You may also have drug or alcohol problems. You have trouble with control and self-esteem, and you blame your mate for things that he or she is not responsible for. You have a distorted vision of reality and a double standard of behavior for you and your partner. Seek treatment immediately from a psychologist, and let him know that this is an emergency.

- **If you are the abused:** You also need to see a psychologist immediately to get help. Check into services for abused people in your area, and take measures to save yourself. Your relationship isn't worth saving, but you are. Act now to change your present and your future. To read more about physical abuse, see Chapter 20. You can also find a wealth of advice on this topic at my `www.drkate.com` and *AOL Keyword: DrKate* Web sites. I have written many advice letters to abused people, coaching them on what to do about their situations. Use the *Dr. Kate Search* function on the sites to locate those letters and learn from the mistakes of others.

Appendix B

The Dr. Kate Communication Quiz

● ●

How are your communication skills? Would your partner agree? Answer these questions as they relate to your opinion of your communication skills, and then follow the instructions at the end to improve your romantic relationship. Of course, this is a fun quiz, not a psychological test, but what do you have to lose? You'll have fun taking it, and you just might learn something valuable! (As in **The Dr. Kate Compatibility Quiz** in Appendix A, I use the pronoun "he" to refer to your partner throughout. However, this quiz applies to both men and women.)

The Quiz

Choose the answer that comes closest to describing your communication skills.

1. **When I was growing up:**

   A. My parents communicated with each other very well, and I learned a lot from them.

   B. My parents really didn't communicate well; I learned a lot of bad habits from them.

   C. Everyone yelled one minute, then forgot it the next.

   D. No one really talked about problems.

   E. I learned a lot of bad communication habits, but have since improved/corrected them through reading, classes, or psychotherapy.

2. **In regards to my feelings, I usually:**

   A. Have a hard time telling my loved one what I think or feel.

   B. Tell it like it is, and let the chips fall where they may.

   C. Believe that my loved one should know what I'm feeling without me telling him.

    D. Express myself in a way that is direct and straightforward, but also shows respect for my partner.

    E. Believe that what my partner doesn't know won't hurt him. After all, you have to keep some things to yourself.

3. When my partner expresses feelings, I usually:

    A. Try to paraphrase or reflect back what he says *("So what you're saying* is_____" or, *"Sounds like that was really hard for you")* to show understanding.

    B. Show emotional support by saying things like: *"I'm sorry you had a rough day."*

    C. Show support by telling him why he shouldn't feel badly.

    D. Think about how his feelings might affect my future, and choose my response accordingly.

    E. Let it go in one ear and out the other. My partner never listens to me, so why should I listen to him?

4. In general, when I talk to my partner:

    A. I try to take responsibility for my feelings by saying: *"I feel_____ when you _____."*

    B. I usually phrase remarks: *"You (or it) made me _____."*

    C. Let's not split hairs. I have no idea how I phrase things; I just *talk*.

    D. I'm frequently not sure how I should feel about anything, so I just don't bring it up.

    E. I try to be subtle. So I say: *"We/they feel _____"* or, *"In this situation, most people would feel _____."*

5. When we disagree, I generally:

    A. Try to help my partner by telling him what he should and shouldn't do, and how to do things the right way.

    B. Share my feelings in a direct, calm way, and allow my partner to do the same. Then I suggest compromises.

    C. Give in. I don't speak up well, and I *hate* fighting.

    D. Let my partner think I'm agreeing with him, then do what I want.

    E. Am very indirect about voicing my feelings. But if I don't get my way, I later *show* my displeasure (for example, by sulking, coming home late, or withholding sex).

6. Usually, when our argument escalates, I:

A. Raise my voice, talk faster and faster, cut off (interrupt) my partner, and end up yelling. I may also pound my fist, gesture emphatically, point my finger, throw something, or punch the wall.

B. Try to have the last word, even if I have to stomp out of the house to get it.

C. Use words like "right/wrong," "good/bad," "always/never," "everyone/no one," "have to/can't." I also criticize my partner by saying things like: ***"You're so _____*** *(stupid, ridiculous, pathetic, or some other negative word)."*

D. Keep my voice calm and modulated, and suggest tabling the discussion for now and agreeing to disagree.

E. Can hardly speak; I just give in. I can't stand it when my partner is mad at me.

7. When I don't like something my partner is doing, I usually:

A. Just cry and feel useless.

B. Give him the "silent treatment," but complain to anyone else who will listen.

C. Pick and choose my battles carefully, and praise him often before requesting any behavioral change.

D. Let him know about it, in no uncertain terms. I say: ***"You _____*** *(always do that wrong),"* or, ***"You are _____*** *(the worst housekeeper I've ever seen)."*

E. Describe the behavior I find objectionable, rather than attacking my partner.

8. When I am offended by something my partner has done, I usually:

A. Tell my partner right away, no matter where we are or who is around.

B. Make time to discuss it when we are both rested, calm, and alone, turning off the TV and any other distractions.

C. Suffer in silence. Life is too short to disagree about things.

D. Tease about it when he can't really fight back (in front of a business client, for example), or ask my in-laws or others to pressure him into giving me what I want.

E. Only bring it up if/when I think it's in my best interest to do so.

9. **In terms of praise, I usually:**

   A. Reward my mate generously and often with praise and physical affection (like hugs and kisses).

   B. Don't praise my partner. He never praises me, so why should I?

   C. Praise my partner to get something I want. When I want something really big, I can be extremely charming.

   D. Show my mate I care by doing nice things, rather than saying anything.

   E. Don't. In my opinion, he gets way too much praise as it is.

10. **When it comes to apologies, I usually:**

   A. Don't apologize; it's a sign of weakness.

   B. Apologize, whether or not it's my fault; I can't stand conflict.

   C. Apologize if I think it will get me what I want. After all, all that matters is the final outcome.

   D. Apologize if I have done something inappropriate or hurtful, even unintentionally.

   E. Pretend like the incident never occurred, rather than apologizing; that really gets him!

11. **When it comes to saying, "I love you," I:**

   A. Don't tell my partner, "I love you," because he never says it to me.

   B. Don't say, "I love you," because I find it hard to talk about feelings in general.

   C. Don't say, "I love you," because I find it easier to say what I don't like rather than what I do like.

   D. Say, "I love you," when I want something or if I'm in the mood, but behave differently later.

   E. Say, "I love you," when I feel that way, and demonstrate behavior consistent with that message.

12. **In terms of honesty, I generally:**

   A. Tell my partner the truth, even when it's difficult.

   B. Tell little white lies that won't matter down the road if I think it will serve my purpose.

   C. Lie whenever I feel like it. My partner is too stupid to know the difference, and besides, I really don't care if he finds out.

   D. Lie (or just imply an untruth through my silence) to make my partner feel better, or just because it's easier.

   E. Lie whenever I feel like it. After all, he lies to me, so why shouldn't I?

13. **I usually:**

   A. Love talking with my partner about all kinds of things. I can't wait to share things with him.

   B. Get tired of constantly having to set my partner straight about his priorities.

   C. Prefer the company of my friends, and love to make my partner jealous by talking about them.

   D. Think talking is overrated. My partner can tell how I feel just by watching my actions.

   E. Talk whenever necessary to achieve my needs. Communication is a great tool.

14. **When it comes to asking for help:**

   A. I ask for too much help. Sometimes I solicit so many opinions, I get totally confused as to what I should do.

   B. I don't really have a problem. My mate is the one with the problem. If he would only change . . . .

   C. I don't really need therapy. Normal people solve their own problems.

   D. I try to solve my problems with my partner, but would consider therapy before the situation got out of hand.

   E. Why should I go to therapy? He won't go anyway, and he's the one who needs the shrink!

15. **You want me to ask my partner to complete this questionnaire and discuss it with me?**

   A. I would feel comfortable asking my partner; I believe in self-help.

   B. I am apprehensive about asking my partner. He might do it, but I wouldn't want him to find out about all my insecurities and faults.

   C. I wouldn't want to admit I actually took this questionnaire. There are a lot of crazies out there, but I'm not one of them!

   D. I wouldn't want to share such personal information with my partner. He might use it against me later.

   E. I would not feel comfortable, because I wouldn't want to reveal my hand. It might ruin a future plan.

You've finished the quiz! Great! Now score your results!

Your Score

Using Table B-1, score your responses by drawing a circle around the appropriate number of points for the answer you chose. Note the behavior or attitude assessed by each item to the right of the scoring.

Table B-1						Communication Quiz Scoring
Q	**A**	**B**	**C**	**D**	**E**	**Behavior/Attitude Assessed**
1	10	0	0	0	10	Early learning
2	0	0	0	10	0	General communication pattern
3	10	10	0	0	0	Reflective/supportive listening
4	10	0	0	0	0	Take responsibility for feelings
5	0	10	0	0	0	Handling disagreement
6	0	0	0	10	0	Choice of words, tone of voice
7	0	0	10	0	10	Asking for behavioral change
8	0	10	0	0	0	Choose time/location to talk
9	10	0	0	0	0	Ratio of positive reinforcement
10	0	0	0	10	0	Willingness to apologize
11	0	0	0	0	10	Saying, "I love you!"
12	10	0	0	0	0	Honesty, respect, and maturity
13	10	0	0	0	0	Attitude toward communication
14	0	0	0	10	0	Attitude toward help/therapy
15	10	0	0	0	0	Openness and trust

Add up your points.

Write your total communication score here: _____.

Now, read on to discover how well you communicate!

The Results

Look for your total communication score in the following sections. Note that these results address behaviors and attitudes important to good communication as measured by quiz questions. The sections are ordered from the highest possible score to the lowest possible score.

Great communicator: Score of 120–150

Congratulations! You scored in the range of great communicators, and you probably love communicating, too. Now you weren't just picking the ones that sounded right, were you?

If you were objective: You enjoy expressing yourself in a direct, straightforward, honest manner that shows respect for your partner. You are able to say, "I love you," and show it through praise and affectionate gestures. You respect your partner's right to hold an opinion that is different from yours. You're able to take responsibility for your own feelings and behavior, rather than blaming your partner. You pick and choose your battles wisely, and give lots of reinforcement before asking for a behavioral change. When you and your partner have a conflict, you remain calm, discuss your feelings, listen attentively to your partner's feelings, and make supportive statements, then look for ways to compromise. If an argument escalates and you're unable to reach an agreement, you calmly suggest tabling the discussion for another time. You're able to apologize and ask for help when you need it.

If your mate is also assertive, you're likely to share good communication and a healthy relationship together. However, whether your relationship is successful is not completely dependent on you; it's an *interaction*. So, if your relationship doesn't seem to be going well, talk to your partner and work on your communication together.

Ask your partner to complete this questionnaire. Then both of you can retake it as if you were each other. Make time to calmly discuss your answers to each question, using them as jumping-off points to discuss your helpful and problematic behaviors. Talk about the answers you gave as yourselves and as each other. You may be surprised to find that your partner holds a different view of your behavior and vice versa. Your ability to communicate will serve you well. Keep up the good work!

Good communicator: Score of 90–110

Congratulations! Although you didn't score in the top category, you still did very well. You're a good communicator and getting even better. You selected many answers which suggest that you often behave assertively. You tend to express your feelings, both pleasant and unpleasant, in a direct, honest, straightforward way, while also showing respect for your partner's rights.

At times, however, you do make mistakes. You may sometimes act *aggressively* (taking advantage of the other person's rights when expressing your feelings), or *passively* (not standing up for your feelings at all). You may also act out in *passive-aggressive* ways (indicating displeasure by doing something indirectly aggressive). Or you may act *politically* (using communication to manipulate your partner into doing something you desire). However, practice makes perfect! To make your communication even better, try the following three tips:

✔ With your partner, read Chapters 11 through 13 on communication. Find out more about reflective listening, supportive statements, facilitative agreement, assertiveness, negotiation, compromise, and other communication skills.

✔ If your partner tends to be respectful of your feelings, ask him or her to complete this questionnaire. Then you can each retake it as if you were the other. Make time to calmly discuss your answers to each question, using them as jumping-off points to discuss your helpful and problematic behaviors. Talk about the answers you each gave as yourself and as your partner. You may be surprised to find that your partner holds a different view of your behavior and vice versa.

✔ You may also benefit from assertiveness classes (taught by local colleges, park districts, and private firms — see Chapter 5 for more on this), and by reading books on assertiveness and communication skills. If you have a computer, access my Web sites (www.drkate.com or **AOL Keyword: DrKate**), and read the letters and articles I've written about communication. Use **Dr. Kate Search** to locate them. You're well on your way to becoming a great communicator. Keep up the good work!

Average communicator: Score of 60–80

You selected many answers which suggest that you sometimes behave assertively. That is, you sometimes express your feelings, both pleasant and unpleasant, in a direct, honest, straightforward manner, while also showing respect for your partner's rights.

At times, however, you do make mistakes. You may sometimes act *aggressively* (taking advantage of the other person's rights when expressing your feelings), or *passively* (not standing up for your feelings at all). You may also act out in *passive-aggressive* ways (indicating displeasure by doing something indirectly aggressive). Or you may act *politically* (using communication to manipulate your partner into doing something you desire). So try these three tips:

✔ With your partner, read Chapters 11 through 13 on communication. Find out more about reflective listening, supportive statements, facilitative agreement, assertiveness, negotiation, compromise, and other communication skills.

✔ If your partner tends to be respectful of your feelings, ask him or her to complete this questionnaire. Then you can each retake it as if you were the other. Make time to calmly discuss your answers to each question, using them as jumping-off points to discuss your helpful and problematic behaviors. Talk about the answers you each gave as yourself and as your partner. You may be surprised to find that your partner holds a different view of your behavior and vice versa.

✔ You may also benefit from assertiveness classes (taught by local colleges, park districts, and private firms — see Chapter 5 for more on this), and by reading books on assertiveness and communication skills. If you have a computer, access my Web sites (www.drkate.com or *AOL Keyword: DrKate*), and read the letters and articles I've written about communication. Use *Dr. Kate Search* to locate them. You're well on your way to becoming a great communicator. Keep up the good work!

Mediocre communicator: Score of 30–50

Your answers suggest that you behave assertively once in awhile. That is, you occasionally express your feelings, both pleasant and unpleasant, in a direct, honest, straightforward manner, while also showing respect for your partner's rights.

However, you're not acting assertively most of the time. You may sometimes act *aggressively* (taking advantage of the other person's rights when expressing your feelings), or *passively* (not standing up for your feelings at all). You may also act out in *passive-aggressive* ways (indicating displeasure by doing something indirectly aggressive). Or you may act *politically* (using communication to manipulate your partner).

The good news is that with practice, you can significantly improve your communication style and, at the same time, your intimate relationship. To become a better communicator, I suggest the following:

✔ With your partner, read Chapters 11 through 13 on communication. Find out more about reflective listening, supportive statements, facilitative agreement, assertiveness, negotiation, compromise, and other communication skills.

✔ If your partner tends to be respectful of your feelings, ask him or her to complete this questionnaire. Then you can each retake it as if you were the other. If you feel that the two of you can discuss the questionnaire productively, ask your mate to discuss the results with you.

✔ Remember not to take any remarks personally. Focus on the behaviors being discussed, and try to understand how your partner views your behavior. Be sure to thank him or her for the help. You may be surprised to find your mate holds a different view of your behavior, and vice versa.

✔ You may also benefit from assertiveness classes (taught by local colleges, park districts, and private firms — see Chapter 5 for more on this), and by reading books on assertiveness and communication skills. If you have a computer, access my Web sites (www.drkate.com or **AOL Keyword: DrKate**), and read the letters and articles I've written about communication. Use **Dr. Kate Search** to locate them. You're well on your way to becoming a great communicator. Keep up the good work!

✔ Finally, I encourage you to consult a psychologist for individual sessions and/or couples counseling. The psychologist can give you personalized instruction and help you apply what you've read, so you can practice good communication skills. If you follow these suggestions, you should eventually be able to enjoy your romantic relationships (as well as those with close family and friends) — more than you ever thought possible! You've already begun the journey by taking this quiz. Now, keep the momentum going!

Poor communicator: Score of 0–20

Cheer up! Although your low score may have you believing that no one will talk to you anymore, keep in mind that communication skills can easily be improved — if you're motivated and get the help you need.

You do have lots of room for improvement. Your answers suggest that you rarely behave assertively. That is, you rarely express your feelings, both pleasant and unpleasant, in a direct, honest, straightforward manner, while showing respect for your partner's rights.

Instead, you may act *aggressively* (taking advantage of the other person's rights when expressing your feelings), or *passively* (not standing up for your feelings at all). You may also act out in *passive-aggressive* ways (indicating displeasure by doing something indirectly aggressive). Or you may act *politically* (using communication to manipulate your partner into doing something you desire).

However, the good news is that with practice, you can significantly improve your communication style and, at the same time, your intimate relationship. Here are my suggestions:

✔ With your partner, read Chapters 11 through 13 on communication. Find out more about reflective listening, supportive statements, facilitative agreement, assertiveness, negotiation, compromise, and other communication skills.

✔ You may also benefit from assertiveness classes (taught by local colleges, park districts, and private firms — see Chapter 5 for more on this), and by reading books on assertiveness and communication skills. If you have a computer, access my Web sites (www.drkate.com or *AOL Keyword: DrKate*), and read the letters and articles I've written about communication. Use *Dr. Kate Search* to locate them. You're well on your way to becoming a great communicator. Keep up the good work!

✔ Ask your mate to complete this questionnaire. Then you can each retake it as if you were the other. Since you do have so much trouble communicating, however, don't discuss your results together unless you're in the presence of a psychologist who can keep the discussion positive, assertive, and productive (see the following bullet).

✔ I strongly encourage you to consult a psychologist — by yourself for individual sessions — and/or with your partner for couples counseling. Do this as soon as possible so you can learn better communication skills. Discuss your responses to this quiz in therapy, and learn to be more assertive. By working hard, you should eventually be able to enjoy your romantic relationships (as well as those with close family and friends) — more than you even imagined! You've already started your journey by taking this quiz. Now, keep the momentum going!

Index

• S •

Notes

Notes

Notes